Introduction to Theology

BENJAMIN WEAVER, 1853-1928

*Beloved Bishop in the Lancaster Mennonite Conference
Biblical Scholar, Gifted Leader, Man of God*

INTRODUCTION TO THEOLOGY

A BRIEF INTRODUCTION TO THE
DOCTRINAL CONTENT OF SCRIPTURE
WRITTEN IN THE
ANABAPTIST-MENNONITE TRADITION

J. C. Wenger
Goshen Biblical Seminary

*Prepared at the request
of the Publishing Committee of
Mennonite Publication Board*

HERALD PRESS
SCOTTDALE, PENNSYLVANIA
KITCHENER, ONTARIO

INTRODUCTION TO THEOLOGY
Copyright © 1954 by Herald Press, Scottdale, Pa., 15683
  Published simultaneously in Canada by Herald Press,
  Kitchener, Ont. N2G 4M5
Library of Congress Catalog Card Number: 53-9049
International Standard Book Number: 0-8361-1791-3
Printed in the United States of America

Fourth Printing, 1976

Preface

Since 1938 I have been attempting to teach God's Word to successive classes of students in Goshen College and in its Bible School which is now known as the Biblical Seminary. No course have I enjoyed more than Systematic Theology. Yet it has always been a problem as to what textbook to use: Baptist? Christian Reformed? Nazarene? No book available contained the emphases and the point of view that I wanted to communicate to my students. The request from the Publishing Committee of the Mennonite Publication Board that I write a "Mennonite theology" was therefore welcome. It was the desire of this committee that the work should be thoroughly saturated with the doctrines of the Anabaptists, and yet that it should be more directly Biblical than historical in character. With this desire I was warmly in accord.

One of the justifications for a new work in theology is the surrender of the Biblical view of inspiration by many contemporary Christian writers. Fundamentalist theologians who still retain a high view of inspiration nevertheless present various doctrines which clash sharply with the most cherished convictions of the Mennonite brotherhood—such convictions as Biblical love and nonresistance, the importance of strict standards of church discipline, the literal observance of every New Testament commandment even to the refusal to wear "gold, or pearls, or costly array," etc.

Because I accept the Bible as the very Word of God I have sought to make this work truly Biblical in character, not philosophical. While I am much interested in philosophy, and teach courses in that field, yet it is my earnest conviction that men need more than philosophy: they must have the eternal verities of divine revelation. Man needs the "Word of God which will more surely and safely carry him," as Plato stated in the *Phaedo* (Jowett translation, Dial Press, N.Y., III, p. 226). And man needs to come to this Word of God with an open mind; no other attitude is justifiable. We must approach the Bible without preconceived ideas as to how God needed to have His Word written: we are not called to instruct Him on this matter! In this as in other doctrines of the faith we may safely follow the Lord Jesus and His inspired apostles: and both He and they regarded the Scriptures as the divine oracles of God, as a sure revelation from the Father.

And how badly our world needs this note of certainty which can be found only in divine revelation! Neither Plato, Augustine, Luther, nor Einstein is able to heal our sin-sick generation; only Christ and His Gospel can restore health to the race. We need theologies to placard the truth of God before our generation. God's truth is eternal, but it needs to be stated afresh in every generation to meet the particular needs, and to overcome the peculiar errors, of each era. The awful blight of our day is secularism: not Russia, but the secularism in the heart of the western world. Bullets cannot stop ideas; only the truth is able to overcome error.

It is also my conviction that although Bible students cannot be indifferent to critical questions such as authorship, date, etc., yet the power of God's Word is not dependent upon our knowledge of such matters. I have not the slightest idea who wrote Hebrews and yet I am much indebted to that great book for its clear presentation of the priesthood of Jesus Christ. A study of anatomy does not account for man's ability to construct a cathedral or to direct a symphony; Socrates playfully ridiculed any attempt to account for his "curved posture," as he sat in prison, by a study of how the muscles and ligaments move the bones, when the real reason lay in the ill will of the Athenians toward him (*Phaedo,* III, p. 244). Men do not need to know the answer to every critical question in order to experience the truth of God's Word and the power of His Gospel to redeem them from sin. It is a tragedy to observe theological students become panic-stricken over problems of textual or literary criticism. One does not need to be a master of biochemistry in order to enjoy good food, and one can learn to play a piano without knowing how mind can operate upon matter. Similarly, one can enter into a faith union with Jesus Christ and experience His power to redeem from sin without having all the answers to the problems of epistemology which are associated with the process of divine revelation. This is not to suggest that these problems are not important, nor that they do not deserve study but they call for patient scholarship, not panic and doubt.

My senior colleague and teacher, Harold S. Bender, Dean of Goshen College Biblical Seminary, has shown in his splendid booklet, *The Anabaptist Vision,* that the Anabaptists thought of the church as a brotherhood, of the Christian life as discipleship to Christ, and of the Christian ethic as the adoption of a life of absolute love and nonresistance. They were convinced of the centrality of divine love in redemption, and of the ability of God to infuse that same redeeming love for men into the hearts of His regenerated children. Christ not only justifies: He also transforms men, taking away their stony heart of selfishness and sin, and putting in its place a heart of love and good will toward all men. The Christian life is therefore one of "redeemed discipleship." Union with the Lord Jesus and being filled and controlled by His Holy Spirit produces a genuine spirituality which is the Biblical and the only real answer to secularism, worldliness, legalism, emotionalism, and intellectualism. Redemption means genuinely redeemed lives, not the justification of unconverted subscribers to a creed.

During the last century, when Mennonites in North America made the transition from German to English, they suddenly found themselves cut off from the writings of Menno Simons, Dirck Philips, T. J. van Braght, and Thomas von Imbroich, as well as their confessions of faith, catechisms, and devotional literature. This brought about a certain disorientation, a cutting loose from the historical moorings. Although the brotherhood was saved by the introduction of the Sunday school, and was greatly revived by the ensuing interest in Bible study and missions, there arose a generation of leaders who were but superficially acquainted with the fundamental doctrines and insights of their Anabaptist forefathers. These new leaders attempted to formulate singlehandedly the outlines of a theology which would give our people a renewed sense of mission and thus prevent the further exodus of the ablest young people, and subsequent disintegration of the group. These formulations tended to cluster about nonresistance, nonconformity, and the ordinances: but nonresistance was thought of too exclusively in terms of a rejection of military service in time of war and little effort was made to develop a broad social ethic in terms of New Testament Christianity; nonconformity was often misunderstood as involving merely the maintenance of a cultural *status quo* rather than a dynamic spiritual tension with a Christ-rejecting world; and there developed an enumeration of "ordinances" which was utterly foreign to the Anabaptist tradition, as well as an undue emphasis on outward forms. The Mennonite of 1900 would have been shocked to read in Menno Simons: "My faithful reader, think not that we put great stress upon the elements and rites"; also that the ceremonies of the New Testament "are but two in number, being baptism and the Supper." (It should be noted that Menno believed in keeping every New Testament command, even to observing the holy kiss in the brotherhood, but he recognized that there were but two sacramental signs.)

PREFACE

I recognize freely that no human being is worthy to write of the doctrinal content of God's Word. Historical research, a mastery of the tongues of the Bible, a knowledge of the history of theology: none of these suffices. Unless one is anointed of God, and is blessed with the illumination and guidance of His Spirit, the resultant work will be spiritually barren and ineffective. I can only hope that God heard my constant prayer for divine guidance and blessing as I wrote.

It will be recognized in the reading of this book that there are various questions which are not discussed exhaustively, or perhaps not treated at all: my reason being that I wanted to produce a book which would be readable, and which would serve as an introduction to larger and more comprehensive works in theology. I also attempted to make central those major doctrines of the Bible which relate to God and His salvation, and which exalt the Lord Jesus Christ. Theology must edify, not confuse; it must be Biblical, not philosophical; it must report on divine revelation, not on human insights. I therefore sought to be as nontechnical as possible. Too long has the world thought of theology as being dry as dust and unrelated to life, whereas theology relates to life both here and hereafter, to eternal life and divine salvation, to Jesus Christ and how to become united with Him.

It was my intention to give credit to other writers whenever I borrowed from them. It is possible, however, that due to many years of reading, and of teaching theology, I have picked up thoughts from various authors and no longer recall their sources. If I have therefore been guilty of plagiarism anywhere I would welcome being informed of my fault so that in any future editions of this work proper credit may be extended. In the broadest sense I cannot record the recognition which I ought to, for the simple reason that I owe such a debt to my teachers in Eastern Mennonite College, Goshen College, Westminster Theological Seminary in Philadelphia, and the universities of Zürich, Basel, and Michigan, as I can never express. As to quotations, I have felt free to quote from older, standard works at length, being careful only to indicate the sources. When I quoted at any length from recent books bearing a copyright notice I have done so only with the permission of the publishers. This latter class of quotations are labeled "used by permission." I am indeed grateful to the publishers who have kindly permitted me to use their materials. For the sake of clarity and good English I have generally quoted from the Revised Standard Version of the English Bible, published by Thomas Nelson & Sons of New York, and copyright 1946

PREFACE

(N.T.) and 1952 (O.T.) by the Division of Christian Education of the National Council of the Churches of Christ in the United States of America. I want to express my appreciation for the privilege of doing so. Occasionally I quoted from another version, or adapted a reading on the basis of the original Greek or Hebrew; in these cases I attempted to indicate what had been done.

I am grateful to A. J. Metzler, the Publishing Agent of Mennonite Publication Board, to Paul Erb, Chairman of the Publishing Committee, to Beulah Stauffer Hostetler, to Lenora Dietzel, and to many other friends for the co-operation which has made possible the publication of this book. My wife has been of much help and encouragement to me in the entire project. For the defects and errors of judgment or fact, I alone am responsible. If God can use this effort to strengthen the Christian faith of any of His children, or to lead anyone to accept Christ as Saviour and Lord, I shall truly be well repaid for the many hours of study and labor which went into it. *Soli Deo Gloria!*

Those who did more than any one else to teach me the love and mercy of God, and what Christian discipleship means, must yet be mentioned: my beloved parents, Aaron Martin and Martha A. (Rock) Wenger. It is to me a blessed symbol of my indebtedness to them to be writing this preface, and completing this assignment, on my father's sixty-ninth birthday anniversary.

Goshen, Indiana　　　　　　　　　　　　　　J. C. Wenger
April 17, 1953

PREFACE TO FOURTH PRINTING

Issuing a fourth printing of this volume has once more made it possible to correct a few minor points. The same doctrinal perspective has been maintained. This perspective is that the God who spoke fragmentarily through Israel's prophets has made a final, full, and definitive revelation of Himself in His incarnate Son, Jesus Christ our Lord. I have sought to write a theology which stands squarely in the Anabaptist-Mennonite tradition.

Dozens of doctoral dissertations have been written on Anabaptism. In 1963 a new *Mennonite Confession of Faith* was adopted. The third printing of the Verduin translation of the *Complete Writings*

PREFACE

of Menno Simons was made in 1974. And the monumental and scholarly four-volume *Mennonite Encyclopedia* has been reprinted, volume by volume. The sales of the *Martyrs Mirror* are phenomenal. Although I am deeply immersed in Anabaptist studies my final appeal in this work has been to the living "Oracles of God," especially to the books of the New Testament. Although I am a Mennonite, I have learned much from the other historical traditions of the church: Roman, Orthodox, Anglican, Lutheran, Reformed, Wesleyan, and Quaker.

My final appeal to the reader may be made in the words of Paul as rendered by Luther: *Prüfet aber alles, und das Gute behaltet* (Now test everything, and hold to that which is good)!

Soli Deo Gloria!

Goshen, Indiana   J. C. Wenger
October 9, 1975

Contents

xi

CONTENTS

PROLEGOMENA

PROLEGOMENA

1. *THE FIELD OF THEOLOGY*

The whole field of theology, covering the entire curriculum of theological training, has traditionally been divided into four major blocks. By way of introduction there is first of all the general subject of theological orientation which includes such topics as the Christian concept of revelation, the nature of Christian experience, Christianity and mysticism, Christianity and other religions, law and Gospel, etc. The remainder of the field of theology is divided into four groups of subjects as follows:

I. EXEGETICAL THEOLOGY
  1. Biblical Philology
     a. Hebrew
     b. Aramaic (Chaldee)
     c. Koine Greek
  2. Biblical Archaeology
     a. Geography of Bible lands
     b. Flora and fauna
     c. Domestic and social life in Israel
     d. Civil and political institutions
     e. Religious rites and ceremonies
  3. Biblical Introduction
     a. Origin of Biblical books
     b. Revelation
     c. Inspiration
     d. Canon
     e. Versions
  4. Biblical Criticism
     a. Textual or lower criticism
     b. Literary or higher criticism
  5. Hermeneutics or Principles of Interpretation
  6. Exegesis of the Old and New Testament Books

II. HISTORICAL THEOLOGY
1. Preparatory Studies
   a. Ancient man. Genesis 1-11
   b. History of Israel
   c. Life of Christ
   d. Apostolic history
2. Church History
   a. Ancient, A.D. 30-590.
   b. Medieval, A.D. 590-1517
   c. Modern, 1517-
   d. Special fields
      (1) Persecution
      (2) Development of organization and polity
      (3) Church councils
      (4) Forms of worship
      (5) Patristics
      (6) Symbolics
      (7) Denominational histories
      (8) Missions and charities
      (9) Statistics
      (10) Art and architecture
3. History of Doctrine
4. Biblical Theology
   a. Old Testament: Mosaism wisdom and poetical literature; prophetism
   b. New Testament: Synoptic, Johannine, Pauline, Petrine, Hebrews, James, and Apocalyptic theology

III. SYSTEMATIC THEOLOGY
1. Apologetics
2. Polemics
3. Irenics
4. *Dogmatics or Systematic Theology*
5. Christian ethics
6. Theological encyclopedia

IV. PRACTICAL THEOLOGY
1. Homiletics
2. Evangelism
3. Missions
4. Pastoral theology
5. Christian education
6. Sacred music

7. Church government and polity
8. Christian service institutions
9. Liturgics

2. THE MEANING OF SYSTEMATIC THEOLOGY

The above outline will help the reader to see the setting of this study in reference to the total curriculum of theological study. By systematic theology we mean the comprehensive statement of the truth of God as revealed in His Word. In other words, systematic theology does not relate basically to human insights or philosophy but to the content of the revealed Word of God. Perhaps it will be of some value to examine here the relation of systematic theology to certain other Biblical disciplines. *Exegesis* is the careful analysis of a portion of the Word of God in the original tongues. Ultimately all systematic theology must rest upon exegesis if it is truly to be theology. *Biblical theology* takes the fruits of the exegetical study of a portion of God's Word and combines them into a unit, such as the doctrine of God in Mosaism, or the Messianic hope as found in Isaiah. *Systematic theology* then takes the Biblical teaching which has been derived from exegesis and from Biblical theology and combines the fruit of these studies into one comprehensive statement of the truth. *Practical theology* studies how best to teach and proclaim the truth about God as found in His Word. *Church history* traces the life of the people of God on earth.

The systematic theologian must be careful to indicate that which is clearly revealed as the truth of God's Word and that which is merely his understanding of the relation of various truths of divine revelation. Only God's Word remains completely authoritative and inspired. Theology is a human work, it is not infallible, and it does not possess divine authority. Nevertheless it has value in holding before each generation the great truths of the divine Word of God as found in the Scripture.

3. WHY MEN STUDY THEOLOGY

It is impossible to understand many statements in the Bible apart from a knowledge of the Bible as a whole. This is no denial of the basic clarity of Scripture, but simply an acknowledgment that interpretation enters into more of Scripture than is commonly recognized. For example, when John states that "the blood of Jesus his Son cleanses us from all sin,"[1] he is not asserting that if a sinner

1 I John 1:7.

stands under the cross and allows the blood of the Saviour to flow over his body, he is thus spiritually renewed. Theology tells us that the meaning of that sentence is that faith in the crucified Saviour cleanses from sin. When Paul speaks of glorying in the cross,[2] he does not mean glorying in a physical item but in that which was accomplished by Jesus in His death on the cross in A.D. 30. When the Apostle John speaks of Satan being bound with a great chain,[3] theologians do not understand this to refer to a chain made of iron but to a limitation of Satan's power. When Jesus said: "This cup is the new covenant in my blood,"[4] He certainly meant, "The contents of this cup symbolize the covenant which I am making with believers on me by means of my death at Golgotha." In fact, the general rule could be made that all spiritual truth is stated in such a way as to require interpretation. Ordinarily a devout heart and a mind illuminated by the Holy Spirit are entirely adequate for the average man to become "wise unto salvation."[5] Nevertheless, the church also needs a type of scholarship which can come only from regenerated Christians who have had the benefit of sound training in the study of God's Word and who have spent many years in Biblical study. This is not in the sense of delivering an authoritative message *ex cathedra,* but as thinking through the issues faced by each generation and interpreting the Word of God to meet and overcome the unsound doctrines of each period. Christian scholars and uneducated church members constitute, of course, one united Christian brotherhood.

Men study theology because they are not satisfied to view the Bible as a disorganized collection of religious literature. The human mind is so constituted as to crave for an overview which sees each item in its relation to the whole. Perhaps a comparison with nature will help to make this truth more clear. Take trees, for example. God has not planted all the trees of the world in neat scientific arrangements, with the firs, sycamores, etc., arranged according to family and genus. Rather, nature presents to us a glorious lack of organization. The human mind, however, is not satisfied merely to note the aesthetic beauty of a forest; men want to know what kind of tree this is and to what family it belongs. Men desire to get the helps to understanding which such organization of the data of nature provides. This is true not only of trees but of all forms of life. Scientists have organized everything into systems: minerals, plants, animals, bacteria, heavenly bodies. Scientists take animals or plants having similar characteristics and group them into the largest pos-

2 Gal. 6:14.   4 I Cor. 11:25.
3 Rev. 20:1, 2.   5 II Tim. 3:15, AV.

sible class, the *phylum*. Each *phylum*, in turn, is progressively sub-divided into subgroups in this order: *subphylum, class, subclass, order, suborder, family, genus, species,* and *subspecies* or *variety*. Modern classifications of biology are based on the work of Linnaeus, 1735.[6] The plant kingdom, for example, is divided into four *phyla* and the animal kingdom into twelve or more *phyla*.

Scientists, however, have not been satisfied merely to study biology and to divide life forms into units. They also wanted to know what everything was made of, and thus the science of chemistry was born. And so were all the other sciences: aerodynamics, anthropology, archaeology, astronomy, bacteriology, biochemistry, etc. The outcome of all this organization and study has been not merely the satisfying of the human mind's hunger for ultimate understandings but also profound practical benefits such as X rays, insulin, automobiles, and electrical appliances, etc.—all give witness to the value of science.

And so with theology. The human mind is not satisfied to read the narratives of Moses, the psalms of David, the letters of Paul, and the Apocalypse of John. Men want to understand each truth given in relation to the whole: this is the task of theology. In the field of theology the more or less standard organization goes back at least to Peter Lombard (A.D., c. 1100-1160), the Scholastic theologian.[7] Ever since the earliest centuries of the Christian era theologians have been laboring to interpret the raw materials of the Bible into an organized system, just as scientists have interpreted the data of nature in terms of various classifications.

It is indeed true that individual Christians can receive salvation and understand much of the Bible without studying theology. But the church as such must be clear in its doctrinal message. Its teachers and ministers must know the content and the significance of the Biblical *kerygma*. And just as there are some scientists who specialize in studying a given genus, while others labor in the field of classification and write treatises on the interpretation of nature, so in theology some specialize in narrow fields while others give themselves to theology proper.

The study of science has not driven all the quacks out of business, but it has accomplished wonders in changing the patterns of

6 "Classification." *The World Book Encyclopedia* (Chicago: Field Enterprises, Inc., 1950), Vol. 3, C, p. 1468.

7 Emil Brunner, *The Christian Doctrine of God* (Philadelphia: The Westminster Press, 1950), p. vi.

life for the race and delivering the masses from the fears which had enslaved them for most of human history. In the same way the study of theology has not eliminated heretics and heresies from the church, but the neglect of theology has promoted unsound doctrine. And just as scientists have done much to conquer the physical world, so the theologians of each age are responsible to meet the attacks of the anti-Christian philosophies of each era, as well as to give positive guidance to the lay-thinkers and leaders of the church by assisting them to formulate the message of the Word of God in such a way as best to be understood by each generation. It is to be hoped also that some progress is being made through the centuries in developing a more perfect theology.

4. *THE VALUES OF THEOLOGY*

The study of the doctrinal content of the Word of God has value for the building of spiritual life. Some people emphasize emotion and the stirring of the heart as being a major factor in Christian growth. There is undoubtedly some truth to this point of view. It does people good to be stirred up by sound Gospel preaching. The Word of God must not only reach the understanding but also the emotions if it is to be most effective. Other people emphasize activity as being a prime factor in Christian growth. They point to the strengthening effect in faith and character which witnessing has: speaking to unsaved persons about salvation, seeking to win the lost to Jesus Christ, and testifying to the goodness of God. But neither emotion nor activity alone is the full answer to human need in relation to Christian growth. A third major factor relates to the intellect and the apprehension of the glorious truths of God and His salvation as revealed in Scripture. Getting a good grasp of the full truth which God has revealed to mankind has great value in increasing Christian faith.

Systematic theology also assists in proclaiming the truth of the Gospel. One does not really know God's Word as long as he is acquainted only with isolated verses or partial statements of the truth. To really know the Bible one must know it in its entirety. One must have a good grasp of the entire history of salvation as revealed in Scripture, from the Garden of Eden to the Book of Revelation. One must be familiar with the promises and conditions of salvation, as well as the warnings of God's Word. No one really knows the Word of God until he has a good grasp of its truth and of the relationship of each part of Scripture to the central message of the Bible.

In the third place, the study of systematic theology helps to protect one from heresy. Every unsound doctrine which is current in each age is unsound precisely for the reason that it is a deviation from the clearly revealed truth of Scripture, or is a distortion of the truths which are given to men in the Bible. Some believers are not aware, for example, that the institutions of Moses have had their day and been abolished by Jesus. Other believers do not seem to be familiar with the contrast between those who lived before and those who lived after the day of Pentecost and yet who were in possession of saving faith.

Systematic theology also helps one to be God-centered in his thinking and living. If this study is carried on with a spirit of humility and an earnest seeking of God's will it draws one closer to Christ and gives one that daily guidance and assurance which is essential to fullness of power and joy in Christian living. As one grows in one's understanding of the truth of God's Word one comes to see more clearly how completely dependent men are upon God, how utterly unworthy all people are, and how much they stand in need of the grace of God. The Christian life is founded on truth, the truth of Scripture.

Unfortunately, it is also possible to abuse this great study of theology. One can make of systematic theology an intellectual system without obedience and without humility and reverence. Christianity comes then to be misunderstood and to be conceived of basically as some sort of philosophy which even unsaved intellectuals can study and delight in. This study, which ought to glorify Jesus Christ and enable humble believers to rejoice in the adequacy of God's plan of salvation and in the fullness of His grace, can lead one away from simplicity of heart and from a childlike faith to a barren intellectualism. The sure way to prevent this great study from becoming unfruitful and cold is to spend much time in meditation on God's Word in secret prayer. Otherwise one can become a proud intellectual, given over to controversy about obscure points of theology, and thus lose all usefulness as far as the service of Christ is concerned. Concretely this means that one ought to spend at least as much time in direct reading and study of the Word of God as one spends in reading theological books. The theological student should also read the biographies of great men of God such as Paul, Augustine, Luther, Calvin, Grebel, Menno Simons, Wesley, Spurgeon, Finney, Moody, J. S. Coffman, etc. Christian biography has tremendous value for the illumination of systematic theology and for the development of personal piety.

5. OUTSTANDING WORKS IN SYSTEMATIC THEOLOGY

Perhaps the most important sources of Roman Catholic theology are the canon, decrees, and catechism of the Council of Trent, the sessions of which were held intermittently from 1545 to 1563.[8] One of the more important sets of Catholic theology, written in English, is that of Sylvester Joseph Hunter, a Jesuit, *Outlines of Dogmatic Theology*, three volumes, Benziger Brothers, New York, Cincinnati, Chicago, 1894-96. Valuable also is the two-volume set edited by G. D. Smith: *The Teaching of the Catholic Church*, Macmillan, 1949. The best work for the refutation of Roman Catholicism is that of Professor Karl von Hase (1800-90): *Handbook to the Controversy with Rome,* published in London in 1909 as a translation from the seventh German edition, the original of which was published in 1862. This work probably remains the most solid contribution on the subject. Of great value, however, is the modern reprint, *Infallibility of the Church,* by George Salmon, Baker Book House, Grand Rapids, Michigan, 1951. This work was originally issued in 1888. Valuable also is *A Catholic Dictionary*, edited by Donald Attwater, Macmillan, 1942; as well as the more comprehensive *Catholic Encyclopedia* published by Appleton about 1910.

One of the finest works in the Anglican-Episcopalian tradition is *Theological Outlines*, by Professor Francis J. Hall, Morehouse-Gorham Co., New York 1933; Professor Hall also wrote a ten-volume *Dogmatic Theology,* of which this one-volume *Outlines* is a condensation.

Among the more important works in the Reformed tradition should be mentioned the *Institutes of the Christian Religion* by John Calvin, 1536, now available in the English translation made by John Allen and published in two large volumes by the Westminster Press, 1935. A most significant writer was Charles Hodge (1797-1878), "The Chief Figure in the Group of Theologians Known as the Princeton School," author of a three-volume *Systematic Theology*, 1872-73. Fairly satisfactory also is the *Systematic Theology* of A. H. Strong (1836-1921), originally issued in 1886 but revised in 1907. Strong was a Baptist. The most complete modern Reformed work in systematic theology is that of Professor Louis Berkhof (1873-1957), *Reformed Dogmatics,* four volumes, Eerdmans, 1932-37. Of value also are the *Outlines of Theology* by A. A. Hodge (1823-86), published in 1860, revised 1878, and reprinted by Eerdmans, 1949, and by Zondervan, 1972. See also G. C. Berkouwer's (1903-) books.

8 See, e.g., "The Canons and Dogmatic Decrees of the Council of Trent, A.D. 1563," in Philip Schaff, *The Creeds of Christendom* (New York: Harper and Brothers, 1919), II, pp. 77-206.

The outstanding theologian of the strictest Lutheran body in America, the Missouri Synod, was undoubtedly Dr. Francis Pieper (1852-1931) whose set of German theological volumes was published between 1917 and 1924, and issued in English under the title, *Christian Dogmatics,* three volumes, by the Concordia Publishing House, St. Louis, Missouri, beginning in 1950. Professor John Theodore Mueller has issued a one-volume *Christian Dogmatics,* published by Concordia in 1934. A most useful encyclopedia is that issued by Charles Scribner's Sons, New York, 1899, *The Lutheran Cyclopedia,* edited by H. E. Jacobs and John A. W. Haas.

The most basic source of information about Arminianism, of course, is *The Works of James Arminius* (1560-1609), translated from the Latin and published by Derby, Miller and Orton, Auburn and Buffalo, 1853, in three volumes. The most complete work of theology by an Arminian theologian is the *Theological Institutes* of the Methodist theologian, Richard Watson (1781-1833), originally published in 1823; the thirtieth edition of this work was issued in 1850. In 1869 Samuel Wakefield (1799-1895) issued *A Complete System of Christian Theology,* which was a condensation of Watson's *Institutes.* William B. Pope (1822-1903) published his *Compendium of Christian Theology* in 1879; and John Miley (1831-95) issued his two-volume *Systematic Theology,* 1892-94. Henry C. Sheldon's *System of Christian Doctrine* appeared in 1903. The most comprehensive modern statement of Arminian theology was issued 1940-42 by H. Orton Wiley; *Christian Theology,* Nazarene Publishing House, Kansas City, Missouri. Useful also is the condensation of Wiley's three volumes, *Introduction to Christian Theology,* by H. Orton Wiley and Paul T. Culbertson, Beacon Hill Press, Kansas City, Missouri, 1946.

Perhaps the most important modern volume on the theology of the Society of Friends is Howard Brinton, *Friends for 300 Years,* Harper & Brothers, New York, 1952. The standard work historically is *The Apology,* by William Penn's colleague, Robert Barclay (1648-90).

In the Anabaptist-Mennonite tradition chief emphasis has always been placed on simplicity of faith and obedience to the Scriptures, rather than on systematic formulations and a development of theology. To date no systematic theology has been written by a Mennonite, and few books on Bible doctrine have appeared. Mention should be made of the *Complete Works* of Menno Simons (c. 1496-1561), issued in English at Elkhart, Ind., 1871, and Scottdale, Pa.,

1956, especially of his *Foundation and Plain Instruction*, 1539-40. Menno's colleague, Dirck Philips (c. 1504-68), also produced a number of booklets which have been gathered together under the title, *Enchiridion or Handbook of the Christian Doctrine and Religion* [English], Elkhart, Indiana, 1915. In Germany a Mennonite author and elder, Emil Haendiges, has written a brief historical theology entitled, *Die Lehre der Mennoniten*, 1921. Actually the only man who has written comprehensive books on Bible doctrine for the Mennonites is Daniel Kauffman (1865-1944); his *Bible Doctrine* was published at Scottdale, Pennsylvania, in 1914, and his *Doctrines of the Bible* appeared at the same place in 1928.

One of the most powerful movements in theological thinking today is that led by Karl Barth and Emil Brunner of Switzerland, commonly called Barthianism, the Dialectical Theology, or Neo-Orthodoxy. Perhaps the more prominent leader is Barth, whose *Kirchliche Dogmatik* (set of church dogmatics), although unfinished, has extended to twelve huge tomes, plus a slender but significant thirteenth volume. Dr. Brunner's three solid volumes on systematic theology, *Die Kirchliche Lehre von Gott*, etc., appeared 1946, 1949, and 1960, in German, and 1950, 1952, and 1962 in English (Westminster Press). Worthy of note also is the Lundensian school of theology represented by Gustaf Aulen whose systematic theology is entitled, *The Faith of the Christian Church*, the Muhlenberg Press, Philadelphia, 1948. Recent theological works in America worthy of mention are *The Nature and Destiny of Man* by Reinhold Niebuhr, the Gifford Lectures of 1931, Scribner's, 1951, and Paul Tillich, *Systematic Theology*, Volumes I-III, University of Chicago Press, 1951-63.

Neither the Barthian nor the Lundensian nor the American dialectical theologians recognize the Bible *per se* as being the infallible Word of God.[9] They believe in divine revelation, to be sure, but they do not regard it as being identical with the words of Scripture.[10] Divine revelation is not so much a matter of content as it is contact with God Himself. The Scriptures are the human witness to the experience of encounter with God and Christ. Much of modern Protestant theology, indeed, is moving away from belief in special creation, the fall of man as a historical fact, and belief in the reality of Biblical miracles, as well as the doctrine of eternal punishment. Many theologians set up rigid philosophical limitations as to

9 Cornelius Van Til, *The New Modernism, An Appraisal of the Theology of Barth and Brunner* (Philadelphia: The Presbyterian and Reformed Publishing Co., 1947).
10 For a defense of the Bible as God's very Word, see *The Infallible Word, A Symposium*, by the Members of the Faculty of Westminster Theological Seminary (Philadelphia: The Presbyterian Guardian Publishing Corporation, 1946).

what they believe the Bible can actually reveal and what would indeed be possible for God to say or do. While still professing to take divine revelation seriously, they nevertheless feel free to reject more or less of what the Scriptures actually say. In other words, much of current theological thought has not overcome the older modernism which had its roots in the thinking of Schleiermacher (1768-1834) and Ritschl (1822-89), and other liberal theologians. Barthianism has done much to overcome the unsound theology of the Ritschlians by taking seriously man's sin and need of redemption, by overcoming the man-centeredness of modernism, by stressing the reality of the Saviourhood of Jesus Christ, by emphasizing the crisis into which one comes when he meets Jesus Christ. It is indeed unfortunate that Barthianism has not also overcome the liberal attitude toward the Bible which has for generations characterized modernists. It is to be feared also that many modern theologians in their peculiar views of what is and of what is not possible in divine revelation have seriously distorted the doctrinal content of the revealed Word of God as found in the Scriptures.

In opposition to the older modernism[11] and also to the modern Barthian movement there have been a large number of American Bible teachers who have become known as Fundamentalists. Among the theological writers of these strict evangelicals should be mentioned P. B. Fitzwater of the Moody Bible Institute, whose *Christian Theology* was published by Eerdmans in 1948, and Professor Henry C. Thiessen of Wheaton College, whose *Introductory Lectures in Systematic Theology* was issued in 1949, also by Eerdmans. Fundamentalists accept the Bible as being the very Word of God and hold to a theory of inspiration known as plenary and verbal. Bible believers of various denominations, therefore, are united in holding to a high view of inspiration as represented by such theologians as Fitzwater and Thiessen — as well as James O. Buswell, Jr.

Fundamentalism as a movement, however, has not challenged current thinkers in at all the same way as has Barthianism. Furthermore, Fundamentalism has, unfortunately, often shown a certain narrowness of spirit; for example in its attitude toward those who do not hold to the premillennial view of prophecy. It is also remarkably indifferent to or even negative toward those movements for social reform such as the clearing of slums, which much of modern Christendom has felt is a wholesome thing. In other words, modern

11 Represented by such works as William Newton Clarke, *An Outline of Christian Theology* (New York: Charles Scribner's Sons, 1898), and William Adams Brown, *Christian Theology in Outline* (New York, 1906).

Fundamentalism has manifested a rather dull conscience on social issues.[12] Undoubtedly the fear has been that to take an interest in social issues is to become an exponent of the so-called social gospel which has in turn been indifferent to if not critical of the concept of personal regeneration through the work of the Holy Spirit.

In this brief survey of some of the major works of theology mention should also be made of the *Systematic Theology* of Lewis Sperry Chafer (1871-1952) of Dallas Theological Seminary which was published in seven volumes, plus an index volume, by the Dallas Seminary Press, 1947 and 1948. This set is described as "evangelical, premillennial, and dispensational." Dispensationalism denies what might be called the essential unity of the Bible and stresses the Jews as being God's center of interest on earth, with the church being a mere parenthesis between the Jewish Old Covenant and a millennium in which the Jews will again occupy the center of God's stage. Needless to say the Dispensationalism of Chafer stands in sharp contrast to the standard theologies of recent centuries whether Roman Catholic, Reformed, Arminian, or Anglican. Nevertheless Dispensationalism has exerted a considerable influence in America in those churches and sects which are known as Fundamental.

The present work recognizes the Bible as the Word of God, as the final authority in faith and life. While the Bible is not an end in itself, yet it is all inspired of God and profitable for doctrine and teaching. The central purpose of the Scriptures is to present Jesus Christ and His redemption to a lost world. To make the Bible an end in itself and revert to a sort of a Protestant Scholasticism is not to stand in the glorious tradition of the Christian Church, especially of the sixteenth-century reformers. Nevertheless it must be admitted that the Fundamentalist theologians of the twentieth century, in spite of their limitations, stand closer to the great reformers such as Luther and Calvin, than do the modernists and semi-modernists with their undue preoccupation with philosophy and its categories. The theology which is needed today is one which stresses a simple childlike faith in Christ and His Word, one which warms the heart as well as satisfies the understanding.

6. *THE TRADITIONAL THEISTIC PROOFS*

Many years ago the present writer as a young Christian read the *Natural Theology* of Professor Milton Valentine (1825-1906) of the

---

12 Cf. Carl F. H. Henry, *The Uneasy Conscience of Modern Fundamentalism* (Grand Rapids, Mich.: Eerdmans, 1947).

Lutheran Theological Seminary, Gettysburg, Pennsylvania, 1885.
Dr. Valentine attempted to show the reasonableness of believing in
a personal God from the evidence of intelligence which is discernible
in the Creation. What value have the traditional proofs in demon-
strating the existence of God? Logical arguments cannot make a
Christian believer out of an unbeliever, although the Holy Spirit
may use such considerations to bring conviction to an unsaved man.
Theistic proofs cannot in themselves create saving faith. Nevertheless, they can serve as "flying buttresses" to the faith of young
believers. Reading natural theology can strengthen immature believers.

Traditionally there have been five major arguments advanced *not*
for belief in God. The *ethnological* proof of God's existence is
considered merely presumptive. It points out that all peoples everywhere through all human history have tended to believe in the
supernatural. It would therefore seem that deep in the very nature
of man is the conviction that he is not alone but that a higher power
or powers exist. The *cosmological* proof of God's existence is
based on the assumption that a world requires a World-Maker.
In other words, this world with its inhabitants could not have made
itself; therefore there must be a God who created this world and
its race of intelligent beings. The *teleological* argument for God's
existence stresses the point that when one examines the nature
of the universe it gives evidence of great intelligence; design is
everywhere apparent. If the universe shows evidence of design,
there must be a great Mind which has planned it all. The *ontological*
argument for God's existence does not appear to the average mind
of today as being very compelling. In its crudest form the ontological proof states that since God is by definition perfect, perfection
must include existence, hence God must exist. Perhaps a better
statement of this line of thought would be to say that if human
thinking has validity God must exist, because the very thought
of the finite implies the Infinite, the very thought of the creature
implies the Creator, etc. In other words, the basic convictions of
the race are in this argument regarded as in some sense constituting
a source of truth.[18] It is not held, of course, that man can bring into
being a God to satisfy his thought processes. Immanuel Kant was
not convinced by the theistic arguments with which he was familiar
but he in turn created a fifth, the *moral* argument for God's existence. Kant felt strongly that it was entirely evident that man is in

---

13 Leander S. Keyser, *A System of Christian Evidence* (Burlington, Iowa: Lutheran Literary
Board, 1930), p. 199.

a moral arena. He is in a world where moral law reigns. Man may break the moral law of God by way of transgression, but he cannot crush the reign of moral law itself; he cannot escape the consequences of his sin. Now, said Kant, if there is a reign of moral law there must be a great moral Lawgiver and Governor.

If one is to take into account all the facts it does not seem right to omit mention of a very profound truth, namely, the character and testimony of the *Scriptures*. It is evident to every honest person that the Bible has exerted a salutary influence wherever it has gone. As men have heeded the message of this book they have become righteous and good. Now the Bible asserts without equivocation the existence of a great, personal God. It may, therefore, fairly be asked, Upon what foundation may one stand to deny the testimony of this Good Book? There is also the testimony of *Jesus Christ*, He who is acknowledged to have been both a good and great man. Jesus asserted emphatically that He knew by experience and fellowship the reality of God's existence. Again one may ask, Upon what foundation does the unbeliever stand who challenges the testimony of Jesus Christ? Mention should also be made of *Christian experience*. Throughout the history of the Christian Church there have been millions of good and honest people who have testified that they have known by experience the sweetness of fellowship with God through Jesus Christ, that they are truly aware of the reality of God and of the eternal world. One may, therefore, again ask whether blindness in one man invalidates sight in another. Does the mere fact that some people have refused to accept Jesus Christ and to give themselves to Him in itself prove that those who have done so have experienced only an illusion?

It appears that theologians have in this matter gone from one extreme to the other. It may be that in past generations both Catholics and Protestants have overestimated the value of the reasoning process as a factor in bringing men to faith. Today, however, the tendency seems to be to quite underestimate the whole matter of rationality and to stress practically a sort of irrationalism, as if man was not a creature who thought at all.

The truth lies between these two extremes. The reasoning process in itself is not adequate to make a man a new creature in Christ. Men become Christians not by a sheer change of intellectual point of view but by becoming aware of their sin and of their need of a redeemer, the Lord Jesus Christ. On the other hand, it is reasonable, and this can indeed be demonstrated, to believe that this world is not a self-created and self-sufficient entity. Belief in God is rational and defensible even to the intellect. But the central message of the Christian Church must continue to remain the proclamation of God's holy law and man's great spiritual need, combined with the remedy for that need, the glorious and saving Gospel of Christ which is offered to everyone on the condition of repentance and faith. The theistic proofs cannot create faith nor can they sustain it, but they can serve in a small way to help immature believers with their intellectual problems[14] (though it must be admitted that frequently the basis of doubt is emotional rather than intellectual in character). We must also bear steadily in mind that the central message of the Bible is not a set of propositions but the proclamation of salvation from sin and the gift of eternal life through Jesus Christ our Lord.

7. THE BIBLICAL SOURCE OF THEOLOGY

The evangelical theologian humbly accepts, in faith, all the plain and clear representations of Scripture. While it is true that Jesus Christ is the central gift of God to mankind, and that the function of the Word of God is basically to bear witness to Christ, nevertheless the Bible does contain much propositional truth, all of which is profitable for doctrine. This is not to suggest, of course, that men cannot abuse the Bible by misinterpretation, e.g., by a gross misunderstanding of Biblical figures such as the windows of heaven, the four winds, etc.

On the authority of Scripture Menno Simons wrote bluntly:

We hope that no one will be so ignorant, who is otherwise of a candid and rational mind, but that he will know that the whole Scriptures, both of the Old and New Testaments, were written for our instruction, admonition, and correction; and that they are the true sceptre and rule by which the Lord's kingdom, house, church, and congregation must be governed and adjusted, II Timothy 3:16. Everything contrary to Scripture, whether it be in doctrines, faith, sacraments, worship, or conduct, should be measured by this infallible rule, and demolished by this just and divine sceptre, without any respect of persons, and brought to nothing.[15]

Menno also makes the following appeal:

Do, therefore, with a meek heart, and in the fear of God, examine these our faithful instructions, and judge by the spirit and word of Christ, as much as in you is; compare them with the doctrine and lives of the apos-

---

14 See J. C. Wenger, *Can a Thinking Man Be a Christian?* (Scottdale, Pa.: Herald Press, 1950).
15 *Complete Works* (Elkhart, Ind.: John F. Funk and Brother, 1871), I, pp. 53, 54.

tles . . . ; I hope, by the grace of God, you may plainly comprehend that our doctrine is the infallible doctrine and ground of the Scriptures.[16]

It is well known that within the last century modernistic theologians have arisen who have denied the infallibility of the Scriptures; they are skeptical of miracles, they do not accept the virgin birth of Christ, they disbelieve the unique deity of Jesus Christ, they reduce the atonement to a matter of moral influence, they reject the Biblical doctrine of the bodily resurrection in favor of the Greek doctrine of the immortality of the soul, they reject the future historicity of the Parousia (Christ's personal return): in short the Bible cannot be regarded fully as the authoritative Word of God.[17] Modernists do not believe that all Scripture is God-inspired and profitable for doctrine (II Timothy 3:16) and that "no prophecy of scripture is a matter of one's own interpretation, because no prophecy ever came by the impulse of man, but men moved by the Holy Spirit spoke from God" (II Peter 1:20, 21).

Roman Catholics and evangelical Protestants agree in this high view of inspiration as the following Catholic definition indicates: "Inspiration is a direct divine charismatic influence on the mind, will, and executive faculties of the human writer by which he mentally conceives, freely wills to write, and actually writes correctly all that God intends him to write and nothing else, so that God is truly author of the book produced."[18] This same writer continues: "Inspiration does not vary in degrees; it is equal in all books and in all parts thereof, and it guarantees absolute inerrancy and divine authorship throughout. As inspiration is no mechanical force but acts through the mind and will of the human writer in a human way, the human author's style, diction, and mental outlook naturally remain in the book produced, though God is the author of all that is written and man only the instrument of his hand."[19] The interested student should also read the excellent little essay by Professor John Murray of Westminster Theological Seminary entitled, "The Attestation of Scripture."[20]

Because the Bible is a truly human book, it gives genuine evi-

---

16 _Ibid._, I. p. 77.

17 See John Horsch, _Modern Religious Liberalism_ (Scottdale, Pa.: Mennonite Publishing House, 1924); J. Gresham Machen, _Christianity and Liberalism_ (New York: The Macmillan Co., 1923); Wilbur M. Smith, _Therefore, Stand_ (Boston: W. A. Wilde Co., 1945).

18 Donald Attwater, General Editor, _A Catholic Dictionary_ (New York: The Macmillan Co., 1942), p. 270.

19 _Ibid._, pp. 270, 271.

20 In _The Infallible Word_ (see note 10, above), pp. 1-52.

dence of its human authorship. One finds, for example, what might be called the conscious exaggeration of common people in Israel's wonder at the plagues of Egypt (Exodus 9:6, 7), as well as expressions of human emotions: disgust, discouragement, hope, aspiration, joy, and sorrow. The Bible contains a record of historical events as seen through human eyes. For example, the parallel accounts of Gospel writers sometimes are difficult for us to reconcile because the authors write freely without any anxiety as to whether or not their account might differ in detail from a parallel account. Style and vocabulary vary sharply from one Biblical writer to the other. Furthermore, the background and experience of each author in the Bible are somewhat in evidence. Belief in the plenary inspiration of Scripture does not at all involve the idea that the Bible was written while the authors were in a state of ecstasy. Furthermore the Scripture is written in common everyday language, not that of science or even of theology. (See *God's Word Written*, Herald Press, 1966, 1968.)

When evangelical theologians insist upon the Biblical source of all theology they mean that it is the task of the theologian to base his doctrine upon the Word of God, nothing more and nothing less than the entire message of Scripture. This position is to be contrasted with two other positions, that of rationalism, and that of Roman Catholicism. Other possible positions such as that of mysticism will be discussed in a subsequent section. Rationalists set up their understanding of what they believe to be possible and make their own intellects the ultimate arbiters of truth rather than the objective Word of God as revealed in Scripture. Rationalists have been much influenced by the various schools of philosophical thought, especially from the days of Immanuel Kant, who flourished in the last half of the eighteenth century. With Luther we say: "We ought not to criticize, explain, or judge the Scriptures by our mere reason, but diligently, with prayer, meditate thereon, and seek their meaning. ... The Holy Ghost must here be our only master and tutor; and let youth have no shame to learn of that preceptor. When I find myself assailed by temptation, I forthwith lay hold of some text of the Bible, which Jesus extends to me; as this: that He died for me, whence I derive infinite hope."[21] Luther also stated: "I have grounded my preaching upon the literal word: he that pleases may follow me; he that will not may stay,"[22] And Conrad Grebel, the founder of the Swiss brethren, wrote in 1524: "I believe the Word of God simply from grace,

21 Thomas S. Kepler, *The Table Talk of Martin Luther* (New York & Cleveland: The World Publishing Co., 1952), p. 6. Used by permission.
22 *Ibid.*, p. 8. Used by permission.

not from learning (Kunst)."[23] The curse of theology today is its reduction to abstract theory and philosophical speculation and system, rather than the simple presentation of the express counsels of God as revealed in His Word.

The Roman Catholic Church does not regard the Bible as the only authority in faith and life. Its position has been stated as follows: "Holy Scripture is profitable to teach, to reprove, to correct, and to instruct in justice, but the reading of it is not necessary to salvation nor is it the only or the direct rule of a Christian's faith. The direct rule is the teaching of the living Church, and divine tradition is with Scripture the joint source of revelation. A Catholic dogma, therefore, does not need any scriptural text for its warrant; dogmas are believed not because they are contained in the Scriptures, but because they are taught by the Church. . . ."[24] Concerning this extra-Biblical body of truth which the Catholic Church calls "Tradition" the following statement has been made: Tradition is "The sum of revealed doctrine which has *not* been committed to sacred Scripture (though it may have appeared in uninspired writing) but which has been handed down by a series of legitimate pastors of the Church from age to age. As revelation it must have come to the Apostle directly from the lips of Christ or been handed down by the Apostles at the dictation of the Holy Ghost.[25]

It is not only on the matter of extra-Biblical tradition that Catholics and Protestants differ; Catholics also deny the right of private interpretation, holding that "It is the office of the Church to declare the sense of any given Scriptural passage."[26] In other words, Catholics are not encouraged to interpret the Bible for themselves and to follow it implicitly according to the guidance of the Holy Spirit. The right of interpretation, according to Catholicism, does not reside with the individual but with the authoritative church, which means concretely the hierarchy. Protestants, on the other hand, hold that the final authority in faith and life is the Word of God as interpreted by the Holy Spirit to the individual conscience. Catholics say that the final authority is the church, never the individual; and the clergy, not the laity.

On a third point the Roman Catholics differ from Protestants as far as the Bible is concerned. Roman Catholics have in the Old

23 Harold S. Bender, *Conrad Grebel, c. 1498-1526* (Goshen, Ind.: The Mennonite Historical Society, 1950), p. iv.

24 *A Catholic Dictionary*, p. 479 (see note 18, above).

25 *Ibid.*, p. 528.

26 *Ibid.*, p. 483.

Testament what they call the *deuterocanonical* books, namely, Tobias, Judith, Wisdom, Ecclesiasticus, Baruch, I and II Maccabees, Esther 10:4 to the end, Daniel 3:24 to 4:3 and chapters 13 and 14. Catholics hold that the authority of these deuterocanonical books is equal with that of the other books of the Bible, although they admit that "they are not included in the Hebrew Bible of the Jews."[27] Protestants reject these extracanonical books because they were not in the Bible of Christ and the apostles, because they contain doctrines not in harmony with Scripture, and because they are nowhere in the New Testament quoted as authoritative: indeed, they are not quoted at all.

There is a fourth point on which Catholics and Protestants differ. Protestants believe that the canon of Scripture is closed and that there are no private revelations which in any way supplement the Word of God. Roman Catholics, however, hold that God on various occasions has given to private individuals genuine revelations which do, in a sense, supplement the Scriptures. For example, the devotion to the sacred heart of Jesus which consists of divine worship being given to His heart of flesh derives its popularity in its present form from the revelations believed to have been given to St. Margaret Mary Alacoque in the years 1673-75.[28] Protestants do not deny that God may give special leadings or visions or revelations to private individuals for their individual guidance but they do deny that any such private communication is in any sense a revelation for the church and therefore an addition to the Word of God.

8. *CHRISTIANITY AND MYSTICISM*

Since mysticism is not one unified movement it is indeed difficult to define it in such a way as to be fair to everyone concerned. Mysticism may refer to a pagan movement which is outside the stream of Christianity or to a heretical type of Christianity within the professing church, or to a type of emphasis which is not unsound in any way but which stresses a particular type of piety or experience. The essence of mysticism is placing stress on an intimate life of fellowship and communion with God or Christ rather than to be content as a humble believer on the Lord Jesus, guided by the Word of God as interpreted by the Holy Spirit. Genuine mysticism as far as the movement in general is concerned, involves, it is said, the three stages of purification, enlightenment, and ecstatic union.[29] Many

---

27 *Ibid.*, p. 153.
28 *Ibid.*, p. 467.
29 See the essay on mysticism by Joseph Bernhart in *Theologica Germanica* (New York:

mystics, some Christian and some pagan, have indeed had these moments of ecstasy in which they experienced an overcoming awareness of a direct and vital union with God. Mystics of this type are apt to become unbalanced in their emphasis and not true to all the teaching of the Word of God on human depravity and the need of a Mediator.

It must be admitted, however, that many Christians who are evangelical, some Catholic and some Protestant, have had moments of great spiritual intensity in which they have come into a tremendous awareness of the immediate presence of God. Charles G. Finney would be a good example of this type of "mysticism." Finney was a young lawyer on October 10, 1821, when he yielded to Christ and accepted Him as his personal Saviour. That very evening he had several hours of intense fellowship with the Lord Jesus Christ in which it seemed to him as if he saw the Saviour face to face. The Lord seemed to be looking at him in such a way that Finney wept like a child. The Holy Spirit came upon Finney with such power that he could feel the Spirit going through him "like waves of liquid love."[30] Other saints of God have had similar experiences. But Charles G. Finney did not become a mystic; he did not stress a particular type of piety, or demand that Christians should seek for an ecstatic union with God. Rather, Finney was a man of sound theology who stressed the austere law of God, the need of repentance from sin, and the obligation to obey Christ from the heart and to live for Him.

True mystics often put too much stress on a particular type of piety, and are sometimes inclined to depreciate the letter of Scripture in favor of emotional experiences. The point of this discussion is not to deny the reality of any ecstasies that God chooses to give His children nor to discourage the reality of heart religion, but to raise a question about what the ultimate authority is for the Christian in matters of faith and life. Is that ultimate authority one's inmost feelings, or one's consciousness of Holy Spirit presence, or what one has learned in moments of ecstatic union with Deity, or is it the Word of God as revealed to mankind by the inspiration of the Holy Spirit in the Scriptures? Menno Simons' sober confession reads as follows:

Brethren, I tell you the truth and lie not. I am no Enoch, no Elias, I have no visions, am no prophet, who can teach and prophesy differently

Pantheon, 1949), pp. 9-109, as well as monographs on the subject in book form as well as in religious encyclopedias. Cf. also J. C. Wenger, "Christianity and Mysticism," *The Christian Ministry* (Scottdale, Pa.: Herald Press), I, 4 (Oct. 1948), pp. 207-11.

30 Richard E. Day, *Man of Like Passions* (Grand Rapids, Mich.: Zondervan, 1942), p. 45.

from what is written in the Word of God (and whoever tries to teach something else will soon miss the right way and be deceived in his learning). I trust that the merciful Father will keep me in His Word so that I shall write or speak nothing but what I can prove by Moses, the prophets, the evangelists, or by other apostolic Scriptures and doctrines, explained in their true sense, spirit, and intent of Christ. Judge ye that are spiritually minded. Again, I have no visions nor angelic inspirations, neither do I desire such, lest I be thereby deceived. The Word of Christ alone is sufficient for me.[31]

9. THEOLOGY AND PHILOSOPHY

Some theologians have abused the Bible by regarding it as a compilation of individual proof texts for the support of some human system of theology. The other extreme, however, is also common, namely, minimizing the doctrinal content of Scripture and regarding the Bible as a mere collection of Hebrew literature. Evangelical theologians believe that the Bible is more than the word of man, that it is also the eternal Word of God. It is not necessary to hold to a particular theory of inspiration in order to recognize from an honest reading of Scripture that the Bible does present a definite point of view on a number of major questions which have confronted the human mind from the beginning of human history.[32]

1. The Bible represents that there does exist a great personal God, the Lord of Abraham, Isaac, and Jacob, the Holy One of Israel, and the Father of our Lord Jesus Christ.

2. There also exists, according to Scripture, a powerful but limited evil spirit, the opponent of God, the devil or Satan. The Christian Church of today stands in need of a deeper awareness of the might of the satanic forces which are at work in the world; needless to say, this is not a plea to return to the Middle Ages caricature of the devil with its strange demonology.

3. The Bible teaches that the universe is not eternal but was created in the beginning by divine fiat. Matter is therefore temporal, not eternal, and the world is completely dependent on God.

4. According to Scripture God is both transcendent and immanent in relation to His creation. He is all glorious in Himself over and beyond His creation, but He is also active in the world as its Sovereign and Sustainer, and His providence extends to all of His creation throughout all history.

5. According to Scripture God created man with a mind capable of thinking His thoughts after Him, and commissioned him to sub-

---

31 *Complete Works*, II, p. 248.
32 Cf. Adam Clarke, *A Commentary* (New York: Eaton & Mains, 1883), VI, pp. 634, 635.

due the earth and to rule over it, to make a victorious conquest of the world.

6. According to the Bible original man was made in the mental, moral, and spiritual image of God, but fell into sin by yielding to the temptation of Satan, and thereby infected the race with "sin and death": since the Fall the race is lost in sin and spiritually alienated from God apart from redemption.

7. According to the Bible, all through human history God has entered into history to bring special redemption to the race, the climax being the redemptive passion of Christ, God's Incarnate Son.

8. The Bible consistently represents God as calling upon men to repent of their sin, to believe on Him, and to obey Him with a surrendered will.

9. According to Scripture, those who surrender to Christ in penitence and faith are spiritually renewed and are progressively transformed into the spiritual image of the Lord Jesus.

10. God hears and answers the prayers of His children. Prayer is the divinely ordained means for the obtaining of blessing from God. Prayer for the sick may include a sacramental anointing. James 5:14.

11. According to Scripture God has a purpose for the race, namely, the formation on earth of His spiritual kingdom, the outward expression of which is the church.

12. The earmarks of true Christianity are: a spiritual separation from evil, i.e., personal holiness, a spirit of humility and meekness, an ethic of love and good will, and the inner urge to build and extend the kingdom of God by the conversion of men to Christ.

13. According to Scripture the drama of human history is not endless but temporal. The struggle of the church with the forces of evil will terminate by a divine irruption at the end of the world when Christ will personally appear to raise the dead, to usher His saints into the glories which God has prepared for them, and to judge and punish the wicked.

If one accepts the Bible in simple faith it gives clear answers to such questions as the being and nature of God; the origin of matter, energy, and life; the nature and destiny of man; and the end of all things. It does not, however, deal directly with such speculative questions of philosophy as the ultimate nature of matter, the relationship of the human mind to the body, and the problems of epistemology, nor does it give a detailed preview of the course of human history. Divine revelation answers man's existential questions but it does not treat philosophical or scientific questions as such. All attempts to make it do so discredit theology by the attempt to extract more from Scripture than God was pleased to reveal. On the other hand, many philosophers close their eyes to the light which divine revelation does throw on God, on the world, on man, and on history. Men need both theology and reason if they are rightly to understand themselves and their world. Much of the race has lost the peace and joy which God intended for men because they have rejected science and become unbalanced bigots, or they have neglected Christianity and opened the way to become inhumanly cruel sadists, creators of *Buchenwalds*. God give us the wisdom to use both revelation and reason and thereby achieve happiness in this world and the next.

10. *CHRISTIANITY AND OTHER RELIGIONS*

Christianity is an exclusive religion. Jesus said that He was the Way, the Truth, and the Life and that no man comes to the Father except by Him. All the peoples of today are, according to the Bible, descendants of those who at one time had a true knowledge of God. That is, the Bible teaches the unitary origin of the human race, and the human race at the beginning was in direct and vital touch with God. Paganism is, therefore, really a spiritual declension from an original true knowledge of the Father.[33] The evolutionary theory of the origin of religion is that of a marvelous growth and progress all the way from animism up to monotheism; that is, all religions are a human development and production. But according to the Word of God the most primitive religions are those which have sunk the farthest from an original, true knowledge of God. Since men are sinners by nature they can approach God only through a mediator and according to the Scriptures the only true mediator with God is the Lord Jesus Christ. This position may be offensive to those who stand outside the Christian religion; nevertheless this is the plain representation of the Bible.[33a]

If the Lord Jesus Christ is the only mediator between men and God the question may be asked, Why did God give the Mosaic institutions. The Bible does not answer this question fully. However, theologians would have the following suggestions: God gave the institutions of Moses: (1) to make the Hebrews sin-conscious; (2) to give them an opportunity to express penitence symbolically; and (3) to point them to the coming Messianic redeemer. In other words, the Mosaic institutions were didactic, symbolic, and typical. Only the grace of God enabled Him to accept the spiritual worshipers of

---

[33] Rom. 1:20-32.
[33a] Cf. Schmidt-Rose: *The Origin and Growth of Religion* (Dial Press, 1935).

the Old Testament, since the blood of bulls and of goats can never take away sin.[34] If the question be asked, How then were Israelites of faith saved prior to the true sacrifice of Jesus Christ? the answer certainly lies in the fact that the atonement was retroactive.[35] If one may use a human figure it could be said that salvation is like a check; God in His grace cashed the check before Jesus made the deposit which made the check good. Today, however, neither the preparatory institutions of Judaism nor the ceremonies of any non-Christian religion are able to save men. This is entirely clear in the teaching and preaching of the apostles of Christ. Evangelical Christians are, therefore, not able to participate in the so-called three-faiths movement (Protestantism, Catholicism, Judaism). Only Christ saves.[36] Only He is the acceptable Mediator.

The superiority of Christianity over other religions is fundamentally Jesus Christ. It is not a matter of Christianity's superior philosophy of religion nor the better ethics of Christianity: the superiority of Christianity lies in the person of the Lord Jesus Christ. Only He is able to save men from their sins. Only He is God incarnate. Only He is able to deliver men from sin and from its guilt and power. The angel told Joseph: "You shall call his name Jesus, for he it is[37] that shall save his people from their sins."[38] Other religions contain many truths, good ethical maxims, philosophical propositions of value, etc., but they are totally unable to save men because they lack Christ and His redemptive work. It is in this sense only that they may properly be called "false"; they are false in that they cannot bring eternal salvation to their adherents. This is the reason that Christianity is a faith which stresses missions and the proclamation of the Gospel to the ends of the earth.

11. *LAW AND GOSPEL*

The Protestant church is indebted to the Lutherans for the stress which they have placed on this contrast within the Bible. In the present discussion law means the revealed will of God which holds before man the absolute obedience to the right which God demands of everyone. The Scriptures stress the truth time and again that God's law condemns all men as sinners. Law—any kind of law— is not able to save anyone.[39] The law does have value, however. It drives men to their awareness of their need of a Saviour. The apostle Paul confesses that he would not have known what sin was except for

---

34 Heb. 10:4.
35 Heb. 9:15.
36 Acts 4:12.

37 Force of the Greek.
38 Matt. 1:21.
39 Rom. 3:19-31.

the fact that the law kept saying, "Thou shalt not have evil desire."[40] After a person is a saved Christian the law does have great value, for it serves as an ethical guide for the child of God.

By Gospel in the present discussion is meant the good tidings or the good news that Christ has died for sinners, so that those condemned by the law of God may be saved through faith in the Lord Jesus Christ. In other words, it is the Gospel alone which brings spiritual comfort to men and which saves them.

Some people believe that one finds law in the Old Testament and Gospel in the New. It is true that the Old Testament was much concerned with the law of God. It attempted to make men sin-conscious and aware of their need of divine salvation. The Old Testament prophesied the Gospel of Christ, however. Many New Testament Gospel passages quote Old Testament verses as their foundation. The means of salvation in the Old Testament was, moreover, fundamentally the same as it is now, namely, justification by faith.[41]

The New Testament also contains law; indeed it sharpens the moral law of God, being even more penetrating in its demands than the Old Testament.[42] The New Testament is concerned largely with the presentation of the saving Gospel of Christ, however.

We may, therefore, say that the Old Testament contains salvation by faith, as well as law, and the New Testament contains law as well as salvation by faith. The New Testament difference resides in the fact of its clearer presentation of the Gospel because of the incarnation and passion of the Lord Jesus Christ. Needless to say, this discussion stands sharply in contrast with that of modern dispensationalism, which divides human history into seven dispensations in each of which there are distinctive emphases, promises, and conditions.[43]

12. *THE CHRISTIAN'S RELATION TO THE OLD TESTAMENT*

Just as one finds law and grace both in the Old Testament and in the New, so the Christian does not follow the New Testament only. He also sustains a real relation to the Old Testament. Paul declares that, "All scripture is inspired of God and profitable for doctrine, for reproof, for correction, and for training in righteousness, that the man of God may be complete, equipped for every good work." The revelation of God which we have in the New Testament

40 Rom. 7:7.
41 Rom. 4:1-25.
42 Matt. 5:17-48.
43 Cf. *The Scofield Reference Bible* (New York: Oxford University Press, 1909, 1945); Lewis Sperry Chafer, *Systematic Theology*, (Dallas, Tex.: Dallas Seminary Press, 1947, 1948), I-VIII.

is not totally unrelated to that of the Old Testament, for the New Testament builds squarely upon the Old. Everywhere in the New Testament it is assumed that the Old Testament is the authoritative Word of God. There are hundreds of definite quotations and references to the Old Testament found in the New. Westcott and Hort's Greek New Testament employs uncial type to indicate quotations and phrases from the Old Testament, and there are no less than 1,076 such quotations and phrases according to these scholars. Professor H. S. Miller says, "Hence, the Old Testament is used in the New Testament in a more or less general sense, by direct quotation, and by reference to thought, person, and event, about 1,000 times . . . , and doubtless more if everything were counted closely."[44] There is therefore a marked continuity between the Old Testament and the New.

There is also a continuity between the people of God in the Old Testament and in the New. About two millenniums before Christ, God chose Abraham to make of him a great people for His name and to give to the world through his descendants His two greatest blessings: the Scriptures, and the Christ. Unfortunately, when the Lord Jesus Christ did come as the Messiah of God to save His people, large numbers of the Jews did not receive Him. Paul likens this truth to the cutting away of some of the branches of an olive tree.[45] The Jews, however, who did accept Jesus in repentance and faith constituted a direct continuation of the Israel of God in the Old Testament. The Gentiles in turn to whom the Gospel also was offered and who accepted Christ and entered His church, became joint heirs with the believing Israelites in forming the new Israel of God.[46] In other words, believing Gentiles were grafted into the olive tree, so that the church of Christ, or the Israel of God, now consists of a believing portion of Israel and a believing portion of the Gentiles.[47] Unbelieving Israelites and unbelieving Gentiles are alike lost.

The New Testament, therefore, regards the present church of Christ, composed as it is of both Jewish and Gentile elements, as spiritually continuous with Israel of old. Christians are therefore in the New Testament called "children of Abraham."[48] They belong, not to a Palestinian Jerusalem, but to the heavenly Jerusalem. Spiritually Christians have come, not to an earthly location, but to

44 H. S. Miller, *General Biblical Introduction* (Houghton, N.Y.: The Word-Bearer Press, 1947), p. 49.

45 Rom. 11:17.   47 Rom. 11:17-19.
46 Eph. 2:11-22; Gal. 6:16.   48 Gal. 3:29.

Mount Zion.[49] Christians are, in the New Testament, heirs of the promises made to the fathers.[50] Christians have inherited the central promise of the Old Testament, which was Christ and His righteousness. [51] This truth that Jews and Gentiles were to be fellow heirs of salvation, members of the same body in Christ, Paul calls a "mystery," that is, a truth known only by divine revelation and not hitherto clearly and fully revealed.[52] In the New Testament, therefore, all national distinctions are blotted out.[53] Jews need to accept Christ in order to receive salvation and this is true also for all Gentiles.[54]

Christians shall follow the higher ethical standards of the New Testament rather than revert back to the sub-Christian standards given by God through Moses. Jesus, however, did not regard His teaching as standing in opposition to that of the Old Testament but as fulfilling it. [55] That is, Jesus sloughed off those portions of Old Testament law which were not the final revelation of the will of God and He built upon and even extended those portions of the Old Testament moral law which were a positive and clear statement of God's law.[56] In the Sermon on the Mount Jesus gives a number of illustrations of His relationship to the Old Testament.[57] Not only is all killing wrong, but even anger as expressed by one's language is unbecoming for the members of Christ's kingdom. Not only is adultery wrong, but sins of thought can also violate the holy will of God. Not only is it wrong for a man to divorce his wife without making it legally binding in writing, but Jesus reduced the right of divorce to but one basic occasion. Not only is it wrong to swear a false oath, but Jesus said that all oaths should be eliminated. Not only is personal retaliation wrong, but the Christian shall not take recourse to legal redress. Not only shall Christ's disciples love their neighbors; they shall manifest love to all men. The Old Testament seems to give tacit approval to polygamy, but Christ calls men back to God's original standard of one companion for life.

It is therefore evident that if a Christian wishes to be in the will of God he must diligently study the entire Bible, carefully comparing the Old Testament with the New and taking the New Testament

---

49 Heb. 12:22.
50 Gal. 3:29.
51 Gal. 3:14.
52 Eph. 3:1-6.
53 Gal. 3:28.
54 Rom. 1:16.
55 Matt. 5:17-48.
56 George B. Stevens, *The Theology of the New Testament* (New York: Charles Scribner's Sons, 1927), pp. 17-26.
57 Matt. 5:21-48.

as his final guide in all matters of ethics and theology. He will find, of course, that most of the Old Testament teachings are in complete agreement with the higher standards of the New, but what is temporary in the Old is dropped and not reaffirmed in the New.

The New Testament also teaches clearly that the child of God is now free from all the ceremonial regulations of the Old Testament: ceremonial washings, unclean foods, holy days such as the weekly Sabbath, the monthly Sabbath or new moon, feast days, day of atonement, etc.; indeed, the Christian is free from all human rules which would restrict his freedom in Christ.[58] Undoubtedly the most significant ceremony in the entire Jewish ceremonial law was that of circumcision. It was the sign of the covenant made by God with Abraham.[59] The New Testament indicates clearly that this ceremony has been done away in Christ.[60] But this particular illustration of circumcision also brings to light in a beautiful way the manner in which the apostles of Christ draw upon the deeper spiritual intent of the Old Testament as a foundation for their doctrine. For example, Moses commanded the children of Israel to circumcise the foreskin of their heart and to no longer be stubborn.[61] He also promised that the Lord their God would circumcise their heart and the heart of their offspring so that they would love the Lord their God with all their heart and with all their soul.[62] Consequently when the apostle describes Christians as being circumcised with a circumcision made without hands, in the circumcision of Christ,[63] he is following Old Testament teaching. The writers of the New Testament feel entirely competent and authoritative to record the New Testament revelation of God without apology: in approximately a thousand cases, however, they illustrate their teaching and instruction from illustrations or direct teachings of the Old Testament.

Those portions of the Old Testament which set forth permanent truth as to God's will for men are oftentimes called God's moral law. This moral law is still valid and is reaffirmed in the New Testament as God's final will for men. Jesus Himself interpreted the law of God as being simply a commentary on the great principle of love, love for God and love for mankind.[64] It is perfectly obvious, of course, that these two great commandments, which are clearly stated by Moses, are the foundation of the Ten Commandments as well as of all other ethical instructions in Scripture. Christians are definitely obligated

---

58 Col. 2:14-23; Rom. 14:1-6; Gal. 4:9, 10; 4:21—5:4.
59 Gen. 17:9-14.   62 Deut. 30:6.
60 Gal. 5:2-11.   63 Col. 2:11.
61 Deut. 10:16.   64 Matt. 22:34-40.

to follow the moral law of God, not as hoping to merit salvation thereby, but as an expression of love for God. The New Testament is emphatic in stating that Christians are saved only by faith in Christ, not by obedience to any kind of law.[65] Both the King James and American Standard Versions indicate that Christ is the end of the law for righteousness to everyone who believes.[66] This does not mean that Christ is the end of the law. Christians are not able to dispense with the law of God. It is their ethical guide but Christ is the end of the law for righteousness: that is, Christians do not depend upon their keeping of law for that righteousness which is needed to enter heaven. Christians become righteous by their union with the Lord Jesus Christ who imparts unto them the gift of divine righteousness and transforms them into the image of the Son of God.[67]

The New Testament, especially the Book of Hebrews, indicates that the Old Covenant as a religious system has been done away; it has been superseded by its superior, the New Covenant.[68] This is in fulfillment of Jeremiah 31, which promised the establishment of a new covenant. This means that the priesthood has been changed.[69] Christians are not under an Aaronic priesthood but their priest is the Lord Jesus Christ. The Old Testament employed many sacrifices, namely, the offering of animals. In the New Covenant there is but one sacrifice, namely, Christ Himself.[70] As between the two covenants there has also been a change of law.[71] The New Covenant is also declared to involve better promises. The writer of Hebrews states: "Christ has obtained a ministry which is as much more excellent than the old as the covenant he mediates is better, since it is enacted on better promises. For if that first covenant had been faultless, there would have been no occasion for a second. For he finds fault with them when he says:

> The days will come, says the Lord,
> when I will establish a new covenant with the house of Israel
> and with the house of Judah;
> not like the covenant that I made with their fathers
> on the day when I took them by the hand
> to lead them out of the land of Egypt;
> for they did not continue in my covenant,
> and so I paid no heed to them, says the Lord.

65 Rom. 3:20, 21, 22, 26, 28.
66 Rom. 10:4.
67 Rom. 5:17; II Cor. 3:18.
68 Heb. 8:6, 7.
69 Heb. 7:11, 12.
70 Heb. 7:27.
71 Heb. 7:12.

This is the covenant that I will make with the house of Israel
after those days, says the Lord:
I will put my laws into their minds,
and write them on their hearts,
and I will be their God,
and they shall be my people."[72]

The Old Testament is a rich mine of illustrations for the edifi-
cation of the Christian believer. It contains many examples of faithfulness, of the rewards of righteousness, of warnings against apostasy,
of the blessedness of being a peacemaker, of purity of life, of con-
stancy in temptation, etc. Nicholls, for example, has compiled a
list of twenty-six different proverbs of which the Bible contains concrete illustrations, but this is merely a start in what could be done.[73]
The illustrations of the Old Testament, declares Paul, were written
down for our instruction.[74]

The Old Testament is essential for an understanding of the New
Testament. The New Testament constantly assumes a knowledge of
the story of creation, of the fall, of the entire sweep of redemptive
history, of the law of Moses, of prophecy, etc.

The Old Testament has rich devotional value. Here should be
mentioned not only the Psalms but also the prayers of the various
men of God, Abraham, Jacob, Solomon, etc., as well as the piety and
godly lives of the various patriarchs, prophets, and men of faith.

If the ceremonial regulations of Moses were not an end in themselves, why then were they instituted? It may be that the Christian
of today is not able fully to answer this question. Nevertheless, it can
be pointed out that the regulations as to clean and unclean foods,
holy days, and the like do emphasize that all of life is to be sanctified.
Religion must be made to permeate daily living. This point of view
stood in the sharpest possible contrast with the religion of the
Canaanites which sustained no real relation to morality.[75] The sacrificial system showed Israel that sin was a dreadful and costly thing
which leads to death, as well as pointing forward to that Lamb of
God which was to take away the sin of the world. The institution of
the priesthood illustrated the truth that sinful man does need an
intercessor and a mediator with God, which office was fulfilled in the
Lord Jesus Christ. The laver of the tabernacle was a symbol of

---

72 Heb. 8:6-12.
73 Angus-Green, *The Bible Hand-Book* (New York: Revell, c. 1905), pp. 587-89.
74 I Cor. 10:11.
75 George E. Wright and Floyd V. Filson, *The Westminster Historical Atlas to the Bible*
(Philadelphia: The Westminster Press, 1945), p. 36.

cleansing; the altar, of consecration; the candlestick or lampstand, of divine illumination; the shewbread, of communion with God. The most holy place showed that man's sin bars him from coming into the presence of God without a mediator; the law showed that man is not morally autonomous but responsible to God; and the mercy seat, that God provides an atonement for human sin.[76]

Although the Old Testament is not the full or final or complete revelation of God, yet it is a true revelation and is essential to the New Testament and its understanding. Whatever else is said of the Old Testament, it must be admitted that Christ and the apostles regard it as law, as prophecy, as the oracles of God,[77] an authoritative revelation of the nature and will of God though no longer binding upon God's children except as interpreted by and confirmed by Christ and the apostles.

13. *THE UNITY OF THE BIBLE*

The central purpose of the Word of God is to lead men to faith in the Lord Jesus Christ. It is to bring them to that gift of eternal life which is received through union with Jesus. The Bible may therefore be called the salvation book, not in the sense that the book itself can bring salvation through propositional truth, but that the function of the Bible is to lead men to put their faith in Him who became man and died and rose again in order that man might live. Jesus rebuked the Pharisees for devoting their attention to the Scriptures when he addressed to them these words: "You search the scriptures, because you think that in them you have eternal life; and it is they that bear witness to me; yet you refuse to come to me that you may have life."[78] If one would delete Jesus Christ and His salvation from the Bible it would become a book of despair, for it would point out to man his terrible need, and the requirements of God which man is never able to meet.

The condition of receiving salvation from God is the same from the beginning to the end of the Bible, namely, faith. This is taught not only in such an outstanding chapter as Hebrews 11, but is assumed everywhere in both Testaments. God accepted Abel because of his faith. God translated Enoch to glory without the experience of death because of his faith. It was faith which moved Noah to obey God and build an ark to the saving of his household. Genesis

---

76 Cf. Harold S. Bender, *Old Testament Law and History* (Scottdale, Pa.: Mennonite Publishing House, c. 1936), pp. 43-47.

77 Rom. 3:2.

78 John 5:39, 40; 20:31.

records that Abraham believed in the Lord; and He reckoned it to him for righteousness.[79] The Psalms are such beautiful portrayals of faith and love and devotion toward God that they are beloved by Christians the world around. The Old Testament prophets such as Isaiah and Amos protested in the most vigorous language against making ceremonies a substitute for faith and holiness and obedience.[80] John the Baptist warned the Jews against putting their faith in their membership in the family of Israel and called for the obedience of faith.[81] When the Jews came to Jesus asking what works they should perform in order to receive acceptance with God, Jesus declared: "This is the work of God, that you believe in him whom he has sent."[82] The Apostle Paul declares that the effect of the law of God is to stop every mouth and to make the whole world guilty before Him. "For no human being will be justified in his sight by works of the law since through the law comes knowledge of sin."[83]

One of the finest sections in the entire Scripture on the futility of human works as a means of salvation and an exposition of the way to become righteous in God's sight is found in Romans 3:

But now the righteousness of God has been manifested apart from law, although the law and the prophets bear witness to it, the righteousness of God through faith in Jesus Christ for all who believe. For there is no distinction; since all have sinned and fall short of the glory of God, they are justified by his grace as a gift, through the redemption which is in Christ Jesus, whom God put forward as an expiation by his blood, to be received by faith. This was to show God's righteousness, because in his divine forbearance he had passed over former sins; it was to prove at the present time that he himself is righteous and that he justifies him who has faith in Jesus.[84]

To one who has the simplicity of faith it would be entirely appropriate to say that the Bible is not only the salvation book, but the Jesus book. Of the conversation of the Saviour with the two disciples on the way to Emmaus it is said: "And beginning with Moses and all the prophets, he interpreted to them in all the scriptures the things concerning himself."[85] And to the eleven disciples He declared: "These are my words which I spoke to you, while I was still with you, that everything written about me in the law of Moses and the prophets and the psalms must be fulfilled. Then he opened their minds to understand the scriptures, and said to them, Thus it is written, that the Christ should suffer and on the third day rise from

79 Gen. 15:6; Rom. 4:3.
80 Isa. 1:11-20; 58:4-9; Amos 5:21-24.
81 Matt. 3:7-10.
82 John 6:29.

83 Rom. 3:20.
84 Rom. 3:21-26.
85 Luke 24:27.

the dead, and that repentance and forgiveness of sins should be preached in his name to all nations, beginning from Jerusalem."[86] The ultimate intent, therefore, of the entire Word of God is to witness to the Lord Jesus Christ, first in type and prophecy, and then in fulfillment. Little wonder then that in the revelation to John we are given a vision of a heavenly scene in which "the four living creatures and the twenty-four elders fell down before the Lamb, each holding a harp, and with golden bowls full of incense, which are the prayers of the saints; and they sang a new song, saying,

Worthy art thou to take the scroll and to open its seals,
for thou wast slain and by thy blood didst ransom men for God
from every tribe and tongue and people and nation,
and hast made them a kingdom and priests to our God,
and they shall reign on earth.

"Then I looked, and I heard around the throne and the living creatures and the elders the voice of many angels, numbering myriads of myriads and thousands of thousands, saying with a loud voice, 'Worthy is the Lamb who was slain, to receive power and wealth and wisdom and might and honor and glory and blessing!' "[87]

14. THE RECOGNITION OF GOD'S WORD

Christians are sometimes asked how they know that the Bible is the Word of God. Now it is obvious that Christianity is a closed system of belief, just as naturalism or atheism is also a closed system of belief. One might, therefore, equally well ask the atheist how he knows that no God exists, and why he believes that the Bible is not the Word of God. Nevertheless, it is in order for the Christian to attempt to give a reasonable account of the grounds for his belief.[88] As far as logic itself is concerned Christians would have a right to expect basic comprehensibility, dignity consonant with divine origin, internal harmony, high ethical standards both personal and social, an authority intuitively recognized, and promises verifiable in life and experience, from a book which purports to be the Word of God. Christians claim that the Bible passes these tests beyond a shadow of a doubt.

In recent centuries Protestant apologetes have stressed such arguments as the following for the fact that the Bible is God's Word: its internal harmony, its freedom from the errors of every period of

---

86 Luke 24:44-47.
87 Rev. 5:8-12.
88 Cf. O. Hallesby, *Why I Am a Christian* (Minneapolis, Minn.: Augsburg Publishing House, 1950); and C. S. Lewis, *The Case for Christianity* (New York: Macmillan, 1943).

its composition, its beautiful style, the uplifting influence which it has exerted in society wherever it has gone, its indestructibility in the face of persecution, and its containing truth which obviously had to come to man by special revelation such as the account of the creation of the world.

The factor which Christian apologetes commonly overlook, however, is that the arguments which they marshal in support of Christian and theistic faith in the Word of God appear powerful and convincing to them simply because they have Christian faith. In other words, the Christian believer knows by experience that God exists, and he has found out also by experience that the Bible is the Word of God; therefore every reasonable argument in support of the recognition of the Bible as God's Word appears to him to be powerful and cogent. But to the unbeliever who has rejected faith in God these arguments, no matter how logical, are not enough to convince him, for he is unwilling to grant the very possibility of a divine revelation simply because he is unwilling to acknowledge faith in God. The present writer is therefore in agreement with the following statement from the great Westminster Confession of Faith:

The authority of the holy Scripture dependeth not upon the testimony of any man or church, but wholly upon God . . . and therefore it is to be received, because it is the Word of God.

We may be moved and induced by the testimony of the Church to an high and reverent esteem of the holy Scripture; and the heavenliness of the matter, the efficacy of the doctrine, the majesty of the style, the consent of all the parts, the scope of the whole, (which is to give all glory to God,) the full discovery it makes of the only way of man's salvation, the many other incomparable excellencies, and the entire perfection thereof, are arguments whereby it doth abundantly evidence itself to be the Word of God; yet, notwithstanding, our full persuasion and assurance of the infallible truth, and divine authority thereof, is from the inward work of the Holy Spirit, bearing witness by and with the Word in our hearts.

. . . We acknowledge the inward illumination of the Spirit of God to be necessary for the saving understanding of such things as are revealed in the Word. . . .[89]

Belief in the Bible as the Word of God is therefore not an unmoral and indifferent proposition of philosophy. The Bible is received as the Word of God by him who knows in his heart that God does exist and that He has revealed Himself in His Word. Those who hold to the Christian faith also believe that man in his very

89 Philip Schaff, *The Creeds of Christendom* (New York: Harper & Bros., 1877, 1919), III, pp. 602-4.

nature has some awareness of the existence of God even from a contemplation of the creation of God; his response to God's handiwork is such as to cause him to be aware that a divine Being does exist; and the Holy Spirit, Christians believe, does attest to the conscience of him who is still outside of Christ, his need of salvation from sin, and gives witness to his heart that the message of God's Word is divinely reliable and authoritative. The truth of the Bible is the sword which the Holy Spirit uses to cut down unbelief and self-sufficiency and to bring men in conviction and contrition to the foot of the cross of the Lord Jesus Christ. The truth of God's Word is quick and powerful, whether or not the hearer is fully conscious of the claims of the Bible regarding itself. The basic approach, therefore, of the Christian witness is to attest to the sinfulness of human nature and man's need of redemption, and to point lost sinners to Christ as the Saviour from sin.

SOME BRIEF DENOMINATIONAL ENCYCLOPEDIAS

Mennonite

Harold S. Bender and C. Henry Smith: *The Mennonite Encyclopedia*, 4 vols. (Hillsboro, Kansas; Newton, Kansas; Scottdale, Pennsylvania; 1955-59).

The Complete Writings of Menno Simons, c. 1496-1561. Translated from the Dutch by Leonard Verduin and edited by John Christian Wenger, with a Biography by Harold S. Bender (Scottdale, Pennsylvania: Herald Press, 1956).

Baptist

William Cathcart: *The Baptist Encyclopedia*, 2 vols. (Philadelphia: Louis H. Everts, 1881).

Presbyterian

Alfred Nevin: *Encyclopedia of the Presbyterian Church in the United States of America* (Philadelphia: Presbyterian Encyclopedia Publishing Co., No. 1334 Chestnut St., 1884).

Methodist

Matthew Simpson: *Cyclopaedia of Methodism* (Philadelphia: Everts & Stewart, 1878).

Lutheran

Henry E. Jacobs and John A. W. Haas: *The Lutheran Cyclopedia* (New York: Charles Scribner's Sons, 1899).

Erwin L. Lueker: *Lutheran Cyclopedia* (Saint Louis, Missouri: Concordia Publishing House [1954]).

Episcopalian

A. A. Benton: *The Church Cyclopaedia* (New York: M. H. Mallory & Co. [1883]).

Roman Catholic

Donald Attwater: *A Catholic Dictionary* (New York: the Macmillan Company, 1942).

Pietro Parente, Antonio Piolanti, Salvatore Garofalo: *Dictionary of Dogmatic Theology* (Milwaukee: The Bruce Publishing Company [1951]).

Henry Denzinger: *The Sources of Catholic Dogma* [from the 30th Latin Ed.] (St. Louis and London: B. Herder, 1957.)

PART I

GOD AS CREATOR

I. GOD AS CREATOR

1. DEFINITIONS OF GOD

By God is meant that eternal Being who created all things visible and invisible, He who is absolutely holy and good, ever existing in three Persons: Father, Son, and Holy Spirit. The great Baptist theologian A. H. Strong gives this definition of God: "God is the infinite and perfect Spirit in whom all things have their source, support and end."[1] The Westminster Catechism gives this definition: "A Spirit infinite, eternal, and unchangeable in his being, wisdom, power, justice, goodness, and truth."[2]

The above definitions stress a number of characteristics of Deity. First of all, God is described as a spirit, which means that He does not possess corporeity, shape, materiality, weight, size, or other physical characteristics. As a Spirit, God does not have flesh and bones as do human beings. Secondly, God is a person; that is, He possesses such characteristics as knowledge, will, feeling, purposes, etc. God has plans and is able to carry them out, and He knows what He is doing. In the third place, God is infinite; that is, He is not limited except by His goodness, and the goodness of God must of necessity be stressed because sinful men naturally stand in much awe and fear of the supernatural and tend throughout human history to think of God as a being of wrath, who is to be feared rather than loved. The Word of God, however, constantly stresses the goodness of God, His lovingkindness and steadfast favor toward those who put their faith in Him. Undoubtedly the two major attributes of God in the Bible are love and holiness: love meaning His beneficent intention for His creatures, and holiness meaning His utter separation from all that is finite and evil.

1 Augustus Hopkins Strong, *Systematic Theology* (Philadelphia: The Judson Press, 1907), p. 52.
2 *Ibid.*, p. 52.

2. *BIBLICAL NAMES AND DESCRIPTIONS OF GOD*

God is called by various Hebrew terms in the Old Testament such as *El, Eloah,* and especially *Elohim.* The exact meaning of these various forms cannot be precisely determined. Of the three the second is the least common, being used about fifty-seven times in the Old Testament.[3] *El* is used about 217 times and perhaps has the basic meaning of power. *Eloah* is a somewhat more poetic term. *Elohim* is used about 2,570 times in the Old Testament and is regarded by some scholars as merely a plural of majesty, and by others as being perhaps suggestive of the Trinity since it is a masculine plural noun but is generally used with a singular verb in Scripture. Another common term for God is *Eljon,* used about thirty times in the Old Testament and translated Most High. The word *Shaddai,* used about forty-nine times in the Old Testament, is generally translated "Almighty." It is possible, however, that the real meaning of this word is rather the "Comforting Sovereign." In other words, He is not merely powerful, but the One who uses His power for our love and protection.

By far the most common term for God in the Old Testament, however, is His proper name. The poetic form used about fifty times is *Jah;* this is the word which forms the last syllable of the Hebrew expression "Praise ye the Lord," or "Hallelujah." The more common form of Jah, however, is the so-called *tetragrammaton* which appears in the King James and Revised Standard Versions as the Lord, and in the American Standard Version as Jehovah. It is possible that the original spelling of this word in Hebrew was *Jahweh.* It is used about 6,823 times in the Old Testament. Another common word for God is the expression "Lord" or "Ruler," which in Hebrew is *Adonai,* used about 400 times in the Old Testament.

Then there is a large number of descriptive terms applied to God in the Old Testament such as Lord of Hosts, although it is not clear whether the hosts refer primarily to angels, or to the armies of Israel, or to the stars. Another expression used of God is *Ehjeh,* similar to the proper name *Jahweh.* In Exodus 3:14 this word is translated, "I am that I am." Thomas Rees holds that by a Hebrew idiom the phrase means "I will be all that is necessary as the occasion will arise."[4] Another writer suggests that the phrase indicates "His covenant pledge to be with and for Israel in all the ages to follow."[5]

3 Some of this data is obtained from *The Englishman's Hebrew and Chaldee Concordance* (London: Longman, Green, Brown, and Longmans, 1843), *passim.*

4 *I.S.B.E.* (James Orr, Revised by Melvin G. Kyle: *The International Standard Bible Encyclopedia,* Grand Rapids, Mich.: Eerdmans, 5 vols., 1939), II, p. 1254.

5 *Ibid.,* II, p. 1267.

God is also called by many other names and descriptive terms in the Old Testament: King, Lawgiver, Judge, Rock, Fortress, High Tower or Strong Tower, Deliverer, Shepherd, Great Reward, Shield, Buckler, Sword, Covert, etc. One of the most beautiful expressions is the *Holy One of Israel*, which is used about thirty times. God is also described as the Refuge of the believer.

There are three combinations of the word *Jahweh*, or as it is printed in the American Standard Version, Jehovah; namely, *Jehovah-Jireh* (Genesis 22:14), which means, "Jahweh will see or provide"; *Jehovah-Nissi* (Exodus 17:15), which means "Jahweh is my banner"; and *Jehovah-Shalom* (Judges 6:24), which means "Jahweh is peace."

The New Testament does not contain nearly as many terms for God. In fact, there is only one common word used in the Greek New Testament for God and that is *Theos*, translated God. He is, however, also called *The Almighty* in II Corinthians 6:18, a quotation from the Old Testament, and nine times in the Book of Revelation. The Apocalypse also calls Him *the Alpha and the Omega*, that is, the first and the last. The word *Kurios*, translated Lord, is used in the New Testament of human beings (in expressions like sir), of God, especially in quotations from the Old Testament, and of the Messiah or Christ many times, especially in the Epistles. In fact, the Apostle Paul makes the confession, "Jesus is Lord," a mark of true Christian faith.[6]

Perhaps the most tender term applied to God in the New Testament, indeed the characteristic term of the New Covenant, is *Father*. Although this word is used a few times in the Old Testament it is only in the New that it becomes a characteristic description of God. The word carries with it a connotation of love, providence, tenderness, and protection, and the fact that He will show Himself a beneficent provider and supporter.

Perhaps the three most majestic statements of the New Testament about God are: (1) God is Spirit[7]; (2) God is Light[8]; and (3) God is Love.[9] The Apostle Paul also frequently describes God as the One who raised up Jesus from the dead.[10]

3. *THE ATTRIBUTES OF GOD*

Through all of human history the cry of mankind has been: Can a man know God? The answer to this question is impossible apart

6 I Cor. 12:3. 9 I John 4:8, 16.
7 John 4:24. 10 Rom. 4:24; 8:11 (2); 10:9; etc.
8 I John 1:5.

from divine revelation, but according to the Bible God has truly revealed Himself in two different ways: first, He has given a verbal revelation of Himself through certain persons selected for that purpose; and secondly, He has revealed Himself fully in the person of His Son. The writer of Hebrews says, "In many and various ways God spoke of old to our fathers by the prophets; but in these last days he has spoken to us by a Son, whom he appointed the heir of all things, through whom also he created the world."[11] It is perfectly evident, of course, that a verbal revelation of personality must be inadequate, but in reference to the request of one of His apostles to show to them the Father, the Lord Jesus said: "Have I been with you so long, and yet you do not know me, Philip? He who has seen me has seen the Father; how can you say, 'Show us the Father'?"[12] The only adequate revelation of God has been the revelation which came through Jesus Christ. Jesus showed man all that man needed to know about God. Human philosophy is all too prone to emphasize the difficulties, if not the impossibility, of God entering into relationship with man in history. The Word of God, however, is entirely clear that God has done precisely that: God the eternal Spirit has entered into contact with men for their redemption. He has given a genuine and true revelation of Himself to finite men. Whether or not man is able to understand how this is possible is not the issue. The point is that the Bible asserts plainly and Jesus confirms this, that God has genuinely revealed Himself to men.

The emphasis of Scripture on the superiority of the revelation of God through Christ to that of any merely verbal revelation has not been adequately treated by theologians. It has not been sufficiently shown how Jesus in person and in life situations did reveal those attributes of God which are otherwise presented only verbally in Scripture.[13]

One of the most helpful treatments of the attributes of God is that by the Baptist theologian, A. H. Strong (1836-1921).[14] In a general way, but with some deviation, I have followed his general outline in this discussion.

Strong divides the attributes of God into two classes, those attributes of God which refer primarily to Himself without relation to His creation, called absolute attributes; and those attributes of God which are spoken of in relationship to the creation, especially to man-

---

11 Heb. 1:1, 2.
12 John 14:9.
13 Cf. James Hastings, *A Dictionary of Christ and the Gospels* (New York: Charles Scribner's Sons, 1908), pp. 139-43.
14 *Op. cit.*, pp. 243-303; note p. 248.

kind, called transitive attributes. By the attributes of God, of course, are meant ways of viewing His being. It is not that His being has certain antennae, so to speak, which we can reach out and take hold of; it is rather that God has revealed who He Himself is and we call those various facets or qualities of His being or personality, attributes.

Absolute Attributes

1. One of the first truths about God that must be stressed is His *spirituality*. God is a spirit, according to the testimony of the entire Scriptures and of Christ Himself, and is therefore invisible and incorruptible, nor corporeal. This means that pantheism is a wrong point of view in philosophy and theology. God is not a part of matter and He is not dependent on matter; matter is not necessary to Him. But God is the creator of this material world.

The Scripture represents God as being a living God,[15] the living and true God,[16] the One who has life in Himself;[17] hence Jesus, because He reveals the Father, is able to say: "I am the way, and the truth, and the life; no one comes to the Father, but by me."[18]

During the days of His flesh Jesus also revealed Himself as the source of life, physical and spiritual. To the widow's son at Nain Jesus could say, " 'Young man, I say to you, arise.' And the dead man sat up, and began to speak. And he gave him to his mother. Fear seized them all; and they glorified God, saying, 'A great prophet has arisen among us!' and 'God has visited his people!' "[19]

To the daughter of Jairus Jesus could say in His native Aramaic: " *'Talitha cumi";* which means 'Little girl, [I say to you], arise.' And immediately the girl got up and walked; for she was twelve years old. And immediately they were overcome with amazement."[20]

To one who had been dead four days Jesus could say: " 'Lazarus, come out.' The dead man came out, his hands and feet bound with bandages, and his face wrapped with a cloth. Jesus said to them, 'Unbind him, and let him go.' "[21]

But not only was Jesus the author of physical life; He was able to transform sinners into saints of God. He could take a grasping and avaricious man like Zacchaeus and make of him a humble child of God, willing to make full restitution for all his wrongs.[22] He could take a poor soul like Mary Magdalene, possessed of seven demons,

15 Jer. 10:10. 19 Luke 7:14-16.
16 I Thess. 1:9. 20 Mark 5:41, 42.
17 John 5:26. 21 John 11:43, 44.
18 John 14:6. 22 Luke 19:8-10.

and restore and heal her.[23] He could take a coarse and ungodly fisherman like Peter and make of him a living stone in the foundation of His spiritual temple, the church.[24] Jesus could take a persecutor like Paul and make him the greatest missionary of all time.[25] Truly Jesus revealed the Father by showing that He was in very truth the author of spiritual life and health. As such He was a revelation, *the* revelation, of God.

2. The Bible represents God as possessing *personality,* as being self-conscious and self-determining. This means that God knows and cares and feels and wills. It means that God has plans and He carries them out. Since God has created man as a self-conscious and self-determining personality, made in the very image of God, we human beings are able in some measure to understand what is meant when the Scripture reveals God as being a personality. Because man also is a personality he is able to offer prayer to God, he is able to receive a revelation from Him, he is able to make moral choices, and he is able to ponder and construct a life plan. Man is self-conscious and self-determining in an imperfect sense, but God is infinite. Because God is a personal God He is able to regenerate and sanctify and chasten, hear prayer and guide and comfort and strengthen His people. He is also, by virtue of His being a personality, a God of providence.[26] It is because He is a person that He is to be approached by prayer and not by ceremonies purporting to have magical efficacy or power such as "powwowing," which means the employment of secret formulae calculated to coerce supernatural powers or forces for the healing of the body or the accomplishment of other human ends. In connection with such non-Christian and impersonal conceptions of God the following warning is given in the law of Moses:

When you come into the land which the Lord your God gives you, you shall not learn to follow the abominable practices of those nations. There shall not be found among you any one who burns his son or his daughter as an offering, any one who practices divination, a soothsayer, or an augur, or a sorcerer, or a charmer, or a medium, or a wizard, or a necromancer. For whoever does these things is an abomination to the Lord; and because of these abominable practices the Lord your God is driving them out before you. You shall be blameless before the Lord your God. For these nations, which you are about to dispossess, give heed

23 Luke 8:2.
24 Mark 14:71; Matt. 16:13-20.
25 I Cor. 15:9, 10.
26 See the Reformed theology by G. C. Berkouwer, *The Providence of God* (Grand Rapids, Mich.: Eerdmans, 1952).

to soothsayers and to diviners; but as for you, the Lord your God has not allowed you so to do.[27]

It is because God as a personality respects human beings as responsible personalities, that men are able to exercise moral agency. Consequently any conception of God that makes Him some sort of absolute sovereign, without granting to human beings full responsibility for their moral freedom, is not in line with Scripture. It simply is not true that God has predestined every detail of everyone's life so that men have no choice of their own. Men can spoil God's plans for them. The Bible represents that "men of blood and treachery shall not live out half their days."[28] Furthermore, "the fear of the Lord prolongs life, but the years of the wicked will be short."[29]

The second cluster of divine attributes relates to God's *infinity*. The infinity of God includes His self-existence or absolute independence of being, His immutability or unchangeable being and nature, and His unity or simplicity.

3. The *self-existence* or absolute independence of God in His being means that He is independent in every way: in thought,[30] will,[31] power,[32] counsel,[33] etc. But it must be strongly stressed that the love of God permeates all of His attributes and deeds.[34] His independence does not mean that He is a cold and harsh sovereign. It means rather that He abides. It gives us stability.[35] God's self-existence is what the little girl needed in a bomb-racked city when she prayed: "Dear God, take care of yourself. If anything happens to you, we're sunk."

4. *Immutability.* God is unchangeable in His character and counsel, that is, as viewed in Himself. Many Scriptures assert that God is the same, that He never changes,[36] that with Him there is no variation or shadow due to change.[37] There is no fickleness in God. "By this we shall know that we are of the truth, and reassure our hearts before him whenever our hearts condemn us, for God is greater than our hearts, and he knows everything."[38]

The Biblical teaching on the immutability of God must, of course, not be understood as destroying all that the Word of God has to say about the objectivity and efficiency of prayer and its results. Nevertheless, if we can look at prayer from God's viewpoint, it is not a matter of human beings changing God (who is beneficent by nature

27 Deut. 18:9-14.
28 Ps. 55:23.
29 Prov. 10:27.
30 Rom. 11:33-36.
31 Dan. 4:35; Rom. 9:19-21; Eph. 1:5; Rev. 4:11.
32 Ps. 115:3.

33 Ps. 33:11.
34 Ex. 20:6; I John 4:8, 16.
35 Ps. 46.
36 Mal 3:6.
37 Jas. 1:17.
38 I John 3:19, 20.

and who desires the happiness of His children always), but it is a matter of human beings putting themselves into a position where God is able to bless them and to help them. Thus God told Solomon: "If my people who are called by my name humble themselves, and pray and seek my face, and turn from their wicked ways, then I will hear from heaven, and will forgive their sin and heal their land."[39]

It is freely admitted, of course, that the Bible contains many anthropomorphic expressions, such as God being sorry that He had made man on the earth, and being grieved to His heart[40]; that He came down to see whether the race had done according to the outcry which had come to Him or not[41]; that He would destroy Israel or Nineveh, but later did not do so because of prayer and repentance,[42] etc. These expressions must be interpreted in the light of all the Scripture, rather than contrary to the plain didactic statements of the Bible. For example, Jeremiah speaks of God rising up early to send His prophets on their way,[43] but this Scripture must be interpreted in the light of that Psalm which says that God neither slumbers nor sleeps.[44]

5. One of the main emphases of the Bible is on the *unity* of God: Israel did not have a multitude of gods such as her heathen neighbors did, but Jahweh was one divine being; besides Him there was no other God.[45] The New Testament is just as emphatic as the Old that there is only one God,[46] only one true God,[47] no God but one,[48] the blessed and only Potentate,[49] etc. Paul says: "For there is one God, and there is one mediator between God and men, the man Christ Jesus, who gave himself as a ransom for all."[50] This means that polytheism, which would destroy the unity of the universe, is entirely unscriptural and untrue.

6. The third cluster of divine attributes relates to *perfection*. Perfection has to do with qualitative excellence, and the attributes involved are of course moral attributes. The first of these attributes of perfection is what Strong calls *truth*. By truth he does not mean veracity, but that attribute of God by which His being and knowledge conform perfectly to each other. God knows Himself fully. Ultimately, truth is personal because God is truth and Jesus declared

---

39 II Chron. 7:14.
40 Gen. 6:6.
41 Gen. 18:21.
42 Jon. 3:10.
43 Jer. 44:4.
44 Ps. 121:4.

45 Deut. 6:4; Isa. 44:6.
46 John 5:44.
47 John 17:3.
48 I Cor. 8:4.
49 I Tim. 6:15.
50 I Tim. 2:5, 6.

that He also was the truth.[51] That is, because Jesus is one with God, He may appropriate that divine attribute also to Himself.

7. The second attribute of God relating to perfection is *love*. Here again this term does not refer to mercy and goodness, the love of God to men, but that attitude which exists among the three members of the Trinity, Father, Son, and Holy Spirit, by which God stands "in perfect self-impartation, self-devotion, and communion with Himself."[52] In the great prayer of John 17 Jesus prayed for His disciples, that they might be with Him where He is, to behold His glory "which thou hast given me in thy love for me before the foundation of the world."[53]

8. The third attribute of perfection in God is *holiness*. This term refers to the positive moral excellence and integrity of "the Holy One of Israel." In Him there is no trace of sin. The root idea of the word "holiness" seems to relate to separation. That is, God in His being, in His existence, is completely other than the finite and sinful order with which human beings are acquainted. Hence, the Bible frequently associates the holiness of God with the fact that only He in an absolute sense exists.[54] He is described as glorious in holiness.[55] When Isaiah the prophet had his great vision of God, the seraphim were crying one to another: "Holy, holy, holy is the LORD of hosts; the whole earth is full of his glory."[56] Since only God is holy in an absolute sense, He is therefore also the source of the moral law and the ultimate standard of what is right and wrong. God is not good or holy in the sense that He conforms to a law above Himself, but what He is in His nature determines what is right and holy. That is holy which conforms to the good will and nature of a sinless and transcendent being, God.

Transitive Attributes

Most of the references to God in the Bible have not to do with the absolute attributes, which in human thinking tend to become more or less philosophical abstractions, but with the transitive attributes of God, that is, His relation to time and space, to the creation, and especially to men.

9. *Eternity*. In contrast with human beings who enter into life at a given point of time, and after living in the flesh for a comparatively brief span experience physical death, God has existed forever and will never cease to be. The Bible usually does not state truth in

51 John 14:6.
52 Strong, *op. cit.*, p. 260.
53 John 17:24.

54 I Sam. 2:2.
55 Ex. 5:11.
56 Isa. 6:3.

the form of philosophical absolutes but in terms of concrete realities and illustrations. For example, instead of saying merely that God is timeless, the psalmist exclaims:

> LORD, thou hast been our dwelling place in all generations.
> Before the mountains were brought forth,
>> or ever thou hadst formed the earth and the world,
>> from everlasting to everlasting thou art God.[57]

God, therefore, has existed before the "eternal" mountains, and He will be God forever. He has existed even before the earth:

> Of old thou didst lay the foundation of the earth,
>> and the heavens are the work of thy hands.
> They will perish, but thou doest endure;
>> they will all wear out like a garment.
> Thou changest them like raiment, and they pass away;
>> but thou art the same, and thy years have no end.[58]

For this reason the Old Testament speaks of God as the first and the last,[59] and the New Testament employs the phrase "the Alpha and the Omega."[60]

We have already noted that Jesus spoke of the glory which He had with the Father before the foundation of the world.[61] To the Jews Jesus declared: "Truly, truly, I say to you, before Abraham was, I am." [62] In the Revelation to John, the ascended Lord Jesus declared: "Fear not, I am the first and the last, and the living one; I died, and behold I am alive for evermore, and I have the keys of Death and Hades."[63]

It is because of the eternity of God that the Apostle Peter can declare that with the Lord one day is as a thousand years, and a thousand years as one day.[64] God is not subject to any limitations of time. For this reason Christians may rejoice in His eternity and find in Him comfort and strength and assurance for the future both in this life and also in that which is to come.

10. God's relation to space is called His *omnipresence*. By this is meant that He, without diffusion or division, is everywhere present in His universe. In His remarkable dedicatory prayer Solomon confessed to God: "But will God indeed dwell on the earth? Behold, heaven and the highest heaven cannot contain thee; how much less

---

57 Ps. 90:2.
58 Ps. 102:25-27.
59 Isa. 41:4.
60 Rev. 1:8.

61 John 17:24.
62 John 8:58.
63 Rev. 1:17, 18.
64 II Pet. 3:8.

this house which I have built!"[65] To the philosophers on Mars' Hill the Apostle Paul could declare: "In him we live and move and have our being."[66] One of the psalmists expresses the truth of the omnipresence of God with beautiful concrete illustrations:

> Whither shall I go from thy Spirit?
> Or whither shall I flee from thy presence?
> If I ascend to heaven, thou art there!
> If I make my bed in Sheol, thou art there!
> If I take the wings of the morning
> and dwell in the uttermost parts of the sea,
> even there thy hand shall lead me,
> and thy right hand shall hold me.[67]

It is freely confessed, of course, that all the attributes of God are beyond the human intellect's ability to comprehend. Omnipresence is no exception. Men find it impossible to understand how God can be immediately present everywhere. A human being is capable of being aware of a number of persons who are directly before him at one and the same time. Some people may be able to closely watch the faces of ten or even more individuals. But if an audience enlarges to 25,000 the average speaker sees only a sea of faces with here and there a particular person standing out in his consciousness. God, however, is without human limitations and the whole universe is undoubtedly immediately present before Him in a more vivid way even than one person is aware of another. It was, therefore, no mere figure of speech that Tennyson employed, when he declared: "Closer is He than breathing, and nearer than hands and feet."[68] Anthropomorphic expressions such as God's sitting in the heavens refer not to His great distance and remoteness from us but to His exaltation and glory.[69]

It is because Jesus is a perfect image of the Father that He was able to tell His disciples: "For where two or three are gathered in my name, there am I in the midst of them."[70] This awareness of the omnipresence of God and of Jesus through the Holy Spirit gives to Christians a feeling of security and of their being in the immediate care of God. They are "never alone." But this truth cannot be experienced by intellectual apprehension alone: it requires much feeding on the Word of God, meditation, and secret prayer.

11. The Bible also teaches clearly the *omniscience* of God as to memory, present knowledge, and foreknowledge. This is oftentimes

65 I Kings 8:27.
66 Acts 17:28.
67 Ps. 139:7-10.

68 Strong, *op. cit.*, p. 280.
69 Ps. 123:1.
70 Matt. 18:20.

put in a concrete illustration rather than an abstract doctrine. For example, God is declared in the Psalms as knowing all the stars,[71] in the words of Jesus as caring for sparrows,[72] as concerning Himself with all men,[73] as knowing the human heart,[74] as being aware of our needs,[75] as knowing the future[76] and even the number of our hairs.[77] Because Jesus (as to His spiritual office) was like God, the Apostle John declared that "He knew all men and needed no one to bear witness of man; for he himself knew what was in man."[78] The illustration of Jesus having "seen" Nathanael when he was under the fig tree is probably also given as an illustration of the omniscience of Christ in His Messianic ministry.[79] (As to what might be called the natural life of Jesus, as a man on earth, He seems to have subjected Himself to the limitations of other men.[80])

Concerning the omniscience of God the psalmist cries:

> O Lord, thou hast searched me and known me!
> Thou knowest when I sit down and when I rise up;
>   thou discernest my thoughts from afar. . . .
> Even before a word is on my tongue,
>   lo, O Lord, thou knowest it altogether. . . .
> Such knowledge is too wonderful for me;
>   it is high, I cannot attain it.[81]

12. God is also *omnipotent;* which means that He is able without limitation to accomplish all His purposes. The omnipotence of God does not mean that He is able to do foolish or contradictory things. And He is certainly not able to sin,[82] to be untrue to His nature,[83] or to break His promises.[84] He is a God of absolute faithfulness. In a certain sense He does limit Himself by allowing human unbelief to frustrate His desire to save men, as was indeed the case with the Pharisees and scribes who "frustrated God's purpose for them, by refusing to be baptized."[85] Perhaps a more literal translation would be: "But the Pharisees and the lawyers rejected the purpose of God for themselves, not having been baptized by Him."

The Lord reminded Abraham of His omnipotence when He said: "Is anything too hard for the Lord?"[86] And the psalmist declares:

71 Ps. 147:4.
72 Matt. 10:29.
73 Ps. 33:13-15.
74 Acts 15:18.
75 Matt. 6:8.
76 Isa. 46:9, 10.
77 Matt. 10:30.
78 John 2:25.

79 John 1:49.
80 Mark 11:12, 13.
81 Ps. 139:1-6.
82 Jas. 1:13.
83 II Tim. 2:13.
84 Titus 1:2.
85 Luke 7:30.
86 Gen. 18:14.

> Our God is in the heavens;
> he does whatever he pleases.[87]

Jesus Himself declared that with God all things are possible.[88] The Apostle Paul states that God works all things after the counsel of His will[89]; and Paul wants all believers to see the exceeding greatness of His power in us who believe.[90] God is able to do exceeding abundantly above all that we ask or think.[91] In the New Testament, especially in the Pauline letters, the measure of God's power in Christians is often given as the resurrection of Jesus from the dead.[92] That is to say, the supreme example of God's power is the fact that He was able to bring Jesus back from the dead. Any God who is able to give a dead man life can also enable a weak Christian to stand and to overcome temptation! The omnipotence of God is therefore a bulwark of security and confidence and strength for the Christian believer.

Belief in the omnipotence of God, however, does not deliver Christians from the necessity of quiet endurance in suffering or in persecution. In connection with His teaching on the persistence in prayer that Christians ought to practice, Jesus dropped a remark about the elect "who cry to him day and night."[93] God does not always see fit to come to the immediate aid of Christians who are in difficulty. Sometimes He even allows them to glorify Him by dying a martyr's death. Christians also suffer the same calamities as non-Christians: illnesses, accidents, "untimely deaths," financial reverses, etc. Christianity is therefore not so much a means of escaping the limitations and misfortunes of earthly life as it is a new life in Christ, joy and peace in the midst of tribulation, and victory over discouragement and suffering. Even a cursory reading of Hebrews 11 will reveal the fact that saving faith does not result in escaping suffering: one even gets the impression that in this life it definitely adds to the persecutions that one must endure! How beautiful, therefore, are the words of Isaiah:

> When you pass through the waters
>   I will be with you;
> and through the rivers, they shall not overwhelm you;
> when you walk through fire you shall not be burned,
>   and the flame shall not consume you.
> For I am the LORD your God,
>   the Holy One of Israel, your Savior.[94]

87 Ps. 115:3.
88 Matt. 19:26.
89 Eph. 1:11.
90 Eph. 1:19.
91 Eph. 3:20.
92 Rom. 6:4; 8:11; etc.
93 Luke 18:7.
94 Isa. 43:2, 3.

It must be confessed, of course, that the human mind cannot understand the providences of God. Every Christian has a keen awareness of the goodness of God, of His love and His providential care. Many Scriptures can be cited showing the ability of God to deliver His people from the calamities which strike others, such as the beautiful statement of the psalmist:

> A thousand may fall at your side,
>   ten thousand at your right hand;
> but it will not come near you.
> You will only look with your eyes
>   and see the recompense of the wicked.[95]

And yet another Psalm, attributed to Asaph, confesses the temptations to doubt which assailed him when he observed how the wicked prospered in every way while the saints of God had great difficulty:

> For all the day long I have been stricken,
>   and chastened every morning.[96]

The Apostle Paul, after reviewing the sovereignty of God in human history as it relates to Jew and Gentile, exclaims: "O the depth of the riches and wisdom and knowledge of God! How unsearchable are his judgments and how inscrutable his ways!"[97] This involves two profound truths: first, that the true Christian believes with all his soul that God is absolutely able to accomplish whatever He may wish to do; and second, that human beings simply cannot understand the providences of God, why a young mother will be taken away by death, why a man of God will be struck down at the height of his powers, why God allows wicked nations to crush and destroy entire peoples, etc. God is the absolute sovereign while men are the completely dependent creatures. But the Christian knows that what God does is good. Job exhibited the true attitude of faith when he said: "The Lord gave, and the Lord has taken away; blessed be the name of the Lord."[98]

Jesus was revealing divine omnipotence when He miraculously multiplied the loaves,[99] turned water into wine,[1] stilled the storm on the sea,[2] walked on the water,[3] healed the sick,[4] gave sight to the blind,[5] cast out demons,[6] and sent the Holy Spirit on the day of Pentecost.[7]

95 Ps. 91:7, 8.
96 Ps. 73:14.
97 Rom. 11:13.
98 Job 1:21.

99 John 6:5-14.
1 John 22:1-11.
2 Mark 4:35-41.
3 Mark 6:46-50.

4 Mark 6:56.
5 Luke 7:21.
6 Mark 1:32-34.
7 Acts 2:1-6, 32, 33.

13. Men can rely absolutely on God and His promises. He is true in word and in deed. This basic attribute is spoken of as transitive truth or *veracity* and *faithfulness*. It is taught many places throughout the Scriptures.

> God is not man, that he should lie,
>   or a son of man, that he should repent.
> Has he said, and will he not do it?
>   Or has he spoken, and will he not fulfil it?[8]

The New Testament is also emphatic that God is simply not able to lie, that it is utterly impossible for Him to be untruthful.[9] God is also faithful; that is, He will not desert those whom He has accepted and whom He has promised to stand by.[10] The faithfulness of God is therefore the ground of assurance that His saints will reach glory. Paul could look forward to his converts meeting him on the day of Christ, on the resurrection morning, not because of their own personal stability but because of the faithfulness of God.[11]

Because Jesus reveals God fully, "all the promises of God find their Yes in him. That is why we utter the Amen through him, to the glory of God."[12] When Jesus accompanied Martha and Mary to the tomb of the dead Lazarus, and Martha remonstrated with Jesus about taking away the stone from the tomb after Lazarus had been dead four days, Jesus tenderly rebuked her lack of faith in His words by saying: "Did I not tell you that if you would believe you would see the glory of God?"[13]

The truth of God's Word is an anchor for the souls of men in a day of much uncertainty, of complete relativism in all human thought systems, and of much skepticism and doubt. God's Word is true because He can be depended upon. In a most vigorous exclamation which employs conscious exaggeration for the sake of emphasis in contrast, the Apostle Paul declares: "Let God be true though every man be false."[14] And this is said in a context which is stressing the absolute faithfulness of God.

14. The central attribute of God is *love*. The Apostle John declares that God is love.[15] By love of God in Scripture is meant that attitude of beneficence and kindness toward mankind which led God to give even His only Son in order that the race might be redeemed. "For God so loved the world that he gave his only Son, that whoever

---

8 Num. 23:19.
9 Titus 1:2; II Tim. 2:13; Heb. 6:17, 18.
10 Heb. 13:5.
11 I Cor. 1:7-9; Phil. 1:6.

12 II Cor. 1:20.
13 John 11:40.
14 Rom. 3:4.
15 I John 4:8, 16.

believes in him should not perish but have eternal life. For God sent the Son into the world, not to condemn the world, but that the world might be saved through him."[16] The Apostle Paul points out that very few people have enough love to lay down their lives for one another. "But God shows his love for us in that while we were yet sinners Christ died for us."[17] Calvary thus becomes the measure of the redeeming love of God and consequently of the assurance that God will also give to His children whatever they may need. "He who did not spare his own Son but gave him up for us all, will he not also give us all things with him?"[18] The Apostle John makes the love of God in giving Christ an occasion to urge Christians to love one another also: "Beloved, let us love one another; for love is of God, and he who loves is born of God and knows God. He who does not love does not know God; for God is love. In this the love of God was made manifest among us, that God sent his only Son into the world, so that we might live through him. In this is love, not that we loved God but that he loved us and sent his Son to be the expiation for our sins. Beloved, if God so loved us, we also ought to love one another."[19]

The Apostle Paul calls attention to the wickedness of pre-Christian days and adds: "But when the goodness and loving kindness of God our Savior appeared, he saved us, not because of deeds done by us in righteousness, but in virtue of his own mercy, by the washing of regeneration and renewal in the Holy Spirit, which he poured out upon us richly through Jesus Christ our Savior, so that we might be justified by his grace and become heirs in hope of eternal life."[20] In a similar vein he writes: "And so we were by nature children of wrath, like the rest of mankind. But God, who is rich in mercy, out of the great love with which he loved us, even when we were dead through our trespasses, made us alive together with Christ (by grace you have been saved), and raised us up with him, and made us sit with him in the heavenly places in Christ Jesus, that in the coming ages he might show the immeasurable riches of his grace in kindness toward us in Christ Jesus. For by grace you have been saved through faith; and this is not your own doing, it is the gift of God—not because of works, lest any man should boast."[21] The Apostle Peter exults in his praise to God explaining that "by his great mercy we have been born anew to a living hope through the resurrection of Jesus Christ from the dead, and to an inheritance which is imperishable, undefiled, and unfading, kept in heaven for you. . . ."[22] Even con-

---

16 John 3:16, 17.
17 Rom. 5:8.
18 Rom. 8:32.

19 I John 4:7-11.
20 Titus 3:4-7.
21 Eph. 2:3-9.

22 I Pet. 1:3, 4.

version in the New Testament is declared to be a manifestation of the love of God. "Do you not know that God's kindness is meant to lead you to repentance?"[23]

The Scriptures teach that the central attribute of God is redeeming love as manifested in the giving of Jesus Christ on Calvary. The Apostle Paul reminded the philosophers on Mars' Hill that God "himself gives to all men life and breath and everything."[24] And to his pagan listeners at Lystra he declared that God "did not leave himself without witness, for he did good and gave you from heaven rains and fruitful seasons, satisfying your hearts with food and gladness."[25] Jesus Himself in telling His disciples that they should love their enemies and pray for their persecutors grounded that commandment in the love of God. If we want to be the children of God we must be like God, and God "makes his sun rise on the evil and on the good, and sends rain on the just and on the unjust."[26] The Bible, therefore, does recognize the good hand of God in the natural blessings of this life. Nevertheless, there is enough evil in human life, sickness, calamities, and disappointments, that the mind of man would be puzzled regarding the love of God were it not for Calvary.

In no aspect of God is Jesus a fuller revelation than in this matter of love. Jesus loved the little children, received them into His arms, and blessed them.[27] Jesus showed mercy upon crippled and handicapped people and healed all who came to Him for help.[28] Jesus had mercy even upon contrite sinners such as the woman of sin who anointed the feet of Jesus and washed them with her tears.[29] He wept and sobbed over Jerusalem in its unbelief because He could not bear to think of the awful destruction which would come upon it a generation later.[30] His redeeming love was so great that when the soldiers were nailing Him to the cross He prayed, "Father, forgive them; for they know not what they do."[31] Even in His agony as He hung on the cross Jesus turned to the penitent thief and declared: "Truly, I say to you, today you will be with me in Paradise."[32] When John the Baptist was languishing in prison and began to doubt, he sent disciples to Jesus to ask Him if He truly was the Messiah. Jesus answered them: "Go and tell John what you have seen and heard: the blind receive their sight, the lame walk, lepers are cleansed, and the deaf hear, the dead are raised up, the poor have good news [the Gospel] preached to them."[33]

---

23 Rom. 2:4.
24 Acts 17:25.
25 Acts 14:17.
26 Matt. 5:45.
27 Matt. 19:13-15; Mark 10:13-16; Luke 18:15-17.

28 Mark 6:56.
29 Luke 7:36-50.
30 Luke 19:41-44.
31 Luke 23:34.
32 Luke 23:43.   33 Matt. 11:4, 5.

One of the greatest evidences of human sin and depravity is the widespread ignorance of and indifference toward the love of God. Even at conversion the average Christian is much more conscious of the wrath of God than of His love. Only gradually does the "babe in Christ" become aware of the greatness of God's love toward him in Christ. But as he grows more mature in his Christian life and experience he sees more and more that everything that God has done in his life has been a result of redeeming love. Even the chastisements of the Lord are for the good of the Christian; divine chastening is a token of sonship: God in His love sends into the life of each one of His children those experiences which are needed to purge out the dross and to sanctify the believer.[34] Not only did Jesus take up His cross and bear it to Calvary; each believer must also follow the Saviour in being willing to endure whatever suffering comes by virtue of being a disciple of the Lord Jesus Christ.[35] And whatever God does permit to come into the life of the saints is a result of His love for them:

> For the Lord disciplines him whom he loves,
> and chastises every son whom he receives.[36]

It is redeeming love which makes a father unwilling to give up and abandon the unworthy son who becomes dissolute and unworthy of his family. Christ's parable of the prodigal son[37] was given in protest against the self-righteous attitude of the Pharisees when they condemned Jesus for receiving sinners and eating with them. Jesus first gave the parables of the lost sheep and the lost coin and then told the story of the man who had two sons, the younger of whom took his journey into a far country and squandered all that he had in loose living. When he came into need because of a famine the "lost boy" also came to himself and said, "I will arise and go to my father, and I will say to him, 'Father, I have sinned against heaven and before you; I am no longer worthy to be called your son; treat me as one of your hired servants.' "[38]

But the father's love was too great to demote his son to the status of a bond servant. "While he was yet at a distance, his father saw him and had compassion, and ran and embraced him and kissed him. And the son said to him, 'Father, I have sinned against heaven and before you; I am no longer worthy to be called your son.' But the father said to his servants, 'Bring quickly the best robe, and put

---

34 Heb. 12:5-11.   37 Luke 15:11-32.
35 Mark 8:34, 35.   38 Luke 15:18, 19.
36 Heb. 12:6.

it on him; and put a ring on his hand, and shoes on his feet; and bring the fatted calf and kill it, and let us eat and make merry; for this my son was dead, and is alive again; he was lost, and is found.' " To the older brother (who took the attitude of the Pharisees, and who in his meanness lamented the great celebration which was being held) the father said, "It was fitting to make merry and be glad, for this your brother was dead, and is alive; he was lost, and is found."[39]

The New Testament is able to make much of God's redeeming love because it takes seriously the doctrines of sin and its consequences. Many moderns have minimized sin so much that God's redeeming love means little to them. They then reason that since God is a being of love He will never do anything severe to those who spurn His love. Nothing could be further from the truth of divine revelation. The Bible takes sin seriously and speaks constantly of the wrath of God, even in passages which are dealing primarily with His love. Romans 5 argues that the fact that God sent His Son to die for a lost race is a proof supreme of the love of God. But the apostle does not go on to say, "Therefore the race has nothing more to fear as to divine judgment." On the contrary, the apostle speaks of Christians being justified by the blood of Christ and "much more shall we be saved by him from the wrath of God."[40] It is those who are closest to Christ in fellowship and obedience who fear most for non-Christian society and for those nations who live in disobedience to God and in worldly pleasures, while those who are not Christians are concerned only when God brings judgment upon a nation or an individual for sin. The love of God and the wrath of God are in Scripture a great paradox. To preach only His wrath drives men to despair, but to represent God as a sort of benign simpleton whom one can mock and despise with impunity is an awful error. "He who believes in the Son has eternal life; he who does not obey the Son shall not see life, but the wrath of God rests upon him."[41] The Apostle Paul declares: "Do not be deceived; God is not mocked, for whatever a man sows, that he will also reap."[42] There will be no widespread turning to Christ on the part of our generation until there is a renewed awareness of the awfulness of sin and God's wrath, and of the amazing depth of God's redeeming love to those who are in Christ Jesus. Only he who has caught a glimpse of the enormity of his sin and then experienced the amazing love of God is able to exclaim with the apostle: "Thanks be to God for his inexpressible gift!"[43]

---

39 Luke 15:20-32.
40 Rom. 5:10.
41 John 3:36.

42 Gal. 6:7.
43 II Cor. 9:15.

15. The *righteousness* of God is that attribute which demands of all His creatures conformity to the moral perfection of Deity. In one of the Psalms attributed to David the writer addresses God as, "Thou who triest the minds and hearts, thou righteous God."[44] In another passage the psalmist says: "For the Lord is righteous, he loves righteous deeds; the upright shall behold his face."[45] Also, "Gracious is the LORD, and righteous; our God is merciful."[46] In His great intercessory prayer the Lord Jesus addresses God as "O righteous Father."[47] The Apostle Paul also describes God as "the righteous judge."[48] John also speaks of the Saviour as "Jesus Christ the righteous."[49]

It was the righteousness of Jesus Christ which led Him to warn the disciples, especially Judas, of the peril of avarice,[50] to rebuke the Samaritan woman at Jacob's well for her sensuality,[51] to protest against the desecration of the Lord's temple and to drive out the merchants and money-changers,[52] and to request the rich young ruler to sell all that he had and distribute his wealth to the needy.[53]

To express vividly the absolute righteousness of God the Old Testament frequently speaks of God "hating" evildoers,[54] hating a spiritual dullness which tends to make images,[55] hating all forms of violence in human relations,[56] religious formalism,[57] and the divorce evil.[58] Even more vivid is the expression "the wrath of God," which occurs time and again in the Old Testament and in the New. For example, God warned Israel of His extreme displeasure with any form of economic oppression, promising that if such should take place God would hear the cry of the poor and His "wrath will burn."[59] Such anthropomorphisms are common in the Pentateuch and the entire Old Testament. The Psalms contain many examples of the divine wrath.[60] Isaiah,[61] Jeremiah,[62] Ezekiel,[63] and at least six of the minor prophets make mention of the wrath of God.[64] The expression is also found in the Chronicles,[65] as well as Ezra[66] and

44 Ps. 7:9.
45 Ps. 11:7.
46 Ps. 116:5.
47 John 17:25.
48 II Tim. 4:8.
49 1 John 2:1.
50 Luke 12:15.
51 John 4:18.
52 John 2:13-22.
53 Luke 18:18-30.

54 Ps. 5:5.
55 Deut. 16:22.
56 Ps. 11:5.
57 Isa. 1:14.
58 Mal. 2:16.
59 Ex. 22:24.
60 Ps. 2:5, 12; 78:31; 79:6; 88:16; etc.
61 Isa. 9:19; 10:6; 13:13.
62 Jer. 21:5; 32:37.
63 Ezek. 7:19.

64 Hos. 5:10; Amos 1:1; Nah. 1:2; Hab. 3:2; Zeph. 1:15, 18; Zech. 7:12;.
65 I Chron. 27:34; II Chron. 12:7, 12; 24:18; 28:11, 13; 29:8, 10; 30:8, 25; 34:21; etc.
66 Ezra 5:12; 7:23; 8:22; 10:14.

Nehemiah.[67] Even the New Testament speaks frequently of God's extreme displeasure with sin in terms of divine wrath: "He who does not obey the Son shall not see life, but the wrath of God rests upon him."[68] Paul declares that, "the law brings wrath,"[69] that is, when men insist upon trying to merit eternal life, all they are able to do is manifest their depravity by breaking God's law, and thus incur His displeasure. Hence, human beings are spoken of as "by nature children of wrath."[70] Such sins as immorality, impurity, and covetousness are spoken of as bringing the wrath of God "upon the sons of disobedience."[71] Hence Paul writes: "Put to death therefore what is earthly in you: immorality, impurity, passion, evil desire, and covetousness, which is idolatry. On account of these the wrath of God is coming."[72] The unbelieving Jews are also spoken of as being under the divine wrath.[73]

Quite frequently in the New Testament the expression "the wrath of God" is used of the punishment God will render to the wicked on the day of Christ. Hence, John the Baptist asked the Pharisees and Sadducees: "Who warned you to flee from the wrath to come?"[74] And the Apostle Paul warns the impenitent sinner, you are "storing up wrath for yourself on the day of wrath when God's righteous judgment will be revealed."[75] Jesus is the one who will deliver or save the Christian "from the wrath of God."[76] Hence, Paul describes the Saviour as "Jesus who delivers us from the wrath to come."[77] The Apocalypse contains many references to the wrath of the Lamb or the wrath of God.[78]

It must be remembered, of course, that God is not a human being with a physical organism. Hence, terms of emotion, such as wrath, do not stand in a relation of contradiction to attributes such as love. The Bible is therefore free to speak of the sinner being under the wrath of God and of God loving him at one and the same time. The wrath of God refers to God's displeasure with his disobedience, while the love of God refers to the desire of God to see the sinner redeemed.

16. The *justice* of God is that attribute which punishes disobedience to the divine will of God. It appears that many times the holiness of God and the righteousness of God are used in a more or less synonymous fashion. Similarly, the judgment which God will

---

67 Neh. 13:18.
68 John 3:36.
69 Rom. 4:15.
70 Eph. 2:3.
71 Eph. 5:6.
72 Col. 3:5, 6.

73 I Thess. 2:16.
74 Matt. 3:7.
75 Rom. 2:5.
76 Rom. 5:9.
77 I Thess. 1:10.
78 Rev. 6:16, 17; 11:18; 14:10, 19; 15:1, 7; 16:1, 19; 19:15.

render through Jesus Christ is described indifferently as righteous or just. It was this attribute which Abraham had in mind when he pleaded with the Lord, "Shall not the Judge of all the earth do right?"[79] And Moses sang:

> For I will proclaim the name of the LORD.
> Ascribe greatness to our God!
> The Rock, his work is perfect;
> for all his ways are justice.
> A God of faithfulness and without iniquity,
> just and right is he.[80]

One of the Psalms says beautifully:

> The LORD reigns; let the earth rejoice;
> let the many coastlands be glad!
> Clouds and thick darkness are round about him;
> righteousness and justice are the foundation of his throne.[81]

The Apostle Paul speaks of "the day of wrath when God's righteous judgment will be revealed. For he will render to every man according to his works: to those who by patience in well-doing seek for glory and honor and immortality, he will give eternal life; but for those who are factious and do not obey the truth, but obey wickedness, there will be wrath and fury. There will be tribulation and distress for every human being who does evil, the Jew first and also the Greek, but glory and honor and peace for every one who does good, the Jew first and also the Greek. For God shows no partiality.

"All who have sinned without the law will also perish without the law, and all who have sinned under the law will be judged by the law. For it is not the hearers of the law who are righteous before God, but the doers of the law who will be justified. When Gentiles who have not the law do by nature what the law requires, they are a law to themselves, even though they do not have the law. They show that what the law requires is written on their hearts, while their conscience also bears witness and their conflicting thoughts accuse or perhaps excuse them on that day when, according to my gospel, God judges the secrets of men by Christ Jesus."[82]

4. THE TRINITY

The term "trinity" is not a Biblical term but has been ascribed to Tertullian, who was born about A.D. 160 and who flourished far

---

79 Gen. 19:25.
80 Deut. 32:3, 4.

81 Ps. 97:1, 2
82 Rom. 2:5-16.

into the third century. The data upon which the doctrine of the trinity is based are, however, clearly found in the New Testament and to a certain extent are intimated in the Old.[83] In other words, the New Testament representation is that three are recognized as having divine attributes, and these three are so described that we must conceive of them as Persons. Theologians generally hold that the term "tritheism" should be avoided as too much implying three *different* Gods, and the Bible never speaks in such terms but always refers to there being but one God—Father, Son, and Holy Spirit.

The early Mennonite bishop, Pieter J. Twisck (1565-1636), explained, "That in the only eternal Divine Being there are not three mere names; but that each name has its true signification and attributes; so that there is a true, real Father, of whom all things are; and a true, real Son, by whom are all things; and a true, real Holy Ghost, through whom the Father and the Son operate. . . . Hence there are, in the same divine Essence, in heaven, three true witnesses: the Father, the Word, and the Holy Ghost; of whom the glory of the only begotten Son of God appeared really and distinctively in the form of a servant on earth, and was also seen by John the Baptist at the Jordan. And the Holy Spirit was also distinctively seen by the same John to descend in the form of a dove from God out of heaven, upon Christ and abide upon Him. And the Father who is an invisible Spirit, and cannot be seen by mortal eye, let His voice be heard from heaven: 'This is my beloved Son, in whom I am well pleased.' "[84] Twisck published this in 1617.

It is the conviction of the present writer that the revelation of the trinity is not helped by many of the illustrations which are employed to try to illustrate it. That the one eternal God existing in three persons, Father, Son, and Holy Spirit, is not a matter of human reason was well stated by Gerrit Roosen (1612-1711): "Thus this matter remains to human reason incomprehensible: even as a father who has a son, is not the son, but the father; so also is the son not the father, but the son of the father; and as the Holy Spirit is a Spirit of God and of Christ, so He is neither the Father nor the Son, but the Holy Spirit. But as we are mere natural beings, and this is supernatural and the work of God, we must view it as a Godly mystery and receive it in faith."[85]

83 See the most excellent article, "Trinity," by B. B. Warfield in the *I.S.B.E.*, V, pp. 3012-22.

84 T. J. van Braght, *The Bloody Theater or Martyrs' Mirror* (Scottdale, Pa.: Mennonite Publishing House, 1950; original Dutch, 1660), pp. 374, 375.

85 Cited in J. C. Wenger, *The Doctrines of the Mennonites* (Scottdale, Pa.: Mennonite Publishing House, 1950), p. 129.

The great Presbyterian theologian, B. B. Warfield (1851-1921), has written what is undoubtedly one of the most thorough discussions of the trinity of God.[86] He shows conclusively that the Old Testament does no more than present intimations of the trinity. One of these intimations is the plural form of the Hebrew word for God, *Elohim*.[87] This plural form in itself does certainly not constitute a revelation of the trinity, yet it is of deep interest that it is used regularly with a singular verb.[88] The Old Testament also contains many examples of plural pronouns being used of God, such as, "Let us make man in our image, after our likeness"[89]; and, "the man has become like one of us, knowing good and evil"[90]; and Isaiah heard the voice of the LORD saying, "Whom shall I send, and who will go for us?"[91] The Old Testament also contains threefold liturgical expressions which the Jews certainly did not understand as implying the tri-personality of God but which the Christian may now recognize as possible intimations of the trinity. A good example of this is the Old Testament benediction:

The LORD bless you and keep you:

The LORD make his face to shine upon you, and be gracious to you:

The LORD lift up his countenance upon you, and give you peace.[92]

Of great interest also are the passages which contain the remarkable phenomena associated with the angel of the LORD, such as in the cases of Hagar,[93] Abraham,[94] Jacob,[95] Moses,[96] Joshua,[97] and Manoah's wife.[98] The point of interest in the angel of the Lord is that in some sense the angel of the LORD seems to be totally distinct from the LORD and yet also identical with Him. For example, when Abraham was tested it was God who asked him to sacrifice his son Isaac. But when Abraham was restrained from slaying his son it was the angel of the LORD who called to him from heaven. This angel said: "Now I know that you fear *God*, seeing you have not withheld your son, your only son, from *me*."[99] Devout Christians with the knowledge they now have from the New Testament are inclined to hold that the angel of the LORD may have been the eternal Son of God prior to His incarnation.

86 See note 83, above.
87 A common word for God in the Hebrew O.T.
88 Gen. 20:13; 35:7 (original Hebrew).
89 Gen. 1:26.
90 Gen. 3:22.
91 Isa. 6:8.
92 Num. 6:24-26.
93 Gen. 16:7-13.
94 Gen. 22:11-16.
95 Gen. 31:11-13.
96 Ex. 3:2-6.
97 Josh. 5:13-15.
98 Judg. 13:2, 16, 20-22.
99 Gen. 22:12.

Not to be omitted, of course, is the occasional use of the phrase, the Holy Spirit, in the Old Testament. It is entirely probable that the Jews thought of the Holy Spirit only as a synonym for the term "God," just as we would understand the expression, "My soul delights"[1] to mean, "I myself delight." But since the New Testament speaks of the Holy Spirit in personal terms, Christians feel free to read Old Testament references to God's Holy Spirit as also referring to the third Person of the Holy Trinity. The very first book of the Bible records that in its initial form when the earth had not yet received its present shape and was still without inhabitant, "The Spirit of God was moving over the face of the waters."[2] And Job says: "By his Spirit the heavens are garnished" (or, "were made fair").[3] Prior to the Deluge the LORD said, "My Spirit shall not strive with [or, not abide in] man for ever."[4] The Spirit of the Lord equipped various Old Testament men for service,[5] empowered deliverers such as Samson,[6] and especially came upon the prophets when they received revelations from God.[7]

It is sometimes held today that believers prior to the day of Pentecost did not have the Holy Spirit. But this is nowhere taught in Scripture. On the contrary, the Old Testament specifically states that God marvelously delivered Israel from Egypt, sustained them for forty years in the wilderness, led them by the pillar of cloud by day and the pillar of fire by night, gave His good Spirit to instruct them,[8] and satisfied their physical needs with manna and water. It is, of course, true that since the day of Pentecost the Holy Spirit has had the redemption of Christ to apply to every believer in a fullness of power and blessing not possible before the Passion of our Lord.

Professor Warfield has demonstrated that the New Testament writers do not feel any need of proving the doctrine of the trinity.[9] By the time the New Testament was written the early church already believed in God the Father as the Author and Creator of all things, in Christ as the Redeemer and Saviour of the church, and in the Holy Spirit as Comforter and Guide. In other words, the early church before the writing of the New Testament accepted fully the deity of Jesus Christ and the personality of the Holy Spirit. Christ as the eternal Son came into the world to save the race, and the Holy Spirit came upon the church in fullness of power and blessing on the

1 Isa. 42:1.
2 Gen. 1:2.
3 Job 26:13, ASV (& RSV).
4 Gen. 6:3.
5 Ex. 31:1-5.
6 Judg. 3:10; 6:34; 9:23; 11:29; 13:25; 14:6, 19; etc.

7 Ezek. 2:2; 3:12; 3:24; 11:1, 5; etc.
8 Neh. 9:18-21.
9 Op. cit., pp. 3015, 3016.

day of Pentecost. The revelation of the trinity was fundamentally a revelation in deed rather than in words. The writers of the New Testament were therefore not changing their doctrine of God by adding two deities to the LORD of the Old Testament; rather, they were showing that the God of the Old Testament consisted of three persons, the eternal Father who was the author of the plan of salvation, the eternal Son who came into the world and accomplished redemption, and the eternal Holy Spirit who was applying the redemption of Jesus. Redemption, therefore, was the occasion for the fullness of revelation on the trinity: the revelation of the trinity was incidental to the bringing of salvation to the race. In the final analysis it was the incarnation of the Son at the birth of Jesus and the gift of the Holy Spirit on the day of Pentecost which made clear that the one God of the Old Testament existed in three persons. The Gospels are clear that there was an *I-Thou* relation between Jesus and the Father; the Father and the Son in turn join in sending the Holy Spirit to the church. Not only does the entire New Testament present the Holy Spirit in personal terms of loving, willing, caring, being grieved, etc., but Jesus was so keenly conscious of the personality of the Holy Spirit that He referred to Him as *Ekeinos* (John 14:26) which could be translated "that One or He." And Jesus used the masculine pronoun although the noun for Spirit with which "He" is in apposition is actually a neuter word in Greek.

We have, therefore, this peculiar situation: the doctrine of the trinity is at the most only intimated in the Old Testament, and it is not at all proved in the New Testament. Rather, it is the assumption of the New Testament writers that God exists as Father, Son, and Holy Spirit, although almost every New Testament writer was a Jew and as such was an intense monotheist. The confident manner in which the apostles refer to the three members of the Holy Trinity is more impressive than formal proof would have been.

The New Testament contains numerous references to the three members of the trinity; for example, according to the first Gospel, the last words of Jesus were: "All authority in heaven and on earth has been given to me. Go therefore and make disciples of all nations, baptizing them in the name of the Father and of the Son and of the Holy Spirit, teaching them to observe all that I have commanded you; and lo, I am with you always, to the close of the age."[10]

References of the Apostle Paul to the three members of the Godhead are confident, easy, and frequent. For example, in I Thessa-

10 Matt. 28:18-20.

lonians Paul speaks of giving thanks to God, remembering their steadfastness of hope in our Lord Jesus Christ, and mentioning the fact that the Gospel came to them not only in word but also in power and in the Holy Spirit.[11] In the second Thessalonian letter he again speaks of giving thanks to God, of being saved through sanctification by the Spirit, and of obtaining the glory of our Lord Jesus Christ.[12] In I Corinthians Paul speaks of varieties of gifts but the same spirit, varieties of service but the same Lord, and varieties of working but the same God.[13] And all Christians are familiar with the beautiful apostolic benediction of II Corinthians 13: "The grace of the Lord Jesus Christ and the love of God and the fellowship of the Holy Spirit be with you all."[14] This benediction seems to correspond to the threefold liturgical benediction of Numbers 6.

In Ephesians 2 Paul speaks of Jesus Christ and says that, "Through him [Christ] we both have access in one Spirit to the Father"[15]; and in the third chapter he speaks of his stewardship of God's grace, of his insight into the mystery of Christ, and of the revelation of that mystery to the apostles and prophets by the Spirit.[16] For this reason Paul says that he bows his knees before the Father, praying that the Christians at Ephesus might be strengthened through the Spirit in the inner man, and that Christ might dwell in their hearts through faith.[17] Indeed, Ephesians abounds in trinitarian passages such as that of chapter 4: "There is one body and one Spirit, just as you were called to the one hope that belongs to your call, one Lord, one faith, one baptism, one God and Father of us all, who is above all and through all and in all."[18] In Ephesians 5 Paul urges his readers to be filled with the Spirit, "always and for everything giving thanks in the name of our Lord Jesus Christ to God the Father."[19] In II Timothy 1 Paul gives thanks to God, urges his readers to persevere in the faith and love which are in Christ Jesus, and to guard the truth that had been entrusted to them by the Holy Spirit who dwells within them.[20] And in the letter to Titus Paul speaks of the goodness and loving-kindness of God our Saviour, of the washing of "regeneration and renewal in the Holy Spirit, which he poured out upon us richly through Jesus Christ our Savior, so that we might be justified by his grace and become heirs in hope of eternal life."[21]

The other epistles of the New Testament contain the same trinitarian doctrine as the Pauline letters. In Hebrews 6 the writer

11 I Thess. 1:2-5.
12 II Thess. 2:13, 14.
13 I Cor. 12:4-6.
14 II Cor. 13:14.

15 Eph. 2:18.
16 Eph. 3:2-5.
17 Eph. 3:14-17.
18 Eph. 4:4-6.

19 Eph. 5:18-20.
20 II Tim. 1:3, 13, 14.
21 Titus 3:4-7.

speaks of becoming partakers of the Holy Spirit, tasting the goodness of the word of God, and of crucifying the Son of God.[22] And in chapter 10 he speaks of spurning the Son of God, outraging the Spirit of grace, and falling into the hands of the living God.[23] In contrasting the inadequacy of the Old Testament sacrifices which nevertheless did accomplish ceremonial purification, the writer argues: "How much more shall the blood of Christ, who through the eternal Spirit offered himself without blemish to God, purify your conscience from dead works to serve the living God."[24] In a similar way the Apostle Peter speaks of Christians as being chosen by God the Father, sanctified by the Spirit, resulting in obedience to Jesus Christ.[25] And Jude, the half brother of our Lord, urges his readers to pray in the Holy Spirit, to keep themselves in the love of God, and to wait for the mercy of our Lord Jesus Christ unto eternal life.[26] In I John 2 the apostle says that "he who confesses the Son has the Father also,"[27] and then goes on to explain that he who remains faithful will abide in the Son and in the Father, since the anointing which his readers received from God makes it unnecessary for anyone to teach them[28]—a clear reference to the promise of the coming of the Holy Spirit given by Jesus and recorded by John in his Gospel.[29] The last book of the Bible describes itself as "The revelation of Jesus Christ, which God gave him to show to his servants what must soon take place,"[30] and one of the most common expressions in it is, "He who has an ear, let him hear what the Spirit says to the churches."[31]

There is no hint anywhere in the New Testament that the several members of the trinity differ from one another whatever in their attributes. The Son is no less divine than is the Father, nor does the Holy Spirit lack any of the attributes of the Father and the Son. Theologians have tried to express this by saying that ontologically the members of the trinity are equal. This is not to assert, however, that in the economy of their operations there is no subordination. On the contrary, there does seem to be a sense in which the Father is the ultimate one, the Son came into the world to do the will of the Father, and the Father and the Son join in sending the Holy Spirit into the world to convict of sin and to lead men to repentance and faith. The so-called Athanasian Creed tried to maintain the separate personality of each member of the trinity together with the

22 Heb. 6:4-6.
23 Heb. 10:29-31.
24 Heb. 9:14.
25 I Pet. 1:2.
26 Jude 20, 21.

27 I John 2:23.
28 I John 2:27, 20.
29 John 16:12-15; cf. Jer. 31:33, 34.
30 Rev. 1:1.
31 Rev. 2:7, 11, 17, etc.

full deity of each by stating in language which seems quaint to twentieth-century ears, "Neither confounding the Persons: nor dividing the Substance."[32] The apostles who wrote the New Testament almost uniformly offer prayer to God the Father in the name of Jesus Christ (that is, by virtue of their union with Him), moved by the Holy Spirit.[33] There is one God, and one Mediator between God and man, Himself man, Christ Jesus.[34] It is the office of the Holy Spirit to bring men to God through the Lord Jesus Christ.

Although the Father, the Son, and the Holy Spirit are intimately joined together in the baptismal formula and in the apostolic benediction, there are but few passages which speak of the Son or of the Holy Spirit as God. The Fourth Gospel does say that in the beginning the Word was with God and *the Word was God*.[35] And in Acts 5 Peter accused Ananias of lying to the Holy Spirit, and a moment later said, "You have not lied to men *but to God*."[36] Nevertheless, the term "God" is typically reserved for the Father, while Jesus is spoken of as the Son of God, and the *Paraclete* as the Spirit of God or the Holy Spirit.

The early church had many struggles in its attempt to formulate the doctrine of the trinity in a manner which would do justice to all the representations of the New Testament. Perhaps the two chief deviations from what is now acknowledged to be sound doctrine were Arianism, which made of Jesus only a creature and therefore did not place enough emphasis on what the Greeks would have called the "unity of essence"; and Sabellianism, which did not place enough emphasis on the separate personalities of the Father, Son, and Holy Spirit, but tended to have only what might be called an economical trinity in contrast with the ontological trinity in which evangelical Christians believe. The liberalism of the twentieth century also more or less denies the essential and unique deity of the Lord Jesus Christ and the personality of the Holy Spirit. Confession of faith in the Father, the Son, and the Holy Spirit is therefore one of the first evidences of soundness of Christian faith in contrast with any type of rationalism or unscriptural philosophy which is not content to accept the profound Biblical mystery of one God eternally existing in three Persons, Father, Son, and Holy Spirit. Although the term "trinity" is not Biblical and for that reason there have been simple

---

32 Schaff, *Creeds of Christendom*, II, p. 66.
33 Rom. 1:8; I Cor. 1:4; Eph. 3:14; Phil. 1:3; Col. 1:3; I Thess. 1:2; II Thess. 1:3; II Tim. 1:3; Philemon 4. (I Tim. 1:12 is an exception.)
34 I Tim. 2:5.
35 John 1:1.
36 Acts 5:3, 4.

Biblicists who avoided its use because it seemed too philosophical to them,[37] yet the New Testament is clear that the Son of God existed eternally in full equality with God and that the incarnate Son of God who ascended to heaven began His spiritual reign over the church by sending the Holy Spirit with His transforming power upon the apostles and disciples on the great day of Pentecost, A.D. 30.[38]

5. *THE DECREES OF GOD*

In recent centuries there has been a certain amount of disagreement due to differing emphases between the so-called Reformed or Calvinist theologians and those who are called Arminians. The Reformed, represented by such great denominations as the Presbyterian, Dutch Reformed, and to a certain extent the Baptist, have followed in the tradition established by Augustine (354-430) and John Calvin (1509-64). The Reformed tradition emphasizes the sovereignty of God, the total depravity of man, God's unconditional election of certain chosen individuals to eternal salvation, the fact that Christ died only for the elect ("limited atonement"), the doctrine of efficacious grace, and the perseverance of the saints (commonly called eternal security).

The so-called Arminians are the followers of James Herman or Harmen, who Latinized his name as Arminius (1560-1609). The Arminians believe in total depravity but stress human responsibility more than do the Reformed, believing that when sinners are convicted by the Holy Spirit they either accept Christ or reject Him. Arminians believe in election based upon God's foreknowledge; they believe that the atonement effected by Jesus was universal in its scope but that divine grace is resistible. They believe that the power of God is adequate to keep the saints, and that it is also God's intention to do so, but that it is possible through a neglect of prayer and the other means of grace to grow cold in the Christian life and finally to apostatize. The Arminian tradition has been strongly represented in past centuries in the Methodist Church.

The Anabaptists arose in Switzerland and Holland long before the Calvinist-Arminian controversy had developed. They tended to be somewhat more paradoxical than either the Calvinists or the Arminians, although they would have agreed with the Arminians rather than with the Reformed as to the doctrine of predestination, the scope of the atonement, the possibility of apostasy, etc.

When theologians speak of the decree of God they have in mind

---

37 Van Braght, *Martyrs' Mirror*, 1950, p. 1107.
38 Acts 2:33.

His eternal plan or purpose which embraces everything which comes to pass. Both the Reformed and the Arminians stress that this divine decree is founded in divine wisdom, is eternal, efficacious, and immutable, and that it embraces both the good acts and the bad acts of men though not equally in respect to good and evil, for the decree of God is always permissive in respect to sin.

The main difference between the Reformed and the Arminians is that the Reformed have stressed that all God's decrees are unconditional, whereas the Arminians have divided the various decrees of God into two classes: those which are absolute, such as the decree to create the universe and to send the eternal Son as the Saviour of mankind; while other decrees are regarded as conditional, especially those which pertain to the eternal welfare of men. As a matter of fact, the Bible does teach that there is a universalism in the Gospel as far as God's intention is concerned: it is God's desire that all men shall be saved and come to a knowledge of the truth.[39] It is not God's will that any should perish, but that all should reach repentance.[40] Nevertheless, the Scriptures are paradoxical on this point, for the Bible does ground the acceptance of Christ on the part of the saints in the eternal good pleasure of God.[41] In a general way about as close as Christians can come to an understanding of this mystery is to say that when men are lost it is because of their sin and disobedience; it is not because of a lack of love on the part of God for them. Hence, the apostolic rebuke given to those who rejected the Gospel was: "Since you thrust it from you, and judge yourselves unworthy of eternal life, behold, we turn to the Gentiles."[42] On the other hand, when people accepted the Gospel the apostles recognized the eternal love and grace of God so that Luke is able to record: "As many as were ordained to eternal life believed."[43]

It is certainly true that there is a sense in which God is completely sovereign and that all comes to pass either by His directive will or by His permissive will. Nothing can happen to the Christian without the permission of Almighty God. But any man is able to thwart God's desire to save him, to use him, or even to keep him saved. (Satan uses the unregenerate "flesh," that is, sinful human nature, as a fulcrum to pry the believer off the ground of justifying faith.) God's foreknowledge does not destroy human freedom. In the final analysis the controversy between the Reformed and the Arminians

39 I Tim. 2:4.
40 II Pet. 3:9.
41 Rom. 8:28-30; Acts 16:14.
42 Acts 13:46.
43 Acts 13:48.

is due largely to dissimilar emphases. The differences are relative, not absolute.

Historically a controversy arose within the camp of the Reformed between the so-called supralapsarians and the infralapsarians or sublapsarians. According to the supralapsarians the logical order of the divine decrees would have been, first, to save some and reject others, then to create both classes, then to permit the fall, and finally to save the elect through Christ. The infralapsarians, however, held that the decrees should be given the following order: first, to create, second, to permit the fall, third, to provide salvation in Christ (sufficient for all), and finally to elect some to eternal salvation.[43a] If Arminians would have created a logical order to these decrees they would undoubtedly have been arranged as follows: first, to create, second, to permit the fall, then to provide a universal atonement in Christ, then to offer the Gospel to all men, and finally to save all those who accept Christ. Actually it seems presumptuous and ridiculous to attempt to discuss the order of the decrees in the mind of God even if it is called logical rather than chronological.

On the providence of God, the election of believers, and the rejection of unbelievers, the Mennonite bishop, P. J. Twisck (1565-1636), wrote in his famous Confession of 33 Articles, 1617:

As we believe and confess that God is omnipotent; and that with Him nothing is impossible; so likewise is He also prescient and omniscient, so that nothing is hid from Him in heaven and in earth, neither that which is to take place until the end of all things, nor that which has taken place from all eternity. And through this exceeding high prescience, knowledge, and wisdom of God, which are unfathomable, He very well saw and knew from the beginning in eternity until the consummation of the world, who would be the truly believing recipients of His grace and mercy; and, again, who should be found unbelieving despisers and rejecters of said grace. And, consequently, He from the beginning and from eternity knew, foresaw, elected, and ordained all true believers to inherit eternal salvation through Christ Jesus; and, on the other hand rejected all unbelieving despisers of said grace to eternal damnation. Hence, the perdition of men is of themselves, and their salvation only through the Lord their God, without whom they can do nothing that is good.[44]

In recent generations it would appear that in the Mennonite tradition there has been such a strong reaction to the Reformed doctrine of election that there has been a somewhat inadequate emphasis on the grace of God, on the bondage of men in sin, and on the Bibli-

---

cal teaching that God did choose His saints before the foundation of the world. This subject of election, however, will be given a fuller treatment under soteriology. The subject which concerns us at this point is God's decree to create the universe. Naturally the Bible confines its attention almost exclusively to this earth since this is the planet on which our race dwells, and where the Biblical theme of divine redemption from sin has its locus. Let us, therefore, turn at this point to a study of the Biblical account of the creation, including that of our first parents.

6. *THE BIBLICAL DOCTRINE OF CREATION*

Professor A. H. Strong has defined creation as "That free act of the triune God by which in the beginning for his own glory he made without the use of pre-existing materials the whole visible and invisible universe."[45] This doctrine is known technically as creation *ex nihilo,* that is, the personal and glorious God depicted throughout the Scriptures created out of nothing all that now exists both in the material and spirit worlds. The doctrine of creation is a part of *Christian theism* and is to be contrasted with *evolutionary naturalism;* the latter rejects the supernatural and attempts to account for all forms of life which now exist by the theory of organic evolution, according to which the higher forms of life have all evolved from lower forms by means of resident forces.

It will help the reader of the Bible to understand the character of the first few chapters of Genesis if he bears in mind that the basic purpose of the Bible is to lead men to that redemption which God offers to them in Christ. It was, therefore, necessary that Moses by divine inspiration give a brief account of the origin of matter, energy, life, consciousness, and human personality, together with human sin, before beginning the story of God's redemptive history. Genesis is, therefore, first of all theocentric. The entire account has its center of emphasis in God, rather than in any details of method which God may have employed. In the second place, the account is geocentric as far as standpoint is concerned. In the very first verse of the Bible Moses reports that, "In the beginning God created the heavens and the earth." From then on the entire account is earth-centered as to interest, which, to be sure, is entirely natural since the human race dwells on the earth. The account is further colored by the fact that it is written from what might be called a phenomenal rather than a scientific point of view. This does not mean that the account is in any sense untrue, or a matter of mere myth, but it does mean that it

45 Strong, *op. cit.,* p. 371.

is written in common everyday language for ordinary readers; it is therefore extremely simple. But this very simplicity occasions extreme difficulty when men of a scientific turn of mind attempt to extract from the account that which it does not particularly purport to give: namely, exact details describing in scientific language the creative process employed by God. The account is highly poetic. Indeed, the entire first chapter of Genesis could be set up as a sort of blank verse running somewhat as follows:

> And God said, "Let there be . . ."
> And there was . . .
> And God saw that it was good.
> And there was evening
> And there was morning, a . . . day.

Since the whole account is theocentric as to emphasis, geocentric as to standpoint, written in nonscientific language, and highly poetic in character, it is evident that scientists will be disappointed if they seek information concerning God's creative process from the record in Genesis 1.

One of the peculiar characteristics of Genesis 1 is that the six creative days show continual progress in a twofold pattern. On the first day God made light to appear on the earth; on the fourth day He made the luminaries or light-bearers, sun, moon, and stars, to appear in the sky. On the second day God divided the waters which were above the firmament, that is to say, He caused the clouds above the open expanse of the sky to be separated from the waters on the earth; on the fifth day God made birds to fly across the face of the heavens, and He made water animals to dwell in the seas. (Incidentally, it is of interest though perhaps the explanation is not apparent, that the term *create* is employed of the universe in Genesis 1:1, of marine life in 1:21, and of human beings in 1:27; whereas the less specific term *made* is used of the firmament in 1:7, of sun, moon, and stars in 1:16, and of land animals in 1:25). On the third day God made dry land to appear and caused vegetation to grow thereon; on the sixth day God made the land animals and mankind.

There are a number of questions about which there has been much speculation and argument but which Genesis does not answer to the complete satisfaction of human curiosity. One of these is the meaning of the term "day." There are some writers who hold that the entire account in Genesis 1 is so strongly pictorial and poetic that the term "day" cannot be pressed at all. In the judgment of the present writer, however, this view is to be rejected as hardly doing justice to the language of Genesis 1. Other writers believe that the chapter can only be interpreted as meaning six twenty-four-hour days in succession. Indeed, this is a natural way to understand the language, and were it not for the evidence which Christian men of science are now accepting, this would be undoubtedly the common belief of Bible-believing Christians. Nevertheless, in reference to this world there are two sources of truth: the first is those broad metaphysical foundations sketched for us by the Word of God indicating that God is the Creator of all things, that He is the Preserver of His universe, that He is sovereign in all things, and that He is both transcendent and immanent in reference to His creation. The other source of truth is the research and investigation of men of science. This is God's world and He has seen fit to allow created human be-ings minds which are able to unlock many of the mysteries of His creation.

The Bible helps believing Christians who are working in the field of science to avoid the mistakes and false theories of unbelieving scientists who do not accept the revelation which God has given to men in the Scriptures. In other words, the Bible throws light on the creation. But the opposite is also true: that which is learned by scientists about the creation also helps us to understand, or at least not to misinterpret, the revelation contained in the Scriptures. The evidence from science seems to be that this world is older than was held by Archbishop Ussher (1581-1656), whose chronology was added to the King James Version in 1701. It is not a question as to whether God *could* have created the universe and performed His activity in reference to this earth in six twenty-four-hour days or in six seconds; the only question is, What did God do?[46]

A very real possibility is that Genesis 1 should be understood as meaning that there were six creative days (ordinary days of twenty-four hours, but not following each other in immediate succession). The Hebrew actually says: "And there was evening and there was morning, one day; . . . a second day . . . ; a third day . . . , etc." Is this carefulness of statement in Genesis 1 perhaps deliberate and there-fore remarkably accurate in reference to what scientists now believe about the age of the earth? It is also held by some devout Christians, especially those who are much interested in the relationship of the revelation of God in the Bible to that which has been learned about God's world through scientific study, that the six days of Genesis 1 were not six diurnal days, that is twenty-four-hour days, but six crea-

46 Cf. *Modern Science and Christian Faith*, by Members of the American Scientific Affiliation (Wheaton, Ill.: Van Kampen Press, 1948).

tive days or epochs. According to this explanation the terms "evening" and "morning" would not refer so much to the setting and rising of the sun but to the beginning and the ending of each creative epoch.

This matter of how best to interpret the term "day" in Genesis 1 is not one over which evangelical believers should quarrel; the point is, and all evangelical Christians accept this, that Genesis does teach that God is the creator of all which exists, that He effected this creation in six "days," and that He is a personal God embracing His entire creation in His providential care.

Another point on which the record is not clear is the number of specific life forms which God created on the earth in the beginning. For example, today there are various types of hares, owls, bears, violets, wrens, etc. Did God create an Arctic hare as well as the ordinary North American hare in the Temperate Zone? Or, did God create one type of rabbit which in turn branched out into the several varieties which now are scattered over the face of the earth? Are the number of species on the earth now approximately the same as were created or did certain life forms become extinct, while other new varieties arose? It should be carefully observed that this is not a question of naturalistic evolution; it is simply whether God may not have allowed numerous life forms to become extinct, while also allowing new varieties to arise through the millenniums since the time of the creation. Certain it is that there have been many fossils discovered for which there do not seem to be extant any living specimens. Why should any Christian attempt to limit God and undertake to assert that He could not have allowed new varieties to develop through the influence of climate, etc.? The aim of all honest study is to arrive at the truth. Christians need to have no fear of any truth either from the Bible or from true science.

As was indicated above, *the real struggle today is between evolutionary naturalism and the theistic doctrine of creation*. Most of the arguments for evolution historically fell into about five main classes. The argument of *morphology* holds that similarity of structure points to a common evolutionary origin. *Embryology* maintains that during the development of a fetus at least a part of the evolutionary history of that life form tends to be duplicated. *Paleontology* holds that the fossil forms found in the rocks would support the elaborate theories of origin proposed by evolutionists. The argument from *vestigial* organs proposes that the structures found in some forms of life, though no longer of functional value to that life, are evolutionary remnants of organs which at one time were of value to the ancestor of the present life form. The general point of view is that *natural variations* in life forms, by accumulative addition, and by numerous mutations, ultimately produce new species.

It should be carefully noted that the question is not whether God could have used evolution as His method; the only question is whether He did. In all honesty, it should be noted that organic evolution is not a matter of science; it is strictly a philosophical interpretation of the data. For example, similarity of structures can just as well point to a common Creator as to a common evolutionary ancestor. The embryological development of a fetus must of necessity proceed from the simple to the complex, resulting in a superficial resemblance to simpler forms of life. Fossil forms prove only that a large number of life forms have become extinct; they do not indicate that the present forms were descended from older and simpler forms. The argument from vestigial organs was at one time much more compelling than it is now for the simple reason that many of the organs formerly regarded as vestigial have now been found to play a highly significant role. (The evangelical Christian has the same right to bring his faith to bear at this point by holding that every structure or form which the Creator has given to an animal has now, or has had, some useful function, as does the organic evolutionist have the right to interpret the data in terms of his fundamental assumptions.)

The present writer joins a host of evangelical Christians in rejecting naturalistic evolution for two reasons: (1) Genesis 1 represents God as creating successively by fiat a variety of life forms, both flora and fauna, each to reproduce "after its kind." This simple description is still found to be true by observation. God seems to have set certain limits, though not always known by man, as to what can or cannot be done with a given life form. For example, all kinds of dogs have been produced both by nature and under the artificial program of men, but whether the dog weighs ten pounds or one hundred, he is still quite recognizable as a dog and has not been transformed into a sheep or a wildcat. Life forms still reproduce after their kind. Occasionally, indeed, a life form discovered in the fossils and thought by evolutionists to have been extinct for "fifty million years" is found to be alive and unchanged, such as the coelacanth, discovered in 1952 and thought to have been extinct for a vast period of time.[47] (When this form was brought to light Dr. E. I. White of the British Museum's Geology Department said, "It's as if a live dinosaur had suddenly appeared.") Life forms are still reproducing after their kind, though this is no denial of natural variation, muta-

47 Note the various accounts in the press: e.g., *Time*, LXI, 2 (Jan. 12, 1953), p. 60.

tions, and the effect of climate, etc., upon animals and plants. (2) The other argument against naturalistic evolution is the information provided by science itself, particularly in the field of genetics. There is no known way for one species to be transmuted into another. In other words, genetics supports entirely the Biblical representation that life forms reproduce themselves in a remarkably accurate fashion.

If the historic arguments for evolution have been largely discredited by further investigation, and if there is no absolute proof of the transmutation of one species into another in science, why then does the theory of evolution continue to be the accepted hypothesis? The answer seems to be that the nerve of organic evolution is naturalism; that is, it has an antisupernaturalistic bias. It must be stressed repeatedly that the real foes are *Christian theism,* the view of God and the world taught in the Bible, and *evolutionary naturalism,* which is the point of view which consistently rejects God and the Bible.

According to theism the ground of all existence is an almighty, personal God; whereas according to naturalism no supernaturalistic being shall be accepted. According to theism Genesis gives us an inspired account of the creative work of God, but according to evolutionary naturalism the origins of the world, of matter, energy, life, and mind, are inexplicable. According to theism God created self-perpetuating life forms, which are still relatively fixed. Naturalism holds that nature is very dynamic and by means of resident forces has produced the forms of life which we now know, together with vast numbers which have become extinct. According to theism man was created in God's image, with a capacity for intelligent thought and divine communion; he is a responsible creature, being called upon by God to accept the redemption which Christ provided. Naturalism, however, holds that man is a direct descendant of the lowest forms of life, is merely a highly developed mammal, and is without any legitimate right to faith in God. According to theism God actively controls and sustains the world and is guiding it to its purposed goal. Naturalism holds that the world is entirely self-contained, operates rigidly by its own laws, and is controlled by blind mechanism, not by a beneficent heavenly Father. *If one accepts Christian theism there cannot be any objection whatever to the doctrine of creation as presented in the Word of God. Evangelical Christians have nothing to gain by accepting organic evolution except to be in fashion with those scientists who are more concerned to be regarded as up-to-date than to align their thinking with divine revelation.*

What should the Christian theist who accepts the Biblical doctrine of the special creation of man say as to the so-called prehistoric races of men who once inhabited this earth? What about the *Neanderthal (Homo neanderthalensis)* type of men? And what of the *Cro-Magnon* man? It is indeed true that various skulls, skeletons, or portions of skeletons, have been found in various parts of the earth, some of which are undoubtedly of ancient origin. Nevertheless, the tools and artifacts found in close proximity with these ancient skeletons or parts of skeletons would indicate that the races represented by these bones led about the same type of life as primitive people do today. *There is no evidence that man was ever inferior mentally, spiritually, or physically to what he now is.* In other words, from the very beginning man has had the divine image; he has been truly *Homo sapiens.* From the scientific point of view, some of the main distinguishing characteristics of *Homo sapiens* are: "his completely erect posture and gait, from which follow the modification of the feet for walking instead of prehension . . . and the greater development of certain muscles . . . which hold the body erect; the shortness of the arms and the size and perfect apposability of the thumb; the distinctness of the chin; the comparatively uniform size and even arrangement of the teeth; and most of all, the enormous development of the brain, especially of the cerebrum, and the smooth rounded skull and high facial angle. Man alone has the power of articulate speech, and largely by reason of this power the capacity of abstract reasoning."[48] No evidence whatsoever has thus far been produced to show that any man ever differed substantially from the races which are now on earth. In other words, man always had the divine image; he was always truly human. It is indeed true that some races have disappeared or lost their identity. It is also true, of course, that there have always been occasional abnormalities or freaks. Unfortunately, the tendency has been for evolutionists to seize upon any oddly formed skull or bone and to use the evidence therefrom in support of the evolutionary theory. No more variation exists among the various skeletons and skulls which have been found from antiquity than that which obtains now among the various races, especially among the various individuals, of the earth today.

Byron C. Nelson, Th.M., in his excellent little book, *Before Abraham, Prehistoric Man in Biblical Light,* states that he has two deep convictions: "The first is that mankind is very old—how old the writer does not know or even try to imagine. The second is that

---

48 From the article on "man" in *Webster's New International Dictionary of the English Language* (Springfield, Mass.: Merriam Co., 1917), p. 1307.

man has always been man. Man is not a product of evolution but of creation, exactly as described in the Book of Genesis, which, the writer is glad to say, he accepts as true in a literal sense."[49]

7. THE CONSTITUTION OF MAN

Scientific anthropology is the study of man as such, not particularly from the religious point of view, but from the standpoint of the characteristics of the various cultures in which man has lived, the several races which have appeared during man's history on earth, etc. Biblical anthropology, however, is the study of man as found in Scripture: his special creation by God, his constitution, conscience, sin, the divine image, etc. Historically the two main schools of thought in Biblical anthropology, as to the constitution of man, have been trichotomy and dichotomy.

Trichotomy holds that man is according to the Scriptures composed of body, soul, and spirit. This tripartite division of the human personality is based chiefly upon two Scriptures, I Thessalonians 5:23 which speaks expressly of man's "spirit and soul and body"; and Hebrews 4 which states that the Word of God is so sharp as to divide soul from spirit.[50] It is, of course, evident from these two Scriptures that the terms "soul" and "spirit" are at least not always used in identical senses. However, there are other passages such as Matthew 22 which speak of the heart, soul, and mind, not to mention body and spirit.[61] It, therefore, becomes a question as to how far one may press such expressions as body, soul, and spirit to prove a tripartite nature. By this type of reasoning one could conclude that man really has a fivefold nature: body, soul, spirit, mind, and heart. Is it not more reasonable to believe, however, that by expressions like heart, soul, and mind the Scripture attempts to denote total personality and self rather than the delineation of "parts" of the human personality? Nevertheless, the terms "soul" and "spirit" are not used entirely synonymously in Scripture. The word "soul" seems to refer primarily to the principle of animate life, to the difference between a living being and a dead one. This is why the books of Moses in the original Hebrew speak of the "souls" of animals.[52] The Bible also frequently refers to persons as souls; for example, eight souls were saved in the ark, that is, eight people. The term "spirit" in the Scripture refers to

49 Byron C. Nelson, *Before Abraham, Prehistoric Man in Biblical Light* (Minneapolis, Minn.: Augsburg Publishing House, 1948), p. 96.

50 Heb. 4:12.

51 Matt. 22:37.

52 Gen. 1:20, 21, 24, 30; 2:19; 9:4, 10, 12; etc. See *The Englishman's Hebrew and Chaldee Concordance*, pp. 829-33.

that capacity which human beings have for fellowship with God. God's Spirit bears witness with our spirits, not with our souls. However, the Old Testament (in the Hebrew) speaks also of the "spirits" of animals,[53] yet evidently not in the same sense as human beings, for the spirit of man ascends to God, whereas the spirit or breath of animals descends to the earth[54] (perhaps in the sense of terminating at the death of the organism).

It is therefore obvious that the Biblical doctrine of man does not depend upon the term "soul," for the Hebrew Bible calls the marine animals which were created on the fifth day "souls of life,"[55] as well as the land animals. When Moses, therefore, reports that the LORD God formed man of dust from the ground, and breathed into his nostrils the breath of life, and man became a "soul of life," the significant thing is not the fact that man became a living soul (living being, RSV); rather it is the divine image and the divine inbreathing that are significant. God created man in His moral and spiritual image, and no animate life preceded the divine inbreathing. Man's differentiation from the beasts of the field lies not in the fact that he become a living being, but in the characteristics which God gave him, mental, moral, and spiritual, and which are summed up under the phrase, "the image of God."

Dichotomists hold that if man is to be divided at all it must be in terms of his material body and the spiritual self which indwells the body. Indeed, this is the very distinction frequently made by the Bible itself. For example, the writer of Ecclesiastes describes death as the dust returning to the earth as it was, and the spirit to God who gave it.[56] And when Jesus wanted to teach the principle of complete trust He told His disciples not to be anxious about the soul, what to eat or drink, nor about the body, what to wear[57]: that is, God is able to make provision for the total needs of man, both for the sustenance of life and for the protection of the body. Jesus also told His disciples not to fear those who are able to kill the body but cannot destroy the soul; rather, said He, we should fear Him who is able to destroy both soul and body in Gehenna.[58] Paul frequently makes the same distinction between body and soul or body and spirit.[59] Indeed, the Bible frequently speaks of death indifferently as the giving up of the spirit,[60] or as the giving up of the soul.[61] This fact helps to convince the dichotomist of the essential correctness of his position.

53 Gen. 6:17; 7:15, 22; Eccl. 3:19, 21; etc. *Ibid.*, pp. 1160-62.
54 Eccl. 3:21.
55 Gen. 1:20.
56 Eccl. 12:7.
57 Matt. 6:25.
58 Matt. 10:28.
59 Rom. 8:10; I Cor. 5:5; 7:34; II Cor. 7:1; Eph. 2:3.
60 Ps. 31:5; Luke 23:46; Acts 7:59.
61 Gen. 35:18; I Kings 17:21, 22; Acts 15:26.

It would seem that the only way to do full justice both to those Scriptures that speak of the contrast between man's body and his inner personality, often described indifferently as spirit or soul, and to those Scriptures which do differentiate between soul and spirit, is to give up both dichotomy and trichotomy and to emphasize the essential oneness or unity of the human personality. Actually, man is not composed of a loose union of a soul and spirit with a body, but is a psychophysical personality, made in the mental and spiritual image of God. There is a continuity of one's identity after the death of the physical organism, however. At the return of Jesus God will provide a resurrection body for each saint, thus reconstituting the full personality. In other words, man is a united personality having both material and spiritual elements.

When we speak of man's *body* we have in mind the physical organism which in many respects resembles that of the higher mammals. When we speak of the capacity of man to understand abstract thought we refer to his *mind*. When we speak of that capacity of man which enables him to enter into fellowship with God, we refer to man's *spirit*. When the Bible speaks of man's *soul* it generally means the animate life of the body, but in the Christian world of today, which has been somewhat influenced by Greek philosophy, the term *soul* has come to mean the responsible inner self which survives the death of the body and meets God at the judgment. Thus many Christian hymns refer to the "never dying soul," meaning that aspect of the human personality beyond the material. Perhaps it would help clarify this discussion if one would say that body, soul, spirit, mind, and heart are not the names of loose entities tied together inside one's skin, but are rather capacities of the total personality. Conceiving of soul and spirit as the names of capacities which human beings possess obviates such puzzling questions as just where to draw the line between body and soul, of how great the division must be in Siamese twins before there are two souls, etc. One cannot be Biblical in his thinking and deny that man has material, intellectual, social, spiritual, etc., facets to his personality. Stressing the essential oneness of human personality, of body, mind, and soul, is both Biblical and in harmony with the best current thinking.

The Origin of the Individual Soul

Theologians tend to discuss a number of questions to which the Bible does not give a totally clear answer. One of these obscure points relates to the origin of the individual soul. Traditionally there has been a controversy between the Creationists and the Traducians. The Creationists hold that God creates a soul for each child that is conceived and born. The time of this creation is, of course, unknown. Creationists point to Scriptures which refer to the body returning to the earth at death and the spirit going to God who gave it[62]; to the creation of the heavens and the earth and of God's giving breath or spirit to the people on the earth[63]; and to the comment of the writer of Hebrews that men respect the fathers of their flesh, shall they not much more be subject to the Father of spirits,[64] a passage which is regarded as contrasting men and God as being respectively the sources of our bodies and of our spirits. Creationism, however, seems to make the inheritance of some traits a bit difficult to understand. Perhaps more serious is how to account for depravity if only the body is inherited.

Those who hold to Traducianism believe that in a general way God ceased from His creative work after the original six creative days. In fact, Genesis seems to imply precisely that.[65] Traducians also point out that the entire creation was made to reproduce "after its kind," and that this principle evidently applies to man, also. For example, Scripture reports that God made man in His image, after His likeness, in the beginning.[66] And later Adam "became the father of a son in his own likeness, after his image."[67] Moses in Genesis 5 seems to stress the tremendous significance of God creating Adam in His likeness, and of Adam in turn begetting a son in his own likeness. Traducianism seems to account for all the Biblical descriptions and assertions in reference to man better than does Creationism.

It is doubtful, however, whether Scripture ever intends to speak on this particular question. The Bible is content to report that man has originated by a special creative act on the part of God, that he is a responsible moral agent able to make genuine moral choices, that he possesses a capacity for fellowship with God, that by the gracious work of the Holy Spirit he is able to lay hold on eternal life, and that he is destined to live forever. Such philosophical questions as the relation of the mind to the body, the origin of man's "soul," and the like, are not discussed at all in Scripture. The Christian believer should, therefore, respect the silence of the Bible on these questions and not enter too deeply into speculation about them.

62 Eccl. 12:7.
63 Isa. 42:5.
64 Heb. 12:9.
65 Gen. 2:2 (cf. Leupold's commentary).
66 Gen. 1:27.
67 Gen. 5:3; cf. 5:1.

The Divine Image

Frequent mention has been made in the discussions thus far about man having been created in the image of God. Just what does the Bible mean by the divine image? According to the Roman Catholic point of view a distinction is to be made between the image of God and the divine likeness. The image is thought of as such natural gifts as the spirituality of the soul, the freedom of the will, and the immortality of the soul. The likeness of God is then regarded as a supernatural gift, consisting of original righteousness, which was given to man to keep down his lower nature, his "concupiscence." According to this point of view the divine image has been retained but the likeness has been lost. Therefore man has been plagued with sensuality ever since the Fall.[68]

Lutheran theologians in their strong emphasis on man's sin and his need of redemption have tended strongly toward an identification of the divine image with that knowledge, righteousness, and holiness which original man possessed and which is now restored in the Christian believer through redemption. The divine image has thus been basically lost although natural man still retains traces of it. The Christian believer is gradually being transformed once more into that perfect image of God in which Adam was created.[69]

Reformed theologians tend to distinguish between the divine image in a broad and in a narrow sense. The broad meaning includes intellect, moral nature, and immortality; that is, rationality, morality, and the endless existence which the inner self possesses. The divine image in this formal sense has been retained. In the narrow sense of the content of the divine image, namely, true knowledge, righteousness, and eternal life, however, the divine image has been lost.[70]

It should be observed that these differences are largely matters of words: all Biblical theologians agree that original man was created with a mind capable of thinking God's thoughts after Him, with a nature which is truly moral in character, and with an inner self which shall endure forever. As far as Genesis is concerned the words "image" and "likeness" are undoubtedly synonymous. The repetition of the phrase, "after our likeness," is undoubtedly simply to

---

68 *A Catholic Dictionary:* articles, "Concupiscence," "Fall of man," "Sin, Original," etc. See also Pietro Parente, Antonio Piolanti and Salvatore Garofalo, *Dictionary of Dogmatic Theology* (Milwaukee: Bruce Publishing Co., 1952), articles, "Image," "Sin, Original," etc.

69 Henry E. Jacobs and John A. W. Haas, *The Lutheran Cyclopedia* (New York: Charles Scribner's Sons, 1899), p. 241.

70 Louis Berkhof, *Reformed Dogmatics* (Grand Rapids, Mich.: Eerdmans, 1932), I, pp. 191-99.

emphasize the similarity of the divine image. All Biblical theologians also acknowledge that the Fall did not change man into an irresponsible animal. Man is still to be contrasted with the brute; he still has rationality, moral nature, and immortality. Nevertheless, the Fall did mar and blur the divine image. First of all there was the noetic effect of the Fall: man can still think, but his knowledge of God and salvation is blurred by his sin-darkened mind. Man still has a moral nature but he is depraved, with an unfortunate balance of power on the side of his lower nature. Man still is a spiritual being, being immortal, but he is doomed to an eternity in Gehenna unless he is in Christ. It should be noted that regeneration and sanctification largely cancel the effect of the Fall as far as the divine image is concerned. Original man was innocent, intelligent, holy (though unconfirmed therein), and enjoying communion with God.[71]

Only God is unable to sin. Adam was able either to sin or not to sin. But the Fall changed all this. Natural man now is unable not to sin: he stands in terrible need of redemption.

Conscience

By conscience is meant that God-given monitor within us which passes judgment on the moral character of what we are, what we think and say, and what we do. According to the Bible the conscience is not an accretion which man somehow developed in the course of an evolutionary history, but an aspect of human personality from the beginning.

Although the Old Testament does not employ any specific word for conscience it does give many examples of it: Adam and Eve after their disobedience to God hid behind the trees of the garden dreading to meet their Maker[72]; Cain also displayed the behavior of a man with a bad conscience[73]; Joseph's brothers turned to one another in their distress a score of years after they had sold Joseph into slavery and confessed that their difficulties were due to their great sin[74]; and David's "heart" smote him after he had humiliated the king of Israel.[75]

Of all the Biblical writers none gives as much attention to conscience as Paul. He speaks of conscience as bearing witness continually,[76] of it being either good[77] or bad, even defiled and seared,[78] etc. Paul himself had a good conscience, although he was not introspec-

---

71 Here again the Biblical view clashes with the theory of evolution.
72 Gen. 3:8.
73 Gen. 4:13.
74 Gen. 42:21.
75 I Sam. 24:5.
76 Rom. 2:15.
77 Acts 23:1; 24:16; cf. I Pet. 3:16, 21.
78 Titus 1:15, 16; I Tim. 4:2; cf. Heb. 10:22.

tive.[79] He teaches that if the Christian wishes to be happy he must follow his conscience.[80] The Christian is also obligated by love to respect the scruples of his fellow believers.[81] At the same time the apostle stresses the fact that Christianity is not a self-imposed asceticism, although Paul has nothing but praise for voluntary self-denial which is based on fraternal love. The apostle displays vigorous mental and spiritual health when he reports that he relies entirely upon the Holy Spirit to call his attention to any matter in his life which requires correction rather than himself becoming an introspective person.[82] The other apostles agreed perfectly with the teaching of Paul. Peter speaks also of conscience being good,[83] and John indicates that the approval of God is vastly more significant than that of our own hearts.[84]

It is highly significant that the Bible represents the standing of Christian believers as not depending upon the witness of their own conscience but upon their faith in Him who declares the Christian believer righteous, that is, as having a perfect standing with God.[85] After describing the wonderful redemption which Christians enjoy in Christ, Paul declares: "There is therefore now no condemnation for those who are in Christ Jesus. For the law of the Spirit of life in Christ Jesus has set me free from the law of sin and death. For God has done what the law, weakened by the flesh, could not do: sending his own Son in the likeness of sinful flesh and for sin, he condemned sin in the flesh, in order that the just requirement of the law might be fulfilled in us, who walk not according to the flesh but according to the Spirit."[86] It should also be noted that the apostles of Christ had full confidence in the ability of the Holy Spirit to bring such truth to the minds of real Christians as they may need for the saving apprehension of the Gospel of Christ and for making their lives pleasing in His sight. In a certain sense the individual Christian therefore does not stand in any need of a teacher because he himself has an anointing from God, he is taught of God.[87]

One of the finest discussions of conscience is that of Stalker[88] who distinguishes between sequent conscience, that which follows an act,

79 I Cor. 4:3, 4; cf. 10:25.
80 Rom. 14:22.
81 I Cor. 10:27-29.
82 I Cor. 4:3, 4.
83 I Pet. 3:16, 21.
84 I John 3:20.
85 Rom. 1:17; 3:21, 22, 24, 26, 30; 4:3, 5; 5:1; etc.
86 Rom. 8:1-4.
87 I Thess. 4:9; I John 2:20, 27.
88 James Stalker, "Conscience," in the *I.S.B.E.*, II, pp. 701-3.

and antecedent conscience which precedes the moral choice and which unfortunately is much weaker than sequent conscience. Much could be said about the punitive character of sequent conscience, about the mental pain and anguish on the part of a Herod or a Judas for the awful sins which they committed. But it should also be noted that conscience is not infallible and hence is not the direct voice of God. The Holy Spirit does speak through the human conscience, but the conscience is not identical with the Holy Spirit. Nevertheless, conscience must be followed to have peace. This means that the Christian has two duties in reference to his conscience: first, to educate his conscience by the Word of God; and second, to obey his conscience.

The education of conscience is necessary because by previous training some Christians are too scrupulous, while others are actually careless. The means of the education of conscience is fervent Bible study, earnest prayer, obedience to the Word of God, and a full use of the means of grace.

The question is sometimes raised as to how to account for those who are overly scrupulous. This condition is sometimes due to early teaching, to an inner sensitivity or temperamental instability, to a lack of understanding of God's method of justification, and unfortunately it is sometimes a mask by way of compensation for hidden sin.

Where then does the final authority rest: with the conscience, the Bible, or the Holy Spirit? The Protestant position is that the final authority in faith and life is the Word of God as interpreted by the Holy Spirit to the individual conscience. There is a wholesome objectivity about this position; it avoids the subjectivity of those who would look to the conscience rather than to God's Word as the final authority. Perhaps the Protestants of today, however, should be reminded that where the church speaks, and conscience permits, the Christian should render cheerful obedience. It is possible for the principle of individual interpretation of the Scripture to be misunderstood so as to minimize the significance of church standards of faith and life.

8. *THE FALL*

The Book of Genesis is the book of beginnings: the origin of the universe, of all forms of life including man, and of sin. The story of the fall of original man is recorded in Genesis 3. Perhaps the ablest interpretation of Genesis 3 is that of Professor Geerhardus Vos who served as Professor of Biblical Theology in Princeton Theological Seminary for almost forty years.[89] Professor Vos holds in effect that the tree which Adam and Eve ate from in the Fall should be called the maturity tree. It could not have meant the temptation tree because God tempts no one to evil.[90] Undoubtedly full moral maturity would have been reached not only by falling into sin but also by obedience. In other words, God created man holy in the sense that he was sinless and yet he was merely innocent, not positively holy. It was the intention of God to bring man to full maturity and to confirm him in holiness by providing for him an experience which would enable him to confirm his holiness by a free choice of obedience to God.

Vos demonstrates that there are three levels of goodness in choosing the right. The lowest level is to obey out of fear of punishment. A bit better is that type of obedience which results from a reasoned insight into the nature of the good; although this may turn out in the end to be a form of prudence. The highest level of goodness is that which springs from a personal love for God, in the absence of any insight as to the reason for the divine commandment. It was precisely in this respect that Adam was given the opportunity to obey God. There was no insight possible as to the reason for the prohibition not to eat of the particular tree. The tempter, however, was immediately ready with a false interpretation of the prohibition. The tree, said he, had of itself magical powers to confer a knowledge of good and evil. Vos holds that this was a reduction of the religious and moral to the pagan and the magical. Satan also attributed to God the motive of envy; it was God's will, he said, to keep man down and to prevent him becoming like Himself. The Biblical account makes clear that although God intended the prohibition to be a blessing to man, even to prevent his dying, the old serpent made of the prohibition a temptation and thereby designed evil for man. The narrative identifies the physical medium of the tempter as a serpent, and undoubtedly a real serpent was there. But the Bible as a whole makes clear that the real tempter was none other than the devil.

The tempter may have approached the woman not because she was weaker in character or intellect, or had a greater proneness to sin, but because she had not personally received the prohibition not to eat of the tree.

The first stage of the temptation was apparently an innocent form of doubt: "Did God indeed say . . . ?" In other words, did He

89 Geerhardus Vos, *Biblical Theology, Old and New Testaments* (Grand Rapids: Eerdmans, 1948), pp. 37-51.
90 Jas. 1:13.

actually offer the prohibition? But the tempter hastened on to say that if He did, then the prohibition was certainly too severe, for man would thereby be deprived of the fruit of every tree. This latter expression, every tree, is ambiguous in the Hebrew. It could either mean that man could not eat from a single tree of the garden, or that there was one or more trees from which no food was to be taken. Perhaps the tempter was purposely ambiguous so as to confuse the woman. In any case, she at once insisted on the fact of the divine prohibition, but did perhaps weaken a bit by adding that God certainly was strict, for they were not allowed even to touch the tree—a prohibition which the Scripture does not otherwise mention.

Satan thereupon boldly declared that what God had said was not true; man would not die! The devil took what would be the ruin of man and represented it to him as his good. The woman seems to have fallen because of three factors: (1) the attractive appearance of the fruit, that is, the lust of the eyes; (2) belief in the delicious flavor of the fruit, that is, the lust of the flesh; (3) and an eagerness for the enlightenment which the tempter promised, that is, the pride of life.[91] The central sin of the woman consisted of putting the tempter in the place of God. She was so confused that she thought the serpent willed her good, while God wished to keep the best from her! This is still the essence of temptation: the belief that obedience to God will deprive one of good, while committing an act of sin will bring great personal benefit.

Adam quickly followed the example of Eve with perhaps even greater guilt than she.[92] Scripture does not indicate what the motives of Adam were. It may have been that he had the same intellectual curiosity which prompted Eve to sin; or perhaps it was attachment to her which moved him to participate in disobedience with her. Sin often has social implications.

The Fall was followed immediately by a sense of guilty self-consciousness and shame. The minds of Adam and Eve were contaminated by sin. Their smitten consciences drove them to avoid communion with God. They therefore sought to provide coverings for themselves. They could not bear to think of meeting God; they wanted to hide; they wanted to get inside of something so as to avoid the eye of their Maker.

The result of the Fall was that man suffered spiritual death, that is, alienation from God; he also became mortal physically; and he started down the road to eternal death. The phrase "in the day,"

91 Gen. 3:6; I John 2:16.
92 I Tim. 2:14.

which promised death in the event of transgression, seems according to its use in I Kings to mean, "As surely as you eat of it,[93] you shall die." Each of the partners received a punishment related to his or her distinctive function.[94] The punishment of the woman involved the partial loss of full partnership with man, that is, a sense of subjection, as well as severe suffering in childbirth. Nevertheless, the woman will be able by God's grace to bring life into the world. The distinctive punishment of man is a weary struggle with nature in the acquisition of a livelihood. Woman is the life-bearer while man is the life-sustainer. Man's struggle with the soil will eventually end in the victory of the soil over man. Nevertheless, the man will be able to support life by his toil.

In the meeting with God both the man and the woman sought to shift the blame for the transgression. It is to the serpent that God gave what has been called the *Protevangelium,* that is, the first prophetic proclamation of the Saviour. God Himself promised that the Seed of woman[95] would crush the head of the tempter, although the tempter would himself wound the Saviour. It should be carefully noted that it was God who took the initiative in the work of redemption. Furthermore, God had to reverse the attitude of man: man must side with God and oppose the tempter.

The account ends with God supplying animal-skin tunics for the first pair: perhaps for the comfort of the body, and the maintenance of morality in a race which is now depraved by sin. Nowhere in the Bible is the suggestion given that the animals were slain for the expiation of the sin of original man. Following the Fall, God expelled man from the Garden of Eden (Eden, incidentally, means pleasure) and withheld from him the tree of life. The Book of Revelation, however, again pictures redeemed man in the eternal paradise of God with its "tree of life."[96] Redemption thus annuls the awful consequences of sin.

9. *THE NATURE OF SIN*

In the Bible sin is regarded as any transgression of, or any lack of conformity to, the holy will and nature of God, the basic cause being the lack of a perfect love for God. Sin may consist of deeds, thoughts, attitudes, or even states of character. The Bible teaches not only that all men have sinned, that is, have committed acts that

93 I Kings 2:37, 40-46. Vos, *op. cit.,* p. 49.
94 Vos, *op. cit.,* p. 55.
95 Grammatically, a collective noun; prophetically used of Christ, however. Cf. Heb. 2:14; I John 3:8.
96 Rev. 22:2.

are wrong, but that all are sinners in their nature: all men are by nature "children of wrath,"[97] that is, they have a nature which if followed places them under the disfavor of God. The Bible nowhere attempts to give a formal or comprehensive definition of sin. On this subject as on all others the Scripture is concrete and specific rather than philosophical and abstract. The Apostle John calls sin lawlessness,[98] by which he undoubtedly means an attitude of defiance to the commandments of God. He also speaks of sin as unrighteousness or wrongdoing,[99] a lack of that positive moral excellence which God desires to see in men. Paul declares that any action which does not spring from faith is sin:[1] God wants man to live with a face continually turned toward Him in love, devotion, and obedience. The Apostle James indicates that not only are there sins of commission but also of omission, for whoever "knows what is right to do and fails to do it, for him it is sin."[2]

Throughout the Bible much stress is placed on sin as being a condition of one's nature, rather than viewing it atomistically. The prophet Jeremiah stated that "the heart is deceitful above all things, and desperately corrupt; who can understand it?"[3] With deep pessimism Bildad asks: "How then can man be righteous before God? How can he who is born of woman be clean?"[4] When Isaiah received a vision of the Holy One of Israel he cried: "Woe is me! For I am lost; for I am a man of unclean lips, and I dwell in the midst of a people of unclean lips; for my eyes have seen the King, the LORD of hosts!"[5] The reaction of Peter to the Lord Jesus when He displayed His deity was similar: "Depart from me, for I am a sinful man, O Lord."[6] David becomes the mouthpiece of the race in conviction for sin when he cries:

> Behold, thou desirest truth in the inward being;
> therefore teach me wisdom in my secret heart.
> Purge me with hyssop, and I shall be clean;
> wash me, and I shall be whiter than snow.
> Fill me with joy and gladness;
> let the bones which thou hast broken rejoice.
> Hide thy face from my sins,
> and blot out all my iniquities.
> Create in me a clean heart, O God,
> and put a new and right spirit within me.

97 Eph. 2:3.
98 I John 3:4 (Greek)
99 I John 5:17.
1 Rom. 14:23.
2 Jas. 4:17.
3 Jer. 17:9.
4 Job 25:4.
5 Isa. 6:5.
6 Luke 5:8.

Cast me not away from thy presence,
    and take not thy holy Spirit from me.
Restore to me the joy of thy salvation,
    and uphold me with a willing spirit.[7]

The letter to the Hebrews warns against anyone having "an evil, unbelieving heart."[8] And Jesus declared that "what comes out of the mouth proceeds from the heart, and this defiles a man. For out of the heart come evil thoughts, murder, adultery, fornication, theft, false witness, slander. These are what defile a man . . . ."[9] Sin is, therefore, not merely the characterization of an act; it is the evil condition of the unregenerated man's inner self, his true character. This inner depravity condemns all men outside of Christ. More exactly, all men outside of Christ are condemned for their sin of choosing to remain unregenerate rather than being willing to accept the free salvation which is offered them in Christ. This is what Menno Simons meant when he declared that only one sin can damn a man, namely, unbelief.[10] What man needs is the creation within him of a new nature, a nature which inclines one to love God and to desire to do His will. This is exactly what was prophesied through the prophet Jeremiah: "I will put my law within them, and I will write it upon their hearts; and I will be their God, and they shall be my people."[11] This is what Jesus meant when He told Nicodemus that "unless one is born of water and the Spirit, he cannot enter the kingdom of God."[12]

Theologians have somewhat tended to emphasize sin in the formal sense as being a transgression of law, rather than to view it as a lack of love for God. Augustine, for example, said that sin was "any thought, word, or deed against the law of God."[13] Presbyterian standards define sin as "any want of conformity unto, or transgression of the law of God."[14] Similarly, the Lutheran theologians define sin as "a departure from the divine law."[15] It should be noted, however, that when Jesus was asked what sort of commandment in the law was the greatest He replied: "You shall love the Lord your God with all your heart, and with all your soul, and with all your mind. This is the great and first commandment. And a second is like it, You shall love your neighbor as yourself. On these two commandments depend all the law and the prophets."[16] Since the entire moral

7 Ps. 51:6-12.
8 Heb. 3:12.
9 Matt. 15:18-20.

10 *Complete Works*, I, p. 159.
11 Jer. 31:33.
12 John 3:5; cf. Titus 3:5.
13 *A Catholic Dictionary*, p. 490.

14 A. A. Hodge, *Outlines of Theology* (Grand Rapids, Mich.: Eerdmans, 1949), p. 316.
15 *The Lutheran Cyclopedia*, p. 447.
16 Matt. 22:37-40.

law of God is according to the words of Jesus merely a commentary on the great principles of love, is it not the case that sin ought to be defined in terms of a lack of love, rather than as a formal transgression of a code? According to this point of view sin is any failure to love God and man with a perfect heart, which lack of love leads to attitudes and deeds which are displeasing to God.

If an Israelite loved the Lord with his whole being he would not wish to worship any other deities, nor would he want to materialize that worship by making an image of his god, nor would he take His name in vain, nor violate His Sabbath. If a person loves his neighbor as himself he will give honor to whom honor is due, he will not take life, nor commit adultery, nor steal, nor bear false witness, nor covet."[17] This is the meaning of Paul when he writes: "Owe no one anything, except to love one another; for he who loves his neighbor has fulfilled the law. The commandments, 'You shall not commit adultery, You shall not kill, You shall not steal, You shall not covet,' and any other commandment, are summed up in this sentence, 'You shall love your neighbor as yourself.' Love does no wrong to a neighbor; therefore love is the fulfilling of the law."[18] And in the Galatian letter Paul writes: "For you were called to freedom, brethren, only do not use your freedom as an opportunity for the flesh, but through love be servants of one another. For the whole law is fulfilled in one word, 'You shall love your neighbor as yourself.' "[19] In a similar way James declares: "If you really fulfil the royal law, according to the Scripture, 'You shall love your neighbor as yourself,' you do well. But if you show partiality, you commit sin, and are convicted by the law as transgressors."[20]

10. ADAM AND HUMAN DEPRAVITY

As a consequence of the Fall man became mortal, spiritually alienated from God, and doomed to eternal death. Because of the Fall Adam's descendants are born with the seeds of a sinful nature, with a corruptible and mortal body, and apart from Christ are doomed to divine wrath. And yet, apart from Genesis 3 the Old Testament says practically nothing of the Fall. Rather, it deals directly with human sin and with sinners. Only after the Saviour brought redemption to the race was there any point to a reference to Adam and the awful consequences of his sin in the race. The historical Adam is mentioned in Luke 3,[21] is alluded to in Matthew

17 Ex. 20:2-17; Deut. 5:6-21.   20 Jas. 2:8, 9.
18 Rom. 13:8-10.   21 Luke 3:38.
19 Gal. 5:13, 14.

19,[22] Jude 14, and I Timothy 2[23]; while Eve is mentioned by name in II Corinthians 11.[24] Scripture refers to Adam, therefore, as a historical person. The crucial passages of the Bible on the subject of Adam and human sin are I Corinthians 15[25] and Romans 5,[26] especially the longer discussion in the letter to the Romans. The passage in Romans 5 is one of the most controversial sections of the Bible. Theologians of the most varied types are forced to reckon seriously with Paul's discussion in this chapter. What does the apostle say?

First of all, Paul indicates that it was the historical Adam who introduced sin into the world, that is, into human nature, by his act of disobedience to God. Paul speaks of the Fall as "the trangression of Adam," "one man's trespass," "that one man's sin," "one man's disobedience," etc. The inspired apostle accepts the Mosaic account as historical truth.

In the second place Paul regards death in the fullest sense, physical and spiritual, as the penalty of sin, not in the sense that Adam fell and that a whole race of innocent people are, therefore, doomed to death, but in the sense that Adam introduced into human nature an element of evil which causes all men to follow in his footsteps by also sinning. It was Adam who introduced sin into the world and thereby brought death also, but each man confirms this penalty by his own individual sin. The apostle does not merely indicate a bad example on the part of Adam but the infection of the race. He is stressing the solidarity of the Adamic race in sin and death. Paul indicates that even in the era of no written law, in the period between Adam and Moses, all men continued to sin, undoubtedly in the sense of transgressing the light of conscience, and death continued to reign universally even over those who had not sinned against a revealed law of God. The words "sin" and "death," therefore, refer respectively to the sinful nature which each man has by virtue of Adam's fall, and the consequences of sin, namely, spiritual alienation from God or "death."

What kind of imputation does this passage indicate? The doctrine of immediate imputation is that the guilt of Adam's sin was at once imputed to all his descendants. The fact remains, however, that this teaching is not explicitly stated in Romans 5. It seems more in harmony with the general teaching of personal accountability in the Scripture to hold that Adam was responsible for his own sin, as is each man since that time responsible for his personal sin.[27] Nevertheless,

---

22 Matt. 19:4-6.   23 I Tim. 2:13, 14.   25 I Cor. 15:22, 45.
                         24 II Cor. 11:3.   26 Rom. 5:12-21.
27 Deut. 24:26; II Kings 14:6; Jer. 31:30; Ezek. 18:4, 19, 20, etc.

each man since the Fall is born with a nature which will inevitably lead him to commit acts of sin. The race is not guilty of Adam's sin; each man is guilty for his own sin, yet he is a sinner because of Adam's transgression. This view is commonly called mediate imputation. If an act is to be sin in the full sense of a conscious rejection of obedience to God from a heart of love, the apostle indicates that there must be a clear apprehension of God's will. Hence, he states simply that "sin is not counted where there is no law." And yet Paul indicates also that "law came in, to increase the trespass."[28] In this same Letter to the Romans the apostle indicates that the heathen who have never been confronted with a clear written revelation of God's will, are nevertheless responsible for the sin of rejecting the God who is revealed in His creation, "so they are without excuse."[29] But where a person is confronted with special revelation, where an individual knows what God's will is, and still continues to choose sin rather than God, the effect is to "increase the trespass."[30] It should be noted, however, that the contrast between those who sin like Adam against the revealed word of God, and those who live in heathen darkness so as to not be guilty of sin in the fullest sense, is only a secondary comparison in this discussion. The main point of Romans 5 is the contrast between Adam who brought sin and death to the race, and Christ who brought righteousness and eternal life.

The contrast in Romans 5 between Adam and Christ is sharp and pronounced. Adam was guilty of disobedience to the will of God and all that he brought upon the race was due to this disobedience. Christ, however, brought His blessings by virtue of His obedience to God. Paul represents the ground of our blessings in Christ as resting upon "one man's act of righteousness," upon "one man's obedience." This obedience was, of course, Christ's lifelong obedience which culminated in His redemptive death: He "became obedient unto death, even death on a cross." The note and mood of Romans 5 is not one of gloom because of Adam's sin but exultation because of "the free gift," "the free gift in the grace of that one man Jesus Christ," "the free gift of righteousness," and "acquittal and life for all men," the total effect of Christ's gift being that "grace also might reign through righteousness to eternal life through Jesus Christ our Lord." Although God's judgment followed the one sin of Adam and involved condemnation for all, because all men are sinners, the gracious gift of God follows upon the many transgressions of all men, and involves through union with Christ the acquit-

---

28 Rom. 5:20.   29 Rom. 1:20; cf. 2:12.   30 Rom. 5:20.

tal of all. The Fall, one trespass, led to condemnation; the free gift is given to all in spite of many transgressions; the gift is out of all proportion to the curse.

There is a sense in which the theologian is not obligated to justify the economy of God: He is omniscient and absolutely good, while man is limited in judgment and in goodness. The true child of God can but bow his head in reverence before God and acknowledge that His ways are higher than our ways. It is, therefore, not necessary to ask, Why did God permit the Fall? Nevertheless, the true child of God is able to see certain benefits that come out of redemption. Among these should be mentioned: (1) Because of Calvary the Christian has a keener sense of God's love than if there had been no need for redemption. (2) The Christian has the blessed privilege of membership in a redeemed brotherhood, the church of the Lord Jesus Christ. (3) The Christian becomes, by virtue of being an ambasador for Christ, a fellow worker with God in the Salvation of men (4) The Christian has an overwhelming sense of God's grace because of an utter lack of personal merit; he knows that salvation can be for him only a free gift and never a matter of merit. (5) The Christian also has the prospect of glorious deliverance from sin and death in the ages to come in glory.

Romans 5 teaches a solidarity in sin resulting from the transgression of Adam, but much more gloriously does it teach a solidarity in redemption through the Lord Jesus Christ who died as a ransom for all. There are many statements in this chapter that the free gift of grace abounded to many, that the free gift brings justification, that the free gift of righteousness leads to a reign in life through Jesus Christ, that one man's active righteousness leads to acquittal and life for all men, by one man's obedience many will be made righteous, etc.: and yet these very expressions of universal justification in Christ lead to a new difficulty. The question is, How are these expressions to be understood? Is the whole race to be saved? Is the effect of the Fall canceled for all men everywhere?

It would seem that the justification of all men as set forth in this discussion in terms of "acquittal and life for all men" must be limited in one of three ways: (1) the doctrine of universalism, which indicates that all men will ultimately be saved: (2) Calvinism, which would limit this acquittal to the elect, to those chosen in Christ before the foundation of the world; all men then means the elect as representative of the race; or (3) Arminianism, which limits this justification in character, holding that the atonement of Christ is adequate for all men, is intended for all, and is offered to all, but is actually efficacious only for those who believe. Which of these three best comports with the general teaching of Scripture? In the opinion of the present writer the answer is the third. Scripture asserts emphatically that Christ did die for all, that those for whom Christ died may perish, that all are urged to accept Gospel salvation, and that the reason not all are saved lies not in a lack of election on the part of God but in that stubborn and wicked unwillingness to yield to God which in Scripture is called "unbelief." The Bible also teaches emphatically that not all men will ultimately be saved; rather, there will be a great and eternal separation made at the second coming of Christ when the wicked "will go away into eternal punishment, but the righteous into eternal life."[31] The teaching of universalism that all men will ultimately be saved is utterly unscriptural.

11. *THE NATURE OF DEPRAVITY*

In what sense is man "totally depraved"? It has been pointed out that there are four possible relations to sin: (1) God is unable to sin, but this is not true of any man; (2) Adam and Christ, as well as the new nature of the Christian, are able not to sin; (3) original man as well as all men since that time, including Christians, are able to sin; (4) the natural man, however, he in whom the Spirit of God is not operative, is unable not to sin: he sins continually because he is a sinner by nature.

The natural man is totally depraved in the following senses: (1) He is unable to eradicate sin from his heart; (2) he is unable to act from pure love for God, being selfish; (3) he is unable to accept Christ apart from the work of the Holy Spirit, this according to the express word of Christ[32]; (4) sin has also discolored every area of his personality, so that no aspect of his nature has escaped depravity. Nevertheless, depravity should not be understood as meaning that human nature has become completely devilish, so that men are as wicked as they could possibly be, and therefore beyond redemption.

Menno Simons describes the unsaved and depraved man thus: "A carnal man cannot understand spiritual things, for he is by nature a child of the devil, and is not spiritually minded, hence, he comprehends nothing spiritual; for by nature he is a stranger to God; has nothing of a divine nature dwelling in him, nor has communion with God, but is much rather at enmity with Him; he is unmerciful, unjust, unclean, not peaceable, impatient, disobedient, without understanding, and unhappy. So are all men by nature according

---

31 Matt. 25:46.   32 John 6:44, 65.

to their birth and origin after the flesh. This is the first or old Adam, and is comprised in the Scriptures in a single word, ungodly, that is, without God, a stranger and destitute of the divine nature."[33]

The main message of the Bible, however, is not concerning the hopelessness of man in his sin, but the glorious possibility of his redemption in Christ. On the regenerating work of the Holy Spirit Menno Simons wrote: "The new birth consists, verily, not in water nor in words, but it is the heavenly, living, and quickening power of God in our hearts which comes from God, and which by the preaching of the divine Word, if we accept it by faith, quickens, renews, pierces, and converts our hearts, so that we are changed and converted from unbelief into faith, from unrighteousness into righteousness, from evil into good, from carnality into spirituality, from the earthly into the heavenly, [and] from the wicked nature of Adam into the good nature of Jesus Christ."[34]

The subject of the believer's relation to his sinful nature will be taken up more fully under the topics of regeneration and sanctification. Nevertheless, it may be observed here that the Christian retains after the new birth what the Bible calls "flesh," that is, a certain propensity toward sensuality, pride, self-seeking, spiritual coldness, etc., so that even the apostle could confess: "I know that nothing good dwells within me, that is, in my flesh."[35] The hymns and prayers of Christendom through the centuries which cry for more holiness are a vivid attestation of the fact that the regenerated child of God is still dwelling in fallible "flesh," needing to take advantage of every means of grace, to watch and pray, and to give diligence to persevere by God's grace unto a happy end in Christ.

Menno Simons held that there are four kinds of sin.[36] First, there is the inherent depravity of nature which is retained even in the child of God, but which is not reckoned to his account. "There is no condemnation for those who are in Christ Jesus." It is fortunate, indeed, that Christ is "our wisdom, our righteousness and sanctification and redemption,"[37] otherwise no Christian could have any ground of hope for eternal life. In the second place, says Menno, there are major acts of sin such as lying, stealing, swearing, etc., and these require conscious repentance. If a Christian has grown sufficiently cold in his walk with God as to fall into major transgressions of God's holy law, he will be smitten with conviction as soon as he realizes the tragedy which has overtaken him, and he will in humility

---

33 *Complete Works*, I, p. 232; cf. II, pp. 312, 313.
34 *Ibid.*, II, p. 215.
35 Rom. 7:18.
36 *Complete Works*, II, pp. 312, 313.
37 I Cor. 1:30.

and contrition hasten to his Saviour for forgiveness and restoration to full fellowship. Thirdly, Menno spoke of the shortcomings of the saints, a hasty word, an unworthy thought, and the like, which are, of course, sufficient to destroy the peace and joy of every child of God if he puts his eyes on himself rather than on the Saviour. These, however, are not held against the believer, but are covered by Calvary. This is precisely the glory of the grace of God, that He is able to receive and justify those whose lives are still imperfect but who are born again, who love the Saviour, who delight in His law, and who crave above all things to please Him, and yet who fall short of God's glory.

Menno's fourth type of sin is commonly called the unpardonable sin or the blasphemy against the Holy Spirit. What is the meaning of these expressions? The New Testament contains a number of warnings against blasphemy of the Holy Spirit or the sin unto death. When the Pharisees slandered the work of Christ by attributing it to the devil, an awful sin which was undoubtedly against the witness of their own hearts, Jesus warned them: "Therefore I tell you, every sin and blasphemy will be forgiven men, but the blasphemy against the Spirit will not be forgiven. And whoever says a word against the Son of man will be forgiven; but whoever speaks against the Holy Spirit will not be forgiven, either in this age or in the age to come."[38] A parallel account states: "Truly, I say to you, all sins will be forgiven the sons of men, and whatever blasphemies they utter; but whoever blasphemes against the Holy Spirit never has forgiveness, but is guilty of an eternal sin . . . ."[39] In his First Letter John speaks of a sin unto death or a mortal sin,[40] indicating that he does not place his readers under obligation to pray for him who is guilty of that type of transgression.

The Letter to the Hebrews also contains at least two possible references to this unpardonable sin. In chapter six the writer states, "It is impossible to restore again to repentance those who have once been enlightened, who have tasted the heavenly gift, and have become partakers of the Holy Spirit, and have tasted the goodness of the word of God and the powers of the age to come, if they then commit apostasy, since they crucify the Son of God on their own account and hold him up to contempt."[41] The point of this discussion in Hebrews 6 is the danger of apostasy. The illustration which follows about land having often received rain becoming unfruitful and in need of being burned would support this interpretation. Never-

38 Matt. 12:31, 32.
39 Mark 3:28, 29.
40 I John 5:16.
41 Heb. 6:4-6.

theless, the last phrase is in the Greek ambiguous. The sentence could either mean: (1) It is impossible to restore apostates *because* they recrucify the Son of God; or (2) it is impossible to renew apostates to repentance *as long as* they recrucify the Son of God. The latter interpretation would mean that as long as men reject the Lord Jesus Christ there is no hope for them. The former interpretation which is the reading of the King James Version, the American Standard Version, and the Revised Standard Version, makes the last clause causal, explaining *why* it is impossible to restore apostates to a living faith in Christ: namely, they are crucifying the Son of God afresh. If this former interpretation is adopted, and it does seem to be the more natural rendering of the Greek, this passage becomes an additional discussion on the unpardonable sin. It would then be similar to the statement in Hebrews 10: "For if we sin deliberately after receiving the knowledge of the truth, there no longer remains a sacrifice for sins, but a fearful prospect of judgment . . . ."[42] In this case the Greek really means, "If we be found to be sinning deliberately," if we persist in sin, "if we go on willfully sinning" (Williams). There is no hope for the salvation of anyone who permanently reverts to a life of sin after having once become a disciple of Christ.

What can be said further about the unpardonable sin?[43] (1) First of all, it is man's act, not God's. In view of the character of God being one of love and mercy, the impossibility of forgiveness is never due to God's anger or limited mercy, but to man's stubborn "unbelief" and deadened conscience which can actually get beyond the capacity of repentance. (Passages such as Genesis 6:3 and Ephesians 4:30 do not refer to the blasphemy against the Holy Spirit. Genesis 6 is a prediction of the divine judgment of the Deluge while Ephesians 4:30 is an appeal to Christians to avoid grieving the Holy Spirit by acts of sin. Similarly, Hebrews 12:17 seems to refer to the irrevocable decision which Isaac had made about Esau's birthright, not to Esau's inability to repent and be forgiven by God.) (2) The unpardonable sin is something more than a sin of the flesh such as adultery or the like. (3) It is also more than the postponement of accepting Christ; many people delay responding to the Holy Spirit until late in life and are still accepted of God when they repent. (4) It is more than a verbal sin; the Scripture does not represent that there are certain magical words the saying of which forever makes it impossible to be forgiven by God. (5) In a positive way it can be said that the unpardonable sin involves a radical slander of the Holy Spirit in the face of overwhelming external evidence, as well as the conviction of one's

42 Heb. 10:26.   43 Cf. L. Berkhof, *op cit.*, I, pp. 240, 241.

own heart; this seems to have been the situation which Christ originally warned against.

The Bible would indicate that the person guilty of the unpardonable sin is hardened and impenitent, absolutely without desire to come to Christ. This point is of crucial importance, for the average person who worries about having committed this sin is giving evidence by his concern that he has not committed it.

The Bible does not specify that only apostates can commit this sin. It would seem as though people can be close enough to genuine Christianity to know in their own heart that Christianity is true, and they can so persist in sin and so slander Christianity as to become hardened beyond the capacity to respond to the Holy Spirit's call. Nevertheless, only God knows when this awful state has been reached, and Christian workers should never threaten the unsaved with the danger that God might cast them off in His anger. To do so is to upset some people, as well as to misrepresent the mercy and love of God. The fact that people are capable of getting into a hopeless state is never due to limited mercy on God's part, but to a violation of the laws of our own being; *the hopelessness resides in us rather than in God.* It can be said, of course, that this very fact is a judgment of God on sin. It is evident that the uncertainty of life, as well as the law that the longer one waits to become a Christian, the harder it becomes, should be sufficient factors to persuade men of the urgency of coming to Christ without resorting to a misrepresentation of God to do so. It was Jeremy Taylor who thus described the downward progress of the apostate in his sin: "First it startles him, then it becomes pleasing, then delightful, then frequent, then habitual, then confirmed; then the man is impenitent, then obstinate, then resolved never to repent, then damned."[44]

Catalogues of Sin

The Bible never gives a systematic listing of various sins. Theologians sometimes divide sins into sins of omission and sins of commission; sins against self, against one's fellow man, and against God; etc. According to Matthew, Jesus gave the following list of sins: evil thoughts, murder, adultery, fornication, theft, false witness, and slander.[45] The parallel passage in Mark lists: evil thoughts, fornication, theft, murder, adultery, coveting, wickedness, deceit, licentiousness, envy, slander, pride, and foolishness.[46] When Paul reminds his readers that the unrighteous will not inherit the king-

44 A. H. Strong, *Systematic Theology*, p. 651.   45 Matt. 15:19, 20.   46 Mark 7:21-23.

dom of God he lists by name the following examples: "Neither the immoral, nor idolaters, nor adulterers, nor homosexuals, nor thieves, nor the greedy, nor drunkards, nor revilers, nor robbers will inherit the kingdom of God." (But he graciously adds, "And such were some of you. But you were washed, you were sanctified, you were justified in the name of the Lord Jesus Christ and in the Spirit of our God.")[47] In the letter to the Galatians Paul lists the works of the flesh as: "Immorality, impurity, licentiousness, idolatry, sorcery, enmity, strife, jealousy, anger, selfishness, dissension, party spirit, envy, drunkenness, carousing, and the like." And then he adds: "I warn you, as I warned you before, that those who do such things shall not inherit the kingdom of God."[48] The Revelation to John warns: "As for the cowardly, the faithless, the polluted, as for murderers, fornicators, sorcerers, idolaters, and all liars, their lot shall be in the lake that burns with fire and brimstone, which is the second death."[49]

According to the Bible sin is an awful reality which alienates from God, brings one under His wrath, and dooms one to an endless Gehenna of fire. There will never be a revival in our world until men again take seriously the Word of God on the subject of sin. The Christian Church has failed terribly to proclaim boldly and without apology the nature and consequences of sin. Without a conviction for sin men are not going to turn to the Saviour in contrition and in the surrender of faith. Only he who trembles at the wrath of God with sin and at the future retribution which awaits him becomes sufficiently desperate to make the leap of faith. Before one can appreciate the comfort of the Gospel he must become fully aware of the exceeding sinfulness of sin.

12. FREE WILL

One of the most knotty problems in theology is the question of human free will. Theological writers of the most varied complexions agree fairly well in their definitions of free will but argue about the significance of it. Jonathan Edwards (1703-58), the great Congregational clergyman and theologian, defines free will thus: "The plain and obvious meaning of the words freedom and liberty, in common speech, is the power, opportunity, or advantage, that any one has to do as he pleases. . . ."[50] Samuel Wakefield (1799-1895), the Methodist theologian, says: "A free moral agent is one who is the real author of his own moral actions, without being determined to will or to act

---

47 I Cor. 6:9-11.   48 Gal. 5:19-21.   49 Rev. 21:8.
50 Samuel Wakefield, *A Complete System of Christian Theology* (Cincinnati: Cranston and Stowe, 1869), p. 313.

by any extrinsic cause."[51] *The Lutheran Cyclopedia* defines freedom of the will as applying only to the natural life, but not to spiritual matters, man "being in thought and will helpless and in contradiction with divine salvation."[52] In 1525 Martin Luther wrote his severe critique of human freedom entitled *De Servo Arbitrio*. The Augsburg Confession of Faith defines free will in Article XVIII by saying, "that man's will hath some liberty to work a civil righteousness, and to choose such things as reason can reach unto, but it hath no power to work the righteousness of God, or spiritual righteousness, without the spirit of God."[53] The Formula of Concord of 1577, Art. II, represents that in the natural man there is not even a spark of saving knowledge and power because in reference to grace man is as dead as a stone, even worse, for he neglects, if not even opposes, the coming of the grace of God into his life.[54] The *Catholic Dictionary* defines liberty as, "The power of choice," and distinguishes between internal liberty which means "freedom from all necessity," and external liberty which refers to any compulsion or force which would restrain an individual from doing what he wishes.[55]

How then may we define free will today? By free will we mean the capacity which human beings have to make moral decisions without their being determined by any external agent. Free will involves the ability to contemplate ends. It also involves what is called the power of contrary choice; that is, the individual may choose either one of two moral opposites. Free will involves the capacity to be self-determining, to make a life plan. It rests at least in part upon human intelligence, because a normal human being is able to contemplate the consequences of his anticipated deeds and to choose accordingly. Free will means that a man is able to subordinate a present passion to an ideal or to a life goal. Free will becomes, therefore, one of the most distinguishing characteristics of men, for animals are not able to make moral choices, to formulate life plans, or to subordinate physical desires in the interest of morality or ideals, or of eternity.

The Bible continually assumes the truth of two propositions which to human reason are paradoxical: (1) that men are responsible for their moral choices, for their character, and for everything they do including their sinful acts; (2) that men are depraved and hopelessly lost in sin, totally unable to deliver themselves. What is the solution, if any, to this paradox? P. J. Twisck (1565-1636), bishop in the Frisian Mennonite Church of Holland, asserted in 1617:

51 *Ibid.*, p. 314.   53 *Ibid.*, p. 187.   55 P. 309.
52 P. 186.   54 *Ibid.*, p. 187.

That God almighty in the beginning created the man Adam and his wife in His image and likeness, endowing them above all creatures with virtues, knowledge, speech, reason, and a free will or power; so that they could know, love, fear, and obediently serve their Creator; or could voluntarily and disobediently forsake their God; as appeared in the first transgression when Adam and his wife through subtlety of the devil, who appeared in the form of a deceitful serpent, departed from the commandment of God; hence they did not sin through the foreordination or will of God; but as they had been created with a free will, and to do as they would, they sinned through their own voluntary desire and transgressed the command of God contrary to His will.

The man Adam and his wife having thus through their own sin fallen under the wrath and disfavor of God, whereby they became sinful and mortal, were again received into favor by God their Creator; so that they were not utterly divested of their former wisdom, speech, and knowledge, above all other creatures, nor of their previous free will or power, as may be seen from their voluntarily accepting God's gracious promises unto life, and obeying the voice of the Lord; and as also clearly appears from the fact that God the Lord very strictly appointed an angel with a flaming sword to keep the tree of life from Adam lest through his free will or power he should eat of the tree of life and live forever; which would have been in Adam's power. And this free will or power has been transmitted to all their descendants, who proceed from them as branches from their stem; so that even as men are endowed of God with knowledge, reason, and voluntary power, by which they can perform manifold works, and seek and desire from God the health of their diseased and infirmed bodies, and are not without action, as the irrational creatures, blocks and stones, so likewise, man, through the grace of God, and the moving of the Spirit, by which men live, and are moved, *may open the door of the heart to the salutary grace of God*—which through the Gospel is offered to all men, and through which death and life are set before man—and seek the health of his wounded soul; or he *may voluntarily resist, reject, and neglect* this offered grace and moving of the Spirit. Thus also, as men have eyes and ears, to see and to hear, yet not of themselves, but only from God the Giver, so they also, through the grace of God, have a free will or power to do the good and to leave the evil.

But men, considered in themselves, seeing they are without the grace of God, *are of themselves incapable of thinking anything that is good, much less are they able to do it.* But it is almighty God, who through His Spirit of grace works in man both to will and to do, moves, draws, and chooses them, and accepts them as His children, so that men are only *recipients of God's saving grace.* Hence, all Christians are in duty bound, to ascribe the beginning, middle, and end of their faith, with all their good fruits thereof, not to themselves, but only to the unmerited grace of God in Christ Jesus.[56]

56 *Martyrs' Mirror*, p. 379.

This means that a truly Biblical theology will acknowledge: (1) that fallen man is depraved, a slave to sin; (2) that the sinner can usually reject any particular evil or choose any particular good, but he cannot of himself renounce sin as such and choose Christ apart from the enablement of the Holy Spirit; hence salvation is wholly of grace; (3) that men are not mere creatures of heredity or environment, but are also responsible for themselves; their destinies are in their own hands, for they are able to accept or reject the grace of God when convicted by the Holy Spirit.

All through the Bible God appeals to men to recognize sin, and to reject it. Before Cain murdered Abel, God told him that sin was couching at the door, desiring Cain, but he was to master it.[57] Paul tells his readers to consider themselves dead to sin and alive to God in Christ Jesus.[58] In another letter he writes: "Put to death therefore what is earthly in you: immorality, impurity, passion, evil desire, and covetousness, which is idolatry."[59] Many times the Bible commands men to choose righteousness and to overcome sin.

The Scripture also confronts men with moral choices and appeals to them to choose well. In one of his farewell addresses Moses exclaimed: "I call heaven and earth to witness against you this day, that I have set before you life and death, blessing and curse; therefore choose life, that you and your descendants may live, loving the LORD your God, obeying his voice, and cleaving to him; for that means life to you and length of days, that you may dwell in the land which the LORD swore to your fathers, to Abraham, to Isaac, and to Jacob, to give them."[60] In his farewell address Joshua also commanded Israel to fear the Lord, to serve Him in sincerity and faithfulness, to put away all idols, etc., and concluded with the ringing declaration, "As for me and my house, we will serve the LORD."[61] The prophet Ezekiel cried to Israel: "Cast away from you all the transgressions which you have committed against me, and get yourselves a new heart and a new spirit! Why will you die, O house of Israel?"[62] And in a similar manner, "Turn back, turn back from your evil ways; for why will you die, O house of Israel?"[63] Through the prophet Jeremiah God promised: "If at any time I declare concerning a nation or a kingdom, that I will pluck up and break down and destroy it, and if that nation, concerning which I have spoken, turns from its evil, I will repent of the evil that I intended to do to it."[64]

57 Gen. 4:7.
58 Rom. 6:11.
59 Col. 3:5.
60 Deut. 30:19, 20.

61 Josh. 24:15.
62 Ezek. 18:31.
63 Ezek. 33:11.
64 Jer. 18:7, 8.

Jesus Himself said: "Come to me, all who labor and are heavy-laden, and I will give you rest. Take my yoke upon you, and learn from me; for I am gentle and lowly in heart, and you will find rest for your souls."[65] One of the last messages of the Bible is: "The Spirit and the Bride say, 'Come.' And let him who hears say, 'Come.' And let him who is thirsty come, let him who desires take the water of life without price."[66]

The Scripture is also clear that all men will be judged for the decisions they have made and for the life they have lived. Jesus declared, "For the Son of man is to come with his angels in the glory of his Father, and then he will repay every man for what he has done."[67] Paul also says that God "will render to every man according to his works."[68] To the Corinthian church Paul wrote: "For we must all appear before the judgment seat of Christ, so that each one may receive good or evil, according to what he has done in the body."[69] And John in picturing the last judgment says: "And the sea gave up the dead in it, Death and Hades gave up the dead in them, and all were judged by what they had done."[70] I Samuel 23 provides an excellent illustration of divine foreknowledge and human freedom. David asked God whether the men of Keilah would deliver him over to Saul if he remained where he was, and the Lord said they would. Whereupon David departed and escaped.[71] But if David had remained he would have certainly been taken prisoner.

According to the Word of God men are not lost for having depravity, a situation for which they are not responsible, but they are guilty for choosing to follow their sinful nature rather than to surrender to a good and merciful God who calls them. When men do sin they are acting according to their inner nature but they are responsible for this. When men are saved, however, it is only because of the goodness of God. Jesus declared that no one could come to Him except the Father draw him, except it be given him of the Father.[72] Scripture also speaks, however, of the Pharisees and lawyers frustrating God's purpose by refusing to be baptized.[73] The awful fact is that finite men, because of the mystery of free will, are able to frustrate the will of a good and holy God whose will it is to save them. Free will is, therefore, both the hope of man and the despair of the wicked.

65 Matt. 11:28, 29.
66 Rev. 22:17.
67 Matt. 16:27.
68 Rom. 2:6.
69 II Cor. 5:10.

70 Rev. 20:13.
71 I Sam. 23:8-14.
72 John 6:44, 65.
73 Luke 7:30.

13. *DIVINE PRESERVATION*

The Bible teaches that all things visible and invisible have been created by God through Jesus Christ.[74] It also asserts that the heavens and the earth ever since their creation in the beginning have been under the watchful care of an almighty God. In one of his prayers Ezra confessed: "Thou art the LORD, thou alone; thou hast made heaven, the heaven of heavens, with all their host, the earth and all that is on it, the seas and all that is in them; and thou preservest all of them."[75] In describing Christ the Apostle Paul says: "He is before all things, and in him all things hold together."[76] Paul also describes God as the one who gives life to all things,[77] which is reminiscent of his remark when he stood in the Areopagus: "Yet he is not far from each one of us, for

'In him we live and move and have our being.' "[78]

The letter to the Hebrews describes Christ as "upholding the universe by his word of power," or, more literally, "upholding all things by the word of his power."[79]

In an era of great anxiety caused by atomic fission, when dire prophets of doom are warning about the possible destruction of the world by evil men, this Biblical assurance of the complete sovereignty of God and of His watchful care over His creation ought to bring to the hearts of His children a feeling of calm and security. Our God is not an absentee Deity who looks the other way while wicked men or demons set the world on fire. This world is destined to stand until that hour of which no man knows when the Son of Man will be revealed "in flaming fire, inflicting vengeance upon those who do not know God and upon those who do not obey the gospel of our Lord Jesus . . . when he comes on that day to be glorified in his saints . . . ."[80] The return of Christ, an event which will be unforeseen by the scientists of the world, will usher in the renovation of the earth by fire. This will not be the first time that the uniformity of nature was interrupted by a divine intervention: witness the Deluge. Peter declares: "The day of the Lord will come like a thief, and then the heavens will pass away with a loud noise, and the elements will be dissolved with fire, and the earth and the works that are upon it will be burned up . . . . The heavens will be kindled and dissolved, and the elements will melt with fire! But according to his promise we

74 John 1:3; Col. 1:16.
75 Neh. 9:6.
76 Col. 1:17.
77 I Tim. 6:13.

78 Acts 17:28.
79 Heb. 1:3.
80 II Thess. 1:7-10.

wait for new heavens and a new earth in which righteousness
dwells."[81]

Because of God's sovereignty and of His ability and intention to
preserve His creation the child of God can joyfully sing:

> God is our refuge and strength,
>   a very present help in trouble.
> Therefore we will not fear though the earth should change,
>   though the mountains shake in the heart of the sea;
> though its waters roar and foam,
>   though the mountains tremble with its tumult.

*   *   *

> Be still, and know that I am God.
>   I am exalted among the nations,
>   I am exalted in the earth!
> The LORD of hosts is with us;
>   the God of Jacob is our refuge.[82]

14. *THE PROVIDENCE OF GOD*

All the Word of God is a unit in teaching that God has a hand
in all which comes to pass so that everything contributes to the fulfillment of the divine plan for history. This is no denial of secondary
causes, nor of human responsibility for sin. One of the psalmists
sang:

> Whatever the Lord pleases he does,
>   in heaven and on earth,
>   in the seas and all deeps.
> He it is who makes the clouds rise at the end of the earth,
>   who makes lightnings for the rain
>   and brings forth the wind from his storehouses.
> He it was who smote the first-born of Egypt,
>   both of man and of beast.[83]

When Daniel interpreted King Nebuchadnezzar's dream he
said: "You, O king, the king of kings, to whom the God of heaven
has given the kingdom, the power, and the might, and the glory, and
into whose hand he has given, wherever they dwell, the sons of men,
the beasts of the field, and the birds of the air, making you rule over
them all . . . ."[84] And four times in Daniel 4 Daniel declares, "to the

81 II Pet. 3:10, 12, 13.
82 Ps. 46:1-3, 10, 11.
83 Ps. 135:6-8.
84 Dan. 2:37, 38.

end that the living may know that the Most High rules the kingdom of men, and gives it to whom he will, and sets over it the lowliest of men."[85] Through the prophet Jeremiah the Lord says: "It is I who by my great power and my outstretched arm have made the earth, with the men and animals that are on the earth, and I give it to whomever it seems right to me."[86] The Lord Jesus also said: "Are not two sparrows sold for a penny? And not one of them will fall to the ground without your Father's will. But even the hairs of your head are all numbered. Fear not, therefore; you are of more value than many sparrows."[87] Paul describes God as He "who accomplishes all things according to the counsel of his will."[88] And all Christians are familiar with Romans 8:28: "We know that in everything God works for good with those who love him, who are called according to his purpose." This passage, however, is set in a soteriological context; it does not refer to the physical or economic or social welfare of men. In the lives of the elect God makes all things work for their eternal and spiritual good.

The Old Testament contains many examples of the providence of God. When Abimelech took Sarah, Abraham's wife, it was God who withheld the king from sinning against Sarah. When the king discovered the deception which had been practiced against him he took the matter to the Lord in prayer. "Then God said to him in the dream, 'Yes, I know that you have done this in the integrity of your heart, and it was I who kept you from sinning against me; therefore I did not let you touch her.' "[89] One of the most wicked acts in Old Testament history was the sale of Joseph at the hands of his wicked brothers. Yet Joseph himself, after he came to great success in Egypt, was able to say to his brothers: "As for you, you meant evil against me; but God meant it for good, to bring it about that many people should be kept alive, as they are today."[90]

Another example of the providence of God is the way He gave the Israelites favor in the sight of the Egyptians so that whatever the Israelites asked for God caused the Egyptians to give to them. "Thus they despoiled the Egyptians."[91] When Samson took such a remarkably disobedient attitude toward his father and mother by persisting in asking for a Philistine wife the Scripture explains: "His father and mother did not know that it was from the LORD; for he was seeking an occasion against the Philistines."[92] And when Rehoboam rejected

---

85 Dan. 4:17, 25, 32, 35.
86 Jer. 27:5.
87 Matt. 10:29, 30.
88 Eph. 1:11.

89 Gen. 20:6.
90 Gen. 50:20.
91 Ex. 12:36.
92 Judg. 14:4.

the wise counsel of the older men in favor of the rash advice of the young men the Word of God reports: "So the king did not hearken to the people; for it was a turn of affairs brought about by the LORD that he might fulfill his word, which the LORD spoke by Ahijah the Shilonite to Jeroboam the son of Nebat."[93]

It is necessary to emphasize the fact that the Bible never interprets the providence of God as destroying human freedom and responsibility. Asaph represents God as saying:

> But my people did not listen to my voice;
>   Israel would have none of me.
> So I gave them over to their stubborn hearts,
>   to follow their own counsels.
> O that my people would listen to me,
>   that Israel would walk in my ways!
> I would soon subdue their enemies,
>   and turn my hand against their foes . . . .
> I would feed you with the finest of the wheat,
>   and with honey from the rock I would satisfy you.[94]

When the lustful king of Israel seduced Bathsheba and arranged for the destruction of her husband, Uriah the Hittite, the Scripture does not present God as preventing the fulfillment of these evil plans. Instead, it reports simply: "But the thing that David had done displeased the LORD."[95] And thus it often appears both in Biblical history and in our own day: God sometimes seems to stand by silently and merely disapprove the wicked deeds of men who are in places of great power.

In Exodus, after Moses and Aaron had demonstrated with miracles their divine commission, the Scripture reports: "And the people believed; and when they heard that the LORD had visited the people of Israel and that he had seen their affliction, they bowed their heads and worshiped."[96] It is with somewhat of a shock that the reader soon learns that the lot of the Israelites immediately became so much worse that the divine promises fell upon deaf ears. God told Moses to tell the Israelites: "I am the LORD, and I will bring you out from under the burdens of the Egyptians, and I will deliver you from their bondage, and I will redeem you with an outstretched arm and with great acts of judgment, and I will take you for my people, and I will be your God; and you shall know that I am the LORD your

93 I Kings 12:15.   95 II Sam. 11:27.
94 Ps. 81:11-14, 16.   96 Ex. 4:31.

God, who has brought you out from under the burdens of the Egyptians. And I will bring you into the land which I swore to give to Abraham, to Isaac, and to Jacob."[97] The Bible reports that Moses brought this message to the people of Israel, "but they did not listen to Moses, because of their broken spirit and their cruel bondage."[98]

The fact of the goodness of God to His children, and the truth that He many times permits evil to triumph while He seems to do nothing at all to rescue His suffering and broken children, is one of the mysteries of God. Those who rely upon human observation and their reason are apt to become cynical and believe either in a finite deity or deny His immanence. When James Russell Lowell (1819-91) considered the awful evil of human slavery which America was tolerating, he cried:

Careless seems the great Avenger; history's pages but record
One death-grapple in the darkness 'twixt old systems and the
     Word;
Truth forever on the scaffold, Wrong forever on the throne.

This is a vigorous expression of the seeming triumph of evil in human history. But the poet continues:

Yet that scaffold sways the future, and, behind the dim unknown,
Standeth God within the shadow, keeping watch above His own.[99]

When the Apostle Paul had finished his survey of the problem occasioned by God's seeming rejection of the Jews he exclaimed: "O the depth of the riches and wisdom and knowledge of God! How unsearchable are his judgments and how inscrutable his ways!"[1] And after showing the sovereignty of the Lord he added: "For from him and through him and to him are all things. To him be glory forever. Amen."[2]

The only solution to the paradox of the apparent silence of God when evil is sweeping over the earth is the surrender of faith. This is undoubtedly the central message of the Book of Job. Job could not understand why all his children had to perish, why he was stripped completely of his economic security, and why even his health collapsed. Scripture represents, however, that behind all this awful series of events stood a good and loving God who was vindicating

97 Ex. 6:6-8.
98 Ex. 6:9.
99 Roy J. Cook, *One Hundred and One Famous Poems* (Chicago: The Cable Co., 1929), pp. 34, 35. Used by permission.
1 Rom. 11:33.
2 Rom. 11:36.

the character of His servant by showing Satan the victory of faith.[3] The providence of God is not an item of human reason or insight, but simply an aspect of the faith of a finite creature in a kind heavenly Father.

With just such childlike faith Menno Simons writes:

I do not esteem my life to be better and dearer than the beloved men of God did their lives. I can only be deprived of perishable and mortal flesh, which must once die, and return to dust, though I should live to be as old as Methuselah; not a hair can fall from my head without the will of my heavenly Father; if I lose my life for the sake of Christ and His testimony, and on account of my sincere love for my neighbor, I certainly know that I will save it in life eternal; therefore I cannot conceal the truth, but I must testify and reveal it without hypocrisy in the true fear of God, to my beloved lords.[4]

15. ANGELS

The acceptance of the Biblical doctrine of angels is somewhat of a test as to whether one regards the Bible as a record of the evolutionary development of religion by mankind, or whether one accepts the Scripture as the Word of God inspired by the Holy Spirit. The doctrine of angels is not the result of logical deduction made from an occasional figure of speech in the Bible but is built upon many clear references to angels describing their nature and function as spirit beings who serve God and minister to His children. The Bible speaks of angels as being wise,[5] as speaking,[6] as being curious,[7] as striving,[8] as worshiping and praising God,[9] as rejoicing when converts to Christ are made,[10] as watching over little ones,[11] as receiving dying saints,[12] as mediating Old Testament revelation,[13] as communicating God's blessings to the saints,[14] as ministering to all Christian believers,[15] and as executing the judgments of God.[16] The Scripture represents that angels are spirit beings, not possessing corporeity and therefore as not marrying.[17]

The Bible teaches also that angels are in two classes, the good angels who serve God and minister to the saints,[18] and the evil angels

3 Job 1:8-12; 2:3-6.
4 *Complete Works*, I, pp. 78, 79.
5 II Sam. 14:20.
6 Zech. 1:9; Luke 1:13.
7 I Pet. 1:12.
8 Jude 9.
9 Luke 2:13; Heb. 1:6; Ps. 103:20; 148:2; Rev. 5:11; etc.
10 Luke 15:10.
11 Matt. 18:10.
12 Luke 16:22.

13 Dan. 9:21-23; Zech. 1:12-14; Acts 7:38, 53; Heb. 2:2.
14 Ps. 91:11, 12; Dan. 6:22; Acts 5:19; Matt. 4:44; Luke 22:43.
15 Ps. 34:7; Heb. 1:14; Acts 27:23.
16 II Kings 19:35; Matt. 13:41, 42; Acts 12:23.
17 Matt. 22:30.
18 Mark 8:38; II Cor. 11:14; I Tim. 5:21; Rev. 14:10.

who fell from the holy estate in which they had been created and whose head is Satan.[19]

The Bible also speaks of two orders of angels. There are the cherubs (cherubim is the Hebrew plural of cherub) who guarded Paradise,[20] and who were represented by beautiful figures of gold over the mercy seat in the most holy place of the tabernacle.[21] From their function in the Garden of Eden and from their being placed over the ark where God dwelt symbolically it has been concluded that the cherubs reveal the power and majesty of God and especially that they are guardians of His holiness. Isaiah 6 also speaks of seraphs (seraphim is the Hebrew plural of seraph) praising God and doing His bidding.[22] There are a number of Scriptures in the New Testament which would somewhat confirm the conclusion that angels differ in rank and dignity (but not necessarily in kind). When Paul speaks of the spirit realm he mentions "all rule and authority and power and dominion,"[23] also "principalities and powers in the heavenly places,"[24] again, "thrones or dominions or principalities or authorities,"[25] and Christ is "the head of all rule and authority."[26] Peter also speaks of Christ who has gone "into heaven and is at the right hand of God, with angels, authorities, and powers subject to him."[27] Since the Scripture does no more than merely mention the orders of angels, the humble theologian will be content with the declarations of God's Word and will respect the silences of the Bible.

The Bible also gives the names of two angels. Gabriel appeared to the prophet Daniel, to Zacharias, father of John the Baptist,[28] and to the virgin Mary.[29] Another angel is called Michael, also described as the Archangel.[30]

Both the Old and New Testaments speak of the angels of God as being a means of blessing to the saints. The psalmist declares that "the angel of the Lord encamps around those who fear him, and delivers them."[31] And the Letter to the Hebrews in speaking of the superiority of Christ to angels says:

> But to what angel has he ever said,
> "Sit at my right hand,
> till I make thy enemies
> a stool for thy feet"?[32]

19 II Pet. 2:4; Jude 6.
20 Gen. 3:24.
21 Ex. 25:18-22; II Sam. 22:11; etc.
22 Isa. 6:2, 3, 6.
23 Eph. 1:21.
24 Eph. 3:10.
25 Col. 1:16.
26 Col. 2:10.
27 I Pet. 3:22.
28 Dan. 8:16; 9:21; Luke 1:19.
29 Luke 1:26, 27.
30 Dan. 10:13, 21; Jude 9; Rev. 12:7.
31 Ps. 34:7.
32 Heb. 1:13.

And then the writer to the Hebrews adds concerning the angels: "Are they not all ministering spirits sent forth to serve, for the sake of those who are to obtain salvation?"[33] The Scriptures do not specify clearly what the nature of the ministry of angels to the saints is. The Bible indicates merely the fact of their ministry but does not reveal its manner. Perhaps it is significant that when Jesus was undergoing His Gethsemane experience the third Gospel reports that angels came and ministered to Him.[34]

In Matthew 18 Jesus describes proper conduct toward immature believers, those who "like children are limited in experience or strength or knowledge or opportunity,"[35] and yet who are true believers on Christ.[36] Jesus gave special warning against causing such "little ones" to stumble, explaining that even such immature believers are precious to God. "He declares that the angels who serve, or protect or represent them, are nearest to the throne of God, and therefore His followers cannot think lightly of those who are so dear to God."[37]

We may therefore conclude that the angels are spirit beings, created by God, possessing personality, and divided into two classes: the good angels who serve God and whose ministry includes giving help to Christians, and the evil spirits who are aligned with Satan in the spiritual struggle going on between the kingdoms of God and Satan through all human history. The Bible, however, nowhere explicitly asserts that God assigns a particular angel to each individual Christian believer.

16. SATAN

The Old Testament has very little to say of Satan or the devil. He is not mentioned by name in the Pentateuch nor in the four historical books which were called the former prophets by the Jews: Joshua, Judges, Samuel, and Kings. The word "Satan" is actually a Hebrew term meaning adversary, and there are a number of passages in the Old Testament where it is a question whether it is Satan or a human adversary that is spoken of; for example, Psalm 109:6. In I Chronicles 21:1 Satan moved David to take a military census of Israel, but quite strangely the parallel passage in II Samuel 24:1 speaks of this plan as having its source in God. (Evidently the tempta-

---

33 Heb. 1:14.
34 Luke 22:43.
35 Charles R. Erdman, *The Gospel of Matthew, An Exposition* (Philadelphia: The Westminster Press, 1933), pp. 146, 147.
36 Matt. 18:1-14, especially verse 6.
37 *Op. cit.*, p. 147.

tion of David and his fall played a role in the plan of God, difficult as it may be to understand this.) The latter prophets, both major and minor, make very little mention of Satan except the postexilic Zechariah, who mentions Satan as resisting the high priest.[38] In Job 26 a Hebrew term for destruction is used which is quoted in Revelation 9 in the form *Abaddon* and is there applied to Satan.[39]

Of all the Old Testament books only one makes frequent mention of Satan and it clearly represents him as the archenemy of God, as the slanderer of God's saints, and as the executor of various calamities: the Book of Job, especially the first two chapters.[40]

In addition to Job there are two passages in the major prophets which seem to contain meanings deeper than the superficial descriptions of kings which they purport to be. These passages are found in Isaiah 14 and Ezekiel 28. Isaiah 14 is directed to the king of Babylon and yet the following passage seems to refer to someone beyond the Babylonian king:

> How you are fallen from heaven,
>   O Day Star, son of Dawn!
> How you are cut down to the ground,
>   you who laid the nations low!
> You said in your heart,
>   "I will ascend to heaven;
> above the stars of God
>   I will set my throne on high;
> I will sit on the mount of assembly
>   in the far north;
> I will ascend above the heights of the clouds,
>   I will make myself like the Most High."
> But you are brought down to Sheol,
>   to the depths of the Pit.[41]

And does not the following description seem to refer more to Satan than to the king of Tyre:

> You were the signet of perfection,
>   full of wisdom
>   and perfect in beauty.
> You were in Eden, the garden of God;
>   every precious stone was your covering,
> carnelian, topaz, and jasper,
>   chrysolite, beryl, and onyx,

38 Zech. 3:1, 2.
39 Job 26:6; Rev. 9:11.
40 Job 1:6-12; 2:1-7.
41 Isa. 14:12-15.

sapphire, carbuncle, and emerald;
and wrought in gold were your settings
and your engravings.
On the day that you were created
they were prepared.
With an anointed guardian cherub I placed you;
you were on the holy mountain of God;
in the midst of the stones of fire you walked.
You were blameless in your ways
from the day you were created,
till iniquity was found in you.
In the abundance of your trade
you were filled with violence, and you sinned;
so I cast you as a profane thing from the mountain of God,
and the guardian cherub drove you out
from the midst of the stones of fire.
Your heart was proud because of your beauty;
you corrupted your wisdom for the sake of your splendor.[42]

In the New Testament Satan is called the devil,[43] which means a slanderer; the evil one[44]; or the tempter.[45] Paul hints that the cause of Satan's downfall was pride.[46] He is represented as having tempted Jesus,[47] as being the head of an empire or house,[48] as causing a case of prolonged illness,[49] as resisting the conversion of sinners,[50] as having led Judas to betray Christ,[51] as having moved Ananias to lie,[52] as holding sinners under his power,[53] as disguising himself as a good being,[54] as placing hindrances in the Christian's life,[55] as being the real tempter of Genesis 3,[56] and as persecuting Christians.[57] Our Lord declared that hell was prepared for him and his angels.[58] Paul stresses the fact that Satan is a cunning being.[59] By the power of the Holy Spirit Christians are able to rout the devil and put him to flight.[60] The New Testament stresses especially the fact of the deliverance of Christians from Satan's power.[61] Paul declares that God "has delivered us from the dominion of darkness and transferred us to the kingdom of his beloved Son, in whom we have redemption, the forgiveness of sins."[62]

42 Ezek. 28:12-17.
43 Matt. 13:39.
44 Matt. 6:13.
45 Matt. 4:3.
46 I Tim. 3:6.
47 Matt. 4:1, 8, 10.
48 Matt. 12:36.
49 Luke 13:16; cf. I Cor. 5:5.
50 Matt. 13:39; Mark 4:15; Luke 8:12.
51 Luke 22:3; John 13:27.
52 Acts 5:3.
53 Acts 26:18.
54 II Cor. 11:14.
55 I Thess. 2:18.
56 II Cor. 11:3; Rev. 12:9; 20:2.
57 Rev. 2:10; cf. Dan. 7:25.
58 Matt. 25:41.
59 Eph. 6:11; I Tim. 3:7; II Tim. 2:26.
60 Jas. 4:7; I Pet. 5:8, 9.
61 Col. 1:13; Heb. 2:14; I John 3:8.
62 Col. 1:13.

In giving the reason for the incarnation of Jesus Christ the Letter to the Hebrews says: "Since therefore the children share in flesh and blood, he himself likewise partook of the same nature, that through death he might destroy [render powerless] him who has the power of death, that is, the devil, and deliver all those who through fear of death were subject to lifelong bondage."[63] The Apostle John also says: "The reason the Son of God appeared was to destroy the works of the devil."[64] Because Satan is powerful though· limited, Christians are told to pray to God for deliverance from him."[65]

The picture of Satan which the New Testament presents is certainly that of an intelligent and powerful being, yet one from whom Christians have been completely redeemed so that they need not fear him. The New Testament stresses also the fact that Satan approaches people as an angel of light; that is, he disguises the evil into which he seeks to lead the saints. Needless to say, this viewpoint stands in total contrast with the Middle Ages concept of playful and malicious imps which are active, especially during the night, but which are not to be taken very seriously.

There is also a sense in which Satan is undoubtedly misrepresented: that is, when he is regarded as leading people only into the most bestial and sensual forms of living. As a matter of fact Satan is probably ashamed of some of his followers who create a nauseating picture of sin by the very depths to which they sink. Those who are the most effective servants of Satan are those who live respectable lives, while refusing to surrender to Jesus Christ and to unite with His church. Satan wants men of social status and upright lives to represent the cause of morality, humanistic philosophy, and perhaps even religion if divorced from the blood of Christ. It is also probable that Satan does not exert very much influence as long as an individual makes no move toward becoming a Christian. But let a man accept Jesus Christ and seek to live a life of earnest discipleship and as a Christian worker to make inroads into the kingdom of evil: it is then that Satan exerts the greatest effort to lead the Christian into discouragement or sin, and to provoke hostility and opposition to his work.[66]

Not until Christ has held the final judgment and the devil has been thrown into the lake of fire, where he will be tormented day and night for ever and ever, will the children of God be entirely

63 Heb. 2:14, 15.
64 I John 3:8.
65 Matt. 6:13.
66 Cf. C. S. Lewis, *Screwtape Letters* (New York: Macmillan, 1951).

free from the opposition and the agonies of temptation into which Satan is able to bring them. Nevertheless, the New Testament promises Christians here and now victory over Satan as far as a spiritual triumph in Christ is concerned. The Lord sometimes allows Satan to put Christians to death physically, but spiritually they are ultimately victorious, for they depart to be with Christ even from their death of martyrdom, and enter into that life of glory which is vastly superior to the joy of union with Christ in this world.[67] Certain it is that Satan, according to God's Word, is a real personality and a dreadful foe, and therefore not a subject for humor or ridicule.

67 Phil. 1:21, 23.

PART II

GOD AS REVEALER

II. GOD AS REVEALER

1. *THE MEANING OF DIVINE REVELATION*

By divine revelation in this discussion is meant that process whereby Almighty God has entered into human history to communicate a true knowledge of Himself to mankind for the redemption of the race. Divine revelation implies the miracle of an eternal God entering into temporal human history. The Bible manifests no anxiety as to this possibility. The same God who created man in His own image is the God of redemption who manifested Himself to Adam and Eve following the Fall, to selected individuals from Adam to Abraham, to the patriarchs as the fathers of His holy people Israel, to the prophets of old, to the apostles of Christ after Pentecost, and supremely in the person of His own beloved Son, the Lord Jesus Christ. According to the Bible the God of creation is also the God of history, and the God of history is also the God of revelation and redemption.

No evangelical theologian can write on revelation and inspiration without manifesting his indebtedness to two great theologians, Professors B. B. Warfield [1] (1851-1921) of Princeton Seminary, and James Orr [1,a] (1844-1913) of Glasglow, Scotland. No theologian has ever had deeper insights or greater loyalty to God's Word than these two giants. (See also my "Attempt at a Synopsis" in *God's Word Written*, Scottdale, Pa.: Herald Press, second printing, 1968, pp. 139-144).

It should also be noted that the present discussion accepts the truth of the Biblical representation that the religion of the Old and New Testaments is not a matter of human development, or of insights borrowed from the neighbors of Israel, but of divine revelation. It was God Himself who entered into contact with selected in-

1 Benjamin B. Warfield, *Revelation and Inspiration* (New York: Oxford University Press, 1927); also *The Inspiration and Authority of the Bible* (Philadelphia: the Presbyterian and Reformed Publishing Co., 1948).
1a James Orr, *Revelation and Inspiration* (Eerdmans, 1952).

dividuals to receive His Word and to become His chosen instruments for the bringing of divine salvation first to the family of Seth, later to Israel, and finally to the whole world through the Christian Church. This view stands in sharp contrast with the theory of the evolution of religion, according to which all the religions of the world are to be put in one group and regarded as a phenomenon of human culture. According to this evolutionary view man created God, not *vice versa*. This evolutionary point of view stands diametrically opposed to that of the prophets and apostles and of the Lord Jesus Christ Himself. For it is entirely clear that Jesus Christ believed in a personal God who had revealed Himself to the patriarchs and prophets of old and to Himself as the Messiah, and that He would further reveal Himself through the Holy Spirit to the apostles whom He had chosen. If one believes in the Biblical doctrines of a personal God, of His creation, and of the divine image in man, all difficulties connected with epistemology, in reference to divine revelation, vanish completely.

2. *EDENIC REVELATION AND THE PROTEVANGELIUM*

Without going into any details it is obviously the intention of Moses to picture in the early chapters of Genesis the beautiful and happy estate of original man. At that time there was not yet a cloud of sin above him to hide the face of his God. Adam and Eve evidently had walked with God in the paradise of Eden prior to their fall into sin. Prior to the fall of man the noetic effect of sin was, of course, not yet in existence. The curse of God had also not yet been placed on the ground. For these reasons there was undoubtedly a closer sympathy between man and the remainder of the creation than that which now obtains. There was no particular contrast between the revelation of God to original man through nature and in word. Rather, Adam undoubtedly saw the entire creation as the handiwork of God. Ever since the time of the Fall, however, although the Bible recognizes the fact of natural revelation, apart from Scripture, that revelation is blurred by sin and is not able to save. The Bible does clearly teach that there is such a thing as a natural revelation of God, however. Psalm 19 expresses the fact of this revelation in a beautiful way:

> The heavens are telling the glory of God;
>   and the firmament proclaims his handiwork.
> Day to day pours forth speech,
>   and night to night declares knowledge.

There is no speech, nor are there words;
    their voice is not heard;
yet their voice goes out through all the earth,
    and their words to the end of the world.[2]
Another Psalm says rather sharply:
Understand, O dullest of the people!
    Fools, when will you be wise?
He who planted the ear, does he not hear?
He who formed the eye, does he not see?[3]
That great man of faith David also confessed to God:
I remember the days of old,
    I meditate on all that thou hast done;
    I muse on what thy hands have wrought.
I stretch out my hands to thee;
    my soul thirsts for thee like a parched land.[4]
In one of his numerous speeches Job declares:
. . . Ask the beasts, and they will teach you;
    the birds of the air, and they will tell you;
or the plants of the earth, and they will teach you;
    and the fish of the sea will declare to you.
Who among all these does not know
    that the hand of the Lord has done this?[5]
Through the prophet Isaiah the Lord exclaims:
Lift up your eyes on high and see:
    who created these?
He who brings out their host by number,
    calling them all by name;
by the greatness of his might,
    and because he is strong in power
    not one is missing.[6]

To the pagans at Lystra Barnabas and Paul cried: "We also are men, of like nature with you, and bring you good news, that you should turn from these vain things to a living God who made the heaven and the earth and the sea and all that is in them."[7] And to the Athenians Paul said: "The God who made the world and everything in it, being Lord of heaven and earth, does not live in shrines made by man, nor is he served by human hands, as though he needed anything, since he himself gives to all men life and breath

2 Ps. 19:1-4.   5 Job 12:7-9.
3 Ps. 94:8, 9.   6 Isa. 40:26.
4 Ps. 143:5, 6.   7 Acts 14:15.

and everything."[8] And in the Letter of Paul to the Romans he asserts vigorously: "For what can be known about God is plain to them, because God has shown it to them. Ever since the creation of the world his invisible nature, namely, his eternal power and deity, has been clearly perceived in the things that have been made. So they are without excuse; for although they knew God they did not honor him as God or give thanks to him, but they became futile in their thinking and their senseless minds were darkened."[9] Paul also explains: "All who have sinned without the law will also perish without the law, and all who have sinned under the law will be judged by the law."[10]

The dimness of spiritual perception with which sinners view God's creation is to be accounted for by the darkening effect of sin on man's mind, and the inability of this natural revelation to save man is due to the fact that man needs more than intellectual insights; he now needs a divine Mediator and Saviour.[11]

Immediately following the Fall of the original pair, God pronounced His judgments on the offenders and to the serpent He said:

I will put enmity between you and the woman,
  and between your seed and her seed;
he shall bruise your head,
  and you shall bruise his heel.[12]

There is not a single verse in the entire Bible which better illustrates the need of seeking the deep spiritual significance of the Word of God than the profound statement which here lies before us. A mere literal reading sees neither Satan nor divine redemption in this passage but merely an agelong struggle between serpents and mankind, "The seed of the woman." Many liberal commentators deny, in fact, that this passage has anything to do with Christ and His redemption. Here God announces that it is He Himself who will arouse undying opposition on the part of the human race to the Tempter. God will not allow the race to serve sin to the limit without divine interference. It must be admitted that a simple reading of the Hebrew in this statement would produce the impression that God is addressing only a literal serpent and referring to the fact that the seed of the woman (i.e., human beings) would crush the head of the serpent, while it in turn would attack the heel of the race. The devout child of God sees more in this passage, however, than what a

8 Acts 17:24, 25.
9 Rom. 1:19-21.
10 Rom. 2:12.

11 Rom. 1:21; I Cor. 2:14; etc.
12 Gen. 3:15.

superficial reader would observe; he believes that ultimately the reference is not to men fighting with serpents, but to a struggle which would transpire between one Man, the Messiah, and the devil.

Bishop Ryle writes: "The victory of the Cross contains, in its fullest expression, the fulfillment of the conflict, which God here proclaims between Mankind and the symbol of Evil, and in which He Himself espouses the cause of man."[13] There seems to be no more reason to deny that Genesis 3:15 is a genuine Protevangelium, than to deny that Isaiah 53 is also Messianic. Indeed, Genesis 3:15 introduces the glorious theme of redemption which is the central message of the entire Bible. With deep spiritual insight Martin Luther declared: "This text embraces and comprehends within itself everything noble and glorious that is to be found anywhere in the Scriptures."[14] According to the Jewish Targums even the Jews regarded this passage as Messianic.

It should be noted that the Douay version of the Roman Catholic Church follows an error in the Latin vulgate by reading: "She shall crush thy head and thou shalt lie in wait for her heel." Professor H. C. Leupold translates the Hebrew with his usual scholarship as follows: "And enmity will I put between thee and the woman, between thy seed and her seed; he shall crush thee in respect to the head, thou shalt bruise him in respect to the heel."[15] Dr. Leupold comments: "In other words, we can and must subscribe to the statement that this word held up the Savior before their eyes, and so made it possible for men to believe on Him."[16]

If the Bible is inspired of God by the Holy Spirit, why should one stumble even at believing that the expression, "Seed of the woman," is a veiled reference to Mary and the virgin birth of Christ?[17] In other words, the very being whom Satan deceived and ruined, so he thought, is to be used of God to bring about his own ruin: that is to say, just as woman introduced sin into the world, so it was also ordained of God that a woman, the virgin Mary, should give birth to Him who was destined to be the Saviour of the world.[18] As Professor Leupold again accurately states: "The expression used does not specifically prophesy the virgin birth, but it coincides and agrees with it under divine providence."[19]

13 Herbert E. Ryle, *The Book of Genesis*, The Cambridge Bible for Schools and Colleges (Cambridge: at the University Press, 1914, 1921), pp. 54, 55.

14 H. C. Leupold, *Exposition of Genesis* (Columbus, Ohio: The Wartburg Press, 1942), p. 163. This commentary is superb, both evangelical and scholarly.

15 *Ibid.*, p. 163.   18 Perhaps alluded to in I Tim. 2:15.

16 *Ibid.*, p. 164.   19 *Op. cit.*, p. 169.

17 *Ibid.*, pp. 169, 170.

3. FROM ADAM TO ABRAHAM

We have already observed that the central theme of the Bible is redemption, and that this redemptive work of God was carried out in the Old Testament era through Israel and since Pentecost through the church. The Bible, therefore, quickly passes over a vast segment of history in order to come quickly to Abraham and his family. The first three chapters of the Bible describe the creation and fall of man, chapters four and five quickly summarize antediluvian history, chapters six through eight are devoted to the Flood, chapters nine to eleven tell of the new beginnings of the three great branches of the human race, and chapter twelve records the call of Abraham: whereupon Hebrew history has begun. The rest of Genesis is then devoted to the stories of Abraham (chapters 12-24), Isaac (25-27), Jacob (28-38), and Joseph (39-50). The exact length of this period of time is not known. Modern evangelical scholars are inclined to believe that it was substantially longer than the chronology of Archbishop Ussher would indicate, but that it was vastly shorter than the evolutionists claim.

The Book of Genesis indicates that true faith in the Lord did not begin with Abraham. When Adam and Eve became the parents of their first son they named him Cain, which by a sort of alliteration meant "gotten," for Eve declared, "I have gotten a man with the LORD."[20] Luther translated this passage: "I have the man, the Lord," a translation which has perhaps given rise to the conclusion that Eve regarded Cain as the Messiah who was to crush the head of the serpent.[21] It is entirely possible, however, that the word "with" in Hebrew in this case means, "with the help of," so that Eve is really giving thanks to God for the safe delivery of her son. Childbirth would thus be regarded as a pledge of divine favor, and a fulfillment of the promise that the woman would be able to bring forth life in spite of the curse for the Fall. In any case the passage would indicate that Adam and Eve were people of true faith in the LORD.

The very next paragraph in Genesis 4 reports that Adam's son Abel was also a man of faith and that he brought to the LORD an acceptable sacrifice, acceptable because of his true faith.[22] Since the godly line from Adam to Abraham was cut off with the murder of Abel, God raised up Seth in his stead. This conclusion is not based on the joyful remarks of Eve at the birth of Seth, but upon the name which Seth in turn gave to his son. In the Hebrew this boy's name was given as Enosh, which seems to mean, "the frail or mortal one."

---

20 Gen. 4:1.   21 Leupold, *op. cit.*, p. 190.   22 Heb. 11:4.

This would seem to indicate that Seth had meditated upon the fact of mortality and upon the eternity of God, and by giving his son this name was giving a witness to his awareness of the reality of the eternal world.[23] If this conclusion seems farfetched, one should note that immediately following this name the remarkable sentence occurs: "At that time men began to call upon the name of the LORD." What is the meaning of this particular expression? It cannot be that Moses means that the name LORD is now new, for he has been using it repeatedly in his narrative prior to this. Nor can it mean that for the first time men truly turned to God in faith. The answer is probably given us by Dr. Johann Peter Lange (1802-84), who writes in his great commentary: "Moreover, it must be that here is narrated the beginning of a formal divine worship . . . the language undoubtedly refers to a general honoring of the name Jehovah among the pious Sethites."[24] Professor Leupold comments: "The thing that the name stood for was known. Men do not first in the age of Abraham or Moses begin to comprehend God's faithfulness, unchangeableness, and mercy. Since this calling out by the use of the name definitely implies public worship, we have here the first record of *regular public worship*."[25] Dr. Ryle admits that the Hebrew expression, "to call upon," always means to use in invocations, "especially at times of sacrifice."[26] Moses is telling us that very early in human history there was a godly line of men who called upon God in formal worship.

The next individual who is singled out for special mention as to his piety is Enoch, father of Methuselah. Of Enoch it is twice recorded that he "walked with God."[27] The narrative hastens on to Noah, who "found favor in the eyes of the Lord," and who also "walked with God."[28] When God was ready to destroy the whole human race with the flood He was able to say to Noah: "Go into the ark, you and all your household, for I have seen that you are righteous before me in this generation."[29] Prior to the Deluge the LORD promised Noah: "But I will establish my covenant with you,"[30] and after the flood the LORD said: "I establish my covenant with you, that never again shall all flesh be cut off by the waters of a flood, and never again shall there be a flood to destroy the earth."[31] God selected the rainbow to be the sign of this Noachian covenant.[32]

Genesis 10 gives the story of the main branches of the families of Shem, Ham, and Japheth, Noah's sons; while chapter 11 reports

23 Leupold, *op. cit.*, p. 227.
24 *Commentary on . . . Genesis* (Grand Rapids, Mich.: Zondervan, n.d.), p. 262.
25 *Op. cit.*, p. 228.   28 Gen. 6:8, 9.   31 Gen. 9:11.
26 *Op. cit.*, p. 83.   29 Gen. 7:1.   32 Gen. 9:13.
27 Gen. 5:22, 24.   30 Gen. 6:18.

the dispersion of the human race at the tower of Babel. This brings Moses to the point he has been rapidly striving to reach, namely, the call of Abraham and the beginning of the Hebrew race. "Now the LORD said to Abram, 'Go from your country and your kindred and your father's house to the land that I will show you. And I will make of you a great nation, and I will bless you, and make your name great, so that you will be a blessing. I will bless those who bless you, and him who curses you I will curse; and by you all the families of the earth will bless themselves [or, be blessed].' "[33]

It should be noted, however, that at various points all through the Old Testament God did make occasional revelations of Himself to selected individuals outside of the family of Abraham. Thus we have Melchizedek, who was priest of the most high God in the days of Abraham[34]; Abimelech, to whom God spoke in a dream by night[35]; Pharaoh, who received revelations of the famine to come[36]; Balaam, who was used of God to bring true revelations to Balak[37]; the dream of the Midianite soldier in the Book of Judges[38]; Cyrus,[39] Nebuchadnezzar,[40] and Belshazzar,[41] as well as the Magi at the birth of Jesus.[42] Mention should also be made of Jonah's divine mission to Nineveh, capital of Assyria, in the latter eighth century B.C.[43] In a general way, however, God did confine special revelation to the nation of Israel prior to the coming of the Saviour.[44]

4. PATRIARCHAL REVELATION

One of the modes of special revelation on the part of God to His chosen people is that which Warfield has called patriarchal.[45] God appeared to Noah both before and after the flood, made a covenant with him never again to destroy the earth, and designated the rainbow as the sign of the Noachian covenant. God also appeared to the patriarchs Abraham, Isaac, and Jacob, making His covenant with Abraham to give him the land of Canaan and promising that in his seed all the nations of the earth would be blessed: the sign of the Abrahamic covenant being circumcision.[46] The Noachian and Abrahamic covenants, however, were merely preparatory for the great old covenant made by God with Israel through Moses and rati-

---

33 Gen. 12:1-3.
34 Gen. 14:17-24.
35 Gen. 20:6.
36 Gen. 41:1-32.
37 Num. 24:2, 3 ff.
38 Judg. 7:9-14.
39 Ezra 1:1-4.
40 Dan. 2:28-45.
41 Dan. 5:5-9, 17-28.
42 Matt. 2:1, 2.
43 Jon. 3:1-10.
44 Deut. 10:15; Ps. 147:19, 20; Deut. 4:7, 8, 32-34.
45 *The Inspiration and Authority of the Bible*, pp. 83-86; *Revelation and Inspiration*, pp. 15-18.
46 Gen. 17:11.

fied with blood.[47] The sign of the Mosaic covenant was the weekly Sabbath.[48]

All through the period from Abraham to Amos God sent prophets on occasion to reveal His will to His people Israel. To none of them, however, did God reveal Himself in any such manner as He did to Moses. This is stressed especially in two passages from the Pentateuch: "Thus the LORD used to speak to Moses face to face, as a man speaks to his friend."[49] The Lord Himself commented on the matter thus: "Hear my words: If there is a prophet among you, I the LORD make myself known to him in a vision, I speak with him in a dream. Not so with my servant Moses; he is entrusted with all my house. With him I speak mouth to mouth, clearly, and not in dark speech; and he beholds the form of the LORD."[50] If one accepts the Bible in simple faith it is as clear as language can make it that God truly revealed Himself to the patriarchs.

One of the main characteristics of patriarchal revelation was theophany. For example, in Genesis 15 the Lord caused Abraham to see a burning pot and a flaming torch; and in chapter 18 the Lord appeared to Abraham in the form of three men. The patriarch Jacob saw a ladder set up to heaven and the angels of God ascending and descending.[51] When the Lord called Moses He appeared to him in a burning bush which was not consumed.[52] Perhaps one could say that the characteristic manifestation of patriarchal revelation was the theophany.

It has become fashionable in many circles to scoff at the Mosaic authorship of the Pentateuch. A recent writer, however, has pointedly shown that the most natural thing in the world for an educated man to do, when entrusted with the leadership of God's people, and when he is the recipient of special revelations from God, is to write down those revelations from time to time as they are received.[53] We know that Moses was an educated man, that writing was an old art in Canaan long before the time of Moses, that Moses would have had animal skins to use for parchment, that he did receive special revelations from God, that Israel was the people of God, and that Moses was the divinely appointed leader of Israel. When one actually examines the Pentateuch he finds precisely the type of document that would have resulted from the piecing together of the records of spe-

---

47 Ex. 24:3-8.
48 Ex. 31:12-17.
49 Ex. 33:11; cf. Deut. 34:10.

50 Num. 12:6-8.
51 Gen. 28:10-17.
52 Ex. 3:1-6.

53 J. Stafford Wright, "Some Thoughts on the Composition of the Pentateuch," *The Evangelical Quarterly*, London, XXV, 1 (Jan. 1953), pp. 2-17.

cial revelation which Moses received and the historical notes which a man of the type of Moses would have kept on the journeys of the children of Israel on the way from Egypt to Canaan.

While it is true that the Old Testament shows evidence of progressive revelation as between Moses and the writing prophets, yet it must be admitted that the Pentateuch does contain a lofty theology, an ethical monotheism of the highest order, and it gives abundant testimony to the love and mercy and grace of God. There seems to be no good reason for denying the Mosaic authorship of the Pentateuch, unless one is unwilling to accept the picture of Old Testament history and revelation which the Word of God presents. At this point the evangelical theologian pleads for a willingness to allow the Bible to speak for itself, rather than to approach it with a dogmatic bias which insists on reconstructing the history of Old Testament revelation along the lines of the evolutionary development of religion.

One of the most interesting phenomena of the Old Testament is that associated with "the angel of the LORD." Again and again the reader of the Old Testament meets this specific angel of the LORD. He appeared to Hagar,[54] to Abraham,[55] to Jacob,[56] to Moses,[57] to Samson's parents,[58] etc.; and he is also mentioned by the prophet Zechariah.[59] The peculiar thing about the angel of the LORD is that in some sense he bears the name of the LORD, being at one and the same time identical with the LORD and yet distinct from Him. For example, Genesis 22 gives the account of how God put Abraham to the test to see whether he really loved Him. When Abraham proved to be faithful and was about to slay his son Isaac, it was the angel of the LORD who called to him from heaven saying, "Abraham, Abraham! . . . Do not lay your hand on the lad or do anything to him; for now I know that you fear God, seeing you have not withheld your son, your only son, from me."[60] In this conversation the angel of the LORD identifies himself with God by reporting that he himself is now satisfied of Abraham's love; the angel now knows that Abraham fears God, because Abraham did not withhold his only son from the angel of the LORD! The question which persists is this: Who could the angel of the LORD be? Who is the Being who is one with the Father, and yet a distinct personality from the Father? Is it possible that the angel of the LORD is the second member of the holy Trinity, the preincarnate and eternal Son of God?

54 Gen. 16:7.
55 Gen. 18:2, 10, 13; 22:1, 11.
56 Gen. 31:11; 32:24, 28.
57 Ex. 3:2; 23:20; 32:34; Josh. 5:13—6:2; Judg. 2:1.

58 Judg. 13:3-20; cf. 6:11-24.
59 Zech. 3:1.
60 Gen. 22:11, 12.

The great Methodist commentator Adam Clarke does not hesitate to assert that the angel of the LORD is "the very person who was represented by this offering; the Lord Jesus who calls Himself Jehovah, . . . and on His own authority renews the promises of the covenant. He was ever the great Mediator between God and man."[61] With cautious reserve Professor Leupold states: "This Angel of the Lord is in a class by Himself and distinctly recognized as a superior being by the writers of Old Testament books."[62] Dr. Leupold also states that "His identity with Yahweh is fully established by v. 13."[63] In connection with our passage in Genesis 22 Leupold writes: "He who speaks to Abraham is here designated as 'the Angel of Yahweh.' As 16:7-11 and 21:17, 18 already indicated, this person is divine and specifically the one who later assumed the form of man. . . . That one can be God and yet so distinct from Him in one sense as to be able to say, 'I know that thou fearest God,' is to be explained on the ground of the distinction of divine persons."[64]

The genuineness of patriarchal revelation, and the maturity of the faith of the patriarchs, is attested by Hebrews 11:

By faith Abraham obeyed when he was called to go out to a place which he was to receive as an inheritance; and he went out, not knowing where he was to go. By faith he sojourned in the land of promise, as in a foreign land, living in tents with Isaac and Jacob, heirs with him of the same promise. For he looked forward to the city which has foundations, whose builder and maker is God. . . .

By faith Abraham, when he was tested, offered up Isaac, and he who had received the promises was ready to offer up his only son, of whom it was said, "Through Isaac shall your descendants be named." He considered that God was able to raise men even from the dead; hence, figuratively speaking, he did receive him back. By faith Isaac invoked future blessings on Jacob and Esau. By faith Jacob, when dying, blessed each of the sons of Joseph, bowing in worship over the head of his staff. By faith Joseph, at the end of his life, made mention of the exodus of the Israelites and gave directions concerning his burial.[65]

Concerning such men of faith as Abel, Noah, Abraham, and Sarah the Letter to the Hebrews states:

These all died in faith, not having received what was promised, but having seen it and greeted it from afar, and having acknowledged that they were strangers and exiles on the earth. For people who speak thus

---

61 Commentary on Gen. 22:11 (I, p. 138).
62 H. C. Leupold, *Exposition of Genesis* (Columbus, Ohio: The Wartburg Press, 1942), p. 501.
63 *Ibid.*, p. 500 (on Gen. 16:7).
64 *Ibid.*, p. 628.
65 Heb. 11:8-10, 17-22.

make it clear that they are seeking a homeland. If they had been thinking of that land from which they had gone out, they would have had opportunity to return. But as it is, they desire a better country, that is, a heavenly one. Therefore God is not ashamed to be called their God, for he has prepared for them a city.[66]

5. MOSAISM

If one accepts the testimony of the Bible one is compelled to believe that the God of the Pentateuch is also the God of the prophets and of the apostles. Moses presents in the first two chapters of the Bible a picture of a personal God who in an orderly fashion created the heavens and the earth and made of this world a beautiful dwelling place for the human race. There is no question but that Moses presents God continually as a personal God. He is also a holy God. Statements such as the following occur time and again: "And the LORD said to Moses, 'Say to all the congregation of the people of Israel, You shall be holy; for I the LORD your God am holy.' "[67] Because God is a holy God He is also a God of judgment, the One who destroyed the world in Noah's day because of its sin,[68] the One who scattered the race at the tower of Babel,[69] the One who rained fire and brimstone on Sodom,[70] the One who destroyed the Canaanites when their cup of iniquity became full,[71] the One who punished Nadab and Abihu for their lack of reverence,[72] the One who took the children of Israel out of Egypt after He had judged the Egyptians.[73]

The LORD is also a God of providence. This appears plainly in the lives of the patriarchs Abraham, Isaac, Jacob, Joseph, and in a multitude of incidents such as that associated with the Jewish midwives in Egypt,[74] the miraculous deliverances of the children of Israel on the way to Canaan,[75] and the providing of manna[76] and water[77] for the people of Israel. This personal and holy God is the one who entered into covenant relationships with Noah,[78] Abraham,[79] Isaac,[80] Jacob,[81] and supremely with the children of Israel under Moses, in the Old Covenant.[82]

When Moses desired of the Lord to behold His glory, Scripture records: "And the LORD descended in the cloud and stood with him

66 Heb. 11:13-16.
67 Lev. 19:1, 2.
68 Gen. 6.
69 Gen. 11.
70 Gen. 19.
71 Gen. 15:16; Num. 31; Deut. 7:1-5; Josh. 6-13; etc.
72 Lev. 10.
73 Ex. 7—12.
74 Ex. 1:15-21.

75 Ex. 14.
76 Ex. 16:4-8, 13-21; Josh. 5:12.
77 Ex. 17; Num. 20.
78 Gen. 6:18; 9:9-17.
79 Gen. 12:2, 3; 15:18; 17:2.
80 Gen. 17:19; 17:21; 26:3, 4.
81 Ex. 2:24; cf. Gen. 32:12.
82 Ex. 24:7, 8; Heb. 9:17-20; Ex. 31:12-17.

there, and proclaimed the name of the LORD. The LORD passed before him, and proclaimed, 'The LORD, the LORD, a God merciful and gracious, slow to anger, and abounding in steadfast love and faithfulness, keeping steadfast love for thousands, forgiving iniquity and transgression and sin, but who will by no means clear the guilty, visiting the iniquity of the fathers upon the children and the children's children, to the third and the fourth generation.' "[83] Here is evident the steadfast love and mercy and faithfulness of God as well as the justice which He manifests toward those who disobey Him and live in sin.

In Mosaism the LORD is also revealed as an electing God, the One who called out Abraham to follow Him to the land to which He would direct him. It was the will of God to make of Abraham a great nation for Himself. Many times in the Pentateuch one finds expressions such as the following: "I am the LORD your God, who have separated you from the peoples."[84] Moses also reminded the children of Israel: "The Lord has taken you, and brought you forth out of the iron furnace, out of Egypt, to be a people of his own possession, as at this day."[85] Moses also interpreted this election in terms of God's love: "And because he loved your fathers and chose their descendants after them, and brought you out of Egypt with his own presence, by his great power, driving out before you nations greater and mightier than yourselves, to bring you in, to give you their land for an inheritance, as at this day; know therefore this day, and lay it to your heart, that the LORD is God in heaven above and on the earth beneath; there is no other."[86] This divine election placed obligations upon Israel: "For you are a people holy to the LORD your God, and the LORD has chosen you to be a people for his own possession, out of all the peoples that are on the face of the earth."[87]

The personal and holy covenant God who elected Israel to be His people also made provision for their sins. Of Abraham it is recorded that when God gave His promises to Abraham, "He believed the LORD; and he reckoned it to him as righteousness."[88] The law of Moses also contains detailed instructions for the procedures to be taken when an Israelite fell into sin, and concerning every type of transgression committed through ignorance or weakness the Scripture promises that if the individual would follow the divine instructions, "It shall be forgiven him."[89]

83 Ex. 34:5-7.
84 Lev. 20:24.
85 Deut. 4:20.
86 Deut. 4:37-39.

87 Deut. 14:2.
88 Gen. 15:6.
89 Lev. 4:20, 26, 31, 35; 5:10, 13, 16, 18; etc.

One of the aspects of Mosaism which is often overlooked is that of the joy which God desired His people to have. The following description of the feast of booths (tabernacles) will illustrate this truth:

> You shall keep the feast of booths seven days, when you make your ingathering from your threshing floor and your wine press; you shall rejoice in your feast, you and your son and your daughter, your manservant and your maidservant, the Levite, the sojourner, the fatherless, and the widow who are within your towns. For seven days you shall keep the feast to the LORD your God at the place which the LORD will choose; because the LORD your God will bless you in all your produce and in all the work of your hands, so that you will be altogether joyful.[90]

One must also believe that the Mosaic benediction would produce joy in Israel:

> The LORD bless you and keep you:
> The LORD make his face to shine
>   upon you, and be gracious to
>   you:
> The LORD lift up his countenance
>   upon you, and give you peace.[91]

The Pentateuch also presents the LORD as a God of revelation. Scripture represents the Lord as speaking and communicating with Adam, with Moses, with Abraham, Isaac, Jacob, especially with Moses, and with the prophets of Israel. God describes the Messiah as a prophet in the following words: "I will raise up for them a prophet like you from among their brethren; and I will put my words in his mouth, and he shall speak to them all that I command him."[92] Concerning Moses God said: "He is entrusted with all my house. With him I speak mouth to mouth, clearly, and not in dark speech; and he beholds the form of the LORD."[93] The Lord also makes the following statement about false prophets: "But the prophet who presumes to speak a word in my name which I have not commanded him to speak, or who speaks in the name of other gods, that same prophet shall die."[94]

The culmination of Mosaic revelation came at Sinai when God revealed the Ten Commandments and other laws to Israel through Moses. "And Moses wrote all the words of the LORD. And he rose early in the morning, and built an altar at the foot of the mountain,

90 Deut. 16:13-15.
91 Num. 6:24-26.
92 Deut. 18:18.

93 Num. 12:7, 8.
94 Deut. 18:20.

and twelve pillars, according to the twelve tribes of Israel. And he sent young men of the people of Israel, who offered burnt offerings and sacrificed peace offerings of oxen to the Lord. And Moses took half of the blood and put it in basins, and half of the blood he threw against the altar. Then he took the book of the covenant, and read it in the hearing of the people; and they said, 'All that the Lord has spoken we will do, and we will be obedient.' And Moses took the blood and threw it upon the people, and said, 'Behold the blood of the covenant which the Lord has made with you in accordance with all these words.' "[95]

Before his death Moses appealed to the children of Israel in the following words: "And now, O Israel, give heed to the statutes and the ordinances which I teach you, and do them; that you may live, and go in and take possession of the land which the Lord, the God of your fathers, gives you. You shall not add to the word which I command you, nor take from it; that you may keep the commandments of the Lord your God which I command you."[96]

It should be noted that the rest of the Bible refers many times to the Mosaic authorship of the Pentateuch. The Hebrew Bible is divided into three parts: Law, Prophets, and the Writings. The Law includes our first five books: Genesis, Exodus, Leviticus, Numbers, and Deuteronomy. The Prophets is divided into two parts, former and latter. The Former Prophets include four books: Joshua, Judges, Samuel, and Kings. The Latter Prophets consist of Isaiah, Jeremiah, Ezekiel, and "The Twelve." The Writings include the following eleven books: Psalms, Job, Proverbs, Ruth, Song of Solomon, Ecclesiastes, Lamentations, Esther, Daniel, Ezra-Nehemiah, and Chronicles. Each of the two other sections attests to the Mosaic authorship of the law: (1) from the "Prophets": Joshua,[97] Judges,[98] Kings,[99] and Malachi[1]; and (2) from the "Writings": Psalms,[2] Daniel,[3] Ezra-Nehemiah,[4] and Chronicles.[5] In the New Testament the Pharisees,[6] Sadducees,[7] and the Jews in general[8] accepted the Mosaic authorship of the Law, as well as Philip,[9] James,[10] Peter,[11] Paul,[12] Stephen,[13] John,[14] the au-

---

95 Ex. 24:4-8.
96 Deut. 4:1, 2.
97 Josh. 1:7, 8; 8:30-35; 22:5; 23:6.
98 Judg. 3:4.

99 I Kings 2:3; II Kings 14:6; 23:25.
1 Mal. 4:4.
2 Ps. 103:7.
3 Dan. 9:11, 13.

4 Ezra 3:2; 6:18; 7:6; Neh. 1:7, 8; 8:1, 14; 9:14; 10:29; 13:1.
5 I Chron. 15:15; II Chron. 23:18; 25:4; 34:14; etc.
6 Matt. 19:7.
7 Matt. 22:23, 24.
8 John 9:29.

9 John 1:45.
10 Acts 15:21.
11 Acts 3:22.

12 Rom. 10:5; 10:19; I Cor. 9:9; II Cor. 3:15; etc.
13 Acts 7:37.
14 John 1:17.

thor of Hebrews,[15] and Jesus Himself.[16] Ethical monotheism is not only the religion of the writing prophets in the last centuries of the Jewish nation's history, but is clearly taught in the Pentateuch of Moses. The Old Testament prophets regard their function as that of calling the people of Israel back to the law of Moses, and as interpreting that law for the people.

What were the requirements which God made upon Israel as to religious life and service? One of the main emphases of the Law is that God looks for singlehearted devotion to Himself because He is a "jealous" God.[17] The Lord promised Moses that He would drive out before Israel the various peoples of Canaan, and Israel was to tear down the altars of those pagans, break up their religious pillars, and cut down every idolatrous grove, "For you shall worship no other god, for the LORD, whose name is Jealous, is a jealous God."[18] The most significant commandment which God gave His people was this: "Hear, O Israel: The LORD our God is one LORD; and you shall love the LORD your God with all your heart, and with all your soul, and with all your might. And these words which I command you this day shall be upon your heart; and you shall teach them diligently to your children, and shall talk of them when you sit in your house, and when you walk by the way, and when you lie down, and when you rise. And you shall bind them as a sign upon your hand, and they shall be as frontlets between your eyes. And you shall write them on the doorposts of your house and on your gates."[19]

The singlehearted love and devotion which God asked of His people proscribed the worship of any other deity. The Book of the Covenant included this warning: "Take heed to all that I have said to you; and make no mention of the names of other gods, nor let such be heard out of your mouth."[20] In one of his farewell addresses Moses gave a special warning against false prophets who would arise to call Israel to the worship of other deities; he also warned the Jews against dealing lightly with a brother or son or wife or friend who would seek to entice Israel to the worship of other gods. Such false prophets and such seductive persons were to be executed by public stoning. "And all Israel shall hear, and fear, and never again do any such wickedness as this among you."[21] Needless to say, this singlehearted love for God excluded any attempt to establish contact with evil spirits: "A man or a woman who is a medium or a wizard shall

15 Heb. 7:14; 8:5.
16 Matt. 8:4; Mark 7:10; Luke 20:37; John 5:46; 7:19.
17 Ex. 20:5.   20 Ex. 23:13.
18 Ex. 34:14.   21 Deut. 13:1-11.
19 Deut. 6:4-9.

be put to death; they shall be stoned with stones, their blood shall be upon them."[22]

In this connection special mention should be made of the prohibition in Leviticus 17:7 which forbids the offering of sacrifices to "devils" (AV), "he-goats" (ASV), or "satyrs" (RSV). The Hebrew word which is here perhaps rendered most accurately by *satyrs* is translated in this passage in the Septuagint by the expression "vain thing," while the German has "field devils." It must be admitted that there is a certain amount of obscurity about the word, the most probable meaning of the passage being the forbidding of worship to demons under the form of a being partly human and partly goatlike known as a "goat" or "satyr." In any case it is a form of evil idolatrous worship which the Lord will not tolerate.

Not only did God call for Israel to love Him, but they were to practice love and social justice among themselves: "You shall not steal, nor deal falsely, nor lie to one another. And you shall not swear by my name falsely, and so profane the name of your God: I am the Lord. You shall not oppress your neighbor or rob him. The wages of a hired servant shall not remain with you all night until the morning. You shall not curse the deaf or put a stumbling block before the blind, but you shall fear your God: I am the Lord. You shall do no injustice in judgment; you shall not be partial to the poor or defer to the great, but in righteousness shall you judge your neighbor. You shall not go up and down as a slanderer among your people, and you shall not stand forth against the life of your neighbor: I am the Lord. You shall not hate your brother in your heart, but you shall reason with your neighbor, lest you bear sin because of him. You shall not take vengeance or bear any grudge against the sons of your own people, but you shall love your neighbor as yourself: I am the Lord."[23]

"And if your brother becomes poor, and cannot maintain himself with you, you shall maintain him; as a stranger and a sojourner he shall live with you. Take no interest from him or increase, but fear your God; that your brother may live beside you. You shall not lend him your money at interest, nor give him your food for profit. I am the Lord . . . ."[24]

God did not go into detail in telling Abraham how he ought to live. He simply said: "I am God Almighty; walk before me, and be blameless. And I will make my covenant between me and you, and will multiply you exceedingly."[25] And to all Israel God promised:

22 Lev. 20:27.   23 Lev. 19:11-18.   24 Lev. 25:35-37.   25 Gen. 17:1, 2.

"If you will diligently hearken to the voice of the LORD your God, and do that which is right in his eyes, and give heed to his commandments and keep all his statutes, I will put none of the diseases upon you which I put upon the Egyptians; for I am the LORD, your healer."[26]

A good summary of the moral requirements of belonging to the Holy One of Israel is found in Exodus 20 and Deuteronomy 5: the well-known Ten Commandments. The first commandment is a call for the whole loyalty of Israel to the LORD: there are to be no other deities worshiped. The second commandment calls for a spiritual worship without any sensuous aids such as images of Deity. The third commandment demands reverence for the name of God, and the fourth requires the setting aside of the seventh day for rest from earthly toil. The fifth commandment requires the rendering of honor to one's parents, while the sixth forbids the taking of human life. The seventh recognizes the sanctity of marriage by forbidding adultery. The eighth recognizes the property rights of others by proscribing thievery. The ninth commandment calls for absolute truthfulness, rather than the bearing of false witness against one's friends. The tenth commandment is a recognition that one ought to be content with such blessings as God has given rather than to have an evil desire for the property of others.

The Book of Deuteronomy contains a number of other excellent summaries of what God asks of His people, together with a reminder of the solemn outcomes of obedience and disobedience: "Behold, I set before you this day a blessing and a curse: the blessing, if you obey the commandments of the LORD your God, which I command you this day, and the curse, if you do not obey the commandments of the LORD your God, but turn aside from the way which I command you this day, to go after other gods which you have not known."[27]

"And now, Israel, what does the LORD your God require of you, but to fear the LORD your God, to walk in all his ways, to love him, to serve the LORD your God with all your heart and with all your soul, and to keep the commandments and statutes of the LORD, which I command you this day for your good? Behold, to the LORD your God belong heaven and the heaven of heavens, the earth with all that is in it; yet the LORD set his heart in love upon your fathers and chose their descendants after them, you above all peoples, as at this day. Circumcise therefore the foreskin of your heart, and be no longer stubborn. For the LORD your God is God of gods and Lord of

---

26 Ex. 15:26.   27 Deut. 11:26-28.

lords, the great, the mighty, and the terrible God, who is not partial and takes no bribe. He executes justice for the fatherless and the widow, and loves the sojourner, giving him food and clothing. Love the sojourner therefore; for you were sojourners in the land of Egypt. You shall fear the Lord your God; you shall serve him and cleave to him, and by his name you shall swear. He is your praise; he is your God, who has done for you these great and terrible things which your eyes have seen. Your fathers went down to Egypt seventy persons; and now the Lord your God has made you as the stars of heaven for multitude.

"You shall therefore love the Lord your God, and keep his charge, his statutes, his ordinances, and his commandments always."[28]

It should also be noted that the Bible frequently speaks of God in terms of human situations and emotions, such as that God came down to see whether the wickedness of man was a great as had been reported to Him,[29] that God was dissuaded by Moses from destroying Israel after He had made up His mind to do so,[30] that God warned of His wrath burning if Israel would sin,[31] etc. These ascriptions of human emotions and forms to God are called anthropomorphisms, and are to be understood figuratively, of course. The Bible does not mean to tell us that God has material eyes or hands or feathers. When the Scripture states that "the eyes of the Lord run to and fro throughout the whole earth, to show his might in behalf of those whose heart is blameless toward him,"[32] this is simply a vivid and beautiful way of expressing the fact of the good providence of our heavenly Father toward those who have genuine faith. When the psalmist writes,

> He will cover you with his pinions,
> and under his wings you will find refuge[33]

these words should not be understood as describing God in terms of physical feathers, but as a refuge for frightened children of God to resort to in times of danger just as chicks flee to the wings of their mother.[34] When God did not carry out His warning that Nineveh was to be destroyed in forty days,[35] it was the Ninevites who repented, not God. By their repentance the people of Nineveh transferred themselves from the sphere of God's displeasure to the sphere of His favor. Hence, God was able to cancel the announced judgment because of *their* change, not because of any change in Him. Further-

---

28 Deut. 10:12—11:1.
29 Gen. 18:21.
30 Ex. 32:7-14.
31 Ex. 22:24.

32 II Chron. 16:9.
33 Ps. 91:4.
34 Cf. Matt. 23:37.
35 Jon. 3:4.

more, devout Christians believe that the entire event was foreknown by God, so that the announced judgment was really a divinely ordained means to bring about repentance on the part of the wicked Assyrians. And thus with all the other anthropomorphisms of Scripture: far from being unworthy, they add literary beauty and vividness to the Word of God.

Works in the field of Biblical Theology should be consulted for detailed studies of those institutions which God used Moses to set up: tabernacle, priesthood, sacrificial system, religious calendar, civil law, ceremonial regulations, and the moral law of God. At this point, however, a few remarks must be made about certain sub-Christian ethics which one finds in the law of Moses. Both Exodus and Leviticus allow polygyny[36]; Deuteronomy permits divorce and remarriage[37]; Exodus 21 and 22 prescribe capital punishment for a variety of sins[38]; and the Pentateuch seems to anticipate and to permit the waging of war by Israel.[39]

In view of the teaching of the New Testament on the fact and permanence of monogamy,[40] on the insistence on the practice of absolute love, etc., how are these sub-Christian standards of Mosaism to be interpreted? We reject, of course, the modernistic view that God never told Moses to give such instructions to Israel. We also find it impossible to adopt the historic Protestant view which insists that the Bible teaches clearly from beginning to end a single ethic, a view which is generally employed to justify the swearing of oaths, participation in the military, the divorcing of one's companion, the right of the "innocent party" to remarry, etc. We also feel compelled to reject the Dispensational view that God changes both the terms and obligations which He lays upon His people from each "dispensation" to the next. We believe that the only satisfactory answer to this difficulty is that given by Jesus in connection with the matter of divorce in Matthew 19:

And Pharisees came up to Him and tested Him by asking, "Is it lawful to divorce one's wife for any cause?" He answered, "Have you not read that he who made them from the beginning made them male and female, and said, 'For this reason a man shall leave his father and mother and be joined to his wife, and the two shall become one'? So they are no longer two but one. What therefore God has joined together, let no man put asunder." They said to Him, "Why then did Moses command one to give a certificate of divorce, and to put her away?" He said to them,

36 Ex. 21:10; Lev. 18:17, 18.   38 Ex. 21:12, 15, 16, 17; 22:18, 19.
37 Deut. 24:1-4.   39 Deut. 7:1-3; cf. Judg. 1:1-4.

40 Matt. 5:32; 19:6-8; Mark 10:2-12; Luke 16:18; Rom. 7:1-3.

"For your hardness of heart Moses allowed you to divorce your wives, but from the beginning it was not so. And I say to you: whoever divorces his wife, except for unchastity, and marries another, commits adultery." Some ancient manuscripts add at this point: "And he who marries a divorced woman commits adultery," a phrase which is found in Matthew 5.[41]

6. WISDOM LITERATURE AND POETRY

Evangelical Christians accept the Bible as the inspired Word of God. They, therefore, do not feel any necessity of justifying God for employing various types of literature; it is not within the province of faith to offer criticisms on any type of literature which God chooses to use. Certain difficulties do arise, however, as to the interpretation and meaning of certain books, particularly the group before us in this section.

Certain characteristics run through much of the poetry of the Old Testament, although not altogether confined to the poetical sections. These characteristics include an ornate style, literary exaggeration for the sake of emphasis, multitudes of figures which add beauty and vividness to literature, parallelism of various kinds, a rather large number of acrostics,[42] etc. One finds in the poetry of the Old Testament prayer, praise, aspiration, the struggles of faith, gems of ethical and religious truth, etc. In these books there is also a large element of what might be called human reflection in contrast with direct prophetic messages from God. Israel is never mentioned in Proverbs and the LORD does not appear in Ecclesiastes.[43] Much of the poetry of the Old Testament, if not all, is intended for use in religious devotion.

Job

The Book of Job deals with the problem of suffering: Why must the righteous suffer? The unknown author begins by giving the reader an insight into what was going on in the eternal world before the plans there discussed transpired on earth. God is seen vindicating the character and faith of His good servant Job. The LORD allowed Satan to strip Job of all his possessions and to bereave him of all his children, and finally to take away his health also. In a remarkable literary structure and with keen philosophical insights the author records the reasonings of three of Job's friends and finally

---

41 Matt. 19:3-9.
42 Acrostics in the Hebrew O.T.: Psalms 9 & 10, 25, 34, 37, 111, 112, 119 (8 verses for each letter); Lam. 1, 2, 3, 4; Prov. 31:10-31.
43 Joseph Angus, revised by Samuel G. Green, *The Bible Hand-Book* (New York: Revell, c. 1905), p. 583.

of a fourth. In brief, the point of view of the three men is that suffering is penal and therefore indicates that Job is a sinner. Since his outward life is blameless, however, it must be that Job is a secret sinner or hypocrite. This point of view is highly offensive to Job, who fumes at his former friends for their false accusations. In the end the LORD Himself speaks to Job and brings him to a more appropriate humility.

In the final analysis the book does not solve in a philosophical manner the problem with which it deals. It does not reveal why the righteous have to suffer. The solution rather seems to reside in submission to the will of a righteous and good God. This is the message which Christians can profitably learn from the Book of Job. There is no place, therefore, for the bringing of accusations against those who suffer as if their suffering was evidence of particular blameworthiness. One may also observe in this book how intimately God is concerned with the lives of His children, a point which Jesus stressed vigorously in His teaching. Needless to say, the disapproval of God with the reasoning of Job's friends makes it impossible to regard their remarks as a source or norm of Christian truth.

Psalms

The Psalms are not one unified book but a collection of writings from different persons. It is believed that the superscriptions to the Psalms are not original; they vary, for example, as between the manuscripts of the Hebrew and those of the Septuagint. In the Hebrew Old Testament, seventy-three Psalms are ascribed to David, twelve to Asaph, eleven to the Sons of Korah, one to Moses, etc. The Septuagint adds twelve to those ascribed to David but takes away three from those which are ascribed to David in the Hebrew. In the original Hebrew the Psalms are divided into five books: 1-41, 42-72, 73-89, 90-106, and 107-150. In Books I, IV, and V the predominant name for deity is the LORD; in Book II the usual term is God (Elohim), while in Book III both the LORD and God are employed.

Various classifications of Psalms have been given such as the didactic or teaching Psalms, Psalms of praise and adoration, thanksgiving, devotional, penitential, historical, and Messianic.[44] Professor Franz Delitzsch (1813-90) comments thus on the nature of this collection: "The psalter is also a Pentateuch; the echo of the books of Moses from the heart of Israel. . . . It is the five books of the church to Jehovah as the law is the five books of Jehovah to the church."[45]

44 See listings, *Ibid.*, p. 579.   45 *Ibid.*, p. 569.

And Richard Hooker (c. 1554-1600), the English theologian, describes the Psalms thus: "Heroical magnanimity, exquisite justice, grave moderation, exact wisdom, repentance unfeigned, unwearied patience, the mysteries of God, the sufferings of Christ, the terrors of wrath, the comforts of grace, the works of providence over this world, and the promised joys of that world which is to come; all good, necessary to be either known, or done, or had, this one celestial fountain yieldeth. Let there be any grief or disaster incident into the soul of man, any wound or sickness named, for which there is not in this treasure-book a present comfortable remedy at all times ready to be found."[46] In other words, the Psalms are the outstanding devotional collection of the Old Testament. It should also be mentioned that the New Testament contains a large number of quotations from the Psalms, both as to general doctrinal teaching, and as to the Messiah.

Song of Songs

The Song of Solomon, called in the Hebrew the Song of Songs,[47] is a book which has occasioned perhaps more disagreement among theologians than any other in the Old Testament. The primary question is not so much whether this is a drama or a simpler composition, whether it is the love of Solomon for a Shulammite maiden or a collection of love songs (Canticles), etc., but rather whether the composition is primarily a description of human love or an allegory setting forth the love of God for Israel. Many Bible students who hold the allegorical interpretation also regard it as Messianic, as prefiguring the love of Christ for the church. This is the view which is found in the chapter summaries of some editions of the King James Version. Although various writers in the Old Testament and in the New do compare the relationship of God to His people as that of a husband to his wife, it must be admitted that there is not a word in the book itself which would indicate that it is Messianic or even allegorical. Rather, we must agree with Joseph Angus (1816-1902), who states: "Literally, the whole is a description of wedded love, one of the noblest of human affections. In this aspect the book gives a beautiful representation of the sentiments and manners which prevailed among the Israelites on conjugal and domestic life."[48]

This beautiful little book with its oriental exaggerations and literary embellishments gives the full approval of God to married

---

46 *Ibid.*, p. 568.
47 That is, the greatest or most beautiful song.
48 *Op. cit.*, pp. 595, 596.

love and the sanctity of the home. It therefore becomes a protest against a low view of sex and marriage which would regard them as unworthy of the people of God. And how needful this message is in a world which holds such low views of sex as to be a curious combination of prudery and sensualism. Sanford Calvin Yoder writes: "Almost every writer of the Scripture has something to say about marital loyalty and devotion, and recognizes the fact that these virtues obtain their highest perfection when they are rooted in deep affection and love for each other out of which grow ties that hallow and sanctify relationships that would ordinarily be debasing and degrading. Hence, to accept this song in a literal sense does not lower it to a level that makes it unworthy of a place in the Scripture."[49]

Proverbs

The Book of Proverbs consists of a collection of terse, self-evident, and easily remembered gems of practical wisdom to give a young man the knowledge and discretion needed to attain to a happy and successful life. Dr. Angus observes that the Book of Proverbs is for practical ethics what the Book of Psalms is for devotion.[50] There is a certain universality about the Proverbs which gives the book value for all peoples everywhere. Furthermore, permeating all the writings "strictly religious motives are either presupposed or expressly enjoined."[51] The aim of the book, it should be noted, is practical rather than theological. Concerning its value Dr. Adam Clarke writes: "It is impossible for any description of persons to read the book of Proverbs without profit. Kings and courtiers, as well as those engaged in trade, commerce, agriculture, and the humblest walks of life, may here read lessons of instruction for the regulation of their conduct in their respective circumstances. Fathers, mothers, wives, husbands, sons, daughters, masters, and servants, may here also learn their respective duties; and the most excellent rules are laid down, not only in reference to morality, but to civil piety and economy. Many motives are employed by the wise man to accomplish the end at which he aims; motives derived from honor, interest, love, fear, natural affection, and piety towards God. The principal object he has in view is to inspire deep reverence for God, fear of His judgments, and an ardent love for wisdom and virtue. He exhibits injustice, impiety, profligacy, idleness, imprudence, drunken-

---

49 Sanford Calvin Yoder, *Poetry of the Old Testament* (Scottdale, Pa.: Herald Press, 1948), p. 380.
50 *Op. cit.*, p. 585.
51 *Ibid.*, p. 585.

ness, and almost every vice, in such lively colours as to render every man ashamed of them who has any true respect for his interest, honour, character, or health."[52]

Ecclesiastes

A more difficult book is Ecclesiastes or The Preacher. Undoubtedly the major theme of this book is the emptiness or vanity of life apart from God. The very first chapter stresses this point, showing that all of life has a monotonous and wearisome sameness to those who live without true faith—though it must be admitted that the positive requirement of faith is generally not stated in the book in connection with the negative theme of the emptiness of life. The writer, traditionally Solomon, speaks much of the natural life as such, employing for this purpose the phrase, "under the sun," about twenty-eight times. He describes, in terms which accurately reflect Solomon's experience, how he gave himself to intellectual pursuits, to all kinds of pleasure, always followed with discretion; to a building program of houses, vineyards, gardens, and parks with pools of water, to the acquisition of wealth, and to cultural items such as choruses: "Then I considered all that my hands had done and the toil I had spent in doing it, and behold, all was vanity and a striving after wind, and there was nothing to be gained under the sun."[53] From time to time throughout the book the voice of pessimism, a sort of practical deism, is allowed to express itself, even to the point of denying any consciousness in the afterlife.[54]

A second theme which is expressed from time to time, however, is positive, the enjoyment of the natural blessings of food, labor, and love. "There is nothing better for a man than that he should eat and drink, and find enjoyment in his toil."[55] ". . . it is God's gift to man that every one should eat and drink and take pleasure in all his toil."[56] "Every man also to whom God has given wealth and possessions and power to enjoy them, and to accept his lot and find enjoyment in his toil—this is the gift of God."[57] "Enjoy life with the wife whom you love, all the days of your vain life which he has given you under the sun, because that is your portion in life and in your toil at which you toil under the sun."[58]

There is also a third and most significant theme in Ecclesiastes, namely, the putting of one's trust in God and the rendering of obedi-

52 Commentary on Proverbs, III, p. 700.
53 Eccl. 2:11.
54 Eccl. 9:10; cf. 3:19.
55 Eccl. 2:24.
56 Eccl. 3:13.
57 Eccl. 5:19.
58 Eccl. 9:9.

ence to His laws. "Guard your steps when you go to the house of God."[59] "When you vow a vow to God, do not delay paying it."[60] "I know that it will be well with those who fear God, because they fear before him; but it will not be well with the wicked, neither will he prolong his days like a shadow, because he does not fear before God."[61] "Rejoice, O young man, in your youth, and let your heart cheer you in the days of your youth; walk in the ways of your heart and the sight of your eyes. But know that for all these things God will bring you into judgment."[62] "Remember also your Creator in the days of your youth, before the evil days come, and the years draw nigh, when you will say, 'I have no pleasure in them.' "[63] "The end of the matter; all has been heard. Fear God, and keep his commandments; for this is the whole duty of man. For God will bring every deed into judgment, with every secret thing, whether good or evil."[64]

The Book of Ecclesiastes is thus sort of a commentary on the seventy-third Psalm, which vividly describes the arrogant attitude of the wicked and the deep pessimism of the discouraged saint who receives illumination only when he goes into the sanctuary of God, and who concludes his meditation thus:

> When my soul was embittered,
>   when I was pricked in heart,
> I was stupid and ignorant,
>   I was like a beast toward thee.
> Nevertheless I am continually with thee;
>   thou dost hold my right hand.
> Thou dost guide me with thy counsel,
>   and afterward thou wilt receive me to glory.
> Whom have I in heaven but thee?
>   And there is nothing upon earth that I desire besides thee.
> My flesh and my heart may fail,
>   but God is the strength of my heart and my portion for
>   ever. . . .
> But for me it is good to be near God;
>   I have made the Lord God my refuge,
>   that I may tell of all thy works.[65]

7. PROPHETISM

The Hebrew language contains an idiom, "to put words in the mouth," meaning "to tell someone what to say." Thus, when Joab

59 Eccl. 5:1.
60 Eccl. 5:4.
61 Eccl. 8:12, 13.

62 Eccl. 11:9.
63 Eccl. 12:1.

64 Eccl. 12:13, 14.
65 Ps. 73:21-28.

sent a wise woman to interview King David he instructed her to "speak thus to him. So Joab put the words in her mouth."[66] When King David discerned the hand of Joab in the matter he forced the woman to confess: "It was your servant Joab who bade me; it was he who put all these words in the mouth of your handmaid."[67]

The Lord prepared Isaiah to be His mouthpiece when He had one of the seraphs touch the mouth of the prophet with a burning coal in a vision as he said: " 'Behold, this has touched your lips; your guilt is taken away, and your sin forgiven.' And I heard the voice of the Lord saying, 'Whom shall I send, and who will go for us?' Then I said, 'Here I am! Send me.' And he said, 'Go, and say to this people . . . .' "[68] When Jeremiah received his call he protested to the Lord that he did not know how to speak. Whereupon "the LORD put forth his hand and touched my mouth; and the LORD said to me,

'Behold, I have put my words in your mouth. . . .' "[69]
In a similar passage the Lord also told Isaiah:

And I have put my words in your mouth,
    and hid you in the shadow of my hand . . . .[70]

And to Ezekiel the Lord said: "Son of man, go, get you to the house of Israel, and speak with my words to them."[71] The Lord also told Ezekiel that He would at times close his mouth so that he could not prophesy; "but when I speak with you, I will open your mouth, and you shall say to them, 'Thus says the Lord GOD . . . .' "[72]

The Pentateuch indicates that it was to Moses that God gave His revelations for Israel, for the Lord said to Moses: "See, I make you as God to Pharaoh; and Aaron your brother shall be your prophet."[73] This statement is explained further by the words of the Lord: "And you shall speak to him and put the words in his mouth; and I will be with your mouth and with his mouth, and will teach you what you shall do."[74] In other words, the prophets were God's spokesmen; they did not themselves undertake to be prophets, but God selected them and used them, sometimes contrary to their own wishes. The true prophet was a man who had received a message from God to pass on to His people. "But the prophet who presumes to speak a word in my name which I have not commanded him to speak, or who speaks in the name of other gods, that same prophet shall die."[75] Through Jeremiah the Lord also protested against the

66 II Sam. 14:3.
67 II Sam. 14:19.
68 Isa. 6:7-9.
69 Jer. 1:9.
70 Isa. 51:16.
71 Ezek. 3:4.
72 Ezek. 3:27.
73 Ex. 7:1.
74 Ex. 4:15.
75 Deut. 18:20.

false prophets by saying: "I have heard what the prophets have said who prophesy lies in my name, saying, 'I have dreamed, I have dreamed!' How long shall there be lies in the heart of the prophets who prophesy lies, and who prophesy the deceit of their own heart, who think to make my people forget my name by their dreams which they tell one another, even as their fathers forgot my name for Baal? Let the prophet who has a dream tell the dream, but let him who has my word speak my word faithfully."[76]

When the Lord came upon His prophets and authorized them to deliver a given message, the Scripture often describes this experience as the hand of the Lord coming upon them. For example, it is said of the prophet Elisha that "the hand[77] of the LORD came upon him. And he said, 'Thus says the LORD . . . .' "[78] And of Ezekiel it is said: "The word of the LORD came to Ezekiel the priest . . . and the hand of the LORD was upon him there."[79] Again, "the Spirit lifted me up and took me away . . . the hand of the LORD being strong upon me; and I came to the exiles."[80] "And the hand of the LORD was there upon me; and he said to me . . . ."[81] Ezekiel tells the story of how he received a visitor from Jerusalem. "Now the hand of the LORD had been upon me the evening before the fugitive came; and he had opened my mouth by the time the man came to me in the morning . . . . The word of the LORD came to me . . . ."[82] Ezekiel also combines the expression "the hand of the Lord" with "the visions of God."[83]

A reading of the Old Testament prophets indicates that many times they experienced some sort of vision in connection with their call. Isaiah says:

> For the LORD has poured out upon you
>   a spirit of deep sleep,
> and has closed your eyes, the prophets,
>   and covered your heads, the seers.[84]

The prophets in some cases seem to have seen their messages. "The word which Isaiah the son of Amoz saw concerning Judah and Jerusalem."[85] "The oracle concerning Babylon which Isaiah the son of Amoz saw."[86] "The words of Amos . . . which he saw concerning Israel . . . ."[87] "The word of the LORD that came to Micah . . . which

76 Jer. 23:25-28.
77 Hebrew, "hand"; RSV: "power."
78 II Kings 3:15.
79 Ezek. 1:3.
80 Ezek. 3:14.
81 Ezek. 3:22.

82 Ezek. 33:22, 23.
83 Ezek. 40:1, 2.
84 Isa. 29:10.
85 Isa. 2:1; cf. 1:1.
86 Isa. 13:1.
87 Amos 1:1.

he saw concerning Samaria and Jerusalem."[88] "The book of the vision of Nahum of Elkosh."[89] "The oracle of God which Habakkuk the prophet saw."[90] "This is the vision which the LORD has shown to me,"[91] declared Jeremiah.

The Old Testament also speaks of the spirit of the Lord coming upon His prophets: "Then the spirit of the LORD will come mightily upon you, and you shall prophesy with them and be turned into another man,"[92] said Samuel to Saul. "When they came to Gibeah, behold a band of prophets met him; and the spirit of God came mightily upon him, and he prophesied among them."[93] Zechariah lamented the sin of Israel thus: "They made their hearts like adamant lest they should hear the law and the words which the LORD of hosts had sent by his Spirit through the former prophets."[94] When God shall pour out His spirit upon all men the result will be prophesying.[95]

Because the prophets received their message from the Spirit of God they are sometimes spoken of as men of the spirit:

> The prophet is a fool,
> the man of the spirit is mad.[96]

It was evidently because the Messiah was to be the Lord's great prophet that Isaiah prophesied for God: "I have put my spirit upon him."[97] The prophet Micah also declared:

> But as for me, I am filled with power,
>   with the Spirit of the LORD,
>   and with justice and might,
> to declare to Jacob his transgression
>   and to Israel his sin.[98]

Concerning the false prophets the Lord said:

> I did not send the prophets,
>   yet they ran;
> I did not speak to them,
>   yet they prophesied.[99]

"The prophets are prophesying lies in my name; I did not send them, nor did I command them or speak to them. They are prophesying to you a lying vision, worthless divination, and the deceit of their own minds."[1]

88 Mic. 1:1.
89 Nah. 1:1
90 Hab. 1:1.
91 Jer. 38:21.
92 I Sam. 10:6.

93 I Sam. 10:10.
94 Zech. 7:12.
95 Joel 2:28.
96 Hos. 9:7.

97 Isa. 42:1.
98 Mic. 3:8.
99 Jer. 23:21.
1 Jer. 14:14.

Rationalists may say what they please, but the fact remains that the Old Testament claims that a true prophet did actually speak, not his own words, but the message which the Lord gave to him.[2] This agrees exactly with the testimony of the Apostle Peter who declares concerning the origin of the Scriptures: "And we have the prophetic word made more sure. You will do well to pay attention to this as to a lamp shining in a dark place, until the day dawns and the morning star rises in your hearts. First of all you must understand this, that no prophecy of scripture is a matter of one's own interpretation, because no prophecy ever came by the impulse of man, but men moved by the Holy Spirit spoke from God."[3]

8. *THE WORD MADE FLESH*

All the special revelations of God prior to the incarnation of the eternal Son had this in common: they were merely verbal. A verbal description about a person is always seriously inadequate. As long as we merely hear about someone we cannot say that we truly know that individual. But after the Son of God, the Eternal Word, took upon Himself human nature and lived on earth as a man, Jesus was able to say to Philip: "Have I been with you so long, and yet you do not know me, Philip? He who has seen me has seen the Father; how can you say, 'Show us the Father'?"[4]

The Fourth Gospel gives this beautiful description of the eternal Son of God, the Word, and the significance of His incarnation:

In the beginning was the Word, and the Word was with God, and the Word was *God*. He was in the beginning with God; all things were made through him, and without him was not anything made that was made. In him was life, and the life was the light of men. The light shines in the darkness, and the darkness has not overcome it. . . .

He was in the world, and the world was made through him, yet the world knew him not. He came to his own home, and his own people received him not. But to all who received him, who believed in his name, he gave power to become children of God; who were born, not of blood nor of the will of the flesh nor of the will of man, but of God.

And the Word became flesh and dwelt among us, full of grace and truth; we have beheld his glory, glory as of the only Son from the Father. . . . No one has ever seen God; the only Son, who is in the bosom of the Father, he has made him known.[5]

2 Cf. the excellent and stimulating section on prophetic revelation by Dr. Warfield, *Revelation and Inspiration*, pp. 18-26; *Inspiration and Authority of the Bible*, pp. 86-94. Warfield's articles are classics of scholarship, sound and challenging.
3 II Pet. 1:19-21.
4 John 14:9.
5 John 1:1-5, 10-14, 18.

Turning from the Fourth Gospel to the Letter of Paul to the Colossians, we find two wonderful statements made about Jesus Christ: "He is the image of the invisible God,"[6] and "in Him the whole fulness of deity dwells bodily."[7] This means that Jesus is the photograph of the God who cannot be seen, the full personification of those divine attributes such as love and mercy and holiness which characterize the eternal Father.

The Letter to the Hebrews begins with a majestic statement on the superiority of the revelation which we now enjoy through Jesus Christ to the revelation of God in the Old Testament: "In many and various ways God spoke of old to our fathers by the prophets; but in these last days he has spoken to us by a Son, whom he appointed the heir of all things, through whom also he created the world. He reflects the glory of God and bears the very stamp of his nature, upholding the universe by his word of power."[8] Here the identity of the attributes of Christ and of God is brought out by the expression translated, "the very stamp of his nature," or more literally "the very image of his substance."[9]

Perhaps the best description of the personality and character of the Lord Jesus Christ would be a paraphrase of part of I Corinthians 13:

Jesus is patient and kind; He is not jealous or boastful; He is not arrogant or rude. When Jesus was here on earth He did not insist on His own way but allowed even sinners to have their way with Him. He was not irritable or resentful. He did not rejoice at wrong, but rejoiced in the right. Jesus bears with all the imperfections of His disciples, He always believes in His saints no matter how weak they are, He always hopes for their perseverance, and His love for them endures through all their days.

Jesus also exhibited perfectly the fruit of the Spirit as described in the letter of Paul to the Galatians: Jesus was characterized by "love, joy, peace, patience, kindness, goodness, faithfulness, gentleness, and self-control."[10]

When the Apostle John was on the island of Patmos he was privileged to behold a vision of Jesus Christ, "clothed with a long robe and with a golden girdle round his breast; his head and his hair were white as white wool, white as snow; his eyes were like a flame of fire, his feet were like burnished bronze, refined as in a furnace, and his voice was like the sound of many waters; in his right hand he

---

6 Col. 1:15.   8 Heb. 1:1-3.   10 Gal. 5:22, 23.
7 Col. 1:19 (from Greek).   9 ASV, 1901.

held seven stars, from his mouth issued a sharp two-edged sword, and his face was like the sun shining in full strength."[11] To the terrified apostle the resurrected and ascended Lord said: "Fear not, I am the first and the last, and the living one; I died, and behold I am alive for evermore, and I have the keys of Death and Hades."[12]

It dare not be forgotten, of course, that Jesus was also a prophet in a pre-eminent sense, comparable and yet infinitely above the prophets of the Old Testament. That Jesus was a prophet was recognized repeatedly by the people who came in contact with Him,[13] by the Apostle Peter,[14] by Stephen,[15] and it was asserted in the most vigorous language by Jesus Himself. Jesus declared: "My teaching is not mine, but his who sent me."[16] Again, "The word which you hear is not mine but the Father's who sent me."[17] In His great intercessory prayer Jesus could tell the Father: "I have given them the words which thou gavest me."[18] In other words, Jesus in His personality exhibited the very nature of Almighty God: His holiness, His love, His patience, His goodness.

In His teaching Jesus also brought to Israel the message which God saw that they needed. Our Lord showed the people clearly that faith is not a matter of human works, nor of lip profession, but the surrender of the self to God. Jesus taught the people that the only way to be saved was to believe on the incarnate Lamb of God, and that the only way to please God was to be joined in faith and devotion to God's Son.

When Jesus was through with His earthly ministry and ready to ascend to heaven God had revealed to the race all that He could about Himself. Divine revelation, therefore, culminated in Jesus Christ, in a marvelous sense in His words, and in a supernatural sense in His very being. The Old Testament prophets revealed the will of God as to the total life of Israel: political, social, economic, and religious; they interpreted the law of God which had been given through Moses; they protested in the strongest possible language against formalism and sin; and they spoke much of the glorious kingdom of the Christ. In a similar way the Lord Jesus Christ also revealed the will of God: He interpreted the law of God; He, too, protested against formalism and sin; and the very heart of His teaching concerned the kingdom. Divine revelation truly culminated in Jesus.

11 Rev. 1:13-16.
12 Rev. 1:17, 18.
13 Matt. 21:11; Luke 24:19; 7:16; John 6:14; 4:19; 7:40; 9:17; Mark 6:15.
14 Acts 3:22-26.   16 John 7:16.   18 John 17:8.
15 Acts 7:37.   17 John 14:24.

9. *APOSTOLIC REVELATION*

In the good providence of God and through the inspiration of His Holy Spirit it became the glorious privilege of the apostles to record in writing the story of the incarnation, teaching, death, and resurrection of the Saviour, the Lord Jesus Christ, and to interpret for the early church the meaning of Christian discipleship. The Lord also gave through the Apostle John a beautiful drama to assure a persecuted body of Christians of the ultimate triumph of the kingdom of God.

It has become common in Christian circles to speak of the Bible as the Word of God. This does not seem to be the usual sense of the expression in the writings of the apostles, however. Jesus on at least two occasions does seem to refer to the will of God as recorded in the Old Testament as the Word of God.[19] More commonly the expression, "the word," is used in the Gospels to refer to the teaching about God and His kingdom, usually as given by Christ. Typical expressions are the following: "And he was preaching the word to them"[20]; "And these are the ones along the path, where the word is sown"[21]; "With many such parables he spoke the word to them, as they were able to hear it"[22]; "While the people pressed upon him to hear the word of God, he was standing by the lake of Gennesaret"[23]; "Now the parable is this: The seed is the word of God"[24]; "Blessed rather are those who hear the word of God and keep it!"[25]

In the Acts and the Epistles the expression, "the word" or "the word of God," refers primarily to the message of the Gospel and the ministry of preaching that Gospel. Concerning the results of apostolic preaching Luke records: "But many of those who heard the word believed."[26] In days of persecution the saints prayed: "And now, Lord, look upon their threats, and grant to thy servants to speak thy word with all boldness."[27] "And they were all filled with the Holy Spirit and spoke the word of God with boldness."[28] "It is not right that we should give up preaching the word of God to serve tables."[29] "Now those who were scattered went about preaching the word."[30] "When the apostles at Jerusalem heard that Samaria had received the word of God, they sent to them Peter and John."[31] When the Book of Acts three times speaks of the Word of God as growing or increasing it evidently is indicating that the preaching

19 Mark 7:13; John 10:35.
20 Mark 2:2.
21 Mark 4:15.
22 Mark 4:33.
23 Luke 5:1.
24 Luke 8:11.
25 Luke 11:28.
26 Acts 4:4.
27 Acts 4:29.
28 Acts 4:31.
29 Acts 6:2.
30 Acts 8:4.
31 Acts 8:14.

of the Word was occurring more widely and enjoying blessed success.[32]

Several times in the New Testament Christ Himself is spoken of as the Word or the Word of God,[33] especially in the writings of the Apostle John. Nevertheless, the predominant meaning of the Word from Acts to Revelation seems to be the preaching of the Gospel of Jesus Christ. It is thus used in Acts,[34] Galatians,[35] Ephesians,[36] Philippians,[37] and the pastoral epistles.[38] Quite frequently the fuller expression, "the word of God,"[39] occurs or, "the good word of God."[40] But the preaching of the Gospel is also spoken of as "the word of the Lord,"[41] "the word of Christ,"[42] "the word of his grace,"[43] "the word of reconciliation,"[44] "the word of truth,"[45] "the word of life,"[46] and "the living and abiding word of God."[47]

In a number of epistles, however, the "word of God" also seems to refer to the written Old Testament: "For the word of God is living and active, sharper than any two-edged sword, . . . discerning the thoughts and intentions of the heart."[48] "Preach the word . . ."[49] ". . . the sword of the Spirit, which is the word of God."[50]

Peter calls the prophetic message the "word of prophecy."[51] The statement in the Letter to the Hebrews that "the world was created by the word of God,"[52] is apparently a reference to the Old Testament teaching of creation by divine fiat, and is thus an allusion to Psalm 33, which declares

By the word of the LORD the heavens were made,
    and all their host by the breath of his mouth.[53]

It seems therefore to be clear that when the New Testament speaks of the Word of God it is referring fundamentally to the blessed message of salvation, promised in the Old Testament era and fulfilled in the New, which God is offering to the world in Jesus Christ on condition of repentance and faith. The heart of the Gospel, therefore, is not an ethic or a philosophy but the message or word of reconciliation that God has by Christ's death reconciled the world

---

32 Acts 6:7; 12:24; 19:20.
33 John 1:1, 14; Rev. 19:13.
34 Acts 4:4; 4:29; 4:31; 6:2; 6:4; 8:4; 8:14.
35 Gal. 6:6.
36 Eph. 5:26.
37 Phil. 1:14.
38 I Tim. 5:17; II Tim. 4:2.
39 Acts 4:31; 17:13; 18:11; Rom. 9:6; 10:17; Eph. 6:17; etc.
40 Heb. 6:5.
41 Acts 13:49; 15:35, 36; 16:32; 19:10; I Thess. 1:8; 4:15; II Thess. 3:2.
42 Col. 3:16.
43 Acts 20:32.
44 II Cor. 5:19.
45 II Cor. 6:7; Eph. 1:13; II Tim. 2:15.
46 Phil. 2:16; I John 1:1.
47 I Pet. 1:23.
48 Heb. 4:12.
49 II Tim. 4:2.
50 Eph. 6:17.
51 II Pet. 1:19.
52 Heb. 11:3.
53 Ps. 33:6.

unto Himself so that sinners may be saved by accepting Jesus as Saviour and Lord. This was well expressed by the Apostle Paul thus: "The word is near you, on your lips and in your heart (that is, the word of faith which we preach); because, if you confess with your lips that Jesus is Lord and believe in your heart that God raised him from the dead, you will be saved. For man believes with his heart and so is justified, and he confesses with his lips and so is saved. The scripture says, 'No one who believes in him will be put to shame.' For there is no distinction between Jew and Greek; the same Lord is Lord of all and bestows his riches upon all who call upon him. For 'every one who calls upon the name of the Lord will be saved.' "[54] In other words, "the word" is "the word of faith which we preach." The Apostle Peter likewise speaks of "the living and abiding word of God,"[55] "the word of the Lord . . . . That word is the good news [Gospel] which was preached to you."[56]

Apart from the Book of Revelation the writings of the New Testament are of an altogether different character than those of the Old. As they write the apostles exhibit the tremendous significance of Pentecost. The attributes and will of God have been fully revealed in Jesus Christ and they themselves are always "filled" with the Holy Spirit who guides and helps them in their Christian service according to His good pleasure. Ordinarily, there is no need, therefore, for God to give the apostles special revelations and visions for the daily work of leading the church. The apostles are not dependent upon the exceptional manifestation of God's Spirit for the writing of their epistles. They give no evidence that they were instructed in vision or by special revelations from God that they should write the Gospels or the Epistles. Furthermore, when they did decide to write they do not generally seem to have received any particular special revelations from God as to the content of their messages.

A good example of the naturalness of the New Testament writings is found in the prologue to Luke's Gospel. Luke indicates three things: First, the reason he wrote was that it seemed good to him; he does not seem to have been given a special commission like the prophets of old. Secondly, Luke knew what to write because he had as a good historian made an accurate investigation of the facts of Gospel history from the beginning; he does not seem to have sat down and received by special revelations from God the materials of Gospel history. Thirdly, Luke indicates that the facts of the Gospel *kerygma* were reliable because they rest on the accounts of eye-

54 Rom. 10:8-13.   55 I Pet. 1:23.   56 I Pet. 1:25.

witnesses and ministers of the Word; he does not appeal to the fact that he received these facts in visions or otherwise in a miraculous manner from God. The same type of atmosphere seems to pervade the Book of Acts as well as the New Testament epistles. The Book of Revelation, however, does contain the record of a number of visions which the Apostle John received quite in the manner of some of the Old Testament prophets.

There is another factor in the books of the New Testament which merits careful notice. The apostles had the joyful assurance that their Christian readers were in the same possession of the Holy Spirit as they themselves were. The epistles, therefore, do not become official decrees issued by spiritual superiors to helpless infants. Rather, the apostles are conscious that their readers have already been born again by the Holy Spirit, they have been sanctified, and they are being led by the Holy Spirit in such a way that the apostles can have the assurance that their readers are spiritually receptive to the reminders and further suggestions which they are presenting to them. One may indeed say that the apostles seem to assume the spiritual competence of their Christian readers: those who receive the epistles are not in the same need of special revelations from God as was Israel of old. They now have an anointing from the Holy Spirit.

The epistles, therefore, become messages from older brothers to younger believers, to Christians who enjoy the full blessings of the Holy Spirit. Hence, the Apostle Paul is able to tell his readers: "You have no need to have any one write to you, for you yourselves have been taught by God to love one another;"[57] and in a similar way the Apostle John says: "The anointing which you have received from him abides in you, and you have no need that any one should teach you."[58] The apostles do not need to come to Christians with official decrees received from God in visions; all they need to do is remind regenerated believers of their standing in Christ and appeal to them to realize in daily life what they already enjoy in their union with the Lord Jesus Christ. Those who are spiritual will cheerfully accept the instructions of the apostolic writings.

The spiritual hierarchy is therefore gone. There is no longer any need for priests or prophets, for all God's children possess the Holy Spirit as their sufficient guide, and the revelation of God in Jesus Christ is full and complete. Every believer enjoys the same union with Christ as do the ministers of the Word. Pastors and

---

57 I Thess. 4:9.   58 I John 2:27; cf. 2:20.

[handwritten marginal note:] If this be true, can the epistles be used to "convert" non-believers?

teachers enjoy no spiritual superiority over the other members of the church. God has now fulfilled His promise to put His laws on our hearts and to write them on our minds. There is no longer any need for a special prophet to teach his fellow or his brother saying, "Know the Lord," for all believers from the youngest to the most mature already know their God through Jesus Christ. "Christ has obtained a ministry which is as much more excellent than the old as the covenant he mediates is better, since it is enacted on better promises."[59]

10. THE INSPIRATION OF THE SCRIPTURES

The Bible does not present a philosophical exposition of the subject of inspiration[60] any more than it gives a theological doctrine of revelation, of the atonement, of eternity, etc. Nevertheless, the Scriptures do assume their full authority and reliability as viewed in reference to their central purpose, the presentation of divine redemption. The apostles of Christ presented as their final authority, gegraptai, "it is written," indicating that the fact that a statement can be backed up with the authority of the Old Testament settles the matter. The Greek word gegraptai is used seventy-three times in the New Testament exclusive of parallels.[61] The expression is used interchangeably with an appeal to what "the scriptures" state. The phrase, "it is written," is used of each section of the Old Testament: Law, Prophets, and Hagiographa. Paul, for example, describes the Gospel as that which "he promised beforehand through his prophets in the holy scriptures."[62] The basic items of Gospel history were all recorded by God in the Scriptures: "For I delivered to you as of first importance what I also received, that Christ died for our sins in accordance with the scriptures, that he was buried, that he was raised on the third day in accordance with the scriptures, and that he appeared to Cephas, then to the twelve.[63]

The writer of the Letter to the Hebrews begins by stating: "In many and various ways God spoke of old to our fathers by the prophets; but in these last days he has spoken to us by a Son, whom he appointed the heir of all things, through whom also he created the world."[64] In showing the superiority of Christ to all else the writer continues:

---

59 Heb. 8:6.
60 See Warfield's great books on revelation and inspiration: note 2, above, passim; also the Westminster Theological Seminary Faculty symposium, The Infallible Word (Philadelphia: The Presbyterian Guardian Publishing Co., 1946); and Loraine Boettner, The Inspiration of the Scriptures (Grand Rapids, Mich.: Eerdmans, 1940).
61 H. S. Miller, General Biblical Introduction, p. 46. This is a useful and reliable book.
62 Rom. 1:2.   63 I Cor. 15:3-5.   64 Heb. 1:1, 2 (Greek: worlds).

> For to what angel did God ever say,
>   "Thou art my Son,
>   today I have begotten thee"?
> Or again,
>   "I will be to him a father,
>   and he shall be to me a son"?
> And again, when he brings the first-
> born into the world, he says,
>   "Let all God's angels worship him."[65]

It should be noted how easily and naturally this writer assumes that God is the author of the words which he is quoting out of the Old Testament.   He continues:

> And again, when he brings the first-
> born into the world, he says,
>   "Let all God's angels worship him."
> Of his angels he says,
>   "Who makes his angels winds,
>   and his servants flames of fire."
> But of the Son he says,
>   "Thy throne, O God, is for ever and ever,
>   the righteous scepter is the scepter of thy kingdom." [66]

Because the writers of the New Testament regard the Scriptures as given by God and therefore authoritative, and because they recognize Christ as the central gift of God to the world and therefore the center of Biblical interest, the New Testament constantly regards the Old Testament as being fulfilled by Jesus Christ. This is true of every writer.   Matthew records how Jesus indicated the necessity of His going to the cross; He would have been able to have called to His side sufficient angels to rescue Him: "But how then should the scriptures be fulfilled, that it must be so?"[67]   Mark indicates that the Gospel began, "As it is written in Isaiah the prophet."[68]   Luke includes in his Gospel the account of how Jesus read from the prophet Isaiah in the synagogue at Nazareth and said: "Today this scripture has been fulfilled in your hearing."[69]   The Apostle John also says frequently that various events transpired "that the scripture may be fulfilled."[70]   The soldiers did not rend the tunic of Jesus and thus fulfilled the Scripture.[71]   Even the remark of Jesus, "I thirst," is a fulfillment of Scripture.[72]   One of the soldiers pierced the side of

65 Heb. 1:5, 6.
66 Heb. 1:6-8.
67 Matt. 26:54.

68 Mark 1:2.
69 Luke 4:21.
70 John 13:18; 15:25; 17:12.

71 John 19:24.
72 John 19:28.

Jesus with a spear, "that the scripture might be fulfilled."[73] "And again another scripture says, 'They shall look on him whom they have pierced.' "[74] According to the Acts Peter explained the fall of Judas with the expression: "The scripture had to be fulfilled."[75] The tragic events connected with the end of Judas had all been foreseen, "For it is written in the book of Psalms. . . ."[76] After Paul and Silas had been released from prison at Philippi they came to Thessalonica. "And Paul went in, as was his custom, and for three weeks he argued with them from the scriptures, explaining and proving that it was necessary for the Christ to suffer and to rise from the dead, and saying, 'This Jesus, whom I proclaim to you, is the Christ.' "[77] And in the writing of his epistles the Apostle Paul constantly appeals to the Old Testament: "For what does the scripture say?"[78] "Do you not know what the scripture says of Elijah, how he pleads with God against Israel?"[79] According to James, Abraham proved the validity of his faith by his obedience to God, "And the scripture was fulfilled . . . ."[80]

In a recent tabulation it was found: (1) that the five books of the Law are called Scripture ten times in the New Testament; (2) the prophets, mostly Isaiah, are referred to as Scripture eleven times; and (3) the Hagiographa, the third section of the Hebrew Old Testament, is called Scripture eleven times, most of these quotations from the Hagiographa being taken from the Psalms.[81]

Perhaps even more impressive than the phrase, "it is written," or the appeal to Old Testament passages as "Scripture," is the way the writings of the Old Testament are ascribed to the Holy Spirit. According to The Acts Peter said, "The scripture had to be fulfilled, which the Holy Spirit spoke beforehand by the mouth of David."[82] On a later ocasion the apostolic church prayed: "Sovereign Lord, who didst make the heaven and the earth and the sea and everything in them, who by the mouth of our father David, thy servant, didst say by the Holy Spirit . . . ."[83] When the Apostle Paul observed the unbelief of many Israelites he remarked: "The Holy Spirit was right in saying to your fathers through Isaiah the prophet . . . ."[84] When the writer of the Letter to the Hebrews wishes to quote an Old Testament passage he says: "Therefore, as the Holy Spirit says . . . ."[85] In referring to the priestly customs and the construction of the taber-

---

73 John 19:36.
74 John 19:37.
75 Acts 1:16.
76 Acts 1:20.
77 Acts 17:2, 3.
78 Rom. 4:3.
79 Rom. 11:2.

80 Jas. 2:23.
81 H. S. Miller, op. cit., p. 46.
82 Acts 1:16.
83 Acts 4:24, 25, RSV (cf. ASV).
84 Acts 28:25.
85 Heb. 3:7.

nacle the Hebrew Letter also states: "By this the Holy Spirit indicates that the way into the sanctuary is not yet opened as long as the outer tent is still standing."[86] And in discussing the blessings of the New Covenant Hebrews adds: "And the Holy Spirit also bears witness to us . . . . Then he adds . . . ."[87] And the Apostle Peter states, "The prophets who prophesied of the grace that was to be yours searched and inquired about this salvation; they inquired what person or time was indicated by the Spirit of Christ within them when predicting the sufferings of Christ and the subsequent glory."[88] Furthermore, "no prophecy of scripture is a matter of one's own interpretation, because no prophecy ever came by the impulse of man, but men moved by the Holy Spirit spoke from God."[89]

One of the strongest statements of the entire New Testament is that of the Apostle Paul: "All scripture is inspired by God and profitable for teaching, for reproof, for correction, and for training in righteousness, that the man of God may be complete, equipped for every good work."[90]

While it is true that the New Testament writers do not attempt to explain the method employed by the Holy Spirit in the giving of the Scriptures, it is evident that they were assured of their complete reliability by the sheer fact that they were given by the Holy Spirit. The critical attitude toward the Scriptures on the part of some modern theologians stands in sharp contrast to the high view of the Bible found in the Scriptures themselves. Christians of a simple faith will accept the Biblical doctrine of the Scriptures just as they accept the Biblical doctrine of prayer, or miracles, or the atonement, or heaven.

It is possible, however, to go to the other extreme and to regard the Bible only as a sort of divine oracle which came down from heaven through the activity of the Holy Spirit and as therefore having no marks of its human authors. This point of view would also be wrong. The Bible also gives abundant evidence of the fact that it has human authorship. The Bible contains what might be called the conscious exaggeration of common people. One can almost hear the excited comments of the children of Israel when the plague struck the cattle of Egypt but passed over those of the Israelites: "All the cattle of the Egyptians died, but of the cattle of the people of Israel not one died"[91]—and yet in the same chapter the servants of Pharaoh who feared the word of the Lord "made his slaves and his cattle flee

86 Heb. 9:8.

87 Heb. 10:15, 17.

88 I Pet. 1:10, 11.

89 II Pet. 1:20, 21.

90 II Tim. 3:16, 17.

91 Ex. 9:6.

into the houses."[92] The Bible also contains the expression of human emotions such as disgust, discouragement, hope, aspiration, joy, and sorrow, and frequent accounts of the struggles and trials and temptations of various saints of God. Even the accounts of historical events such as are recorded in the Gospels are told in simple honesty as seen by various observers with details which modern readers find difficult to harmonize.[93] The fact that style and vocabulary vary sharply from writer to writer in the Bible is adequate proof that inspiration does not mean mechanical dictation.[94] Furthermore, the background and experience of the writer is somewhat in evidence in various books of the Bible. Mark's account of the woman who had been healed of her hemorrhage indicates with Peter's bluntness[95] that the woman had not only spent all her wealth on various physicians but also that she was growing worse.[96] Luke, himself a physician, records with discreet courtesy that the woman "could not be healed by any one."[97]

It is, indeed, fortunate that the Bible was not written in the form of an oracle from heaven, without any evidence of human emotion or experience. The fact is that the Bible employs the language of common people in everyday life as they experience their trials and difficulties and receive divine grace from God. It is just these truly human factors which make the Bible meaningful to millions of people in all ages of the world. Fortunate, indeed, it is that the Lord did not allow His Word to be written in the language of science, philosophy, and theology. The purpose of the inspiration of the Scriptures is to make the sacred writings able to instruct us for salvation through faith in Christ Jesus, "that the man of God may be complete, equipped for every good work."[98]

If there is any question about the inspiration of any portion of the Bible it would be in the Old Testament. There is universal agreement in Christendom that the relationship of the Old Testament to the New is that of fulfillment. Sixteen centuries ago Augustine said that: "The New is in the Old contained; the Old is by the New explained."[99] It is impossible to understand the true nature of

92 Ex. 9:20.
93 Matt. 8:5-10; Luke 7:2-10, e.g.
94 Not to be confused with verbal inspiration as in Angus-Green, *The Bible Hand-Book*, p. 120. (Otherwise a most useful and fine book.)
95 Papias, A.D. 140, says that Mark had been "Peter's interpreter" and wrote down "such things as he remembered" of Peter's telling of the Gospel narratives. Eusebius, *Hist. Eccles.*, iii, 39.)
96 Mark 5:26.
97 Luke 8:43.
98 II Tim. 3:15-17.
99 "Novum Testamentum in Vetere latet, Vetus in Novo patet." Cited in Agnus-Green, *op. cit.*, p. 226 n. The above is a loose paraphrase.

the Bible without an appreciation of the principle of progressive revelation. The New Testament is obviously superior to the Old in every way: in its ethics, its theology, and in its uniform literary quality. This means that it is the inspiration of the Old Testament which is most in need of demonstration and of that inspiration the New Testament leaves no doubt whatsoever.

Just as God in days of old spoke to Israel through the prophets, so He has spoken to the church through Christ and the apostles of the New Testament. The Gospel of John is especially clear as to the divine authority with which Jesus spoke: "The words that I have spoken to you are spirit and life."[1] Again Jesus said: "I have not spoken on my own authority; the Father who sent me has himself given me commandment what to say and what to speak. And I know that his commandment is eternal life. What I say, therefore, I say as the Father has bidden me."[2] "My teaching is not mine, but his who sent me."[3] "And the word which you hear is not mine but the Father's who sent me."[4] In His high priestly prayer Jesus told the Father: "I have given them the words which thou gavest me, and they have received them and know in truth that I came from thee."[5] "I have given them thy word."[6] For this reason the Letter to the Hebrews begins: "In many and various ways God spoke of old to our fathers by the prophets; but in these last days he has spoken to us by a Son . . . ."[7]

In a general way Jesus told the apostles, "And I will pray the Father, and he will give you another Counselor, to be with you for ever, even the Spirit of truth, whom the world cannot receive, because it neither sees him nor knows him; you know him, for he dwells with you, and will be in you."[8] And then in a more direct way Jesus added: "These things I have spoken to you, while I am still with you. But the Counselor, the Holy Spirit, whom the Father will send in my name, he will teach you all things, and bring to your remembrance all that I have said to you."[9] This is a most significant promise, for it indicates that the Holy Spirit would enable the apostles to teach and write the Word of Christ in a reliable manner. Just before He ascended our Lord again promised the apostles that He would confer upon them power to witness effectively: "But you shall receive power when the Holy Spirit has come upon you; and you shall be witnesses in Jerusalem and in all Judea and Samaria and to

---

1 John 6:63.

2 John 12:49, 50.

3 John 7:16.

4 John 14:24.

5 John 17:8.

6 John 17:14.

7 Heb. 1:2.

8 John 14:16, 17.

9 John 14:25, 26; cf. 16:13.

the end of the earth."[10] In his very first letter the Apostle Paul indicates an awareness of this Holy Spirit enablement: "And we also thank God constantly for this, that when you received the word of God which you heard from us, you accepted it not as the word of men but as what it really is, the word of God, which is at work in you believers."[11] And in a later letter Paul adds: "Now we have received not the spirit of the world, but the Spirit which is from God, that we might understand the gifts bestowed on us by God. And we impart this in words not taught by human wisdom but taught by the Spirit, interpreting spiritual truths to those who possess the Spirit."[12] Because Paul was being used of the Holy Spirit as a teacher and writer in the apostolic church he was able to write: "Finally, brethren, we beseech and exhort you in the Lord Jesus, that as you have learned from us how you ought to live and to please God, just as you are doing, you do so more and more. For you know what instructions we gave you through the Lord Jesus."[13] After giving certain specific directions to the church the apostle continues: "Therefore whoever disregards this, disregards not man but God, who gives his Holy Spirit to you."[14] And when the apostle gave his teaching concerning the return of Jesus he did it "by the word of the Lord."[15] To a somewhat unspiritual church which stood in need of apostolic correction Paul gave a solemn warning that when he would come again he would not spare them, "since you desire proof that Christ is speaking in me."[16] And concerning the preaching of the Gospel by the apostles, the Letter to the Hebrews states: "It was declared at first by the Lord, and it was attested to us by those who heard him, while God also bore witness by signs and wonders and various miracles and by gifts of the Holy Spirit distributed according to his own will."[17]

It is undoubtedly the Book of Revelation which most resembles certain of the Old Testament books, and it is precisely the Revelation which speaks most frequently of its being given by the Holy Spirit or by God or by Jesus Christ: "The revelation of Jesus Christ, which God gave him to show to his servants what must soon take place; and he made it known by sending his angel to his servant John, to bear witness to the word of God and to the testimony of Jesus Christ, even to all that he saw."[18] And John adds: "I was in the Spirit on the Lord's day, and I heard behind me a loud voice like a trumpet saying, 'Write what you see in a book and send it to the seven churches

10 Acts 1:8.
11 I Thess. 2:13.
12 I Cor. 2:12, 13.
13 I Thess. 4:1, 2.
14 I Thess. 4:8.

15 I Thess. 4:15.
16 II Cor. 13:3; cf. II Thess. 3:6, 12, 14.
17 Heb. 2:3, 4.
18 Rev. 1:1, 2.

. . . .' "[19] And a little later the apostle was called up into heaven. "At once I was in the Spirit, and lo, a throne stood in heaven, with one seated on the throne!"[20] "And I heard a voice from heaven saying, 'Write this: Blessed are the dead who die in the Lord henceforth.' 'Blessed indeed,' says the Spirit, 'that they may rest from their labors, for their deeds follow them!' "[21]

The inspiration of New Testament writings is explicitly asserted when Paul quotes the Gospel of Luke as Scripture,[22] and when Peter refers to Paul's epistles as Scripture also.[23] In I Timothy Paul teaches the principles of ministerial support saying: "Let the elders who rule well be counted worthy of double honor, especially those who labor in preaching and teaching; for the scripture says, 'You shall not muzzle an ox when it is treading out the grain' [Deuteronomy 25:4], and, 'The laborer deserves his wages' [Luke 10:7]."[24]

In considering the data of divine revelation and observing how the New Testament builds squarely upon the Old, asserting time and again that the promises and prophecies of the Old Testament were given by God through the Holy Spirit, and in observing how the apostles and writers of the New Testament were given Holy Spirit enablement to write the truth, what name should be given to the view of inspiration which is taught in the Bible? It should be observed that this is a theological rather than a Biblical question, for the Bible nowhere assigns a name to the inspiration which is taught in it.

It has become a commonplace among evangelical Christians to apply the terms "plenary" and "verbal" to the theory of inspiration, by which is meant that all the Scripture is inspired of God (and this is indeed true) and that the very words of Scripture may be relied upon (and this is also true); however, it must be admitted that it is possible to describe inspiration in such a way as to freeze it into a hard and mechanical theory which cannot be completely harmonized with the facts. While it is true that New Testament writers may appeal even to the form of a word on occasion,[25] yet it is also true that they are oftentimes satisfied to give the sense of a passage rather than to quote it verbatim,[26] and furthermore they often quote either verbatim or giving the sense of what is found in the Septuagint rather than the Hebrew original, even when the Septuagint deviates markedly from the Hebrew text as we have it.[27] Dean Burgon

---

19 Rev. 1:10, 11.
20 Rev. 4:2.
21 Rev. 14:13.
22 I Tim. 5:18.
23 II Pet. 3:15, 16.

24 I Tim. 5:17, 18.
25 Gal. 3:16 (Greek: seed, not seeds), e.g.
26 Matt. 2:6, e.g.
27 Heb. 10:5, e.g.

stated the theory of verbal inspiration almost in mechanical terms when he wrote: "The Bible is none other than the voice of Him that sitteth upon the throne. Every book of it, every chapter of it, every verse of it, every word of it, every syllable of it . . . , every letter of it, is the direct utterance of the Most High. . . . The Bible is none other than the Word of God, not some part of it more, some part of it less, but all alike the utterance of Him who sitteth upon the throne, faultless, unerring, supreme."[28] If one would read this statement of Dean Burgon before examining the Bible he would hardly be prepared for the human factors of individual style and vocabulary, the free way the Old Testament is quoted in the New, the expression of various human emotions and attitudes, etc., which one finds in the Bible.

As a matter of fact, the truth about the Bible is that the Scriptures are paradoxically both the Word of God and the word of man. All Scripture is inspired of God and profitable for doctrine, and yet all the Scriptures were written by human beings and on every page contain evidences of human authorship. These evidences of human composition do not amount to misleading teaching or doctrinal error, to be sure. Nevertheless, it is possible to overemphasize the divine factor in the giving of the Scriptures in such a way that honest students are shaken in their faith when they discover what appear to be minor discrepancies in parallel passages, verses which express human emotion rather than a divine word, etc. Perhaps a good name for the view of inspiration which best expresses the high view of the Bible which the Scriptures themselves present, while at the same time recognizing the human factor, would be the term *dynamical*.[29]

An analogy will help to make clear the difficulty which the present discussion is seeking to avoid. It would be possible to collect from the Gospels and Epistles a great array of statements pertaining to the Lord Jesus which would indicate that He was the eternal Son of God, that He came down from heaven, that it was not necessary for Him to ask about anyone because He knew what was in man, that He was able to still the storm, to heal the sick, to raise the dead, etc. If one would consistently speak only of these evidences of the true deity of our Lord, it might come as somewhat of a shock to an immature Christian to learn that Jesus was also human, that He had to sleep, that He needed to eat, that He was tempted, and that He died. The solution, however, does not lie in a denial of the deity of

28 Angus-Green, *op cit.*, p. 119 n.
29 Cf. H. Orton Wiley, *Christian Theology* (Kansas City, Mo.: Beacon Hill Press, 1940), I pp. 176, 177.

Christ nor of His sinlessness. So it is with the Scriptures. One does not need to deny the high view of inspiration in order to acknowledge the evidences of human authorship in the Bible. The fact that Jesus was both human and divine may not be used to deny His sinlessness and His deity. In precisely the same way the fact that the Bible contains a human element should not be pressed to the point of asserting that it contains error or is not able to make people wise unto salvation.[30]

11. *THE CANON OF SCRIPTURE*

Old Testament

The term "canon" means that God gave the Scriptures to mankind and that these Scriptures are qualitatively different from all other books. The term "canon" seems originally to have meant a reed or rod used for measuring, and thus came to signify that which is normative. As George L. Robinson indicates in his excellent article on the canon of the Old Testament, the problem of how the Christian Church came to accept its present list of thirty-nine Old Testament books is "a purely historical investigation."[31]

From some time before the Christian era, down to the present, the Jews have accepted our thirty-nine books of the Old Testament. However, since they counted Ezra and Nehemiah as one book, and since they did not divide the books of Samuel, Kings, and Chronicles, and since the twelve minor prophets were counted as one book, the Jews secured a total of twenty-four books. These books, as was noted earlier, were arranged in the Hebrew canon as follows:

THE LAW: [*five books*]
    Genesis, Exodus, Leviticus, Numbers, Deuteronomy
THE PROPHETS: [*eight books*]
    The Former Prophets: Joshua, Judges, Samuel, Kings
    The Latter Prophets: Isaiah, Jeremiah, Ezekiel, The Twelve
THE WRITINGS (in Greek, Hagiographa):   [*eleven books*]
    Psalms, Job, Proverbs
    The Five Rolls:
      Ruth
      Song of Songs
      Ecclesiastes
      Lamentations
      Esther
    Daniel, Ezra-Nehemiah, Chronicles

30 II Tim. 3:15, ASV and AV.
31 *I.S.B.E.*, I, pp. 554-63; citation from p. 554.

These three divisions of the Jewish canon of the Old Testament seem to have been in existence several centuries before Christ. The *Prologue* to *Ecclesiasticus,* written by Jesus ben Sirach, grandson of the author of the book who bore the same name, uses expressions such as the following in connection with the canonical books: "The Law and The Prophets and . . . others that have followed their steps"; "The Law and The Prophets and other books of our fathers"; "The Law itself, and The Prophets, and the rest of the books."[32] This Prologue is to be dated about 132 B.C.

It is generally believed that the five books of The Law were acknowledged as of divine authority somewhat earlier in the history of Israel than were the books of The Prophets and The Writings. It is perhaps difficult to account for the particular arrangement of The Prophets and The Writings, for the Former Prophets included the historical books of Joshua, Judges, Samuel, and Kings, while the later historical books of Ezra-Nehemiah and Chronicles, and surprisingly the Book of Daniel, are included in The Writings. Some scholars hold that there were three stages in the process of canonization, so that The Law was first canonized, at a later date The Prophets, and still later The Writings. It is indeed likely that The Law was recognized as of divine authority earlier than The Prophets and The Writings, if for no other reason because it was composed so much earlier.[33] There seems to be no direct evidence, however, to indicate any particular difference in point of time as between the canonization of the section known as The Prophets and that of The Writings. There is no satisfactory answer as to why Daniel is included with The Writings rather than The Prophets, except for the fact that Daniel seems to have had the prophetic gift, but not the office of prophet in quite the same sense as did the other writing prophets. Daniel was actually a statesman whom God used to write prophecy, but was not a prophet by profession.[34]

The fact that the canon of the Jews consisted of the twenty-four books listed above, no more and no less, rests upon a firm historical foundation. By the time of Christ, how long before is not known, the Jews had a tradition that inspiration had ceased with Malachi, who prophesied in the fifth century B.C. Mention has already been made of the tripartite division in the Prologue to Ecclesiasticus of approximately the year 132 B.C. Even more definite is the testimony of Josephus (A.D. 37-100), who writes:

32 *The Apocrypha* (London: Bagster, n.d.), p. 59.
33 The Pentateuch is here recognized as Mosaic.
34 Cf. H. S. Miller, *General Biblical Introduction,* p. 94. Post-exilic books of those with the office of prophet are in the section of the "Prophets": Hag., Zech., and Mal.

For we have not an innumerable multitude of books among us, disagreeing from and contradicting one another [as the Greeks have], but only twenty-two books[35] which contain the records of all the past times; which are justly believed to be divine; and of them five belong to Moses, which contain his laws and the traditions of the origin of mankind till his death. This interval of time was little short of three thousand years; but as to the time from the death of Moses till the reign of Artaxerxes, King of Persia, who reigned after Xerxes, the prophets, who were after Moses, wrote down what was done in their times in thirteen books.[36] The remaining four books contain hymns to God, and precepts for the conduct of human life.[37] It is true, our history has been written since Artaxerxes[38] very particularly, but hath not been esteemed of the like authority with the former by our forefathers, because there hath not been an exact succession of prophets since that time; and how firmly we have given credit to those books of our own nation, is evident by what we do; for during so many ages as have already passed, no one has been so bold as either to add anything to them, to take anything from them, or to make any change in them; but it becomes natural to all Jews, immediately and from their very birth, to esteem those books to contain divine doctrines, and to persist in them, and if occasion be, willingly to die for them. For it is no new thing for our captives, many of them in number, and frequently in time, to be seen to endure racks and deaths of all kinds upon the theatres that they may not be obliged to say one word against our laws and the records that contained them. . . .[39]

It would appear clearly that by *The Law* Josephus has in mind the five books of Genesis, Exodus, Leviticus, Numbers, and Deuteronomy. His counting of *The Prophets* as being thirteen books, however, seems to be his own enumeration for the benefit of readers who were not familiar with the Jewish canon; Josephus is giving a topical listing rather than reporting strictly on the tripartite division of the Old Testament. In other words, Josephus reaches into Part III of the Jewish canon and lifts out the five books which are either historical or prophetic in order to get this counting of thirteen. The remaining four books he describes as "Hymns to God and Precepts for the Conduct of Human Life." When Josephus indicates that the writing of the thirteen books of The Prophets ceased in the reign of Artaxerxes, he obviously has in mind Malachi as the last prophet of the Old Testament.

35 The Jews sometimes added Ruth to Judges, and Lamentations to Jeremiah.

36 Josephus adds to the Former and Latter Prophets, Job, Esther, Daniel, Ezra-Nehemiah, and Chronicles.

37 These four would be: Psalms, Proverbs, Song of Songs, and Ecclesiastes.

38 Artaxerxes I reigned 465-425 B.C.

39 *The Works of Flavius Josephus*, Tr. by William Whiston (New York: American Publishers Corp., n.d.), III, pp. 530, 531.

The New Testament frequently refers to "the law,"[40] or "the law and the prophets[41];" on one occasion, however, our Lord did refer to "the law of Moses and the prophets and the psalms,"[42] an obvious allusion to the three divisions of the Jewish canon, taking the largest and most significant book of Part III as the name of the whole. Perhaps even more significant is the remark of Jesus concerning the martyrs of the Old Testament, "From the blood of Abel to the blood of Zechariah, who perished between the altar and the sanctuary,"[43] a sweep of history from Genesis to Chronicles, the first and last books of the Jewish canon.[44]

Origen (c. 185-c. 254) speaks of the Jewish canon as consisting of twenty-two books, while Tertullian (c. 160-c. 230) speaks of twenty-four. (The Jews sometimes attached Ruth to Judges, and Lamentations to Jeremiah, thus getting a total of twenty-two books which they thought corresponded beautifully with the twenty-two letters of their alphabet.) The great church father Jerome (c. 340-420) also speaks of the canonical books as twenty-two in number and rejects the so-called deuterocanonical books explicitly. The Catholic writer, Dr. Gigot, admits: "Time and again this illustrious doctor of the Latin church rejects the authority of the deuterocanonical books in the most explicit manner."[45]

The books of The Law are quoted or are called Scripture thirty-two times in the New Testament, The Prophets forty-three times, and The Writings thirty-seven times,[46] while the Old Testament Apocrypha (the so-called deuterocanonical books of the Catholics) are not even quoted in the New Testament, much less called Scripture. It should be observed that they also contain material which seems not to be in harmony with the canonical books; for example, prayers for the dead (II Maccabees 12:43-45).

According to Jewish tradition two councils of rabbis were held at Jamnia near Joppa on the Mediterranean coast in A.D. 90 and 118, at which time the books of Ecclesiastes and Song of Solomon were discussed as to their canonicity and their canonicity reaffirmed.

The Jewish Apocryphal books were written between 200 B.C. and A.D. 100[47], and were preserved through church history, not by the Jews but by Christians. The influence of Augustine (354-430) seems

40 Matt. 12:5; 22:36; 23:23; Luke 10:26; etc.
41 Matt. 5:17; 7:12; Luke 16:16; etc.
42 Luke 24:44.
43 Luke 11:51.
44 Gen. 4:11 and II Chron. 24:20, 21.
45 *I.S.B.E.*, I, p. 559; H. S. Miller, *op. cit.*, p. 114; etc.
46 H. S. Miller, *op. cit.*, p. 47.
47 Thomas W. Davies, "Apocrypha," *I.S.B.E.*, I, p. 183 (cf. 178-83).

to have been decisive in helping these Apocryphal books to a general acceptance in the Catholic Church. Yet Augustine limited the term "canonical" in its strict sense to the Jewish canon, and refuted an argument for suicide based on II Maccabees by "showing that the book was not received into the Hebrew canon to which Christ was witness."[48] It would appear that in a general way from the time of Augustine to the Council of Trent in the sixteenth century the Apocryphal books possessed an authority more or less inferior to the canonical books of the Old Testament.[49] John Wycliffe in his English Bible of the latter fourteenth century segregated the Apocryphal books at the end of the Old Testament as did Luther later. Luther specifically added a note: "These are books which are not to be regarded as equal to the Holy Scriptures but are yet profitable and good to read." In reaction the Roman Catholic Council of Trent on April 8, 1546, decreed that the Apocryphal books were equal in authority to the other books of sacred Scripture adding: "But if any one receive not, as sacred and canonical, the said books entire with all their facts, as they have been used to be read in the Catholic Church, and as they are contained in the old Latin Vulgate edition, . . . let him be anathema."[50] Most Protestant Bibles continued to print the Apocryphal books between the Old and the New Testament until the British and Foreign Bible Society decided in 1827 to discontinue this indefensible practice.[51] If the Bible of Christ and the apostles did not contain these Jewish Apocryphal writings, it is misleading to include them in the list of authoritative books in the Christian canon of Scripture.

New Testament

The writing of the twenty-seven books of the New Testament was completed between A.D. 45 and 96 (James and Revelation). By the end of the first century or thereabouts it appears that the four Gospels were circulating as a unit, and Tatian made a connected manuscript of the text of the four Gospels in the latter half of the second century.[52] It appears also that at the end of the first century or early part of the second century the thirteen letters of Paul were also circulating as a unit. Irenaeus (c. 130-c. 200) left behind writ-

48 George L. Robinson, "Canon of the O.T.," I.S.B.E., I, p. 562.

49 *Ibid.*, p. 562.

50 Philip Schaff, *The Creeds of Christendom* (New York: Harper & Brothers, 1877, 1919), II, p. 82.

51 *I.S.B.E.*, I, p. 562.

52 J. S. Riggs, "Canon of the New Testament," *I.S.B.E.*, I, pp. 563-66; Henry C. Thiessen, *Introduction to the New Testament* (Grand Rapids, Mich.: Eerdmans, 1943); Paul Feine, rev. by Joh. Behm, *Einleitung in das Neue Testament* (Leipzig: Quelle & Meyer, 1936); etc.

ings which contained 1,800 quotations from the four Gospels, Acts, thirteen Pauline epistles, I Peter, I John, and Revelation. The Syriac Version of the New Testament made about A.D. 150 contains twenty-two books, omitting II Peter, II and III John, Jude, and Revelation. The old Latin version, however, also of the middle of the second century, has twenty-six of our New Testament books, all but II Peter. One of the most learned leaders of the ancient church was Origen (c. 185-c. 254), who was used as a Christian teacher before he was seventeen years of age and became a bishop at the age of eighteen; he accepted as Scripture the four Gospels, the thirteen Pauline epistles, the Book of Acts, Hebrews ("God alone knows who wrote it"), I Peter, and I John. He seems also to have accepted the Book of Revelation and Jude, but was not certain about James, II Peter, and II and III John. From the so-called Muratorian Fragment of about A.D. 170 we have a list containing the four Gospels, the Acts, the thirteen Pauline epistles, I and II John, Jude, and Revelation. Hebrews, I and II Peter, and James seem to be missing. The statement is unclear about III John. It would, therefore, appear that by A.D. 200 the early church was clear on the canonicity of the four Gospels, the Acts, the thirteen Pauline epistles, I Peter, I John, and Revelation. In the fourth century, however, the Book of Revelation was questioned in some quarters.

One of the most interesting testimonies as to the development of the canon of the New Testament comes from Eusebius (c. 260-c. 340), who served as bishop of Caesarea from before A.D. 315. In his *Church History* (Book III, Chapters iii-xxv) he gives a rather detailed report on the state of the canon of the New Testament in his day. First of all Eusebius lists the accepted books which he says include the four Gospels, Acts, fourteen Pauline letters (i.e., Hebrews was considered Pauline), I Peter, I John, and possibly Revelation, though there was some question about the last book. The disputed books were of two kinds, says Eusebius. First of all, those in the better class consisted of James, II Peter, II John, and Jude. The other class of books which were challenged Eusebius regards as spurious, and none of them ever was adopted into the canon.

The earliest church father to give our exact list of twenty-seven New Testament books was the great Athanasius (c. 293-373), bishop and theologian of Alexandria, who wrote to set forth "in order from the first the books that are canonized and handed down and believed to be divine, so that each, if he has been deceived, may detect those which have misled him."[53] After giving this list of twenty-seven books

53 H. S. Miller, *op. cit.*, p. 136.

in A.D. 367 Athanasius adds: "These are the wells of salvation so that he who thirsts may be satisfied with the sayings in these. Let no man add to these; and let nothing be taken away."[54] It should be added, however, that John Chrysostom (c. 345-407), bishop of Constantinople and famous preacher, included in his list of New Testament books only twenty-two, omitting II Peter, II and III John, Jude, and Revelation. However, the church councils of Rome, 382; Hippo, 393; Carthage, 397; and Carthage, 419, all confirmed our twenty-seven books as the New Testament canon. The dominant figure in these church councils was the great father Augustine (354-430).

It should be noted that there is no dispute from the fifth century on in the Christian Church as to the canon of the New Testament. All branches of the Christian Church, Catholic and Protestant, accept the same twenty-seven books of the New Testament.

It may seem strange to modern Christians to discover that the ancient church was slow in coming to any particular conclusion as to the canon of the New Testament. But it must be remembered that the church started out under the blessings of Pentecost, with the great apostles of Christ as its leaders. Only gradually did the appearance of heretics and the exigencies of persecution call for a careful delineation as to what books were canonical, which ones were to be quoted as authoritative, which ones read in the churches, which ones defended and preserved during persecution, and which ones translated into the languages of new mission fields. The evangelical Christian, of course, believes that the good providence of God was in the entire selection so that the truth was reached. The church today could not make a better canon than did the ancient church.

It might! [handwritten marginal note]

12. HERMENEUTICS

It is sometimes said that one can prove anything from the Bible. This silly statement is true only if people sufficiently depart from sound principles of interpretation. What are the basic insights and understandings which are required in order to understand the Word of God aright?

To begin with, it is absolutely essential that the interpreter of God's Word be a regenerated child of God. The Scripture indicates that the natural man, he in whom the Spirit of God is not active, cannot receive or discern the things of the Spirit.[55] Christian humility is another prime essential for the understanding of the divine oracles. Furthermore, one must have a proper understanding of the

54 *I.S.B.E.*, I, p. 566.
55 I Cor. 2:14.

basic purpose which God had in mind in giving His Word to the race. Finally, one must have an open-minded attitude, ready to receive whatever the Scriptures teach, rather than approaching them with various preconceived ideas and points of view for which one is seeking justification.

Those who desire a thorough monograph on the principles of interpretation ought to consult standard works such as those of Terry or Berkhof.[56] All that can be done in the present discussion is to indicate a few of the major principles which must guide the Christian theologian as he seeks to interpret God's Word.

To begin with, it should be borne in mind that Christians are individually taught by the Spirit of God so that they are slaves to no one as they study the Scriptures. Jeremiah prophesied of the blessings of the New Covenant, indicating that in the days of the Messiah there would be no need for mutual teaching.[57] The Apostle Paul tells us that we are now in that era, for we are all taught of God.[58] And the Apostle John indicates also that we have no need of teaching because we have a divine anointing.[59] This does not mean, of course, that Christians cannot learn anything from one another; it simply indicates that each individual believer is able by the grace of God to read the Scriptures for himself, receiving the benefit of divine illumination. The New Testament certainly does recognize the aid which one Christian can render to another in the understanding of the will of God: the very writing of the New Testament epistles is an illustration.

The need of hermeneutics arises from a number of factors such as the individual differences in intellectual power which Christians have, the differences in the knowledge-equipment which Christians bring to the Scriptures, and varying degrees of spiritual maturity.

In a general way the two most divergent methods of interpretation in Jewish and Christian schools of thought have been what might be called the allegorical and the grammatico-historical schools of thought. The allegorical method of interpretation accepts nothing merely at face value, but believes that in Scripture there are three or four senses. In the second century Origen taught that each statement in the Bible had a literal meaning, a moral significance, and finally a mystical or allegorical meaning. Later this threefold sense was expanded to four. It should be noted that the highly subjective method which is latent in the allegorical method of inter-

56 Milton S. Terry, *Biblical Hermeneutics* (Grand Rapids, Mich.: Zondervan, n.d.); L. Berkhof, *Principles of Biblical Interpretation* (Grand Rapids, Mich.: Baker Book House, 1950).
57 Jer. 31:33, 34.   58 I Thess. 4:9.   59 I John 2:27.

pretation really destroys the objective significance of the Scripture, for the interpreter can always insist that the Bible does not mean what it says. It is for this reason that the leading reformers threw the allegorical method overboard; Luther called it *Affenspiel*[60] (monkey business). Luther insisted on the right of each Christian to interpret the Bible for himself, as guided by the Holy Spirit. Luther stressed the point that one should take into account the context, noting the historical circumstances. He recognized that personal faith on the part of the reader was highly essential also. Above all, Luther saw clearly that the central theme of God's Word was Christ and His redemption. He, therefore, insisted that one should seek Christ throughout the Scriptures.[61]

First Principle

Let us now seek to state some of the major principles of interpretation which ought to guide the child of God as he reads the Scripture. The first of these is *grammatical* interpretation. This rule means that one must sincerely ask what the language of a given passage actually means. The meaning, of course, must be that of the original language. Here it should be observed that the meaning of any word is that which it had at the time of the writing of the Scripture, not its classical meaning and not its etymological significance. The reason for this is that Christianity greatly enriched the Greek language. Words such as God, love, cross, redemption, forgiveness, life, heaven, etc., etc., all took on greatly enriched meanings after Jesus had brought redemption to the race.

The Biblical exegete must have a working knowledge of Hebrew, Aramaic, and New Testament Greek if he is to be able to do basic Bible study for himself. He must be in possession of the best Hebrew and Greek lexicons and grammars, and he will derive much benefit from Hebrew and Greek concordances. Commentaries which are based on the Hebrew and Greek are highly useful, and a variety of versions is also helpful. Those who do not possess a knowledge of the original tongues of Scripture can at least get much of the benefit of such study by the use of good commentaries and various translations. Take, for example, a verse such as Romans 12:1. This passage reads thus in the King James Version: "I beseech you therefore, brethren, by the mercies of God, that ye present your bodies a living sacrifice, holy, acceptable unto God, which is your reasonable service." When one turns to the American Standard Version he finds

---

60 Berkhof, *op. cit.*, p. 26.   61 *Ibid.*, pp. 26, 27.

that the translation is practically identical except for the last phrase which reads, "which is your spiritual service." On the meaning of this phrase we turn to the Revised Standard Version and read, "which is your spiritual worship." Weymouth renders the phrase, "a spiritual mode of worship." The Berkeley Version renders the phrase, "your worship with understanding." Williams follows the King James Version, "which is your reasonable service." Phillips says, "as an act of intelligent worship." The Twentieth Century New Testament states, "this is your rational worship." The Roman Catholic Confraternity Revision of the Challoner-Rheims Version renders, "your spiritual service." And Ferrar Fenton translates, "your rational service."

We turn now to a few commentaries to see if we cannot better understand this verse. Adam Clarke points out that the word *therefore* has reference to what precedes in this epistle, and the mercies of God are those benign attributes which have been shown in the previous chapters. Clarke shows that the phrase relating to the presenting of our bodies is taken from the ritual of bringing the Old Testament sacrifices to the altar of God. Christians are now exhorted "to give *themselves* up in the spirit of sacrifice; to be as wholly the Lord's property as the whole burnt offering was, no part being devoted to any other use."[62] The Christian's body shall be a living sacrifice, "in opposition to those dead sacrifices which they were in the habit of offering while in their Jewish state."[63] Clarke continues: "All these phrases are sacrificial, and show that there must be a complete surrender of the person—the *body*, the whole man, mind and flesh, to be given to God; and that he is to consider himself no more his own, but the entire property of his Maker."[64] Finally Clarke says: "We are not our own, we are the property of the Lord, by the right of creation and redemption; and it would be as unreasonable as it would be wicked not to live to His glory, in strict obedience to His will. The Christian service of worship is *logike, rational*, because performed according to the true intent and meaning of the law; the heart and soul being engaged in the service."[65]

Meyer's Commentary also explains that the contrast here is with "the ceremonial character of the Jewish and heathen worship," because the worship which is here meant is, "a spiritual service, fulfilling itself in moral rational activity."[66] Lange's Commentary points

---

62 Clarke's Commentary on Rom. 12:1, VI, p. 75.
63 *Ibid.*, p. 75.
64 *Ibid.*, p. 75.
65 *Ibid.*, p. 75.
66 *Hand-Book to the Epistle to the Romans* (New York: Funk & Wagnalls, 1884), p. 468.

out also that the service or worship which is here described has as its central idea that of an offering. "But this sacrificial worship of believers should be [rational] . . . , that which is inspired by reason, in harmony with real reason, and consequently *spiritual,* real; in antithesis to merely external symbolical service."[67] Lenski explains: "This sacrifice is the cultus and worship that Jesus calls 'worship in spirit and in truth,' John 4:23."[68] *The Expositor's Greek Testament* states: "Such a presentation of the body, as the organ of all moral action, to God, is the only thing that can be characterized as . . . spiritual worship. Any other worship, any retention of Jewish or pagan rites, anything coming under the description of *opus operatum* [a work which of itself confers God's grace] is foreign to the Christian *thusia* [sacrifice]; it is . . . not appropriate to a being whose essence is *logos, i.e.,* reason or spirit."[69] *The Cambridge Greek Testament* states: "This offering to GOD of the life in its daily activities is the service dictated by the reasonable consideration of man's nature and his relation to God."[70] Erdman explains: "Such a sacrifice is further described as a supreme form of religious service; it is 'spiritual' in contrast with offerings which were merely material and physical; it is a 'service,' that is, a cult or priestly ritual; in fact, such an act of consecration forms the most sublime of liturgies."[71]

It is thus obvious that even without any ability to read Greek or Hebrew the earnest Bible student is able by the use of versions and commentaries, especially commentaries based on the original languages of Scripture, to ascertain carefully the exact meaning of any verse in the Bible. One of the many benefits of reading the Bible in various translations is to discover that the understandings previously held of many verses in the English Bible were mistaken, not because the translation was poor but because the English was not properly understood. To use a personal illustration: For many years the present writer understood Romans 3:23 to mean: "For all have sinned, and [have] come short of the glory of God." In the course of reading the American Standard Version of the Bible he discovered the following translation, however: "For all have sinned, and fall short of the glory of God." In other words, the first verb of the sen-

67 *Commentary on the Holy Scriptures* (Grand Rapids, Mich.: Zondervan, n.d.), Romans Vol., p. 382 (Greek term translated within brackets).
68 *Interpretation of St. Paul's Epistle to the Romans* (Columbus, Ohio: Wartburg Press, 1945), p. 748.
69 James Denney, "St. Paul's Epistle to the Romans," *The Expositor's Greek Testament* (New York; Dodd, Mead & Co., 1900), II, p. 687.
70 R. St. John Parry, Romans, *Cambridge Greek Testament* (Cambridge: University Press, 1921), p. 156.
71 Charles R. Erdman, *The Epistle of Paul to the Romans* (Philadelphia: The Westminster Press, 1938), p. 132.

tence refers to the past; the human race has exhibited only a record of universal sin. The second verb, however, is in the present tense; Paul surveys his contemporaries and sees that they also are falling short of God's glory. Williams' translation is excellent: "For everybody has sinned and everybody continues to come short of God's glory."[72] This is, of course, not a matter of anyone missing the way of salvation through a misunderstanding of the King James Version. It is rather a desire to understand as fully as possible the Word of God which the Lord has graciously given to His people. Just because we accept the Bible as God's Word we want to know as fully and as accurately as possible the meaning of every statement in the Bible.

One of the most controversial points in hermeneutics is the proper interpretation of figurative language. All Bible scholars admit that the Bible contains figures of speech and figurative language. Trees of the forest do not clap their hands, and the desert cannot rejoice.[73] Jesus is not a vine,[74] and the "cup" is not the New Testament.[75] Every page of the Bible contains sentences which require interpretation by honest and spiritual students of God's Word. There is no substitute for sound literary judgment in the recognition of what is figurative and what is literal or nonfigurative language. Above all the understanding of each verse in its context, and the basic illumination gained by a constant study of the entire Word of God throw a flood of light on any given statement in the Scriptures. The Bible is its own best interpreter. There is no substitute for a knowledge of the whole Word as one studies the Bible. Almost six hundred years ago John Wycliffe wrote:

> It shall greatly help ye to
>   understande Scripture,
> If thou mark
> Not only what is spoken or wrytten,
> But of whom,
> And to whom,
> With what words,
> At what time,
> Where
> To what intent,
> With what circumstances,

---

72 Charles B. Williams, *The New Testament, A Translation in the Language of the People* (Chicago: Moody Press, 1949), p. 334.
73 Isa. 55:12.
74 John 15:1.
75 I Cor. 11:25.

Considering what goeth before
And what followeth.[76]

Second Principle

The second major principle of Biblical interpretation is called *historical* interpretation. While it is recognized that the Bible is not the product of history in the sense that men produced it apart from the inspiration of the Holy Spirit, yet the principle of historical interpretation accepts and builds upon the truth that the first readers of a Biblical book were in a favorable position to understand the poetical, cultural, geographical, etc., allusions in it. The original readers were in an advantageous position to understand its terminology, the individual words employed, its figures of speech, etc. It is also a well-known principle that the more anyone knows of an author's life and experiences the better position one is in to understand his writing. This is, of course, also true for the entire world in which the author lived. Furthermore, one must try to grasp the basic convictions, concerns, and thought patterns of a Biblical writer in order to better understand his book. It is hardly necessary to add that one must distinguish sharply between truths which the writer himself records and the accounts of speeches which he includes in his book. If a Biblical writing includes a sort of imaginary dialogue, as for example the Book of Ecclesiastes seems to do when it allows the voice of pessimism to speak and then overcomes that point of view with the voice of faith, one must seek to identify each "speaker" in the dialogue. It is also a great advantage to be acquainted with the topography, climate, *flora* and *fauna* of the Bible. The more one knows about the national neighbors of Israel, their history, their religious beliefs and practices, the customs of their daily life, etc., the better one's position for a good understanding of the Biblical books.

Third Principle

The third principle of Biblical hermeneutics is called *theological* interpretation.[77] The meaning of this expression is that to be fully understood the Bible must be recognized as coming ultimately from God. Fundamentally the Scriptures must be recognized as the Word of God, not merely the writings of men of God. Theological interpretation rests upon the principle that there is a unity to the Book beyond the conscious agreement of the writers. It means that the

---

76 Quoted in the splendid volume of the evangelical scholar, Dr. Wilbur M. Smith, *Profitable Bible Study* (Boston: W. A. Wilde Co., 1939), p. 38.
77 Cf. Berkhof's excellent discussion, *op. cit.*, pp. 133-66.

New Testament is the divinely intended fulfillment of the Old Testament. It therefore becomes the task of the devout interpreter of God's Word to seek God's intention in a given passage in the light of the whole body of divine revelation. The final question is not, What did Moses or Isaiah or Paul mean? nor even how they individually understood the words which they wrote, but, What does *God* intend us to take from a given passage or book? Here again one must emphasize the importance of knowing the Bible as a whole, and not abuse it by taking passages out of their context and making collections of verses which originally had no connection with one another in order to prove a given point of view.

It is in this connection also that one must stress the importance of divine illumination in the study and interpretation of the Scriptures. The Holy Spirit knows what the intention of God is in any given portion of His Word, and to the humble and sincere seeker for the truth the Holy Spirit is able to take the Scriptures and make the reader wise unto salvation and to give him that daily guidance which he needs for the living of a rich and effective Christian life.

Fourth Principle

The fourth principle of Biblical hermeneutics is that of *progressive revelation*. Christians believe that there is an ultimate God-given unity to the Bible, and that the canon is a divine intention. God really did inspire holy men to write down His revelation in book form. Throughout the entire Bible, however, from Genesis to Malachi in the Old Testament and extending to Christ and His apostles, there is the principle of progressive revelation. The Bible teaches, to be sure, the same basic doctrinal truths everywhere: the personality, love, and holiness of God; the sinfulness of human nature; the need of a mediated access to God; the demand of the Lord for holiness of heart and life on the part of His people; man's need of a devotional life, of meditation and prayer; the recognition of God as creator; the providence of an Almighty God; the grace of God toward those who have faith in Jesus Christ; the fact of a conscious life in the hereafter; and the need of divine enablement to live a life which is pleasing to God. Since God is the ultimate author of the Scriptures each part must therefore be interpreted in the light of the whole. The darker parts must be illuminated by the plainer sections and the humble Christian reader must be willing to put onto the shelf for the time being that which he does not feel able to interpret.

The principle of progressive revelation is no denial of the basic unity of the Scriptures; it does recognize, however, that through the centuries of Biblical history God did make the revelation of Himself and of His will for men increasingly clear. The institutions, rites, and ceremonies of the Old Testament were both symbolic and typical: symbolic of contemporary spiritual realities, and typical of Christ's coming redemption.

The Bible also teaches that there is a spiritual continuity between Old Testament Israel and the present spiritual bride of Christ, the church. Paul does not hesitate to call the church "the Israel of God."[78] And the Letter to the Hebrews states: "But you have come to Mount Zion and to the city of the living God, the heavenly Jerusalem."[79] Jeremiah promised that God would make a new covenant with the house of Israel, and the New Testament teaches that the church is in a spiritual sense the seed of Abraham and therefore heir to the promises of the Old Covenant blessings.[80] The acceptance of the spiritual seed of Abraham, the believing Gentiles, into the fellowship of the Lord's people is in the New Testament declared not to have been clearly revealed in the Old.[81] Yet Paul asserts in the strongest terms that salvation under both covenants is by grace through faith.[82]

The New Testament also teaches that there is a relation of fulfillment as between circumcision, sacrifices, and Jewish ceremonies on the one hand and the present spiritual blessings of Christians in Christ on the other. Jewish converts were actually circumcised in the flesh but Paul writes to Gentile believers thus: "In him also you were circumcised with a circumcision made without hands, by putting off the body of flesh in the circumcision of Christ."[83] Christ is spoken of in the New Testament as "our paschal lamb."[84] Christians need not keep the Old Testament passover nor is it necessary for them to practice the ceremonial washings of Judaism, because "He saved us, not because of deeds done by us in righteousness, but in virtue of his own mercy, by the washing of regeneration and renewal in the Holy Spirit, which he poured out upon us richly through Jesus Christ our Savior, so that we might be justified by his grace and become heirs in hope of eternal life."[85] The recognition that the institutions of the Old Testament find their ultimate fulfillment in the spiritual realities of Christianity is not to suggest that the Old Testament can be discarded. Not by any means, for the Old Testament

---

78 Gal. 6:16.
79 Heb. 12:22.
80 Gal. 3:29.

81 Gal. 2:11—3:6.
82 Rom. 4; Gal. 3.
83 Col. 2:11.

84 I Cor. 5:7.
85 Titus 3:5-7.

furnishes a background of history and redemption for the understanding of the New. The New Testament also provides what might be called "sample understandings of the true meanings of Old Testament ceremonies, institutions, and prophecies." We do not know how the Jews understood the words of Isaiah the prophet:

> The voice of one crying in the wilderness:
> Prepare the way of the Lord,
> make his paths straight.
> Every valley shall be filled,
> and every mountain and hill shall be brought low,
> and the crooked shall be made straight,
> and the rough ways shall be made smooth;
> and all flesh shall see the salvation of God.[86]

But Luke tells us that the prophecy from Isaiah 40 was fulfilled in the preaching of repentance by John the Baptist.[87]

Again, we may not know how the Jews understood the words of Isaiah 9:

> The people who sat in darkness
> have seen a great light,
> and for those who sat in the region and shadow of death
> light has dawned.[88]

Matthew informs us that this was a prophecy of the ministry of the Lord Jesus Christ.[89] The light which Jesus brought was the illumination of the truth of the Word of God which He proclaimed.

The New Testament also indicates that many of the symbolisms of the Mosaic institutions and ceremonies had spiritual significance for Christians. The fact, for example, of the holy of holies being open only to the high priest,[90] and the sacrificial ritual itself,[91] are used as spiritual lessons in the New Testament. Even historical incidents are used as illustrative of spiritual truth: the offering of Isaac by Abraham,[92] the placing of the brazen serpent on a pole,[93] etc. Occasionally the New Testament interprets an Old Testament passage allegorically,[94] though this is certainly not an endorsement for Biblical interpreters today to allegorize the entire Old Testament.

Before closing this discussion of the interpretation of the Word of God mention should again be made of the fact that the Bible, be-

86 Luke 3:4-6 (from Isa. 40:3-5).
87 Luke 3:4.
88 Matt. 4:16 (from Isa. 9:2).
89 Matt. 4:14.
90 Heb. 9:7.
91 Cf. Heb. 13:11-13.
92 Jas. 2:21.
93 John 3:14.
94 Gal. 4:21-31.

ing the Word of God Almighty, is not completely perspicuous to any Christian interpreter. In various places the Bible contains language which to many readers seems somewhat obscure, such as the baptisms for the dead which Paul mentions in the Corinthian letter,[95] or the veiling of Christian women "because of the angels,"[96] or the preaching of the Gospel to the dead.[97] The Bible also contains what might be called a puzzling human element such as that manifested in the imprecatory Psalms.[98] The Bible also contains remarks which seem to be irreconcilable with the basic doctrinal emphases of Scripture, which would again suggest that the recorded speeches of men who were not inspired apostles or prophets cannot be made a norm of spiritual truth.[99]

God give us the humility of heart to receive whatever from God's Word He sees fit to enable us to receive, and to be willing to wait for more light on those passages which may not seem entirely clear! And how important it is in a society where millions of lost people are groping for the light of divine revelation for the children of God to make their central emphasis the essential verities of God's Word, rather than to specialize in the obscure or difficult sections of the Bible, prophetic or apocalyptic. Let us also "respect the silences of the Bible,"[1] and where the Scripture does not speak let us be content to admit that we have no revelation on the point.

If the Christian student reads God's Word and meditates on it through a lifetime of Christian service, he will discover that the entire message of the Word becomes increasingly clear, and that the light of the whole illuminates remarkably in the course of time those portions which at first seemed altogether closed or obscure. May God give us the humility and faithfulness to receive simply the message of Paul to Timothy:

Indeed all who desire to live a godly life in Christ Jesus will be persecuted, while evil men and impostors will go on from bad to worse, deceivers and deceived. But as for you, continue in what you have learned and have firmly believed, knowing from whom you learned it and how from childhood you have been acquainted with the sacred [Scriptures] which are able to instruct you for salvation through faith in Christ Jesus. All scripture is inspired by God and profitable for teaching, for reproof,

95 I Cor. 15:29.
96 I Cor. 11:10. On this veil see J. C. Wenger, *Separated unto God* (Scottdale, Pa.: Mennonite Publishing House, 1952), pp. 207-12, also *The Prayer Veil*, 1964.
97 I Pet. 4:6.
98 Ps. 137:7-9, e.g.
99 Cf. the speeches of Job's friends which displeased the Lord.
1 An admonition which Dr. O. T. Allis gave his classes at Westminster Theological Seminary, Philadelphia, years ago.

for correction, and for training in righteousness, that the man of God may be complete, equipped for every good work.[2]

And may God save us from a false bibliolatry which makes the Bible an end in itself rather than a witness to Christ and His salvation: "You search the scriptures," declared Jesus to the Jews, "because you think that in them you have eternal life; and it is they that bear witness to me; yet you refuse to come to me that you may have life."[3] The Christocentric character of the Gospel is well expressed by John: "Now Jesus did many other signs in the presence of the disciples, which are not written in this book; but these are written that you may believe that Jesus is the Christ, the Son of God, and that believing you may have life in his name."[4]

Thousands upon thousands of volumes have been written about the Bible and how to study and interpret it. One of the finest of these many volumes is that of the distinguished Bible teacher, Dr. Wilbur M. Smith, entitled *Profitable Bible Study,* which not only discusses the blessings of Bible study but presents eight methods for pursuing the study of God's Word, as well as a catalog of the first one hundred books for the Bible student's library. This fine book also contains quotations from great men of God on the study of God's Word. One of the most excellent is that of Dr. Howard A. Kelly, who says: "The very best way to study the Bible is simply to read it daily with close attention and with prayer to see the light that shines from its pages, to meditate upon it, and to continue to read until somehow it works itself, its words, its expressions, its teachings, its habits of thought, and its presentation of God and His Christ into the very warp and woof of one's being."[5]

2 II Tim. 3:12-17.
3 John 5:39, 40.
4 John 20:30, 31.
5 Wilbur M. Smith, *Profitable Bible Study,* p. 85. Cf. Howard A. Kelly, *A Scientific Man and the Bible* (New York and London: Harper & Brothers, 1925), *passim.*

PART III

GOD AS REDEEMER

III. GOD AS REDEEMER

1. GOD'S EDUCATION OF ISRAEL

According to the Scriptures the Lord preserved a godly remnant from Adam to Abraham who kept alive a true knowledge of God; included in this line were the "sons of God," the Sethites. God finally selected Abraham and his family, about 2000 B.C., to continue the godly line and to be the recipients of the "oracles of God." God used Israel to proclaim the unity, holiness, love, and omnipotence of the Lord. God taught to Israel through its prophets the sinfulness of man, his terrible propensity toward apostasy, and his grave need of redemption: points which were painfully exhibited by Israel herself during her long history. Central in the faith of Israel was the Messianic hope: the kingdom of God shall one day be established on earth by a royal and redemptive Messiah.

Professor A. H. Strong has shown that the divine education of Israel was accomplished through three principal agencies: law, prophecy, and judgment.[1] The patriarchal and Mosaic periods contained numerous theophanies and miracles, the purpose of which was undoubtedly to stimulate God-consciousness. A good example of a miraculous theophany was the manner in which God caused fire to fall for the prophet Elijah when the struggle was on between the prophets of Baal and the true prophet of the Lord, Elijah.[2] The moral and ceremonial law was given to Israel to make vivid the sense of sin and to teach the Jews that all of life is sacred. The priestly and sacrificial system led to faith in a mediated access to God and in the reality of divine forgiveness. For all kinds of transgressions committed through weakness or ignorance, the Lord told Moses precisely what procedures should be followed, and to those who sincerely obeyed the commandments of the Lord the gracious promise was explicitly given: "And it shall be forgiven him."[3]

---

1 A. H. Strong, *Systematic Theology* (Philadelphia: The Judson Press, 1907), pp. 667, 668.
2 I Kings 18.   3 Lev. 4, 5.

In prophecy God employed certain men at special times to be His mouthpieces: (1) to interpret the law; (2) to give total guidance to Israel; (3) to proclaim repentance and faith; (4) to keep alive the Messianic hope.

Throughout the history of the Jews God also employed repeated chastisements including agricultural pests, pestilences and epidemics of sickness, wars, and famine, and finally the judgments of God culminated in exile, the loss of national independence. It was the exile which finally cured the Jews of idolatry and gave them an indelible awareness that they were the people of the LORD.

2. MESSIANIC PROPHECY

It is recognized by every serious student of the Bible that the Old Testament contains a prophetic theme dealing with a personal Saviour, the Messiah. It is also a matter of common knowledge that the language of Messianic prophecy is often somewhat obscure, so that Israel had difficulty in recognizing precisely which passages actually applied to their Messiah, and how they were to be understood. It should be noted that prophecy never has the fullness of detail and the chronological unity which history has; prophecy furnishes what might be called "spot checks" rather than in any sense constituting pre-written history.

It should also be noted that there is a peculiar paradox in Messianic prophecy in two respects: (1) the strange mixture of literal and figurative language in the prophecies; and (2) the puzzling combination of passages which refer to the Messiah as a suffering Mediator, and those which describe Him as reigning on David's throne.

Mention has already been made of the *Protevangelium* in Genesis 3:15, the promise that although the serpent would attack the heel of the Seed of the woman, yet that Seed would destroy the serpent's power by crushing his head. Moses also gave a marvelous prophecy of the Messiah in one of his farewell messages to the children of Israel: "The LORD your God will raise up for you a prophet like me from among you, from your brethren—him you shall heed—just as you desired of the LORD your God at Horeb . . . . I will raise up for them a prophet like you from among their brethren; and I will put my words in his mouth, and he shall speak to them all that I command him."[4]

The greatest Messianic prophet was undoubtedly Isaiah:

4 Deut. 18:15, 18.

Behold, I am laying in Zion for a foundation
a stone, a tested stone,
a precious cornerstone, of a sure foundation:
"He who believes will not be in haste."[5]

Behold, a king will reign in righteousness,
and princes will rule in justice.[6]

Strengthen the weak hands,
and make firm the feeble knees,
Say to those who are of a fearful heart,
"Be strong, fear not!
Behold, your God
will come with vengeance,
with the recompense of God.
He will come and save you."[7]

I am the LORD, I have called you in righteousness,
I have taken you by the hand and kept you;
I have given you as a covenant to the people,
a light to the nations,
to open the eyes that are blind,
to bring out the prisoners from the dungeon,
from the prison those who sit in darkness.[8]

Behold, I made him a witness to the peoples,
a leader and commander for the peoples.[9]

Concerning Israel and her Messiah the prophet Ezekiel says: "And I will set up over them one shepherd, my servant, David, and he shall feed them: he shall feed them and be their shepherd. And I, the LORD, will be their God, and my servant David shall be prince among them; I, the LORD, have spoken."[10]

After tracing the course of world history from his own time to the days of the Messiah the prophet Daniel says: "And in the days of those kings the God of heaven will set up a kingdom which shall never be destroyed, nor shall its sovereignty be left to another people. It shall break in pieces all these kingdoms and bring them to an end, and it shall stand for ever; just as you saw that a stone was cut from a mountain by no human hand, and that it broke in pieces

5 Isa. 28:16.
6 Isa. 32:1.
7 Isa. 35:3, 4.
8 Isa. 42:6, 7.
9 Isa. 55:4.
10 Ezek. 34:23, 24.

the iron, the bronze, the clay, the silver, and the gold. A great God has made known to the king what shall be hereafter. The dream is certain, and its interpretation sure."[11]

Many of the Messianic prophecies are brief, concise, and somewhat obscure, such as that of Zechariah: "Behold, I will bring my servant the Branch."[12]

The Messianic prophecies from Genesis to the great writing prophets portray the Messiah as one who will be a means of universal blessing,[13] who shall have dominion not only over Israel but over all the nations,[14] the true prophet of God, and the redeemer of Israel. The literal translation of Genesis 12:2, 3 is: "And I will make of you a great nation, and I will bless you, and make your name great, so that you will be a blessing. I will bless those who bless you, and him who curses you I will curse; and in you all the families of the earth will be blessed." The similar passages in 22:18 and 26:4, however, render the last phrase: "And by you all the families of the earth will bless themselves," a fact which has led the 1952 revisers to render Genesis 12:3 by the same translation as in the other two similar passages.

In his dying blessings to his sons the patriarch Jacob said:

The scepter shall not depart from Judah,
    nor the ruler's staff from between his feet,
until he comes to whom it belongs;
    and to him shall be the obedience of the peoples.[15]

Under divine inspiration the enigmatical Balaam said:

I see him, but not now;
    I behold him, but not nigh:
a star shall come forth out of Jacob,
    and a scepter shall rise out of Israel . . . .[16]

One of the more explicit prophecies is that of Jeremiah: "Behold, the days are coming, says the LORD, when I will fulfil the promise I made to the house of Israel and the house of Judah. In those days and at that time I will cause a righteous Branch to spring forth for David; and he shall execute justice and righteousness in the land. In those days Judah will be saved and Jerusalem will dwell securely. And this is the name by which it will be called: 'The LORD is our righteousness.' "[17]

11 Dan. 2:44, 45.
12 Zech. 3:8.
13 Gen. 12:3.
14 Num. 24:19; Isa. 55:4, 5; etc.

15 Gen. 49:10.
16 Num. 24:17.
17 Jer. 33:14-16.

The word "Messiah" is used about thirty-eight times in the
Old Testament, of which possibly six refer to the Christ while the
others seem to refer to other anointed persons such as priests of the
family of Aaron. The prayer of Hannah contains this remarkable
prophecy:

> The LORD will judge the ends of the earth;
>   he will give strength to his king,
>   and exalt the power of his *Messiah*.[18]

One of the richest Messianic passages of the Old Testament is
the second Psalm:

> The kings of the earth set themselves,
>   and the rulers take counsel together,
>   against the LORD and his *Messiah,* saying . . . .[19]

The most indisputable passage relating to the Messiah, as contrasted with the mere mention of earthly prophets, priests, or kings,
is that of Daniel 9:25, 26 which reads thus: "Know therefore and
understand that from the going forth of the word to restore and
build Jerusalem to the coming of *Messiah,* a prince, there shall be
seven weeks. Then for sixty-two weeks it shall be built again with
squares and moat, but in a troubled time. And after the sixty-two
weeks *Messiah* shall be cut off, and shall have nothing; and the people of the prince who is to come shall destroy the city and the sanctuary."[20]

By far the richest Messianic chapter in the entire Old Testament is Isaiah 53, part of which reads as follows:

> He was despised and rejected by men;
>   a man of sorrows, and acquainted with grief;
> and as one from whom men hide their faces
>   he was despised, and we esteemed him not.
> Surely he has borne our griefs
>   and carried our sorrows;
> yet we esteemed him stricken,
>   smitten by God, and afflicted.
> But he was wounded for our transgressions,
>   he was bruised for our iniquities;
> upon him was the chastisement that made us whole,
>   and with his stripes we are healed.

---

18 I Sam. 2:10 (from Hebrew).   20 From the Hebrew.
19 Ps. 2:2 (from Hebrew); Acts 4:26.

All we like sheep have gone astray;
    we have turned every one to his own way;
and the Lord has laid on him
    the iniquity of us all.

Therefore I will divide him a portion with the great,
    and he shall divide the spoil with the strong;
because he poured out his soul to death,
    and was numbered with the transgressors;
yet he bore the sin of many,
    and made intercession for the transgressors.[21]

3. PREPARATION AMONG THE GENTILES

In a strict sense the Bible is never concerned with the problem of theodicy, how to justify the providence or economy of God. We should not, therefore, expect to find in Scripture a justification for the fact that God waited so many millenniums before sending the Messiah. Nevertheless the Apostle Paul does use the phrase that God sent His Son into the world, "when the time had fully come."[22] What was it that the Gentiles had to learn before the world was ripe for the coming of the Saviour? First of all, man had to learn his utter helplessness to preserve or to regain a true knowledge of God. This picture is set forth in a pathetic way in the first chapter of the Letter to the Romans.[23] This same chapter would indicate that man had to learn the depth to which sin would degrade him, and the picture in Romans 1 of the awful degradation which sin brings is actually revolting.[24] Three times in the discussion the apostle indicates that God judged the sin of people by giving them up to their sin.[25] Man also had to learn the impossibility of self-redemption by philosophy, by art, by naturalistic religion, or by any human effort: men are simply not able to redeem themselves from sin and to accomplish the regeneration of their natures. The Dispersion of Israel among the Gentiles may have helped to bring to the Gentiles some sort of Messianic hope, though it must be admitted that the evidence on this point is subject to question.

In his excellent, *Modern Student's Life of Christ,* Professor Philip Vollmer discusses the preparation of the world for the coming of Christ as being fivefold: (1) the universal empire of the Romans which welded together the known world with a good govern-

21 Isa. 53:3-6, 12.   23 Rom. 1:18-23.   25 Rom. 1:24, 26, 28.
22 Gal. 4:4.

ment including an excellent system of roads; (2) the universally spoken *Koine* Greek; (3) a condition of universal peace at the time of the birth of the Messiah; (4) a universal need for redemption from sin; and (5) universal expectation: there seems to have been in the time of Jesus a general awareness that something was about to happen.[26]

In the final analysis we must confess by faith alone that it was God who knew when to act; only He knew when the propitious moment in history had arrived for the incarnation of His Son; it is neither possible nor perhaps desirable for finite human beings to inquire too closely into this type of question.

4. *THE INCARNATE SON AND HIS PASSION*

One of the simplest and most beautiful statements of the purpose of the incarnation of Jesus Christ is that given by the Apostle John: " 'And as Moses lifted up the serpent in the wilderness, so must the Son of man be lifted up, that whoever believes in him may have eternal life.' For God so loved the world that he gave his only Son, that whoever believes in him should not perish but have eternal life. For God sent the Son into the world, not to condemn the world, but that the world might be saved through him."[27] In the Gospel of Luke we read the testimony of Jesus Himself as to the purpose of His incarnation: "For the Son of man came to seek and to save the lost."[28] The Letter to the Hebrews states: "Since therefore the children share in flesh and blood, he himself likewise partook of the same nature, that through death he might destroy him who has the power of death, that is, the devil, and deliver all those who through fear of death were subject to lifelong bondage."[29] And John explains that: "The reason the Son of God appeared was to destroy the works of the devil."[30] The Apostle Paul says that the purpose of the incarnation was, "To redeem those who were under the law, so that we might receive adoption as sons."[31]

The reality of the fact of the incarnation is stated many times in Scripture. One of the clearest of these is that of the Apostle John, who writes: "And the Word became flesh and dwelt among us, full of grace and truth; we have beheld his glory, glory as of the only Son from the Father."[32] The word for "dwelt" in this statement refers to dwelling as in a tent or tabernacle and is a reminder that just as the Holy of Holies in the tabernacle of Moses contained the

---

26 Vollmer, *The Modern Student's Life of Christ* (New York: Revell, 1912), p. 35.
27 John 3:14-17. 29 Heb. 2:14, 15. 31 Gal. 4:5.
28 Luke 19:10. 30 I John 3:8. 32 John 1:14.

mercy seat over which God dwelt symbolically, so God in Jesus taber-
nacled in the flesh, His body. Paul says that "God has done what
the law, weakened by the flesh, could not do: sending his own Son
in the likeness of sinful flesh and for sin, he condemned sin in the
flesh, in order that the just requirement of the law might be fulfilled in us, who walk not according to the flesh but according to the
Spirit."[33] John says: "By this you know the Spirit of God: every
spirit which confesses that Jesus Christ has come in the flesh is of
God, and every spirit which does not confess Jesus is not of God."[34]
Also, "For many deceivers have gone out into the world, men who
will not acknowledge the coming of Jesus Christ in the flesh; such a
one is the deceiver and the antichrist."[35]

The most beautiful description of the incarnation of the eternal Son of God is that of the Apostle Paul, who uses it as an illustration of the self-sacrificing spirit which ought to characterize the followers of Christ, "Who, though he was in the form of God, did not
count equality with God a thing to be grasped, but emptied himself, taking the form of a servant, being born in the likeness of men.
And being found in human form he humbled himself and became
obedient unto death, even death on a cross."[36]

Two of the Gospels give rather detailed accounts of the birth
of Jesus, Matthew from the standpoint of Joseph, and Luke from
that of Mary. Matthew writes:

Now the birth of Jesus Christ took place in this way. When his mother Mary had been betrothed to Joseph, before they came together she was
found to be with child of the Holy Spirit; and her husband Joseph, being
a just man and unwilling to put her to shame, resolved to divorce her
quietly. But as he considered this, behold, an angel of the Lord appeared
to him in a dream, saying, "Joseph, son of David, do not fear to take Mary
your wife, for that which is conceived in her is of the Holy Spirit; she will
bear a son, and you shall call his name Jesus, for he [it is who][37] will save
his people from their sins." All this took place to fulfil what the Lord
had spoken by the prophet:

"Behold, a virgin shall conceive and bear a son,
and his name shall be called Emmanuel"

(which means, God with us). When Joseph woke from sleep, he did as the
angel of the Lord commanded him; he took his wife, but knew her not
until she had borne a son; and he called his name Jesus.[38]

33 Rom. 8:3, 4.
34 I John 4:2, 3.
35 II John 7.

36 Phil. 2:6-8.
37 Force of the Greek.
38 Matt. 1:18-25.

Luke reports that in the sixth month of the pregnancy of the mother of John the Baptist,

the angel Gabriel was sent from God to a city of Galilee named Nazareth, to a virgin betrothed to a man whose name was Joseph, of the house of David; and the virgin's name was Mary. And he came to her and said, "Hail, O favored one, the Lord is with you!" But she was greatly troubled at the saying, and considered in her mind what sort of greeting this might be. And the angel said to her, "Do not be afraid, Mary, for you have found favor with God. And behold, you will conceive in your womb and bear a son, and you shall call his name Jesus.

He will be great, and will be called the Son of the Most High;
and the Lord God will give to him the throne of his father David,
and he will reign over the house of Jacob for ever;
and of his kingdom there will be no end."
And Mary said to the angel, "How can this be, since I have no husband?"
And the angel said to her,
"The Holy Spirit will come upon you,
and the power of the Most High will overshadow you;
therefore the child to be born will be called holy,
the Son of God. . . .
For with God nothing will be impossible." And Mary said, "Behold I am the handmaid of the Lord; let it be to me according to your word." And the angel departed from her.[39]

It is perfectly evident that if one is willing to accept the plain testimony of the Gospel writers the fact of the virgin birth of Jesus is indisputable. The fact of the incarnation itself is a tremendous miracle and a profound mystery. This is well stated in what is perhaps the oldest hymn recorded in Christian literature. The Apostle Paul says: "Great indeed, we confess, is the mystery of our religion:

He was manifested in the flesh,
vindicated in the Spirit,
    seen by angels,
preached among the nations,
believed on in the world,
    taken up in glory."[40]

It is simply beyond comprehension how the eternal Son of God could come into the world and be born as a child so that that child should be very God while being at the same time truly human. "Great indeed, we confess, is the mystery of our religion!"

39 Luke 1:26-38.   40 I Tim. 3:16.

The incarnation, suffering, and death of Christ have been described as steps in Christ's state of humiliation. It should be observed that the suffering of Jesus was not confined to the events of the cross. All His life He suffered from awful loneliness, the loneliness of those who hunger for spiritual fellowship but find so few who can understand them or appreciate their concerns. The sense of responsibility which the Lord Jesus bore must have been truly crushing. To realize that the redemption of the world rested on His shoulders, the shoulders of one who was truly man, must have driven the Saviour to prayer for the sustaining power of an Almighty God. The Bible also does not hesitate to state that Jesus was tempted, tempted in every way just as other human beings are tempted, yet He never sinned.[41] The culmination of the suffering of Jesus came during Passion Week and found its climax in His death by crucifixion, the death of a felon. Crucifixion in the time of Jesus meant the same thing as the gallows now signifies: a death of shame and ignominy. The death of Jesus was the supreme proof of His true humanity.

Perhaps just a word should be said about the phrase, "He descended into hell," which is found in the so-called Apostles' Creed. This phrase is taken from Psalm 16, which promises that the Messiah would not be left in Sheol, or as the Greek translation has it, *Hades*. There are passages in Ephesians and I Peter which are sometimes interpreted as referring to a supposed preaching mission which Jesus accomplished in the underworld in the interval between His death on Calvary and His resurrection on Easter morning.[42] Roman Catholics hold that Jesus went to the limbo of the fathers to take the Old Testament saints to heaven. This view has also been held by various Protestant groups. Some scholars hold that Jesus made an exposition of the truth to the righteous souls in Paradise, proclaiming to them the joyful news that He had now accomplished the redemption of the world. Other students understand these verses to express figuratively that Jesus suffered the pangs of hell in His passion.[43] The Greek of the Apostles' Creed reads that Christ descended to the depths [katōtata].

The present writer is inclined to hold that some of these passages from the epistles do teach that Jesus entered the state of the dead and established contact with those who were deceased, though for what purpose is not clear. The safe rule is to leave uninterpreted

41 I Pet. 2:22; Heb. 4:15.
42 Eph. 4:9; I Pet. 4:6; 3:18, 19.
43 Bertram, "Höllenfahrt Christi," *Die Religion in Geschichte und Gegenwart* (Tübingen: J. C. B. Mohr, 1928), II, pp. 1968-70; Stephen A. Repass, "Descent into Hell," *The Lutheran Cyclopedia*, p. 155; cf. *A Catholic Dictionary*, p. 151; etc.

what cannot be clearly understood. This is certainly such a case. There is of course no suggestion in this discussion that the Lord offered salvation in the afterlife to anyone who had died unsaved.

The most difficult question connected with the incarnation of Christ is not that of the so-called descent into Hades but rather the peculiar combination of divine and human attributes which are ascribed to the incarnate Son of God. Many times the Messiah is described as having the divine nature or as being God.

> For to us a child is born,
>   to us a son is given;
> and the government will be upon his shoulder,
>   and his name will be called
> "Wonderful Counselor, Mighty God,
> Everlasting Father, Prince of Peace."[44]

Jeremiah says: "Behold, the days are coming, says the LORD, when I will raise up for David a righteous Branch, and he shall reign as king and deal wisely, and shall execute justice and righteousness in the land. In his days Judah will be saved, and Israel will dwell securely. And this is the name by which he will be called: 'The LORD is our righteousness.' "[45] And Malachi cries: "Behold, I send my messenger to prepare the way before me, and the Lord whom you seek will suddenly come to his temple; the messenger of the covenant in whom you delight, behold, he is coming, says the LORD of hosts. But who can endure the day of his coming, and who can stand when he appears?"[46] The Apostle John declares: "In the beginning was the Word, and the Word was with God, and the Word was God. He was in the beginning with God; all things were made through him, and without him was not anything made that was made."[47] And again: "And the Word became flesh and dwelt among us, full of grace and truth; we have beheld his glory, glory as of the only Son from the Father."[48] On one occasion Jesus told the unbelieving Jews: " 'My Father is working still, and I am working.' This was why the Jews sought all the more to kill him, because he not only broke the sabbath but also called God his Father, making himself equal with God."[49] The Apostle Paul declares that "In him the whole fulness of deity dwells bodily."[50] The Letter to the Hebrews says that, "In these last days he has spoken to us by a Son, whom he appointed the heir of all things, through whom also he created the

44 Isa. 9:6.
45 Jer. 33:14-16.
46 Mal. 3:1, 2.

47 John 1:1-3.
48 John 1:14.

49 John 5:17, 18.
50 Col. 1:19 (from Greek).

world. He reflects the glory of God and bears the very stamp of his nature . . . . "[51] The Gospels contain many examples of the deity of Christ: He manifested His divine power in His control over the forces of nature,[52] over illness,[53] over demons,[54] over life and death[55]; He declared that He would be the final judge of all men,[56] and He consistently represented Himself as the Son of God,[57] the Messiah who was to come.[58]

The Bible is equally clear that Jesus had a human nature. He is described many times as being a man,[59] as having flesh,[60] as having a body and mind[61] and as possessing the attributes of human beings. He became hungry,[62] He grew weary,[63] He needed to eat,[64] He slept,[65] He was tempted,[66] and He died.[67] Although Jesus has now been glorified,[68] He still remains the God-Man forever. At the second coming of Jesus the Lord "will change our lowly body to be like his glorious body, by the power which enables him even to subject all things to himself."[69]

Paul says that our natural body "is sown in dishonor, it is raised in glory. It is sown in weakness, it is raised in power. It is sown a physical body, it is raised a spiritual body. . . . Just as we have borne the image of the man of dust, we shall also bear the image of the man of heaven."[70] The Apostle John says that, "It does not yet appear what we shall be, but we know that when he appears we shall be like him."[71]

When the Lord Jesus had ascended to heaven in the same body in which He suffered, the two angels who appeared to the apostles following the ascension said: "Men of Galilee, why do you stand looking into heaven? This Jesus, who was taken up from you into heaven, will come in the same way as you saw him go into heaven."[72] Nevertheless, the glorification of the body of Jesus, in which His being adjusted to the life of glory, evidently involved a considerable metamorphosis, according to the description of the glorified

51 Heb. 1:2, 3.
52 Mark 4:39.
53 Mark 6:56.
54 Mark 1:32, 34.
55 John 11:43, 44.
56 Matt. 7:22.
57 Matt. 11:27; John 3:35, 36; 5:20; 5:25; 9:35, 36; 10:36; 14:13; etc.
58 John 4:25, 26; Matt. 16:20; 23:8; Luke 24:46; etc.
59 John 8:40; Acts 2:22; Rom. 5:15; I Cor. 15:21; I Tim. 2:5.
60 John 1:14; I Tim. 3:16; I John 4:2.
61 Matt. 26:26, 28, 38; Luke 23:46; 24:39; John 11:33.
62 Matt. 4:2.
63 John 4:6.
64 Matt. 11:19.
65 Mark 4:38.
66 Heb. 4:15.
67 Luke 23:46.

68 John 12:16.
69 Phil. 3:21.
70 I Cor. 15:43-49.
71 I John 3:2.
72 Acts 1:11.

Christ who appeared to the Apostle John: "I saw seven golden lampstands, and in the midst of the lampstands one like a son of man,
clothed with a long robe and with a golden girdle round his breast;
his head and his hair were white as white wool, white as snow; his
eyes were like a flame of fire, his feet were like burnished bronze,
refined as in a furnace, and his voice was like the sound of many
waters; in his right hand he held seven stars, from his mouth issued
a sharp two-edged sword, and his face was like the sun shining in
full strength."[73] It is freely recognized, of course, that one may not
take the details of a vision to press a theological conclusion regarding
the nature of the glorified body of the Saviour.

It should be noted that Jesus always kept His human nature in
full harmony with His divine nature; although He was truly human
He was also without sin: this is taught many times in the Word of
God. The angel told Mary, "The child to be born will be called
holy, the Son of God."[74] With perfect serenity Jesus could honestly
ask the Jews: "Which of you convicts me of sin?"[75] At the end of
His life Jesus declared flatly that Satan "has no power over me."[76]
The Apostle Paul declares that Jesus "knew no sin."[77] The Letter to
the Hebrews declares that Jesus was "in every respect . . . tempted
as we are, yet without sinning."[78] Jesus also, "through the eternal
Spirit offered himself without blemish to God."[79] And Peter says
simply that Jesus "committed no sin; no guile was found on his
lips."[80]

It should be noted that the Bible teaches the divine attributes
and the human attributes of Christ without any attempt to resolve
the logical problems associated with a being having both a human
and a divine nature. Thus, for example, eternity is ascribed to
Christ as well as age in terms of years[81]; He is spoken of as having
had preincarnate existence as well as human birth[82]; He is spoken
of as being omniscient and yet He exhibited limited knowledge[83];
He displayed divine power and also human weakness[84]; absolute life
is ascribed to Him and yet He died[85]; He spoke of His own presence
wherever two or three are gathered in His name and yet He was
physically present at only one place.[86] The controversy among theo-

---

73 Rev. 1:12-16.
74 Luke 1:35.
75 John 8:46.
76 John 14:30.
77 II Cor. 5:21.
78 Heb. 4:15.
79 Heb. 9:14.
80 I Pet. 2:22.
81 John 1:1; 8:58 & Luke 3:23.
82 John 1:14; 1:18; Rom. 8:32 & Gal. 4:4.
83 John 2:24, 25; 1:48, 49 & Mark 11:13; 13:32.
84 Mark 4:39; 5:41 & John 4:6.
85 I John 1:1, 2; John 1:4 & Matt. 16:21; Acts 3:14, 15; I Cor. 2:8.
86 Matt. 18:20; 28:20; Eph. 1:23; 4:10 & Acts 7:56.

logians has related to the question as to whether the attributes of one nature were communicated to the other nature, and similar obscure speculations. It is evident from Scripture that the deity of Christ was no mere additional power conferred at His baptism. Christ was truly God in the flesh. The Messianic consciousness probably arose gradually but was already present when He was twelve years of age. There was no trace of any development in the Messianic conceptions of Christ during His public ministry. The incarnation did involve physical fatigue, weariness, and temptation. And the incarnate Christ chose not to be omniscient on at least one doctrinal point,[87] but Scripture never ascribes any error whatever to the doctrine or knowledge of Jesus. The strange combination of Christ's attributes is explicable only by the fact that He was both true God and true man. Christ had divine attributes as the incarnate Son of God, the Messiah, and as a man He allowed Himself to suffer all our limitations, sin excepted. Farther than this the theologian ought not attempt to go.

A comparable humility and restraint applies also to the question of the *kenosis* or emptying which Jesus experienced when He chose to become a man. Paul states in his Letter to the Philippians that Jesus prior to His incarnation was in the form of God, but He did not count equality with God a thing to be selfishly retained, "but emptied himself, taking the form of a servant, being born in the likeness of men."[88] From the data which is given in Scripture the emptying evidently signified that Jesus divested Himself of the full prerogatives of deity to undergo the experience of being truly human, the result of which was that He could be a sympathetic and faithful high priest to those beset with human weakness and temptations.[89] Jesus actually emptied Himself of glory in becoming man. He did not become a sinner, and His teaching was not tainted with error.

As a matter of fact, both the truth that Jesus possessed human and divine attributes, and the fact that He was a man and the Lord from heaven at one and the same time, constitute paradoxes too deep for logical solution. Again we must confess with the Apostle Paul: "Great indeed . . . is the mystery of our religion."[90]

5. *NEW TESTAMENT INTERPRETATION OF THE CROSS*

Many attempts have been made to give a single interpretation of the purpose and result of the death of Jesus on the cross. The ancient

---

87 Mark 11:13; 13:32.   89 Heb. 4:15.
88 Phil. 2:7.   90 I Tim. 3:16.

church fathers, for example, regarded the death of Jesus as a ransom paid by God to Satan for the release of a sinful race. The modern view in conservative circles is to hold that Jesus died as a substitute, taking the place of sinners by dying in their stead. The New Testament, however, presents six or seven accomplishments of Jesus on Calvary, and it is impossible to reduce these to a single theory without seriously weakening the total significance of Christ's death on the cross.

First of all, the Scripture speaks frequently of the glorious fact that Jesus conquered Satan and the powers of evil through His death. Perhaps the most famous passage is that of the Letter to the Hebrews: "Since therefore the children share in flesh and blood, he himself likewise partook of the same nature, that through death he might destroy [render powerless] him who has the power of death, that is, the devil, and deliver all those who through fear of death were subject to lifelong bondage."[91] A similar statement is found in I John: "The reason the Son of God appeared was to destroy the works of the devil."[92] In connection with the inroads which He was making into the kingdom of Satan Jesus said: "But if it is by the Spirit of God that I cast out demons, then the kingdom of God has come upon you. Or how can one enter a strong man's house and plunder his goods, unless he first binds the strong man? Then indeed he may plunder his house."[93] The commission which Jesus gave the Apostle Paul at his conversion included the Gentiles, "to open their eyes, that they may turn from darkness to light and from the power of Satan to God, that they may receive forgiveness of sins and a place among those who are sanctified by faith in me."[94] The Revelation to John includes a heavenly scene in which the victory of the Christian martyrs in glory is celebrated in song thus: "Now the salvation and the power and the kingdom of our God and the authority of his Christ have come, for the accuser of our brethren has been thrown down, who accuses them day and night before our God. And they have conquered him by the blood of the Lamb and by the word of their testimony, for they loved not their lives even unto death."[95] The redemption which Jesus accomplished on the cross included the complete crushing of the head of the old serpent, the devil.[96]

In the second place, the death of Jesus enabled Christians to become victorious over their own "flesh," over the "old man," over

---

91 Heb. 2:14, 15. See Gustaf Aulén, *Christus Victor* (New York: Macmillan, 1951); also J. K. Mozley, *The Doctrine of the Atonement* (London: Duckworth, 1947).
92 I John 3:8.
93 Matt. 12:28, 29.
94 Acts 26:18.
95 Rev. 12:10, 11.
96 Gen. 3:15.

the lower nature. The Apostle Paul declares that the death of Jesus effected the death of the old self in the child of God,[97] a blessed result which is individually appropriated by faith on the part of the true convert who has turned to Jesus Christ.[98] Such a convert has died with Christ. It is for this reason that Christians are able to consider themselves "dead to sin and alive to God in Christ Jesus."[99] The testimony of Paul himself was: "I have been crucified with Christ; it is no longer I who live, but Christ who lives in me."[1] It is because the children of God are enabled through their faith-union with the Lord Jesus to live a life dead unto sin that the apostle is able to say: "Walk by the Spirit, and do not gratify the desires of the flesh."[2] Also, "those who belong to Christ Jesus have crucified the flesh with its passions and desires."[3] It is quite certain in Scripture that one of the blessed outcomes of the death of Jesus on the cross is the enablement of Christians to live above the desires of their lower nature.

In the third place, Scripture represents the death of Jesus as substitutionary and vicarious. This view is beautifully set forth in the prophecy of Isaiah:

Surely he has borne our griefs
and carried our sorrows;
yet we esteemed him stricken,
smitten by God, and afflicted.
But he was wounded for our transgressions,
he was bruised for our iniquities;
upon him was the chastisement that made us whole,
and with his stripes we are healed.
All we like sheep have gone astray;
we have turned every one to his own way;
and the LORD has laid on him
the iniquity of us all.[4]

The Apostle Paul declares that Jesus "was put to death for our trespasses."[5] And Peter states that "He himself bore our sins in his body on the tree, that we might die to sin and live to righteousness. By his wounds you have been healed. For you were straying like sheep, but have now returned to the Shepherd and Guardian of your souls."[6] The Letter to the Hebrews speaks of the incarnation of the eternal Son of God, "So that by the grace of God he might

97 Rom. 6:4-6.
98 Rom. 6:11.
99 Rom. 6:11.
1 Gal. 2:20.
2 Gal. 5:16.
3 Gal. 5:24.
4 Isa. 53:4-6.
5 Rom. 4:25.
6 I Pet. 2:24, 25.

taste death for every one."[7] Jesus died a substitutionary and vicarious death.

In the fourth place, the death of Jesus can be described by such terms as redemption, reconciliation, propitiation, etc. In other words, through the shedding of His blood Jesus reconciled men to God. This truth is set forth many times in the New Testament. Paul says it is through Jesus that "we have now received our reconciliation."[8] The effect of the death of Jesus was to reconcile both Jew and Gentile to God, making the two classes one.[9] Jesus made "peace by the blood of his cross."[10] Jesus made "expiation for the sins of the people."[11] One of the most beautiful statements of the reconciliation which Jesus accomplished with the Father is given in the Second Letter of Paul to the Corinthians: "Therefore, if any one is in Christ, he is a new creation; the old has passed away, behold, the new has come. All this is from God, who through Christ reconciled us to himself and gave us the ministry of reconciliation; that is, God was in Christ reconciling the world to himself, not counting their trespasses against them, and entrusting to us the message of reconciliation."[12]

In the fifth place, the death of Jesus on the cross was a revelation of the love of God for mankind. This truth should prevent any misunderstanding of God as being a harsh Judge in a supposed contrast with Christ as the loving Saviour. The Scriptures are emphatic that the giving of Jesus on the cross was in itself an act of love on the part of God. "And as Moses lifted up the serpent in the wilderness, so must the Son of man be lifted up, that whoever believes in him may have eternal life.

"For God so loved the world that he gave his only Son, that whoever believes in him should not perish but have eternal life. For God sent the Son into the world, not to condemn the world, but that the world might be saved through him."[13] "But God shows his love for us in that while we were yet sinners Christ died for us."[14]

Since Jesus was a man, and since He voluntarily went to the cross in order that human sin might be forgiven, and that man might be reconciled to God, the writers of the New Testament are much impressed with the love of Jesus which led Him to make the sacrifice of Himself. Hence the Apostle Paul can speak of Christ "who loved me and gave himself for me."[15] In a wonderful way the death of Jesus on the cross reveals His love for us.

---

7 Heb. 2:9.
8 Rom. 5:11.
9 Eph. 2:14-16.
10 Eph. 2:13 (Greek); Col. 1:20.
11 Heb. 2:17.
12 II Cor. 5:17-19.
13 John 3:14-17.
14 Rom. 5:8.
15 Gal. 2:20.

There is one more revelation which the death of Christ on the cross effected: it showed the righteousness of God. This truth is set forth in Romans 3:25. Biblical commentators are sharply divided on the meaning of this phrase. The text actually states that although all men have sinned and fall short of the glory of God, "They are justified by his grace as a gift, through the redemption which is in Christ Jesus, whom God put forward as an expiation by his blood, to be received by faith. This was to show God's righteousness, because in his divine forbearance he had passed over former sins; it was to prove at the present time that he himself is righteous and that he justifies him who has faith in Jesus." The point of disagreement relates to the meaning of the righteousness of God in the phrase that the offering of Jesus on the cross "was to show God's righteousness." Excellent commentators such as Anders Nygren of Sweden and R. C. H. Lenski of America argue stoutly that the passage does not refer to the lack of God's punitive dealing with sin in the Old Testament era. They rather regard the righteousness of God as referring exclusively to "the justifying act of God which declares believers righteous and puts them into that status."[16] On the other hand, so excellent an expositor as Dr. James Denney of the Free Church College, Glasgow, Scotland, holds that the thought relates to the way people had sinned with impunity under the Old Covenant so that the character of God seemed to be compromised. "Such had been the course of Providence that God, owing to His forbearance in suspending serious dealing with sin, lay under the imputation of being indifferent to it. But the time had now come to remove this imputation, and vindicate the divine character. If it was possible once, it was no longer possible now, with Christ set forth in His blood as a propitiation, to maintain that sin was a thing which God regarded with indifference. Paul . . . lays stress . . . on the fact that an essential element in a propitiation is that it should vindicate the divine righteousness. It should proclaim with unmistakable clearness that with sin God can hold no terms."[17] Never again would men be able to charge that God did not take sin seriously: He indeed took sin so seriously as to judge it in the body of His own Son on the cross.

One of the most comprehensive statements of the death of Jesus, its purposes and its results is the poem of Mrs. Cecil F. Alexander, 1848:

16 R. C. H. Lenski, *Romans* (Columbus, Ohio: Wartburg, 1945), p. 260; cf. Anders Nygren, *Commentary on Romans* (Philadelphia: Muhlenberg Press, 1949), pp. 159-62.

17 *Expositor's Greek Testament*, II, p. 612.

There is a green hill far away, without a city wall,
Where the dear Lord was crucified, who died to save us all.

We may not know, we cannot tell, what pains He had to bear;
But we believe it was for us He hung and suffered there.

He died that we might be forgiv'n, He died to make us good,
That we might go at last to heav'n, saved by His precious blood.

There was no other good enough to pay the price of sin;
He only could unlock the gate of heav'n, and let us in.

O dearly, dearly has He loved, and we must love Him too,
And trust in His redeeming blood, and try His work to do.[18]

6. *THE OFFICES OF OUR LORD*

It has been suggested that man as originally created was intended to be prophet, priest, and king: prophet in the sense of having a true knowledge of God, priest in that he possessed righteousness and holiness, and king in that he had dominion over the lower creation. The fall of man, however, brought ruin to him. Instead of being a true prophet of God he became contaminated with error and deception; instead of possessing true righteousness and holiness he became morally polluted; and instead of exercising his dominion as the Lord commanded he became a slave to sin and death. So it was with the first man.

The second Adam, however, the Lord Jesus Christ, fulfilled perfectly the offices of prophet, priest, and king. He was the true Word of God, He did make atonement for the sins of the world, and He did become the sovereign of the universe and the loving Lord of His church.[19]

As to His office as prophet the New Testament recognizes that there was a sense in which even the preincarnate Son of God ministered to Israel.[20] He is also the One who inspired the prophets of the Old Testament era.[21] After Jesus began His public ministry He was recognized again and again by the people of Israel as being a true prophet.[22] Peter speaks of Christ as a prophet,[23] and Stephen does

18 *Church Hymnal, Mennonite* (Scottdale, Pa.: Mennonite Publishing House, 1927), No. 106, p. 78.
19 Cf. John Calvin, *Institutes*, II, p. xv.
20 I Cor. 10:4.
21 I Pet. 1:11.
22 Matt. 21:1; Luke 24:19; Mark 6:15; John 6:14; 4:19; 7:40; 9:17; etc.
23 Acts 3:22-26.

also.[24] Jesus Himself said: "My teaching is not mine, but his who sent me."[25] Again, "The word which you hear is not mine but the Father's who sent me."[26] And in His high priestly prayer Jesus reported to God: "I have given them the words which thou gavest me, and they have received them and know in truth that I came from thee."[27] Jesus was therefore a prophet in the sense that He brought a message from the Father. But in a deeper sense He also was in His person, in His very being, the Word: the vehicle of communication from God. Jesus Himself revealed fully all that God wished to make known to mankind about Himself. "In the beginning was the Word, and the Word was with God, and the Word was God."[28] "And the Word became flesh and dwelt among us, full of grace and truth; we have beheld his glory, glory as of the only Son from the Father. . . . No one has ever seen God; the only Son, who is in the bosom of the Father, he has made him known."[29] Because Jesus was the full revelation of the Father He was able to tell Philip: "He who has seen me has seen the Father."[30]

The New Testament has much more to say about the priestly work of Christ than any other office. The letter to the Hebrews describes the qualifications and services of a priest. It indicates, first of all, that a high priest must be a man. His work is to offer gifts and sacrifices for sins. He must be sympathetic inasmuch as he himself is human. Furthermore, no priest takes this honor upon himself; he must be called by God.[31] In one of the great Messianic psalms the Messiah is prophesied as being an eternal priest, "after the order of Melchizedek."[32] This prophecy is quoted in the Letter to the Hebrews in connection with a discussion of the priesthood of Jesus.[33] The New Testament describes the priestly work of Christ in two ways: first, He is spoken of as the one who "made purification for sins"[34]; and secondly, the unique significance of Christ's priesthood is that He Himself was the sacrifice: "He offered up himself."[35] Christ is, therefore, described as an intercessor or advocate with the Father. "Since then we have a great high priest who has passed through the heavens, Jesus, the Son of God, let us hold fast our confession. For we have not a high priest who is unable to sympathize with our weaknesses, but one who in every respect has been tempted as we are, yet without sinning. Let us then with confidence draw near

24 Acts 7:37.
25 John 7:16.
26 John 14:24.
27 John 17:8.

28 John 1:1.
29 John 1:14, 18.
30 John 14:9.
31 Heb. 5:1-4.

32 Ps. 110:4.
33 Heb. 6:20; 7:11, 17; etc.
34 Heb. 1:3.
35 Heb. 9:26.

to the throne of grace that we may receive mercy and find grace to help in time of need."[36]

We may therefore say that Jesus is the answer to the accusations of conscience, of the law of God, and of Satan. "By this we shall know that we are of the truth, and reassure our hearts before him whenever our hearts condemn us; for God is greater than our hearts, and He knows everything."[37] Our Lord Himself said: "Truly, truly, I say to you, he who hears my word and believes him who sent me, has eternal life; he does not come into judgment, but has passed from death to life."[38] And Paul says: "There is therefore now no condemnation for those who are in Christ Jesus. For the law of the Spirit of life in Christ Jesus has set me free from the law of sin and death. For God has done what the law, weakened by the flesh, could not do: sending his own Son in the likeness of sinful flesh and for sin, he condemned sin in the flesh, in order that the just requirement of the law might be fulfilled in us, who walk not according to the flesh but according to the Spirit."[39] Again, "Christ has entered, not into a sanctuary made with hands, a copy of the true one, but into heaven itself, now to appear in the presence of God on our behalf. Nor was it to offer himself repeatedly, as the high priest enters the Holy Place yearly with blood not his own . . . he has appeared once for all at the end of the age to put away sin by the sacrifice of himself."[40] After describing the plan of salvation as being wholly the work of God the Apostle Paul concludes: "What then shall we say to this? If God is for us, who is against us? He who did not spare his own Son but gave him up for us all, will he not also give us all things with him? Who shall bring any charge against God's elect? It is God who justifies; who is to condemn? Is it Christ Jesus, who died, yes, who was raised from the dead, who is at the right hand of God, who indeed intercedes for us? Who shall separate us from the love of Christ? . . . No, in all these things we are more than conquerors through him who loved us."[41]

The New Testament teaches that the blood of Christ, that is, His death,[42] was efficacious in providing forgiveness and justification for the race on the condition of repentance and faith. The death of Christ effected with the Father a reconciliation, a removal of the occasion for estrangement, that is, sin; it also accomplished our redemption; that is, we again became the sons and daughters of God in Christ; the death of Jesus also brought about the propitiation of the

---

36 Heb. 4:14-16.   38 John 5:24.   40 Heb. 9:24-26.
37 I John 3:19, 20.   39 Rom. 8:1-4.   41 Rom. 8:31-35, 37.
42 R. A. Torrey, *What the Bible Teaches*, pp. 147, 161, 317.

Father, that is, the appeasement of His wrath with sin; the death of Christ is also spoken of as a ransom; that is, we are released from sin through the death of Christ. The blood of Christ also made expiation for our sins, constituting the ground of our acceptance with the Father. Theologians often speak of the perfect life which Jesus led as His "active obedience,"[43] and of His suffering and death as His "passive obedience." As a matter of fact, both His sinless life and His sacrificial death constituted one organic whole, being completely the will of God.

Is it possible to speak of Christ as king just as truly as He was prophet and priest? If by king one means an earthly ruler, occupying a throne, having a physical crown, controlling armies, and ruling over people politically, it is evident that Jesus is not entitled to the term "king," but this is not what the Scriptures mean when they speak of Jesus and His kingdom. Christ is now king in the same spiritual sense that God was king over Israel. All Christians thrill to the acclaim of Psalm 24:

> Lift up your heads, O gates!
>   and be lifted up, O ancient doors!
>   that the King of glory may come in.
> Who is the King of glory?
>   The LORD, strong and mighty,
>   the LORD, mighty in battle!
> Lift up your heads, O gates!
>   and be lifted up, O ancient doors!
>   that the King of glory may come in!
> Who is this King of glory?
>   The LORD of hosts,
>   he is the King of glory![44a]

Other Psalms state that "The LORD sits enthroned as king for ever"[44b]; a Messianic Psalm states: "Your divine throne[45] endures for ever and ever"; also:

> Sing praises to God, sing praises!
>   Sing praises to our King, sing praises!
> For God is the king of all the earth;
>   sing praises with a psalm!
> God reigns over the nations;
>   God sits on his holy throne.[46]

43 Menno Simons, *Complete Works*, I, pp. 44, 113, 154.
44a Ps. 24:7-10.   44b Ps: 29:10.
45 See the confirmation of the RSV rendering in Gesenius, *Hebrew Grammar* (Oxford, 1910), p. 415, Par. 128d. The reference is Ps. 45:6.   46 Ps. 47:6-8.

The Old Testament prophets described the Messiah as the Son of David,[47] as "David the King,"[48] and as sitting on "David's throne."[49] The prophet Nathan told King David that he would establish the throne of David's son for ever,[50] a prophecy which undoubtedly had an immediate reference to Solomon but was ultimately fulfilled in Christ.

One of the greatest Messianic prophecies reads:

> For to us a child is born,
>> to us a son is given;
> and the government will be upon his shoulder,
>> and his name will be called
> "Wonderful Counselor, Mighty God,
>> Everlasting Father, Prince of Peace."
> Of the increase of his government and of peace
>> there will be no end,
> upon the throne of David, and over his kingdom,
>> to establish it, and to uphold it
> with justice and with righteousness
>> from this time forth and for evermore.
> The zeal of the LORD of hosts will do this.[51]

Not only Isaiah but also Jeremiah,[52] Ezekiel,[53] Amos,[54] and Zechariah[55] refer to Israel's coming King and His righteous reign. When we come to the New Testament the very first verse refers to Christ the Messiah as the "son of David." And the angel Gabriel told Mary:

> He will be great, and will be called
>> the Son of the Most High;
> and the Lord God will give to him
>> the throne of his father David,
> and he will reign over the house
>> of Jacob for ever;
> and of his kingdom there will be
>> no end.[56]

Matthew reports that when Jesus was born in Bethlehem wise men from the East came to Jerusalem, saying, "Where is he who has been born king of the Jews? For we have seen his star in the East,

---

47 Matt. 9:27; II Sam. 7:12, 13; Ps: 132:11; Isa. 11:1.
48 Jer. 30:9; Ezek. 37:24, 25.
49 Isa. 9:7; Jer. 17:25; 22:2; 29:16; 36:30; etc.

50 II Sam. 7:12, 13.   54 Amos 9:11.
51 Isa. 9:6, 7.   55 Zech. 9:9.
52 Jer. 30:9.   56 Luke 1:32, 33.
53 Ezek. 37:24, 25.

and have come to worship him."[57] Both John and Jesus began their ministries by teaching that the kingdom had now come.[58] And Nathanael confessed to Jesus: "Rabbi, you are the Son of God! You are the King of Israel!"[59] Concerning the Triumphal Entry of the Lord Jesus into Jerusalem Matthew reports: "This took place to fulfil what was spoken by the prophet, saying,

> Tell the daughter of Zion,
> Behold, your king is coming to you,
> humble, and mounted on an ass,
> and on a colt, the foal of an ass."[60]

The Gospels contain numerous examples of Christ being addressed as "Son of David,"[61] that is, the Messiah. When Jesus rode into Jerusalem on Palm Sunday the multitudes began to cry out: "Blessed be the King who comes in the name of the Lord!"[62] When the Pharisees remonstrated Jesus replied: "I tell you, if these were silent, the very stones would cry out."[63] Furthermore, on several occasions Jesus Himself explicitly referred to Himself as a king: "If it is by the finger of God that I cast out demons, then the kingdom of God has come upon you."[64] On another occasion He said: "The kingdom of God is not coming with signs to be observed; nor will they say, 'Lo, here it is!' or 'There!' for behold, the kingdom of God is in the midst of you."[65] He also acknowledged to Pilate that He did have a kingdom though it was not worldly in nature or origin.[66]

Certain recent writers assert that Jesus offered Himself to Israel as its king but was rejected.[67] The Gospels, however, represent the Jews as desiring to come by force and make Christ an earthly king, which plan *He* rejected.[68]

After Christ's resurrection and ascension came Pentecost when the Apostle Peter preached his great sermon which resulted in the conversion of three thousand. In this sermon Peter declared that in the prophecy David gave that the Messiah should sit upon his throne, "He foresaw and spoke of the resurrection of the Christ. . . . Being therefore exalted at the right hand of God, and having received from the Father the promise of the Holy Spirit, he has poured out this

---

57 Matt. 2:2.
58 Matt. 3:2; 4:17.
59 John 1:49.
60 Matt. 21:4, 5; Zech. 9:9.
61 Matt. 9:27; 21:9, 16; Mark 11:10; Luke 19:38-40.
62 Luke 19:38.
63 Luke 19:40.
64 Luke 11:20.
65 Luke 17: 20, 21.
66 John 18:36, 37.
67 *Scofield Reference Bible,* pp: 723, 998, 1011, 1012, 1022, 1028, 1100, 1132, 1226, 1227.
68 John 6:15.

which you see and hear. . . . Let all the house of Israel therefore know assuredly that God has made him both Lord and Christ, this Jesus whom you crucified."[69] And James declared that the reception of the Gentiles into the church of Christ was the rebuilding of the tabernacle of David which Amos had prophesied.[70] Paul defended the right of Gentiles to hold membership in the church of Christ by quoting the prophecy that Christ was to reign over the Gentiles.[71] Paul also said that God had "delivered us from the dominion of darkness and transferred us to the kingdom of his beloved Son, in whom we have redemption, the forgiveness of sins."[72]

The New Testament represents that Jesus has complete sovereignty over the universe in a general way, and that He is in a special way the beloved Lord of the church. After His resurrection Jesus declared that He had all authority in heaven and on earth.[73] And Paul speaks of God's great power, "which he accomplished in Christ when he raised him from the dead and made him sit at his right hand in the heavenly places, far above all rule and authority and power and dominion, and above every name that is named, not only in this age but also in that which is to come; and he has put all things under his feet and has made him the head over all things for the church, which is his body, the fulness of him who fills all in all."[74] Christ is also "the head of the body, the church; he is the beginning, the firstborn from the dead, that in everything he might be preeminent."[75] Peter states that Jesus "has gone into heaven and is at the right hand of God, with angels, authorities, and powers subject to him."[76]

Perhaps the most significant passage on the mediatorial kingship of Jesus is found in I Corinthians. Paul indicates that Jesus was the first to rise from the dead. Christ is now putting His enemies under His feet. The last enemy which He will destroy is death. The destruction of death will take place at His coming when His saints are raised. "Then comes the end, when he delivers the kingdom to God the Father after destroying every rule and every authority and power. For he must reign until he has put all his enemies under his feet. The last enemy to be destroyed is death. 'For God has put all things in subjection under his feet.' . . . When all things are subjected to him, then the Son himself will also be subjected to him who put all things under him, that God may be everything to every one."[77]

Concerning our risen Lord and Saviour Paul writes: "There-

69 Acts 2:29-36.   72 Col. 1:13, 14.   75 Col. 1:18.
70 Acts 15:13-18.   73 Matt. 28:18.   76 I Pet. 3:22.
71 Rom. 15:12; Isa. 11:10.   74 Eph. 1:20-22.   77 I Cor. 15:24-26, 28.

fore I want you to understand that no one speaking by the Spirit of God ever says 'Jesus be cursed!' and no one can say 'Jesus is Lord' except by the Holy Spirit."[78] It should also be noted that the Apostle John describes Jesus as "the faithful witness, the firstborn of the dead, and the ruler of kings on earth."[79]

7. *PENTECOST AND ITS SIGNIFICANCE*

Since the fall of man human nature is such that the natural man does not receive the things of the Spirit of God.[80] He in whom the Spirit of God has not worked will not respond to the Word of God. A careful examination of the teachings of the Old Testament will reveal that it is hardly correct to hold that no one had the Holy Spirit prior to the day of Pentecost. On the contrary, it would appear from the prayer of Ezra in Nehemiah 9 that Israel as a whole did receive the Holy Spirit as its instructor. Ezra enumerates the many blessings of God: the pillar of cloud by day, and the pillar of fire by night. "Thou gavest thy good Spirit to instruct them, and didst not withhold thy manna from their mouth, and gavest them water for their thirst."[81] Nevertheless, the Scriptures do make a rather sharp contrast between the blessings conferred by the Holy Spirit on the people of God prior to the day of Pentecost and those given afterwards. The Gospel of John indicates that something was lacking in reference to Holy Spirit blessings, "because Jesus was not yet glorified."[82] John the Baptist protested that he was able to baptize with water only but that Jesus would baptize with the Holy Spirit.[83] And just before His ascension the Lord Himself stated: "John baptized with water, but before many days you shall be baptized with the Holy Spirit."[84]

On the day of Pentecost the Holy Spirit inaugurated His full ministry to believing Israel with striking phenomena: there were visible tongues as of fire, a roar as of wind, and supernatural speaking in tongues.[85] It should be observed parenthetically that the Book of Acts is a sort of commentary on the commission of Jesus just prior to His ascension: "And you shall be my witnesses in Jerusalem and in all Judea and Samaria and to the end of the earth."[86] It is of present interest to observe that at each stage of the missionary outreach of the church the Holy Spirit confirmed the outreach by striking phenomena similar to Pentecost. In Acts 8 after Philip had preached to the Samaritans and they had become believers, Peter and John went

78 I Cor. 12:3.
79 Rev. 1:5.
80 I Cor. 2:14.
81 Neh. 9:20.
82 John 7:39; 12:16.
83 Mark 1:8.
84 Acts 1:5, 8.
85 Acts 2:1-4.
86 Acts 1:8.

down and prayed that they might receive the Holy Spirit. When the apostles laid hands on the Samaritan believers, "they received the Holy Spirit,"[87] and there was evidently some external demonstration, for the fact that they had received the Holy Spirit was evident even to a man like Simon, who wanted to purchase the same power. Again, while Peter was in the act of preaching the Gospel to the Gentiles, the Holy Spirit fell upon those who heard the Word and the Jewish believers "were amazed, because the gift of the Holy Spirit had been poured out even on the Gentiles. For they heard them speaking in tongues and extolling God."[88]

On a later occasion Peter declared his interpretation of this event: "As I began to speak, the Holy Spirit fell on them just as on us at the beginning. And I remembered the word of the Lord, how he said, 'John baptized with water, but you shall be baptized with the Holy Spirit.' If then God gave the same gift to them as he gave to us when we believed in the Lord Jesus Christ, who was I that I could withstand God?"[89] The response of the Jerusalem church was gratifying: "They glorified God, saying, 'Then to the Gentiles also God has granted repentance unto life.' "[90] The Book of Acts also indicates that it was not enough for people to have been baptized unto the remission of sins by John the Baptist; it was also necessary to become personal believers on the Lord Jesus Christ, that is, Christians.[91]

The reader will have observed that the pouring out of the Holy Spirit upon Christian believers from Pentecost and onward is spoken of as the "baptism" of the Holy Spirit. Holy Spirit baptism signifies exactly the same thing as the receiving of the Holy Spirit. And the New Testament represents that every Christian has indeed been baptized by the Holy Spirit. One cannot become a believer without receiving the Holy Spirit. "Any one who does not have the Spirit of Christ does not belong to him."[92] And Paul indicates in his letter to the Corinthians that it is the Spirit who inducts every believer into the church of Christ, and everyone who is thus converted by the Spirit of God also receives the Spirit: "For by one Spirit we were all baptized into one body—Jews or Greeks, slaves or free—and all were made to drink of one Spirit."[93] It must be emphasized that the New Testament knows nothing of people being saved but not having been baptized with the Holy Spirit. Everyone who has truly become a believer and been thus inducted into the true body of Christ has, according to Paul, been "baptized" with the Spirit, made to "drink"

87 Acts 8:17.
88 Acts 10:45, 46.
89 Acts 11:15-17.
90 Acts 11:18.
91 Acts 19:1-7.
92 Rom. 8:9.
93 I Cor. 12:13.

of the Spirit. The fact that Christians have been baptized with the Spirit of God does not depend upon a subjective awareness of this truth; Holy Spirit baptism is not a matter of feeling. To be a true believer on the Lord Jesus Christ and to have been baptized with the Holy Spirit are aspects of one and the same experience.

The expression "to be filled with the Spirit" or to be "full of the Spirit" is used a number of times in the Acts. It is said of Christian believers on the day of Pentecost, "And they were all filled with the Holy Spirit."[94] The very same Greek term for "filled" is used soon afterwards of the believers who were undergoing persecution: "And when they had prayed, the place in which they were gathered together was shaken; and they were all filled with the Holy Spirit and spoke the word of God with boldness."[95] It is possible that this latter passage means simply that the disciples were *full* of the Holy Spirit and not that they were again *filled*. In any case it should be observed that the Holy Spirit is a person and that the expression "filling" is not to be understood in a quantitative sense. Dr. Joseph Henry Thayer, translator and reviser of *Grimm's Greek-English Lexicon,* states: "What wholly *takes possession* of the mind is said *to fill* it."[96] To be filled with the Holy Spirit therefore means to receive the person of the Holy Spirit for one's sanctification and guidance, making Christ the Lord of one's life. Ananias could therefore say to Saul: "Brother Saul, the Lord Jesus who appeared to you on the road by which you came, has sent me that you might regain your sight and be filled with the Holy Spirit."[97] The Greek term in Acts 13:9 for filled is an aorist passive participle having the force, "having been filled with the Holy Spirit." The seven stewards in general as well as Stephen in particular are spoken of in the Book of Acts as being full of the Holy Spirit, as is also Barnabas.[98]

A different word from that described above is used in Acts 13:52 for the way the disciples were being full of joy and of the Holy Spirit at Antioch. It is also employed in the command to keep filled with the Spirit in Ephesians 5:18. Dr. Thayer says of this word that it is "used of those who will nothing but what God wills."[99] Again it must be stressed that passages such as Ephesians 5:18 are not to be understood in a quantitative sense, as if one had some Holy Spirit but needed more. The Holy Spirit is not received in terms of vol-

94 Acts 2:4.
95 Acts 4:31.
96 Thayer, *A Greek-English Lexicon of the New Testament* (New York: American Book Co., 1889), p. 509.
97 Acts 9:17.
98 Acts 6:3; 6:5; 11:24.
99 *Op. cit.,* p. 517.

ume, but is a Person who is to be obeyed. To be filled with the Spirit is, therefore, to continually keep open every area of one's personality and life for the inspection and sanctification of the Spirit.

The New Testament gives a number of concrete illustrations of what it means for Christians to live in the fullness of Holy Spirit blessing and power. For one thing this type of rich Christian life involves having the mind of Christ, that is, putting His concerns first in one's life. "For those who live according to the flesh set their minds on the things of the flesh, but those who live according to the Spirit set their minds on the things of the Spirit. To set the mind on the flesh is death, but to set the mind on the Spirit is life and peace."[1] A second effect of being filled with the Spirit of God is that of becoming an effective witness for Christ, that is, being filled with such redeeming love as shall win others to Christ.[2]

When the Apostle Paul described the fruit of the Spirit he did not indicate that believers were individually to experience again those divine attestations to God's *inauguration* of the Holy Spirit age and His reception of Gentiles into the church as recorded in the Book of Acts; indeed, tongues are found in only one of the epistles and are there somewhat depreciated.[3] Paul says rather that the fruit of the Spirit is: "love, joy, peace, patience, kindness, goodness, faithfulness, gentleness, self-control."[4] It should also be noted that he who is filled with the Spirit is not inclined to glorify the Spirit but the Lord Jesus Christ. Jesus Himself testified that the Holy Spirit would not glorify Himself; rather, "He will glorify me, for he will take what is mine and declare it to you."[5] When a man is filled with the Spirit of God, that is, is completely obedient to the Lord and His Word, he will have a joyful awareness of his faith union with Christ so that he can say with the Apostle Paul: "I have been crucified with Christ; it is no longer I who live, but Christ who lives in me; and the life I now live in the flesh I live by faith in the Son of God, who loved me and gave himself for me"[6]; and, "To me to live is Christ."[7] The entire sanctification of Christians for which Paul prays[8] is not achieved by a mere effort of the human will, nor will it, however, be realized apart from our desire; rather it is progressively realized by such an earnest devotional life that love for God progressively expels sin from the heart and enables an ever more perfect yielding to the will of God.

---

1 Rom. 8:5, 6.
2 Acts 1:5-8.
3 I Cor. 14.
4 Gal. 5:22, 23.
5 John 16:13-15.
6 Gal. 2:20.
7 Phil. 1:21.
8 I Thess. 5:23.

Christians should not be encouraged to seek some sort of emotional crisis in the belief that they need "more Spirit." Rather, they should be encouraged to meet the conditions for fullness of Holy Spirit blessing and power, for the Spirit who has baptized them into the body of Christ wishes to become sovereign in their lives. Immature Christians do not need a greater quantity of Spirit; they stand in need of a fuller yielding and of a daily surrender to the will of the Lord Jesus Christ as interpreted to their hearts by the blessed Holy Spirit. There is hardly an area of Christian doctrine on which it is more unfortunate for earnest believers to be misled than that connected with the various unscriptural and fanatical doctrines associated with so-called Holy Spirit baptisms, "second works," etc. New Testament piety has a wonderfully wholesome and sober quality. God is not interested in making fanatics; rather, He wants to transform us into the image of His Son: "And we all with unveiled face, beholding the glory of the Lord, are being changed into his likeness from one degree to another; for this comes from the Lord who is the Spirit."[9] The more perfectly Christians yield to the sanctifying of the indwelling Spirit of God, the more they will become like the Lord Jesus Christ in all His beauty of character, in meekness and love, in patience and kindness, in holiness and goodness, and especially in concern for those who have not yet accepted the reconciliation which is in Christ Jesus.

8. THE NATURE AND FUNCTION OF THE CHURCH

What the Church Is

First of all it is necessary to clarify what the church is not: it is not any sort of political group or theocracy, nor is it a racial body. The concept of a national church does violence to the New Testament presentation of the church as a universal body of Christian believers.

According to the New Testament the true church is composed of all those who are regenerated and who have faith in the Lord Jesus Christ. Our Lord Himself said, following the confession of Peter, "Blessed are you, Simon Bar-Jona! For flesh and blood has not revealed this to you, but my Father who is in heaven. And I tell you, you are Peter, and on this rock I will build my church, and the powers of death shall not prevail against it."[10] The Apostle Paul stated: "For no other foundation can anyone lay than that which is

---

9 II Cor. 3:18.   10 Matt. 16:17, 18.

laid, which is Jesus Christ."[11] Paul speaks repeatedly of Christ as the head of the church.[12] And Peter speaks of the church as a spiritual house, a holy priesthood.[13] It is a divine society of which Christ is the head. The church of Christ is fundamentally a Christian brotherhood rather than an organization, or much less, a hierarchy. Jesus warned in the strongest possible terms against anyone in the church, regardless of his office, assuming dictatorial powers or receiving undue recognition. Jesus explained that the Pharisees seek such honor of men as public salutations, the title of rabbi, etc. "But you are not to be called rabbi, for you have one teacher, and you are all brethren. And call no man your father on earth, for you have one Father, who is in heaven. Neither be called masters, for you have one master, the Christ. He who is greatest among you shall be your servant; whoever exalts himself will be humbled, and whoever humbles himself will be exalted."[14] The Saviour also said: "You know that the rulers of the Gentiles lord it over them, and their great men exercise authority over them. It shall be not so among you; but whoever would be great among you must be your servant, and whoever would be first among you must be your slave; even as the Son of man came not to be served but to serve, and to give his life as a ransom for many."[15] The Apostle Peter gives the same type of instructions to the elders of the church: "Tend the flock of God that is your charge, not by constraint but willingly, not for shameful gain but eagerly, not as domineering over those in your charge but being examples to the flock."[16]

The New Testament uses the term "church" in two ways. First, of the local congregations in the various cities or provinces, such as Corinth, Philippi, Galatia, Ephesus, etc. In the second place, the term "church" is also applied to the entire body of Christian believers: this is especially true of passages which speak of Christ being the head of the church or as giving Himself for the church. The term "church" is never applied to any sort of edifice or building, however; it is the Christians who constitute the church.

Since the church is a brotherhood of Christian love,[17] it should be the concern of each member to do all he can to meet every type of need which he sees in the other members of the body of Christ:

---

11 I Cor. 3:11 (motto of Menno Simons).
12 Col. 1:18; Eph. 5:23; etc.
13 I Pet. 2:5. Cf. Franklin H. Littell, *The Anabaptist View of the Church* (American Society of Church History, 1952); also Ernest A. Payne, *The Fellowship of Believers* (London: Carey Kingsgate Press, 1952).
14 Matt. 23:8-10.
15 Matt. 20:25-27.
16 I Pet. 5:2, 3.
17 Symbolized, e.g., by the holy kiss. Rom. 16:16.

spiritual, material, educational, social, etc. The New Testament recognizes, however, that what may be the general duty of the brotherhood as a whole is not necessarily the calling of the ministry: for example, in the apostolic church the apostles felt that it was not fitting for them to neglect the ministry of the Word in order to take care of the physical needs of the widows; consequently seven stewards were chosen for this task.[18] It is possible also that the apostolic church had an order of deaconesses, older widows who devoted themselves in a special way to a service of love to the other members of the church.[19] Paul states that he himself was eager to keep in mind the poor and help to meet their needs.[20]

Even more significant than the meeting of physical needs is the spiritual concern which each member of the apostolic church was expected to have for the other members of the brotherhood. The apostle gave the following instructions in his Letter to the Galatians: "Brethren, if a man is overtaken in any trespass, you who are spiritual should restore him in a spirit of gentleness. Look to yourself, lest you too be tempted. Bear one another's burdens, and so fulfil the law of Christ."[21] The Letter to the Hebrews calls upon the individual members of the church to exhort one another daily.[22] The Apostle James writes: "My brethren, if any one among you wanders from the truth and some one brings him back, let him know that whoever brings back a sinner from the error of his way will save his soul from death and will cover a multitude of sins."[23] And John states: "If any one sees his brother committing what is not a mortal sin, he will ask, and God will give him life for those whose sin is not mortal."[24] This mutual effort on the part of the rank and file of the members of the church to assist one another seems to have become practically a dead letter in modern Christendom. What a contrast with the warm spirit of love in the apostolic church, a brotherhood which symbolized its love by the greeting of the holy kiss.[25]

Offices and Gifts in the New Testament Church

The New Testament does not prescribe what the various offices of the church shall be for all time. Two general terms for the officers of the apostolic church are used in the New Testament, one of which might be translated *presiders*,[26] the other *leaders*.[27] More specifically

18 Acts 6:2.
19 Rom. 16:1; I Tim. 5:9.
20 Gal. 2:10.
21 Gal. 6:1, 2.
22 Heb. 3:13.
23 Jas. 5:19, 20.
24 I John 5:16.
25 Rom. 16:16.
26 Rom. 12:8; I Thess. 5:16; I Tim. 3:4, 5, 12; 5:17.
27 Heb. 13:7, 17, 24.

the New Testament frequently speaks of bishops or *overseers*.[28] It also refers to *elders*,[29] the term being borrowed from the Jewish synagogue and being frequently used in the New Testament to refer to Jewish synagogue leaders.[30] Within the New Testament itself it seems clear that the terms "bishop" and "elder" are used synonymously. For example, when the Apostle Paul was at Miletus he sent to Ephesus and called to him the elders of the church at that place.[31] When they arrived he made a major address to them in the course of which he said: "Take heed to yourselves and to all the flock, in which the Holy Spirit has made you bishops, to feed the church of God,[32] which he purchased with his own blood."[33] In the Letter of Paul to Titus he instructed him to "appoint elders in every town,"[34] explaining also what type of men they needed to be, "For a bishop, as God's steward, must be blameless."[35]

The epistles of the New Testament also speak of various other gifts and offices in the apostolic church. Some of these offices were related to the great task of enlarging and building the church: apostles, prophets, teachers, evangelists, and pastors;[36] but there were also miraculous gifts to meet the special needs in the life of the infant church: gifts of miracles, healings, tongues, and the interpretation of tongues.[37] At the very beginning the Holy Spirit seems to have given a rich array of gifts to the infant church to get it well established, after which He directed the church into more formal or institutionalized lines. It would seem that by the time of the later epistles of the New Testament there were two permanent offices[38] in the church: bishops or elders, of which there seemed to have been several in each congregation, and who assumed the general supervision and oversight of the church; and deacons who, judging by the qualifications given for them, must have served as pastoral assistants, perhaps preaching frequently, "For those who serve well as deacons gain a good standing for themselves and also great confidence in the faith which is in Christ Jesus."[39] In the apostolic church any one, male or female, seems to have been free to prophesy or to lead in prayer;[40] the Apostle Paul, however, seems to have requested women not to

28 I Tim. 3:1-7; Phil. 1:1; Acts 20:28; Titus 1:7.
29 Acts 11:30; 14:23; 15:2; 16:4; 20:17; 21:18; I Tim. 5:17, 19; Titus 1:5; Jas. 5:14; I Pet. 5:1.
30 Matt. 15:2; 16:21; 21:23; Acts 4:8; 6:12
31 Acts 20:17.
32 The reading of the two oldest manuscripts of the Bible, Vaticanus and Sinaiticus.
33 Acts 20:28.
34 Titus 1:5.
35 Titus 1:7.   38 Phil. 1:1.
36 Eph. 4:11.   39 I Tim. 3:13.
37 I Cor. 12:8-12; 12:28-30.   40 I Cor. 11:5; 14:31.

assume any administrative authority over men in the church; women are to be silent in the administration of the church.[41] The New Testament symbols of man's administrative headship are man's uncovered head in worship, and woman's veiled head. I Corinthians 11:2-16.

Principles of Church Government

The New Testament does not set down a systematic list of principles to serve as a polity for all time in the Christian Church. Nevertheless, it does contain such basic principles as that ministers are fundamentally heralds and teachers of the Gospel and servants of the congregation. The Apostle Paul stated that his primary calling was evangelism, rather than a mere performance of the ceremony of baptism.[42] His basic commission to Timothy was, "Preach the word.[43]

As was noted above, ministers should also avoid assuming excessive authority but should regard themselves as members of the brotherhood on a common level with those whom they are seeking to serve.[44] This means, of course, that the minister will not only avoid becoming a dictator but that he will also seek to enlist the total membership of the church in the work of Christ, rather than attempting to perform a large number of the duties himself. The Book of Acts indicates that when problems arose it was the church, not merely the ministry, that sent delegates to Jerusalem for help.[45] At the apostolic council it was not merely the apostles who made decisions but the whole church took approving action.[46] It is possible that the ministers of the apostolic church were elected by the congregation, perhaps following the pattern of the Jewish synagogue.[47] If ministers have an awareness of being answerable both to God and to the brotherhood for their service and oversight it will help them not to become dictatorial in spirit.

The New Testament is clear that the congregation owes the ministry support in prayer.[48] It also owes the ministry loyal cooperation in the work of God. Christians are God's fellow workers; they are workers together with God.[49] The congregation owes its ministry cheerful obedience. The Letter to the Hebrews states: "Obey your leaders and submit to them; for they are keeping watch over your souls, as men who will have to give account. Let them do this joyfully, and not sadly . . . ."[50]

41 I Cor. 14:34, 15; esp. I Tim. 2:12.
42 I Cor. 1:17.
43 II Tim. 4:2.
44 Mark 10:42-44.
45 Acts 15:2, 3.

46 Acts 15:22.
47 Acts 14:23 (cf. Weymouth); II Cor. 8:19.
48 II Thess. 3:1; Jas. 5:16.
49 I Cor. 3:9; 6:1; Phil. 1:7.
50 Heb. 13:17.

The New Testament is also clear that the congregation owes its ministry financial support. The Apostle Paul argues this point earnestly in I Corinthians 9, using the illustrations of a soldier, a vinedresser, a shepherd, the teaching of the Old Testament, a farmer, the principle of mutual compensation, the general practice in the apostolic church, the supported priesthood of the Old Testament, and the specific ordination of Jesus.[51] The Gospels contain the express instruction of Christ that "The laborer deserves his wages," a passage which the Apostle Paul quotes in proof of the principle of ministerial support.[52] Many Christians are not aware that when Paul states in his first letter to the Corinthians that he had "made no use of any of these rights," that he was referring only to the church in Corinth.[53] This fact comes out in his second letter to the Corinthians where he states: "Did I commit a sin in abasing myself so that you might be exalted, because I preached God's gospel without cost to you? I robbed other churches by accepting support from them in order to serve you. And when I was with you and was in want, I did not burden any one, for my needs were supplied by the brethren who came from Macedonia. So I refrained and will refrain from burdening you in any way. As the truth of Christ is in me, this boast of mine shall not be silenced in the regions of Achaia. And why? Because I do not love you? God knows I do!"[54]

In the Letter to the Galatians the Apostle Paul states frankly: "Let him who is taught the word share all good things with him who teaches."[55] And in the Letter to the Philippians Paul states how much he appreciated the gift which they had sent to him, although he said that he had learned the secret of facing plenty and hunger, abundance and want, without complaint. "Yet it was kind of you to share my trouble. And you Philippians yourselves know that in the beginning of the gospel, when I left Macedonia, no church entered into partnership with me in giving and receiving except you only; for even in Thessalonica you sent me help once and again. Not that I seek the gift; but I seek the fruit which increases to your credit. I have received full payment, and more; I am filled, having received from Epaphroditus the gifts you sent, a fragrant offering, a sacrifice acceptable and pleasing to God."[56]

On the subject of stewardship the apostle writes: "He who sows sparingly will also reap sparingly, and he who sows bountifully will

51 I Cor. 9:1-14.
52 Matt. 10:9, 10; Luke 10:7; I Tim. 5:17, 18. The passage in I Tim. refers to an *honorarium,* financial gifts, not to *honor.*
53 I Cor. 9:15.
54 II Cor. 11:7-11; cf. 12:13.
55 Gal. 6:6.
56 Phil. 4:10-13; 4:14-18.

also reap bountifully. Each one must do as he has made up his mind, not reluctantly or under compulsion, for God loves a cheerful giver. And God is able to provide you with every blessing in abundance, so that you may always have enough of everything and may provide in abundance for every good work."[57]

The New Testament does not specify how ministers are to be chosen. It would seem, however, that the final authority should reside in the Christian Church, which should have the right to examine any individual who professes to have the inner call to preach the Gospel of Christ; that is, the congregation and the conference should be able to prevent unsound or unstable individuals assuming in an irresponsible way the sober yet glorious task of preaching the Word of God. Every effort should be made to encourage qualified individuals having the call of the Holy Spirit to preach the Word, to obey the voice of the Lord by giving their lives to this ministry.

Church Discipline

The Lord Jesus not only established His church on earth and committed to it the ministry of reconciliation: He also invested the church with authority to maintain discipline and to assist the individual members of the body of Christ to live a life which glorifies Christ and gives an effective witness to the power of the Gospel. When Peter had made his great confession at Caesarea Philippi Jesus replied: "Blessed are you, Simon Bar-Jona! For flesh and blood have not revealed this to you, but my Father who is in heaven. And I tell you, you are Peter [the word 'Peter' means stone or rock], and on this rock I will build my church, and the powers of death shall not prevail against it. I will give you the keys of the kingdom of heaven, and whatever you bind on earth shall be bound in heaven, and whatever you loose on earth shall be loosed in heaven."[58] A little later Jesus extended this authority to the entire church. He says if the transgressor "refuses to listen even to the church, let him be to you as a Gentile and a tax collector. Truly, I say to you, whatever you bind on earth shall be bound in heaven, and whatever you loose on earth shall be loosed in heaven."[59] Following the resurrection of Christ He breathed upon them and said: "Receive the Holy Spirit. If you forgive the sins of any, they are forgiven; if you retain the sins of any, they are retained."[60] A good example of the exercise of apos-

---

57 II Cor. 9:6-8.
58 Matt. 16:17-19. The granting of the keys is the foundation of the binding and loosing authority. The translation of Williams seems to be vigorously Protestant, but not sound exegetically.
59 Matt. 18:17, 18.
60 John 20:22, 23.

tolic authority is that of the Jerusalem conference, although the record makes clear that the Christian elders together with the whole church concurred in the decision of the apostles.[61]

Since it is freely acknowledged that technically the church of Christ does not have any members in it today with the rank of apostle, it is especially significant to note the teaching of the epistles of the New Testament on the authority of the church. A good example of the need of church discipline occurred in the church at Corinth where a member of the church was living in an incestuous relation and refusing to repent. In this difficult situation the Apostle Paul instructed the church what its responsibility was. Paul told the church plainly that when an individual is impenitent it becomes necessary to expel him from the body of Christ and to break fellowship with him so long as he is impenitent.[62] The apostle is, however, equally clear that when such an expelled transgressor does come to repentance he shall be fully forgiven by the church and completely reinstated as a member of the brotherhood.[63]

Both the spirit and the letter of the New Testament stress the brotherhood character of the church and this is, of course, highly significant as to any concept or program of church discipline. We need again to remind ourselves at this point of the warning of Jesus against leaders assuming dictatorial power.[64] In many Protestant churches today, however, it is precisely the opposite danger which threatens the church—that of allowing every member to do that which is right in his own eyes, regardless of how unscriptural he may be or how poor his testimony and witness. The New Testament assumes not only the right but the obligation of the brotherhood to apply the principles of God's Word to the age in which one lives. A Christian church has not done its duty when it preaches about the sins of King David and Judas; it is even more important to give a witness against the sins of the age in which one is living. Chief emphasis should, of course, fall on maintaining a discipline which is Scriptural, not merely traditional.

In the exercise of the discipline of the church the ordained brethren must naturally assume the leadership and supervision, but the laity must also take a loyal and co-operative attitude. When the New Testament writers address the elders they say: "Tend the flock of God that is your charge, not by constraint but willingly, not for shameful gain but eagerly, not as domineering over those in your

---

61 Acts 15:6, 22.
62 I Cor. 5:2, 5, 11-13.
63 II Cor. 2:6-11.
64 Mark 10:42-44.

charge but being examples to the flock. And when the chief Shepherd is manifested you will obtain the unfading crown of glory."[65] To the laity the New Testament says: "Obey your leaders and submit to them; for they are keeping watch over your souls, as men who will have to give account. Let them do this joyfully, and not sadly."[66] If the ordained leaders of the congregations of Christendom today would all be humble and faithful spiritual leaders, seeking only to uphold the Word of God and to apply its principles to the contemporary world, and earnestly attempting to assist each member of the Christian Church to realize fully his spiritual resources in Christ, it would be natural for born-again believers to render cheerful obedience to the ministry. But if the ministry is dictatorial, or is seeking to maintain a cultural *status quo* rather than a Biblical discipline, or if the laity is cold spiritually and worldly, there can be only tension and frustration in any attempt to maintain discipline in the church. (See Marlin Jeschke, *Discipling the Brother*, HP, 1972.)

If the church is to be in reality a Christian brotherhood rather than a hierarchy, it should be evident that the interpretation of Biblical principles and their application to the culture of any given era is not the task of a few specialists who would in turn coerce the remainder of the brotherhood into obedience; it rather becomes the responsibility of the entire body of Christ, working naturally through its leadership, but doing so with the approval and consent of the entire body, to make such current applications of the eternal principles of God's Word as shall give the best witness to Christ and Christianity.

As far as printed disciplinary standards are concerned it would seem to be most effective generally to limit such standards to basic principles rather than to minute and detailed applications. If the opposite policy is followed, that of seeking to codify every Biblical principle and to work out its detailed implications, it would appear that a twofold danger would result: (1) there would be a constant need of revision which would become wearisome and frustrating and which would undoubtedly bring the whole matter of discipline into question on the part of thinking people; (2) the minute codification of the principles of church discipline would tend strongly in the direction of legalism. By legalism is here meant a loveless conformity to the letter of the law, rather than a joyful obedience rendered to Christ out of pure love for Him. The quality of life which results from such love for the Lord is infinitely superior to that which comes from a slavish conformity to the letter of human regulations. As a tract from the Reformation period asserts, there are two kinds of obedience: servile obedience which appeals to the flesh and produces proud Pharisees while resulting in a poor quality of performance; and filial obedience, which springs from devotion to God, which does not keep an eye merely on the letter of the law, and which results in a spiritual mode of life and a high quality of obedience.[67]

Having made clear that the Scripture does not promote any type of legalism whatsoever, it should be noted, however, that the New Testament does not hesitate to give what might be called concrete illustrations of basic principles of God's law. It has been the tendency of Christendom through the centuries, apart from certain Catholic orders and a few small Protestant groups, to ignore completely whatever sample illustrations the New Testament does give of basic principles and to allow individual members not only to ignore the concrete illustrations of proscribed behavior but to forget all about the very principles involved. The result has been that the professing Christian church has largely lost its distinctive witness for a high level of Christian behavior; the contrast between the church and the world has been almost obliterated. There is very little difference today between the average church member and the better type of people who make no profession of ordering their lives according to the word of Christ.

What are some of the sample illustrations of the New Testament of the type of behavior which one finds in the world which the Christian may not follow?

1. The New Testament teaches that the adornment of the Christian shall not consist of an artificial adornment of the body through the type of clothing that is worn or through such items as the wearing of pearls or gold; rather, the adornment of the Christian shall consist of the beauty of his spirit, his attitudes of kindness, sincerity, loyalty, humility, and love.[68] Christian women shall wear long hair.[68a]

2. Both Christ and the apostles state that Christian disciples ought not need to fortify their word by the swearing of oaths[69]; furthermore, the life of the child of God should be open before all men. There is therefore no place in the life of the simple follower of Christ for joining secret fraternities. When such fraternities are oathbound, and even promise salvation to their members regardless of

---

67 "Two Kinds of Obedience," *The Mennonite Quarterly Review*, XXI, I (Jan. 1947), pp. 18-22; reprinted by Harry Emerson Fosdick in his excellent anthology, *Great Voices of the Reformation*, New York: Random House, 1952, pp. 296-99.
68 I Tim. 2:9, 10; I Pet. 3:3.
68a I Cor. 11:6, 14, 15.
69 Matt. 5:33-37; 23:16-22; Jas. 5:12.

whether they are believers on Christ or not,[70] the situation becomes truly impossible for those who accept humbly all the commandments of the New Testament at their face value. This means that Christian congregations which seek to follow closely the ethic of the New Testament cannot tolerate lodge membership on the part of their members.

3. The Bible also condemns worldliness in all its forms[71] and this certainly includes the various forms of recreation which are so highly regarded in the culture of today. Naturally, the Bible cannot be explicit, for the prevailing means of entertainment change from age to age. Nevertheless, members of the stricter Christian groups today are keenly conscious that second-century Christians refused to attend the Roman theater or to take part in the sensual activities of their day.[72] Concretely, many believers hold that the avoidance of worldly amusements includes the playing of cards, the modern dance, and the theater.

4. Christ and His apostles assert in the strongest possible way that the only attitude which regenerated Christians can take toward wrongdoing is that of suffering. This is the way Jesus Himself dealt with sin. He followed the principle of redeeming love rather than of force and retaliation, even to the point of meekly allowing Himself to be crucified, and in so doing He destroyed the very power of evil. The New Testament urges Christians to take Christ as their example of nonresistant suffering. This means that both the ancient Christians, for the most part prior to the time of Constantine,[73] as well as various Christian groups down to the present time, have refused to employ force or violence of any kind including participation in the constabulary and in the military.

5. The New Testament also teaches that Christians shall regard their bodies as temples of the Holy Spirit and not use those bodies as instruments of sin. It is the obligation of the child of God to take good care of his physical body and not deliberately damage or poison it in any way.[74] This eliminates every form of intemperance as well as such habits as smoking and drinking, which do no good to anyone, which are milder or more severe cases of drug addiction, which involve the principle of Christian stewardship, and which give a questionable witness on the part of those who seek to take the Christian

---

70 J. C. Wenger, *Separated unto God* (Scottdale, Pa.: Mennonite Publishing House, 1952), pp. 194-96.

71 Rom. 12:2; I John 2:15, 16. Cf. Mary Nance Daniel, *Worldliness Out* (Nashville, Tenn.: Broadman Press, 1942).

72 C. J. Cadoux, *The Early Church and the World* (New York: Scribner's, 1925).

73 C. John Cadoux, *The Early Christian Attitude to War* (London: Allen & Unwin, 1940; Guy Franklin Hershberger, *War, Peace, and Nonresistance* (Scottdale, Pa.: Mennonite Publishing House, 1944).

74 I Cor. 6:9-12; Gal. 5:19-26; Titus 2:2.

life seriously. The age in which we live is a highly secularized and sensual one, and the need of giving a witness to the clean life and to simplicity of life is very great.

6. A particular application of the principle of nonresistant suffering rather than of retaliating or seeking justice against wrongdoers is the matter of litigation. The Apostle Paul does not hesitate to urge Christian believers to "take wrong" rather than to resort to courts of law for the achievement of their rights.[75]

7. Mention has already been made of the swearing of oaths and of the fact that both Christ and the apostles urge Christians to tell the truth always, without resorting to any form of oath to "strengthen" their word. It is obvious that one does not need to swear in order to tell the truth, and it is just as obvious that those who do swear are not always truthful.[76]

8. There seems to be no New Testament passage which warns Christians explicitly against gambling. Nevertheless, there seems to be a rather common conscience on the part of earnest Christian believers against any method of receiving unearned money. Games of chance which involve money are therefore regarded as inconsistent with the spirit of simplicity, industry, and stewardship, which are encouraged in the New Testament.

9. The New Testament also teaches the permanence of the marriage bond.[77] The American attitude which undertakes the obligations of marriage and makes the vows of the marriage ceremony with the mental reservation that if the union is not perfectly happy, the divorce courts will stand ready to dissolve the union: that attitude is completely unchristian and utterly foreign to the spirit and letter of the words of Christ and His apostles. It is the responsibility of the Christian Church to try to lift the current attitude toward marriage up to the level where Christ placed it. It is of course also the obligation of the church to take a redemptive attitude toward every sinner no matter how complicated his situation may have become. No sin of the flesh, not even divorce and remarriage, constitutes an unpardonable sin. It must be admitted, however, that it is sometimes difficult to take whatever steps are necessary to undo as much as possible of the evil which one's sin has occasioned.

A Symbol of Brotherhood and Cleansing

There is a lifelong strife in the child of God between the Spirit of God and the flesh. The flesh craves to have its own way, wants pity

---

75 I Cor. 6:1-9.   76 Menno Simons, *Complete Works*, II, pp. 410; II, pp. 272-75.
77 Matt. 5:32; 19:4-9; Mark 10:2-12; Luke 16:18; Rom. 7:2, 3; I Cor. 7:10-16.

and sympathy, is self-seeking, etc. The night before Jesus was crucified the old struggle for prestige and primacy broke out among the apostles. Luke reports the matter thus:

A dispute also arose among them, which of them was to be regarded as the greatest. And he said to them, "The kings of the Gentiles exercise lordship over them; and those in authority over them are called benefactors. But not so with you; rather let the greatest among you become as the youngest, and the leader as one who serves. . . . But I am among you as one who serves."[78]

The Apostle John also indicates that during the eating of the Passover, Jesus "rose from supper, laid aside his garments, and girded himself with a towel. Then he poured water into a basin, and began to wash the disciples' feet, and to wipe them with the towel with which he was girded."[79] All this was a powerful object lesson on the spirit of service and love which ought to characterize the disciples of Jesus Christ; it was a humiliating rebuke to the rivalry and place-seeking which existed among the Twelve. Peter saw at once the utter incongruity of the Lord stooping down and washing his feet; he therefore remonstrated, declaring with his usual vigor, "You shall never wash my feet."[80]

At this point a new element enters the picture. Up to this moment it had appeared only that Jesus was trying to teach His disciples of the spirit of love and brotherhood which He desired to see in them. But now a quite new truth emerges from the object lesson before them: Jesus must also cleanse His disciples of the guilt involved in daily living in the flesh. "If I do not wash you, you have no part in me."[81] Peter caught the point of spiritual cleansing in a flash. He cried out in all sincerity, "Lord, not my feet only but also my hands and my head!" The reply of Jesus is comforting indeed, "He who has [been] bathed does not need to wash, except for his feet, but he is clean all over."[82]

Marcus Dods explains: " 'He that has been in the bath has no need to wash save his feet, but is all clean.' His feet may be soiled by walking from the public bath to the supper chamber, and it is enough that they be washed. . . ."[83]

Jesus added at this point, "And you are clean, but not all of you." Dr. Dods states: "The added clause discloses that a spiritual sense underlies the symbol. . . . All had been washed: the feet of Judas were as clean as those of Peter. But Judas was not clean. . . .

78 Luke 22:24-27.
79 John 13:4, 5.
80 John 13:8.

81 John 13:8.
82 John 13:9, 10.
83 The Expositor's Greek Testament, I, p. 816.

Jesus thus . . . distinguishes between the offence of the rest and the sin of Judas. All that they required was to have the soil of their present evil temper and jealousy removed: they were true in heart, they had been in the bath and had only contracted a slight stain. But Judas had not been in the bath: he had no genuine and habitual loyalty to Christ. . . ."[84]

In commenting on Jesus' question, "Do you know what I have done to you?" Professor Dods writes: "By washing their feet He had washed their heart. By stooping to this menial service He had made them all ashamed of declining it. By this simple action He had turned a company of wrangling, angry, jealous men into a company of humbled and united disciples."[85]

It is with this understanding of John 13 that Menno Simons describes the bride of Christ as "the dear children of God who have their feet washed and their garments cleansed in the blood of the Lamb."[86] And Menno's good friend and fellow elder, Dirck Philips, explains the symbolism of John 13 thus: "First, he would have us know that he himself must cleanse us after the inner man, and that we must allow him to wash away the sins which beset us (Heb. 12:1) and all filthiness of the flesh and the spirit (Ezek. 36:25; II Cor. 7:1), that we may become purer from day to day, as it is written: He that is righteous, let him become more righteous; and he that is holy, let him become more holy (Rev. 22:11). . . .

"The second reason why Jesus instituted the ordinance of foot-washing is that we shall humble ourselves among one another . . . , and that we hold our fellow believers in the highest respect, for the reason that they are the saints of God and members of the body of Jesus Christ, and that the Holy Ghost dwells in them . . . ."[87]

The Dordrecht Confession of Faith of 1632 states:

We also confess a washing of the saints' feet, as the Lord Christ not only instituted, enjoined and commanded it, but Himself, although He was their Lord and Master, washed His apostles' feet, thereby giving an example that they should likewise wash one another's feet, and do as He had done unto them; which they accordingly, from this time on, taught believers to observe, as a sign of true humility, and especially to remember by this feet washing the true washing whereby we are washed through His precious blood, and made pure after the soul. John 13:4-17; I Tim. 5:10.[88]

84 *Ibid.*, pp. 816, 817.
85 *Ibid.*, p. 817.
86 *Complete Works*, I, p. 53.
87 *Enchiridion*, pp. 388-89.
88 *Martyrs' Mirror*, p. 42.

The Dutch Mennonites recognized this ceremony as an ordinance of the Lord, permanently binding upon His church, to be literally kept as a symbol of the spirit of service and equality in the brotherhood, and "especially" of the believer's cleansing in the blood of Christ. An examination of Dutch Anabaptist sources reveals that this ceremony was observed in the homes of the believers. Menno Simons writes: "Wash the feet of your beloved brethren and sisters who are come to you from a distance, tired. Be not ashamed to do the work of the Lord, but humble yourselves with Christ before your brethren's feet, that all humility according to the divine nature may be found in you. Jn. 13; I Tim. 5."[89]

Twisk's Confession of Thirty-Three Articles of A.D. 1617 states similarly:

Hence, the believers . . . ought also, when time and place permit, practice and observe this ordinance of Christ. When their fellow believers out of love visit them, they shall with heartfelt humility receive them with the kiss of love and peace into their houses, and as a ministration to their neighbors, according to the humiliation of Christ, wash their feet; sincerely considering how the most worshipful Son of God humbled Himself, not only washing the feet of His apostles, but much more, washing and purifying with His precious death and blood, all our souls and consciences from the stain of eternal condemnation. . . .[90]

The Jan Cents Confession of 1630 advises that,

. . . when our fellow believers from distant places come to visit us, we wash their feet . . . thereby declaring our humility toward God and our neighbor, with an humble prayer that the Lord would strengthen us more and more in humility, and that like as we have washed one another's feet He would be pleased to wash and cleanse our souls with His blood and the waters of the Holy Ghost from every stain and impurity of sin, that we may appear pure and blameless before His Father.[91]

Although the early Dutch Anabaptist-Mennonite tradition made feet washing a home ceremony, it was only a half-century (c. 1588) until one of the small Dutch Mennonite groups attached it to the observance of the Lord's Supper.[92] And most of the Mennonite congregations of North America which practice feet washing as a religious rite now do so in connection with the Supper. However, in the Franconia Conference of southeastern Pennsylvania it is observed at the "Preparatory Service" on the day prior to the communion service.

---

89 *Complete Works*, II, p. 449.   90 *Martyrs' Mirror*, p. 399.
                                          91 *Ibid.*, p. 36.
     92 Neff and Hege, *Mennonitische Lexikon* (Weierhof und Frankfurt a. M., 1913, 1924, 19—),
II, p. 23.

It would seem to the present writer that a most appropriate time and place for the observance of the ordinance of feet washing would be at the close of the Counsel Meeting service which is held universally in the Mennonite Church a week or two prior to the Lord's Supper, and at which each member of the congregation is asked to state that he has peace with God and with his fellow man. Then would be an excellent occasion for each member to wash feet with a fellow Christian to signify the intention to render every possible service of love to the other members of the church of Christ. In other words, feet washing is not a ceremony to symbolize that one is more humble than other Christians—if that would be the case, it would come closer to symbolizing a Pharisaical pride—but to symbolize spiritual equality and love in the brotherhood. Feet washing is a pledge to do all in one's power all through the year for the welfare and happiness of one's fellow believers. It is not a sacrament to magically convey grace, but a sign of the love and willing service which one is minded to render to the other members of the church. Further, as was noted above, Mennonites also regard feet washing as a symbol of spiritual cleansing which each believer enjoys in Christ Jesus. I John 1:9.

9. *THE SACRAMENTS OF THE CHURCH*

As will have been noted prior to this point, the early Swiss and Dutch Anabaptists sought to obey every New Testament command: they insisted on going about as missionaries all over central Europe regardless of the mandates of princes or emperors to the contrary; they practiced church discipline with the full knowledge that they were being maligned as fanatics and perfectionists for doing so; they held to a sharp line of separation between spiritual and worldly living, even when to do so was to invite the charge that they went beyond the "papists" in insisting on good works.[93] Nevertheless they understood the New Testament to place into a separate category two particular church ceremonies which they often called sacraments, although it is perfectly evident that they rejected completely the theory that the sacraments were direct and automatic channels of grace. They understood the sacraments to be symbols or *signs* "of the unspeakable grace of God," as Dirck Philips expressed it, "to remind us thereof with visible symbols,"[94] namely, baptism and the Lord's Supper.

93 *Johannes Kesslers Sabbata* (St. Gallen, 1902), p. 148.
94 *Op. cit.*, p. 386.

In reference to baptism and communion Conrad Grebel, the founder of Swiss Anabaptism, wrote of "the only two ceremonies."[95] Dirck Philips, one of the earliest and most effective Dutch Mennonite elders (bishops), also wrote of the "Scriptural use of the sacraments of Jesus Christ, that is, of baptism and the Lord's Supper."[96] Menno Simons referred dozens of times to "baptism and the Lord's Supper," "the baptism of Christ and His supper," "the Lord's holy baptism and supper," "the representation of both signs, under water and bread and wine," "the ordinances of baptism and the Holy Supper,"[97] etc., etc. Menno wrote expressly:

> If God would have his ceremonies under the law (which were numerous, and in one respect attended with trouble and expense, and which he commanded not through Christ, his Son, but through his servant Moses), kept thus strictly and unchanged until the time of Christ; how much more so will he have the few ceremonies of the New Testament kept strictly and unchanged, which are but two in number, being baptism and the Supper, which he has commanded, not through his servant but through his only begotten Son, Jesus Christ; and which are neither attended with trouble nor expense.[98]

Although the original Dutch Mennonite practice of washing the feet of traveling brethren had by 1588 been attached by the Groninger Old Flemish to the Lord's Supper, yet the Dordrecht Confession of Faith of 1632 still speaks of "the Lord's ordinances—baptism and supper" (Article IX).[99]

Baptism

Christian baptism originated with the Lord Jesus Christ, but it had two antecedents: (1) the inter-Testamental baptism of Jewish proselytes,[1] and (2) the baptism of repentance by John the Baptist.[2] Christian baptism, however, was something new. It is to be administered in the name of the holy Trinity to those who become disciples. Prior to His ascension Jesus declared: "All authority in heaven

---

95 "Conrad Grebel's Petition of Protest and Defense to the Zurich Council in 1524," E. H. Correll and H. S. Bender, *The Goshen College Record, Review Supplement*, 27, 4 (Jan. 1926), p. 23.

96 *Op. cit.*, p. 386.

97 *Complete Works*, 1, 4, 5, 48, 50, 63, 67, 76, 144, 147, 156, 158, 168, 175, 177, 214, 228, 242, 265, 280, II, 9, 11, 35, 43, 44, 46, 57, 58, 65, 66, 81, 86, 88, 102, 103, 110, 118, 119, 191, 196, 197, 242, 243, 259, 260, 269, 270, 444.

98 *Ibid.*, II, p. 196.

99 *Martyrs' Mirror*, p. 41.

1 Gerhard Kittel, *Theologisches Wörterbuch zum Neuen Testament* (Stuttgart: W. Kohlhammer, 1949), I, pp. 534-35; Issac Landman, Ed., *The Universal Jewish Encyclopedia* (New York: The Univ. Jewish Encyclo., 1940), II, p. 68.

2 Matt. 3:6; Mark 1:4.

and on earth has been given to me. Go therefore and make disciples of all nations, baptizing them in the name of the Father and of the Son and of the Holy Spirit, teaching them to observe all that I have commanded you; and lo, I am with you always, to the close of the age."[3] This was the instruction which Peter followed on the day of Pentecost. First of all, he preached the Word of God to the people; when they were cut to the heart and cried out for the way to be saved he directed them to Christ and His saving Gospel. Those who accepted his word he baptized. "And there were added that day about three thousand souls."[4]

The apostolic precedent on the day of Pentecost furnishes a beautiful model of correct procedure for the Christian Church in perpetuity: first, there was the declaration of God's Word by a man of God; second, the Holy Spirit convicted many of the hearers of their sin; third, in true contrition and repentance they turned away from their sin; fourth, they accepted the Christ who is offered as Saviour in the Gospel; and finally, baptism was administered to those who turned to Jesus, and they were thus inducted into the membership of the church. The proper steps are therefore as follows: (1) the proclamation of God's Word; (2) conviction of heart for one's sin; (3) contrition and repentance; (4) the acceptance of Jesus as Saviour and Lord; (5) induction into the church of Christ by water baptism. It will be observed at once that these steps presuppose a free church, not a religion established by state law, as well as freedom of conscience, not the employment of force to compel the acceptance of a faith or a creed. Baptism is to be administered to those who desire it, to those who have turned to the Lord in penitence and faith, and to those who are ready to assume the obligations of Christian discipleship. It may be observed in passing that these were the basic convictions of the Swiss Brethren and of the Hutterian Brethren of Moravia, as well as of the Dutch Obbenites later called Mennonites. These so-called Anabaptist groups were therefore the forerunners and founders of the free church movement. The free church concept was regarded as a dangerous and unscriptural heresy, a clever scheme of the devil, by the major groups of Christendom in the sixteenth century. (Compare Luther's polemic against the Anabaptists with their free church and their unrestricted missionary efforts, *Von den Schleichern und Winkelpredigern*, 1532.)

In the teaching of the New Testament baptism signifies at least four things:

3 Matt. 28:18-20.
4 Acts 2:36-41.

1. Baptism is a symbol of cleansing from sin. When Ananias came to the contrite Saul following his Damascus Road conversion he said: "And now why do you wait? Rise and be baptized, and wash away your sins, calling on his name."[5] Dr. A. T. Robertson states that the force of the passage is: "Get yourself baptized and get your sins washed away."[6] Water is in the first place then a symbol of cleansing, the removal of the defilement of sin through the blood of Christ.

2. Baptism also symbolizes one's "death" to sin. Baptism is not a momentary burial of the physical body but the death and burial of the old life of sin. Paul represents baptism as the symbol of what Christ accomplished in this respect by His death on the cross. He begins by asserting that in our baptism we signified our intention no longer to live in sin. Just as Christ died physically and was placed in the tomb, so the Christian is to die with Christ as far as the life of sin is concerned.[7] Following his baptism he is to "walk in newness of life."[8] The death of Jesus is not only the symbol of the Christian's death to sin; it is the means which makes that death possible: "We know that our old self was crucified with him so that the sinful body might be destroyed [rendered powerless], and we might no longer be enslaved to sin."[9] The conclusion is: "So you also must consider yourselves dead to sin and alive to God in Christ Jesus."[10]

3. Peter makes a somewhat obscure statement about baptism in his First Letter. He says that just as the ark saved Noah and his family at the time of the Deluge, so baptism saves Christians now, "not as a removal of dirt from the body but as an appeal to God for a clear conscience."[11] It should first of all be observed in this connection that the Greek word for "appeal" is not at all clear. The King James Version renders it, *answer;* the American Standard Version translates it, *interrogation;* Weymouth and Williams both employ, *craving;* Berkeley uses, *earnest seeking;* while the German has, *covenant.* Dr. Thayer in discussing this passage suggests the translation, "avowal of consecration."[12] It would seem that the most recent scholarship would support the translation of the Revised Standard Version, "*appeal* to God for a clear conscience." In any case, Peter is not representing baptism as a sacrament which automatically conveys divine grace or which washes away sin; it is rather a step which

5 Acts 22:16.
6 A. T. Robertson, *A Grammar of the Greek New Testament in the Light of Historical Research* (New York and London: Harper, c. 1931), p. 808.
7 Rom. 6:1-5.   10 Rom. 6:11.
8 Rom. 6:4.   11 I Pet. 3:21.
9 Rom. 6:6.   12 Thayer, *op. cit.,* p. 231.

one takes in order to have a clear conscience. The step which actually insures a clear conscience is the committal to Christ to live a life of faithful discipleship to Jesus Christ, relying upon Him for cleansing from sin and for enabling grace. It would, therefore, seem that Luther's paraphrase, covenant, is quite apt. Baptism truly constitutes a covenant of discipleship with God through Jesus Christ.

4. Water baptism becomes, therefore, in the final analysis a symbol of the baptism of the Holy Spirit. John the Baptist baptized with water but Jesus promised that He would baptize with the Holy Spirit.[13] This came to pass for the Jews on the day of Pentecost,[14] for the Samaritans a bit later,[15] and for the Gentiles when Peter opened the door of faith to the family of Cornelius.[16] And ever since the founding of the Christian Church on the day of Pentecost individual Christians have been baptized into the true body of Christ, the church, by the supernatural work of the Holy Spirit, who enables lost sinners to turn to Christ in repentance and faith. The Apostle Paul states this truth as follows: "But you are not in the flesh, you are in the Spirit, if the Spirit of God really dwells in you. Any one who does not have the Spirit of Christ does not belong to him."[17] Also, "For just as the body is one and has many members, and all the members of the body, though many, are one body, so it is with Christ. For by one Spirit we were all baptized into one body—Jews or Greeks, slaves or free— and all were made to drink of one Spirit."[18]

The term "baptism" is therefore applied both to water baptism and to Holy Spirit baptism, sometimes in such a general way as to make it difficult to know which baptism the writer has in mind: this because of the fact that water baptism is in very truth a symbol of the baptism of the Holy Spirit. For example, "As many of you as were baptized into Christ have put on Christ."[19] Does the apostle refer to water baptism or to Spirit baptism? Actually, he probably made no such distinction, although in the final analysis since the water is merely a symbol he certainly relied upon the Holy Spirit and not upon any mere ceremony for the accessioning of members to the church.

It should be observed that the description of baptism given in the Scriptures eliminates any thought of infants participating in this ceremony. Infants are not able to hear the Word of God, they are not capable of Holy Spirit conviction, they cannot repent and exercise faith in Jesus Christ. They cannot make the appeal of a good

13 Acts 1:5.
14 Acts 2:4.
15 Acts 8:17.

16 Acts 10:44.
17 Rom. 8:9.

18 I Cor. 12:12, 13.
19 Gal. 3:27.

conscience with God, they cannot promise to renounce sin and live a life of faithful discipleship to Christ. It appears, however, that at least by the latter part of the second century there were cases of infant baptism in the Christian Church, for the leader Origen, who was born about A.D. 185, states that he was baptized as an infant. As late as the fourth century there were still many cases of adult baptism, however.

In the sixteenth century when the Swiss Brethren, often labeled Anabaptists, inaugurated believer's baptism again, the leading reformers were obligated to attempt to justify the baptism of infants. Although Luther could not subscribe to the Roman Catholic doctrine of baptismal regeneration, he did assert that faith was introduced into the infant through prayer and the power of the Word. He also claimed that a baby has hidden faith, somewhat comparable to the faith of a Christian who is asleep. Luther admitted that there was not sufficient evidence from Scripture for the inauguration of infant baptism, but "in our time no one may venture . . . to reject or abandon infant baptism which has so long been practiced."[20] Luther's colleague, Philip Melanchthon, held that just as the infant sons of Israel were to be circumcised as a symbol of the Old Covenant, so Christians shall baptize their children as a symbol of the New Covenant in Christ.[21] The real opponent of the Swiss Brethren, however, was Ulrich Zwingli of Zurich. He employed the circumcision argument, the baptism of households, and the covenant concept which holds that the children of believers are included in the covenant on the basis of such passages as Acts 2:39 and I Corinthians 7:14.[22] It should be observed, however, that neither passage says anything about the baptism of infants. The passage in Acts merely indicates that the Gospel promise applied to the hearers of Peter, to the next generation as well, and perhaps to the Gentiles. Paul's remark in the First Letter to the Corinthians indicates only that a certain sanctifying influence emanates from a Christian parent, an obvious fact.

As far as the baptism of households is concerned it should be observed not only that the household of Cornelius was baptized but that the Holy Spirit fell on all who "heard the word."[23] Those who were thus converted were "speaking in tongues and extolling God."[24] Obviously, these are the people who were baptized. At the time of

---

20 John Horsch, *Infant Baptism* (Scottdale, Pa.: Published by the Author, 1917), pp. 38-42. This is a remarkable collection of source material on the subject.
21 *Ibid.*, pp. 42-45.   23 Acts 10:44.
22 *Ibid.*, pp. 52-68.   24 Acts 10:46.

the baptism of the household of the Philippian jailer Luke reports that the apostles "spoke the word of the Lord to him and to all that were in his house. . . . And he rejoiced with all his household that he had believed in God."[25] There is no evidence at all that Lydia was even a married woman, and therefore the baptism of herself and household[26] is not necessarily relevant to the present question. Scripture indicates not only that the household of Stephanus was baptized[27] but that they had "devoted themselves to the service of the saints."[28]

Many modern theologians assert that baptism is the pledge of a godly rearing. Concerning the necessity of such Christian nurture there is no debate at all. The only question relates to the basic meaning of baptism: Is baptism in the New Testament a pledge of Christian nurture for children or is it the symbol of a personal conversion and commitment to Christ? The basic question is not even whether there were infants in the families which were baptized; it is rather this: Are infants suitable candidates for baptism? Surely not! As to the proper subjects of water baptism see the contrary monographs of Karl Barth (1948, 1969) and Oscar Cullman (1950).

The Bible does not indicate what the mode of baptism shall be. The etymology of the Greek word for "baptize" would suggest in some cases such usages as repeated dippings, to immerge or submerge, for example sunken vessels, etc. A second argument in favor of immersion is drawn from patristic evidence: it is often held that second-century Christian fathers speak of baptism in terms which would suggest immersion. *The Didache or Teaching of the Twelve Apostles,* probably written between A.D. 120 and 180, gives the following instruction for baptism: "After giving the foregoing instructions, 'Baptize in the name of the Father, and of the Son, and of the Holy Spirit' in running water. But, if you have no running water, baptize in any other; and if you cannot in cold water, then in warm. But, if the one is lacking, pour the other three times on the head 'In the name of the Father, and Son, and Holy Spirit.' But, before the baptism, let the one who baptizes and the one to be baptized fast, and any others who are able to do so."[29] While the mode is here not prescribed, many church historians believe that immersion was the usual practice. The present writer, however, knows of no actual

25 Acts 16:32-34.
26 Acts 16:15.
27 I Cor. 1:16.
28 I Cor. 16:15.
29 "The Didache or Teaching of the Twelve Apostles," *The Apostolic Fathers,* Vol. I of *The Fathers of the Church,* Translated by Francis X. Glimm, Joseph M. F. Marique, S. J., and Gerald G. Walsh (New York: Cima Publishing Co., 1947), p. 177. Used by permission.

proof that this was the case. The anonymous *Letter of Barnabas,* written between A.D. 70 and 150, does say: "This means that we go down into the water full of sins and foulness, and we come up bearing fruit in our hearts, fear and hope in Jesus in the Spirit."[30] It is possible, of course, that the writer has in mind only that both the bishop and the convert stood in the water for the ceremony, though most church historians would hardly accept this as the actual practice of the second-century church. A third argument in favor of immersion is that the symbolism of Romans 6 and Colossians 2 which speaks of burial with Christ in baptism requires immersion of the body in water.[31]

It will thus be observed that the three main arguments for immersion are linguistic, historical, and exegetical. And baptism upon confession of faith should always be recognized as valid. The Mennonite Church recognizes immersion as a valid baptism, for it does not require rebaptism of those who have been baptized by immersion and who later desire to transfer their membership to the Mennonite brotherhood. The belief that baptism should be by pouring does not involve a condemnation of immersion as a valid mode. The significance of a sacramental sign does not reside in its material form but in the faith of the recipient who is sincerely looking to Christ for the blessings symbolized.

A number of considerations are also used to justify affusion or pouring as a mode of baptism. As far as the New Testament Greek word for "baptize" is concerned it means neither immerse nor pour as such but rather to *baptize.* (Interestingly enough, the Gospel of Mark seems to use a word which might be translated *baptisms* more or less synonymously with a Greek word which means to *sprinkle.*)[32] Perhaps the main reason that some churches defend affusion as the proper method of baptism is that the baptism of the Holy Spirit is spoken of as a *pouring-out.* When the baptism of the Holy Spirit took place on the day of Pentecost the Apostle Peter in his sermon quoted the prophet Joel as saying that this was a fulfillment of the prophecy that God would "pour out my Spirit upon all flesh . . . I will pour out my Spirit."[33] In the same sermon Peter explains that it was the resurrected Jesus who from the right hand of God had "poured out this which you see and hear."[34] The Greek word for pour out is used a fourth time in connection with the Holy Spirit in Titus 3, where Paul explains that God "saved us, not because of

---

30 *Ibid.,* p. 210. Used by permission.
31 Rom. 6:4; Col. 2:12.
32 Mark 7:4.

33 Acts 2:17, 18.
34 Acts 2:33.

deeds done by us in righteousness, but in virtue of his own mercy, by the washing of regeneration and renewal in the Holy Spirit, which he poured out upon us richly through Jesus Christ our Saviour, so that we might be justified by his grace and become heirs in hope of eternal life."[35]

Those who believe in affusion also appeal to history in support of their view. In 1899 a Christian minister from Pennsylvania[36] visited the catacombs of Rome. One day he walked out the Appian Way to the catacomb of St. Callistus. "I had been in other parts of this catacomb twice before, but this time I told the guide that I wanted to see frescoes of baptism. Soon we reached one of about the end of the second century where a minister is represented as baptizing a young applicant. The minister stands on the bank and the applicant in the water. A handful of water has just been dipped and put on the head of the applicant where the minister's hand still rests, perhaps to pronounce a blessing. Small streams of water are plainly seen falling from the head of the applicant. . . .

"We went a little farther to another fresco very similar to the preceding one, and of about the same age, but the minister's feet appear to be just a little in the edge of the stream and no water is represented as falling from the head of the applicant who is in the water and standing erect.

"We went still farther eastward under the hill and beneath the Appian Way. . . . Here we found the baptism of Jesus by John the Baptist. John stands right at the edge of the Jordan and Christ stands in the water below him. It is also so represented by the picture of it in the museum. Baptism by dipping water on the head with one hand appears to be just completed and John is bending slightly forward with his hand at the elbow of Christ to help Him come 'up straightway out of the water.' . . . This is the fresco of baptism that has been assigned by some to A.D. 107.

"I asked the guide to show me frescoes of other modes of baptism. He said, 'There are no other modes represented in any of the catacombs.' This is really surprising, for we know that Tertullian practiced another mode as early as A.D. 200. . . .

"In Philip Schaff's great work Vol. II, page 249, we read, 'It is remarkable that in almost all the earliest representations of baptism that have been preserved for us, this [the pouring of water from a vessel over the body] is the special act represented.' "[37]

35 Titus 3:5-7.
36 A. D. Wenger, 1867-1935.
37 Six Months in Bible Lands (Doylestown, Pa.: Joseph B. Steiner, Mennonite Publisher, 1902), pp. 102-4.

Those who practice baptism by affusion also regard it as a practical mode for all climates and under all conditions.

What about the argument that the etymology of the Greek word for "baptize" would require immersion? The only answer of those who do not immerse is that the final test of a meaning of a word is what people understand it to mean when it is used. For example, the English word *commencement* would suggest a beginning; as a matter of fact, however, the term is now used of the exercises in a school which celebrate the completion and end of a course of study. When we of today use the word *lunatic* we do not mean one who is moon-struck, although that would be what the etymology of the word would suggest. The Greek word *baptizo* does not mean a physical *immersion or a sprinkling;* it means the use of water to symbolize the Christian induction of a convert into the body of Christ.[38]

We therefore conclude that affusion or pouring is a valid mode of baptism, and can see no reason why any Christian minister should refuse to baptize converts by pouring if they believe that pouring is a correct mode. And those who have been baptized by affusion should not be rebaptized by immersion. The present writer rejoices that there now are Christian denominations who are willing to recognize both immersion and affusion as valid modes of baptism. For the basic fact remains that the validity of a Christian ordinance does not depend upon its material form but upon the spiritual attitude of the person receiving the ordinance.

The Lord's Supper

The other major ordinance of the apostolic church is the communion service or Lord's Supper, instituted by our Saviour on the Thursday night prior to Good Friday, A.D. 30. Jesus indicated that the two emblems of this ceremony each have a dual symbolism. The bread represents the body of Christ which has been broken for us,[39] and also Christian fellowship in the Lord.[40] The fruit of the vine, called "the cup,"[41] symbolizes the blood of Christ which has been shed for us, as well as the New Testament which His death inaugurated.[42]

---

38 See the scholarly monograph by Prof. John Murray, *Christian Baptism* (Philadelphia: Committee on Christian Education, The Orthodox Presbyterian Church, 1952.) *passim.* The author shows that the Greek *baptizo* does not necessarily mean immersion.

39 Matt. 26:26.

40 I Cor. 10:16, 17.

41 Mark 14:25; I Cor. 11:25.

42 I Cor. 11:25; Luke 22:20; Heb. 9:16.

The main question associated with the observance of the Lord's Supper is that of who should be admitted to the table. Those who practice what is called open communion state that no believer of any persuasion should be excluded from the Lord's Supper because it is not a denominational table, it is the Lord's table. Furthermore, they say, it is the individual who shall examine himself, not the church.[43] It is also objected that close communion seems too exclusive within Christendom; it tends to be divisive within the Christian Church. It is also said that close communion reflects on the spiritual Christians of other denominations.

It must be admitted that there is some weight to the considerations which favor open communion. There is another side, however. The assumption of those who defend close communion is that the Lord's Supper requires a common faith and a common separation from the world. Furthermore, the Scriptures teach that, although the individual shall examine himself, the church also does have some responsibility for the Christian life of its members. Paul, for example, requested the church at Corinth to expel from its fellowship the incestuous person.[44] Those who hold to close communion do not claim omniscience; they claim only that there are Biblical requirements for membership in the church and for admission to the Lord's table. A major reason for close communion is that church discipline would be meaningless if only the individual himself were the judge as to whether he enjoyed full fellowship in the congregation. It seems impossible to recognize the norms of all other denominations as satisfying New Testament requirements for church membership. Close communion is therefore in part made necessary by the behavior of some professing Christians, and in part it is occasioned by the sub-Christian standards of some denominations. It would seem inconsistent to refuse communion to a member of one's group for not accepting the discipline of the group, but to offer communion to an individual from another group having no such disciplinary standard.

Adherents of close communion—generally the stricter Christian bodies—therefore regretfully insist that they must continue to offer the emblems of the sacramental signs only to those in full fellowship in their group. They recognize full well of course that other denominations contain many spiritual members who are just as much entitled to come to the Lord's table as their own members. It is not those spiritual and consecrated members who make close communion necessary; it is rather the fact that many professing believers are not

---

43 I Cor. 11:28. 44 I Cor. 5:2, 13.

of that type and yet are rated as communicant in their respective churches because said churches do not strictly insist on Biblical standards of life for their members.

The basic question therefore is whether those groups having their present high requirements for membership and communion shall lower these standards down to the level of a Christendom which too often appears "lukewarm" spiritually. Shall the church succumb to the easygoing type of Christian life which is all too prevalent today, or must it follow the Lord in personal cross-bearing and earnest discipleship at any cost? To ask the question is to answer it. Nevertheless, close communion is not something to gloat about: it is a matter of deep regret. It calls for an even greater manifestation of redeeming love toward all men, and especially toward those who are *in Christ* in the various denominations of Christendom.

10. *THE GREAT COMMISSION*

Mention has frequently been made in this book of the Great Commission which Jesus gave before His ascension. It commissions His disciples to go to the ends of the earth and to make disciples of all nations, baptizing them in the name of the trinity, and teaching them to observe all Christ's commandments.[45]

The apostolic church in Jerusalem seems to have hesitated to embark on a world-wide mission of evangelism. It was actually persecution which thrust out the rank and file of the Jerusalem Christians following the martyrdom of Stephen. In the course of a few generations, however, Christianity spread rapidly over the world. There were local persecutions from Nero to Diocletian, A.D. 64 to 303, the two general persecutions being around the middle of the third century and in the early years of the fourth. The great emperor Constantine, who served as Roman emperor from A.D. 306 to 337, issued his Edict of Toleration A.D. 313. He did not, however, make Christianity formally the state religion of Rome. (Christianity became the state religion of the empire by the joint edict of Theodosius the Great and Gratianus in February, A.D. 380.) Little by little all of Europe was Christianized, the last great nation to accept Christianity being Russia, about A.D. 1000.

Long before the time of the Reformation any thought of missions or evangelism had been largely given up. All Europe was regarded as having long been Christian. Everyone was a Christian because he was christened (by infant baptism) at birth. Almost all

45 Matt. 28:18-20.

adults acknowledged the Roman Catholic Church as their spiritual mother. When the Protestant Reformation broke the unity of the church of Rome in the sixteenth century there was no thought of adopting a policy of individual liberty of conscience. Luther himself set up what was called the *Landesherrliche Kirchenregiment,* that is, a system of territorial churches. According to this plan the ruler of each territory determined the religion of his subjects, who then either had to accept the established faith or emigrate. There was no thought of freedom of conscience. No evangelism was desired or even permitted.

The Anabaptists, however, refused to recognize this system of territorial churches. They denied that the population as a whole was truly Christian; they denied the right of the ruler to determine their faith; and they denied the right of any ruler to forbid them to evangelize wherever the Lord led them.[46] As a matter of history it may be mentioned that there was a widespread popular appreciation for the earnest evangelism of the so-called Anabaptists. For example, by Easter, 1525, the congregation of the Swiss Brethren at St. Gall, Switzerland, had 500 baptized members. Indeed, there are said to have been seventy Swiss Brethren congregations in the canton of Zurich by 1535.[47] It has been estimated that George Blaurock won a thousand converts for the Anabaptists before he was burned at the stake in 1529. Leonard Bouwens, Menno Simons' fellow elder, kept a list of those he baptized in a thirty-year period and the list contains no less than 10,378 names.[48] The evangelistic zeal of the Anabaptists was not merely personal witnessing, although that was certainly the heart of the program, but even involved a systematic sending out of missioners to various parts of Europe. For example, over sixty leaders attended the so-called "Martyrs' Synod" of August 20, 1527, held at Augsburg in South Germany. Missioners were sent out from this point to Basel and Zurich, to the Palatinate, to Upper Austria, to Franconia, to Salzburg in Austria, and to Bavaria, South Germany.

The activity of the Anabaptists, who went everywhere regardless of the established religion and without the official endorsement of either the established church or the state, greatly irritated the leading reformers. Luther, for example, wrote a book *Concerning Sneaks and Hedge Preachers,* 1532.[49] Fierce persecution set in against the

---

46 Cf. Littell, *op. cit.,* 94-112.
47 Robert G. Torbet, *A History of the Baptists* (Philadelphia: The Judson Press, 1950), p. 38.
48 John Horsch, *Mennonites in Europe* (Scottdale, Pa.: Mennonite Publishing House, 1950), p. 217.
49 *Von den Schleichern und Winkelpredigern.*

Anabaptists and they were almost annihilated. The result was that within a few decades the evangelistic witness of the group had practically died out.

The Christian Church today needs a revival of the earnest sense of mission which the ancient Christian Church had in the first century, and which the Anabaptists had in the sixteenth century. Christians need to feel the force of the words of Jesus when He declared: "As the Father has sent me, even so I send you."[50] Paul declares: "Therefore, if any one is in Christ, he is a new creation; the old has passed away, behold, the new has come. All this is from God, who through Christ reconciled us to himself and gave us the ministry of reconciliation; that is, God was in Christ reconciling the world to himself, not counting their trespasses against them, and entrusting to us the message of reconciliation. So we are ambassadors for Christ, God making his appeal through us. We beseech you on behalf of Christ, be reconciled to God."[51]

If the Christian Church is ever to regain the missionary outreach of the apostolic church it needs a deepening of its concern for the unsaved, and a strengthening of the redeeming love which moves people to witness to the whole world of the saving Gospel of Jesus Christ, beginning at home. The nations of the world will never be made disciples by professional missionaries; the only way the church can effectively carry out the Great Commission is by each member of the church becoming an active witness in life and word for the Lord Jesus Christ. The revival which is needed in order to make this type of witnessing possible will also release the personnel needed for the home and foreign fields, and the financial support required to make possible a world-wide witness on a vastly larger scale than is now being realized.

The tragedy of modern Christendom is that the Christian Church has become so lukewarm that the average church member feels no particular concern either to be a good witness himself or to give sacrificially of his means in order to send Gospel witnesses to the ends of the earth. If the rank and file of the members of the professing Christian Church in just one country, the United States of America, e.g., would give but one tenth of their income to the work of the Lord, all the pastors of our nation could be supported, the local church plants maintained, and Christian missionaries could be placed in every sizable city in the world in one generation. The only reason this does not happen is spiritual lukewarmness and a complete

---

50 John 20:21.   51 II Cor. 5:17-20.

lack of serious Christian stewardship. Such spiritual lethargy cannot be anything but a source of grief and a concern for prayer on the part of every true child of God.

11. *THE LAW OF GOD*

By the law of God in the present discussion is meant His absolute and holy will for the moral and ethical life of mankind as it is revealed in the Holy Scriptures; it is that which is violated when men sin. Its foundation is unselfish and complete love for God and men.[52]

Primary emphasis must be placed at this point on the fact that the law of God is the expression of His holy will and nature. It is nothing arbitrary, nor does God conform to the "good." The law of God is universal and absolute, but in the era before Christ the revelation of His will was not made known in full: God revealed His will to mankind progressively.

The New Testament recognizes that the law of God is revealed dimly in the conscience of men, and clearly in the Scriptures, which alone are infallible; conscience may err.

One of the areas which requires the most spiritual discernment is the understanding of the Christian's relation to the Old Testament. In connection with this topic it is useful to divide the law of the Old Testament into three types:

1. The civil law of the Old Testament is that which was intended for Israel as a nation, and it is therefore not binding upon the various nations of the world today, nor upon the church, although the more nearly the nations of the earth conform their civil laws to the basic principles of God's Word the happier their subjects will be.

2. The ceremonial law of Moses governed sacrifices, holy days, sabbatical years, clean and unclean foods, regulations on clothing and agriculture, etc. It has been abolished by the death of Jesus. This truth is set forth many places in the New Testament. Although the apostolic church did make a few temporary concessions at the apostolic council of about A.D. 50, yet the basic decision was clear: Gentiles are not obligated to follow the ceremonial law of Moses.[53] Paul asked the Galatian Christians, now that they have come to know God, "or rather to be known by God, how can you turn back again to the weak and beggarly rudiments, whose slaves you want to be once more? You observe days, and months, and seasons, and years! I am afraid I have labored over you in vain."[54] And again, "Now this is an allegory: these women are two covenants. One is from

---

52 Matt. 22:34-40.   53 Acts 15:28, 29.   54 Gal. 4:9, 10.

Mount Sinai, bearing children for slavery; she is Hagar. Now Hagar is Mount Sinai in Arabia; she corresponds to the present Jerusalem, for she is in slavery with her children. But the Jerusalem above is free, and she is our mother. . . . So, brethren, we are not children of the slave but of the free woman.

"For freedom Christ has set us free; stand fast therefore, and do not submit again to a yoke of slavery.

"Now I, Paul, say to you that if you receive circumcision, Christ will be of no advantage to you. I testify again to every man who receives circumcision that he is bound to keep the whole law. You are severed from Christ, you who would be justified by the law; you have fallen away from grace. . . . For in Christ Jesus neither circumcision nor uncircumcision is of any avail, but faith working through love."[55]

Even more emphatic on the Christian's freedom from the ceremonial law of the Old Testament is Paul's Letter to the Colossians. He states: "Therefore let no one pass judgment on you in questions of food and drink or with regard to a festival or a new moon or a sabbath. These are only a shadow of what is to come."[56] The reason Paul is able to tell Christians that they are free is that Christ has "canceled the bond which stood against us with its legal demands; this he set aside, nailing it to the cross."[57] The consequence is: "Why do you submit to regulations, 'Do not handle, Do not taste, Do not touch' . . . according to human precepts and doctrines? These have indeed an appearance of wisdom in promoting rigor of devotion and self-abasement and severity to the body, but they are of no value in checking the indulgence of the flesh."[58]

Not only is the ceremonial law done away as far as its detailed regulations for life are concerned, but the Old Testament as a religious system, involving animal sacrifices, a Jewish holy calendar, etc., is also done away in Christ: "For Christ is the end of the law, that every one who has faith may be justified."[59] In his Letter to the Galatians Paul says that before the era of Christian faith "we were confined under the law, kept under restraint until faith should be revealed. So that the law was our custodian until Christ came, that we might be justified by faith. But now that faith has come, we are no longer under a custodian; for in Christ Jesus you are all sons of God, through faith. For as many of you as were baptized into Christ have put on Christ. There is neither Jew nor Greek, there is neither

55 Gal. 4:24—5:6.
56 Col. 2:16, 17.
57 Col. 2:14.

58 Col. 2:20-23.
59 Rom. 10:4.

slave nor free, there is neither male nor female; for you are all one in Christ Jesus. And if you are Christ's, then you are Abraham's offspring, heirs according to promise."[60]

3. The third type of law in the Old Testament is the moral law as exemplified in such sections as the Ten Commandments. The moral law of God as found in the Old Testament is basically reaffirmed and even strengthened in the New Testament. Another way to say this is that the writers of the New Testament firmly anchor their great spiritual principles in the revelation of God as found in the Old Testament. Our Lord Himself gave specific teaching on this point:

> And one of the scribes came up and heard them disputing with one another, and seeing that he answered them well, asked him, "Which commandment is the first of all?" Jesus answered, "The first is, 'Hear, O Israel: The Lord our God, the Lord is one; and you shall love the Lord your God with all your heart, and with all your soul, and with all your mind, and with all your strength.' The second is this, 'You shall love your neighbor as yourself.' There is no other commandment greater than these." And the scribe said to him, "You are right, Teacher; you have truly said that he is one, and there is no other but he; and to love him with all the heart, and with all the understanding, and with all the strength, and to love one's neighbor as oneself, is much more than all whole burnt offerings and sacrifices." And when Jesus saw that he answered wisely, he said to him, "You are not far from the kingdom of God."[61]

Perhaps one might say that the New Testament fulfills the Old Testament by dropping whatever from the Old was not a final revelation of the will of God, what was only temporary due to the hardness of heart of Israel, and by reaffirming and extending the basic moral principles of the Old Testament, even making them more penetrating in the New than they had been in the Old. This is essentially what Jesus did in the Sermon on the Mount when He showed that His teaching was really built upon the basic moral principles of the Old Testament, and when He also made His laws more demanding than had been the requirements of Moses and the prophets.

The New Testament is emphatic that it is not the purpose of the law of God to provide a way of salvation for men. It is not possible for men to be saved on the basis of God's law, for that would require absolute perfection in order to reach heaven, an accomplishment of which no human being is capable. According to Christ and

60 Gal. 3:23-29.   61 Mark 12:28-34.

the apostles, therefore, law is excluded as a basis of justification. Christians are forgiven and justified on the basis of the grace of God which accepts and declares righteous every person who is willing to accept Jesus Christ and put his trust in Him. The purpose of law, on the other hand, is: (1) to awaken in the non-Christian an awareness of his sin, his need of divine grace, and the urgency of accepting Jesus Christ as He is presented in the glorious Gospel of our Lord; (2) to serve as a guide in the life of the child of God as to how best to live a life which is pleasing to God and which will give the best possible testimony to the Saviour.

It becomes, therefore, the function of the church to awaken in men a sense of their need by an earnest proclamation of the law of God, preached in the demonstration of the Holy Spirit, and calculated to prepare the way for the joyful acceptance of the Gospel of Christ. The preaching of the law of God, however, requires a good understanding of the principle of progressive revelation, as well as an awareness of what from the Old Testament is binding upon the Christian and what was merely temporary or intended for Israel. In this matter the final authority can be only the New Testament.

The church has not been charged with the responsibility of making additions to the Scriptures; Matthew 23 is relevant to this question. The task of the church is to teach the Word of God with a New Testament understanding of the whole. Where the law of God makes no clear provision, Christians must make decisions through mutual agreement on the basis of brotherly love. After all there are many questions in the daily life of the church upon which the New Testament gives no detailed counsel. Such silence in the New Testament would include the frequency and form of the sacramental signs, the form of church organization, the agencies for Christian education, what church institutions to establish for the best accomplishment of the mission of the church, the building of meetinghouses, the attitude toward art, etc. It should be observed, however, that the authority to bind conduct (though only in harmony with divine law, Acts 5:29) has been given: (1) to civil government, Romans 13:1; (2) to parents, Ephesians 6:1; Colossians 3:20; and (3) to church officials, Matthew 18:15-20; Hebrews 13:17.

Special mention should be made of the frequency with which the New Testament quotes either the commandment to love God supremely, or the commandment to love one's neighbor as oneself: Matthew 22:36-40; Mark 12:28-31; Romans 13:8-10; James 2:8; Galatians 5:13, 14, etc.

12. *THE LORD'S DAY*

A particular application of the law of God relates to the observance of one day of rest in seven. In the Old Testament the observance of the Sabbath is grounded by Moses in the seventh day rest of God at the time of creation.[62] Mention is also made in patriarchal history of seven-day periods but not in the sense of a holy rest day.[63] The first mention of the Sabbath is made in connection with the giving of the manna.[64] The Sabbath was also included in the Ten Commandments.[65] The Book of Nehemiah indicates that it was Moses who made known the Sabbath to Israel.[66] The prophet Ezekiel also intimates that the Jewish Sabbath was Mosaic in its origin.[67] The sanction for Sabbath observance was very strict under the law of Moses, a willful Sabbath breaker having been executed at the command of the Lord.[68]

The Mosaic Sabbath was kept (1) in honor of God, for it was declared to be a sign between the LORD and the children of Israel for ever[69]; (2) for man's good, so that the entire family might have a day of rest[70]; (3) as a memorial of national redemption, to celebrate the glorious exodus of the children of Israel from Egypt in the goodness of God.[71] Such prophets and leaders of Israel as Amos,[72] Isaiah,[73] Ezekiel,[74] Jeremiah,[75] and Nehemiah[76] were much concerned that Israel should keep her sabbaths not only in letter but also in spirit.

Between the time of Ezra and Christ Jewish legalism covered the Sabbath with numberless restrictions and legalistic hair-splitting. The Jewish Mishna gives thirty-nine classes of prohibited actions. This legalistic attitude toward the Sabbath did not commend itself to the Lord Jesus. While it is true that He worshiped regularly in the synagogue on the Sabbath,[77] He also regarded man's needs as taking precedence over the traditional Sabbath restrictions of the Jews.[78] Jesus even went so far as to assert His lordship over the Sabbath.[79] While Christ reaffirmed all the other of the Ten Commandments, making some of them even more penetrating than they had been under Moses, He did defend a more lenient Sabbath observance.[80]

---

62 Gen. 2:3; Ex. 20:10, 11; 31:16, 17.
63 Gen. 7:4, 10; 8:10, 12; 29:27, 28.
64 Ex. 16:5, 21-30.
65 Ex. 20:8.
66 Neh. 9:14.
67 Ezek. 20:10-12.
68 Num. 15:32-36.
69 Ex. 31:17.
70 Deut. 5:12-14.
71 Deut. 5:15.
72 Amos 8:5.
73 Isa. 56:2, 4; 58:13.
74 Ezek. 20:12-24; 43:6.
75 Jer. 17:21-27.
76 Neh. 10:31; 13:15-22.
77 Luke 4:16.
78 Matt. 12:1-14; Mark 2:23—3:6; Luke 6:1-11; 13:10-17; 14:1-6; John 5:1-18; 7:23; 9:16.
79 Mark 2:28; Matt. 12:8; Luke 6:5.
80 Matt. 12:12; Luke 6:11; Mark 2:27.

It should be observed that all the other Ten Commandments are quoted or reaffirmed in the New Testament. Moses commanded Israel to worship no other gods, while Jesus stated sternly:

You shall worship the Lord your God
and him only shall you serve.[81]

The second commandment called for the making of no images of deity, and Jesus said: "God is spirit, and those who worship him must worship in spirit and truth."[82] The third commandment called for the swearing of no false oaths, while Jesus said: "Do not swear at all, either by heaven, for it is the throne of God, or by the earth, for it is his footstool, or by Jerusalem, for it is the city of the great King. And do not swear by your head, for you cannot make one hair white or black. Let what you say be simply 'Yes' or 'No'; anything more than this comes from the evil one."[83] In another statement on the matter of swearing Jesus showed that all oaths are wrong because ultimately they involve God.[84] The Letter of James also condemns all swearing.[85] The fifth commandment, to honor one's parents, is reaffirmed by Christ, and by Paul.[86] The sixth commandment, not to kill, is quoted by Jesus, by Paul, and by John; the latter indicating that the hatred of the heart is equal to the sin of murder, "And you know that no murderer has eternal life abiding in him."[87] The seventh commandment, not to commit adultery, is also reaffirmed by Christ and by Paul.[88] The eighth commandment likewise.[89] The ninth commandment, not to bear false witness, is reaffirmed in Matthew and in Revelation.[90] The tenth commandment, not to covet, is quoted in Luke, Romans, I Corinthians, Ephesians, and Colossians.[91]

In contrast with the New Testament confirmation of these nine commandments we find statements such as the following on the observance of a sabbath, or rest day:

"And he went on from there, and entered their synagogue. And behold, there was a man with a withered hand. And they asked him, 'Is it lawful to heal on the sabbath?' so that they might accuse him.

---

81 Matt. 4:10.
82 John 4:24; Rom. 1:23.
83 Matt. 5:34-37 (RSV, evil; ASV, evil *one*).
84 Matt. 23:16-22.
85 Jas. 5:12.
86 Matt. 15:4; 19:19; Luke 18:20; Eph. 6:2; Col. 3:20.
87 I John 3:15; Matt. 5:21, 22; 19:18; Rom. 13:9.
88 Matt. 5:27, 28; 19:18; Rom. 13:9.
89 Matt. 19:18; Eph. 4:28.
90 Matt. 19:18; Rev. 22:15.
91 Luke 12:15; Rom. 7:7; I Cor. 12:31; Eph. 5:3; Col. 3:5.

He said to them, 'What man of you, if he has one sheep and it falls into a pit on the sabbath, will not lay hold of it and lift it out? Of how much more value is a man than a sheep! So it is lawful to do good on the sabbath.' "[92]

"On a sabbath, while he was going through the grainfields, his disciples plucked and ate some ears of grain, rubbing them in their hands. But some of the Pharisees said, 'Why are you doing what is not lawful to do on the sabbath?' And Jesus answered, 'Have you not read what David did when he was hungry, he and those who were with him: how he entered the house of God, and took and ate the bread of the Presence, which it is not lawful for any but the priests to eat, and also gave it to those with him?' And he said to them, 'The Son of man is lord of the sabbath.' "[93]

"And he said to them, 'The sabbath was made for man, not man for the sabbath; so the Son of man is lord even of the sabbath.' "[94]

It would appear that the Jewish Christian church at first continued to keep the law of Moses, including undoubtedly the seventh-day Sabbath: in any case, the apostles regularly sought out the sabbath meetings of the Jews in order to try to reach them with the Gospel.[95] The New Testament apostles, however, strongly warn the Christian Church against observing the ceremonial law of Moses, including the regulations on food, circumcision, and the Sabbath. With a sort of bland indifference the Apostle Paul remarks: "One man esteems one day as better than another, while another man esteems all days alike. Let every one be fully convinced in his own mind. He who observes the day, observes it in honor of the Lord. He also who eats, eats in honor of the Lord, since he gives thanks to God; while he who abstains, abstains in honor of the Lord and gives thanks to God. None of us lives to himself, and none of us dies to himself."[96] These remarks seem to have been directed to a church where there was some difference of opinion among equally sincere believers, and the apostle manifests no particular anxiety on the point.

When Paul learned that Judaizers were seeking to enslave the churches of Galatia in Jewish ceremonial bondage, however, he vigorously rebuked the Galatian Christians for their fickleness and their spiritual declension. "I am astonished," writes the aroused apostle, "that you are so quickly deserting him who called you in the grace of Christ and turning to a different gospel—not that there is another gospel, but there are some who trouble you and want to

92 Matt. 12:9-12.   95 Acts 3:1; 13:14, 42, 44; 16:13; 18:4.
93 Luke 6:1-5.   96 Rom. 14:5-7.
94 Mark 2:27.

pervert the gospel of Christ. But even if we, or an angel from heaven, should preach to you a gospel contrary to that which we preached to you, let him be accursed. As we have said before, so now I say again, If any one is preaching to you a gospel contrary to that which you received, let him be accursed."[97] Later in the letter Paul exclaims: "You observe days, and months, and seasons, and years! I am afraid I have labored over you in vain."[98] Again, "I testify again to every man who receives circumcision that he is bound to keep the whole law. You are severed from Christ, you who would be justified by the law; you have fallen away from grace."[99]

The Gospels indicate that Christ was crucified on what is commonly called Good Friday and that He arose from the dead on "the first day of the week," that is, on the third day after the crucifixion.[1] It appears that very early the Christian Church began to observe the first day of the week as "the Lord's day,"[2] in honor of the resurrection of the Lord Jesus, which event established the Christian Church itself. For example, in Acts 20 one learns that Paul arranged his stay at Troas so as to participate in the communion service which was evidently held there on the first day of the week. A careful study of the passage indicates that Paul arrived on Monday and left one week later.[3] Another evidence of the fact that the apostolic church may have very early adopted the Lord's day as a time for public worship appears in I Corinthians 16 where the Apostle Paul enjoined the Corinthian Christians to make a weekly relief contribution, so that the church would have sufficient funds ready by the time he arrived. The Greek imperative in the sentence, "On the first day of every week, each of you is to *put something aside* and store it up, as he may prosper," would suggest the laying aside on successive Sundays, perhaps an indication that Sunday by Sunday the Christians were gathering together their relief funds, or that Paul desired them to do so.[4] John 20 also suggests that on successive Sunday nights following the resurrection the disciples met together with closed doors, "for fear of the Jews."[5] It would thus appear that Sunday worship may have apostolic sanction.

In any case the evidence from history is entirely clear that the church from about A.D. 100 did observe the first day of the week as a

97 Gal. 1:6-9.
98 Gal. 4:10.
99 Gal. 5:3, 4.
1 Matt. 27:62 (Preparation is the Greek word for Friday; this is still true); 28:1; Mark 15:42; 16:1; Luke 23:54; 24:1; 24:7-21; John 19:31, 42; 20:1, 19.
2 Mentioned by name in Rev. 1:10.   4 I Cor. 16:2.
3 Acts 20:7.   5 John 20:19, 26.

day of worship. Perhaps it would be of interest to start with Constantine and work backward toward the days of the apostles. The so-called Codex Justinianus, III, 12, 3 of A.D. 321 reads as follows: "All judges and city people and the craftsmen shall rest upon the venerable Day of the Sun. Country people, however, may freely attend to the cultivation of the fields because it frequently happens that no other days are better adapted for planting the grain in the furrows or the vines in trenches."[6] This law seems to have been a sort of concession to the Christian conscience although it must be admitted that it was not very strict. The early Christian book, *The Didache,* written between A.D. 120 and 180, contains the following instruction in chapter 14: "And on the Lord's Day, after you have come together, break bread and offer the Eucharist, having first confessed your offenses, so that your sacrifice may be pure. But let no one who has a quarrel with his neighbor join you until he is reconciled, lest your sacrifice be defiled."[7]

Justin (c. 100-c. 165), commonly known as Justin Martyr because of his death for Christ's sake, wrote the following lovely description of a Christian service about A.D. 150.

On the day which is called Sunday we have a common assembly of all who live in the cities or in the outlying districts, and the memoirs of the Apostles or the writings of the Prophets are read, as long as there is time. Then, when the reader has finished, the president of the assembly verbally admonishes and invites all to imitate such examples of virtue. Then we all stand up together and offer up our prayers and, as we said before, after we finish our prayers, bread and wine and water are presented. He who presides likewise offers up prayers and thanksgivings, to the best of his ability, and the people express their approval by saying "Amen." The Eucharistic elements are distributed and consumed by those present, and to those who are absent they are sent through the deacons. The wealthy, if they wish, contribute whatever they desire, and the collection is placed in the custody of the president. [With it] he helps the orphans and widows, those who are needy because of sickness or any other reason, and the captives and strangers in our midst; in short, he takes care of all those in need. Sunday, indeed, is a day on which we all hold our common assembly because it is the first day on which God, transforming the darkness and [prime] matter, created the world; and our Savior Jesus Christ arose from the dead on the same day. For they crucified Him on the day before that of Saturn, and of the day after, which is Sunday, He appeared to His Apostles and disciples, and taught

6 Joseph Cullen Ayer, *A Source Book for Ancient Church History* (New York: Scribner's, 1913, reprinted 1933), pp. 284, 285. Used by permission.

7 *Op. cit.,* p. 182. Used by permission.

them the things which we have passed on to you also for your consideration.[8]

Ignatius, who wrote his letter, *To the Magnesians*, about A.D. 114, in describing Christians states: "They no longer observe the Jewish Sabbaths, but keep holy the Lord's day, on which, through Him and through His death, our life arose . . . ."[9]

The anonymous *Letter of Barnabas* of about A.D. 100 quotes God as saying: "The present Sabbaths are not acceptable to Me, but that [Sabbath] which I have made, in which, after giving rest to all things, I will make the beginning of the eighth day, that is, the beginning of another world. Therefore, we also celebrate with joy the eighth day on which Jesus also rose from the dead, was made manifest, and ascended into heaven."[10] The expression "Lord's day" is also used by the Apostle John in Revelation 1:10.

Thus we see the Lord's day called *Sunday* by Constantine in A.D. 321, the *Lord's day* in the *Didache* of the middle of the second century, *Sunday* in Justin about A.D. 150, *Lord's day* in Ignatius about A.D. 114, *eighth day* in Barnabas about A.D. 100, and *Lord's day* in the Apostle John about A.D. 96. We, therefore, have the testimony of Christian writers back to the time of the Apostle John indicating that Christians were holding their services weekly on the Lord's day or Sunday.

The New Testament does not attempt to define what are proper activities for the Lord's day. It does indicate that Christians are free from the Sabbath restrictions of the Jews, and from ceremonialism of any kind. Christians, however, do observe one day in seven in a special way, devoting it to the worship of God, to Christian service, and to physical restoration. Man is so constituted as to need a day of rest. God who recognized this need instituted such a day and hedged it in with rather severe restrictions in the Old Testament. Now that Christians are in the age of the Holy Spirit those restrictions have been removed, and yet the Lord's people from the very beginning have seen the need of hallowing one day in seven by meeting together on that day for the worship of the Lord. By doing this the Lord's people are giving a witness through all ages against secularism and materialism. As early as A.D. 200 the church father Tertullian (c. 160-c. 230) opposed Sunday work.

8 *The Fathers of the Church*, Vol. 6: *Saint Justin Martyr*, by Thomas B. Falls (New York: Christian Heritage, Inc., n.d., c. 1949), pp. 106, 107. Used by permission.

9 *The Fathers of the Church*, Vol. 1: *The Apostolic Fathers* (New York, 1947), p. 99. Used by permission.

10 *Ibid.*, p. 216. Used by permission.

There is a sense, therefore, in which Christians keep the Lord's day freely (not as a legal requirement) and joyfully (not as a heavy burden to be borne), and use it for physical refreshment and spiritual strengthening. It must be stressed, however, that there is no ceremonial law in Christianity, and the New Testament nowhere explicitly changes the day of rest from the Sabbath to the Lord's day. Christians, therefore, follow what they believe to be apostolic precedent, and work in agreement with international date lines and established calendars, and keep Sunday as unto the Lord in memory of His resurrection.

It would not be within the spirit of New Testament Christianity to attempt to codify every type of behavior which would be proper or improper for the Lord's day. In a general way, however, most spiritual Christians feel that unnecessary business, work which could be avoided, together with sports and amusements, or anything that would becloud one's Christian testimony against secularism and materialism, would not be proper on the Lord's day. In the legitimate class would certainly belong Sunday-school and church attendance, Christian work, physical rest, the visitation of the sick, and anything which furthers the cause of Christ. In this respect Christians may follow the example of Christ, who although He did not abide by the Jewish regulations of the Sabbath yet perfectly pleased His heavenly Father by using the Sabbath to do good, to worship, and to help mankind.

PART IV

GOD AS SANCTIFIER

IV. GOD AS SANCTIFIER

1. *PNEUMATOLOGY*

Section 3 of Part I was devoted to the doctrine of the trinity. We turn now more particularly to the revelation of the Holy Spirit as it is given in Scripture. The second sentence of Genesis states: "And the Spirit of God was moving over the face of the waters."[1] This is the first mention in Scripture of the Holy Spirit. In connection with the doctrine of creation Job comments: "By his Spirit the heavens were made fair (or garnished)."[2]

In connection with the description of the extreme sinfulness of the world in the days of Noah God is reported as saying: "My Spirit shall not strive with man for ever, for he is flesh, but his days shall be a hundred and twenty years" a warning that the Deluge was only a little over a century away.[3] The Hebrew verb, here translated *strive*, could also quite naturally be rendered *judge*, or *rule in*. This is the reading of the Hebrew text. The Septuagint, the Vulgate, and the Syriac, however, read "abide in," which reading is adopted in the Revised Standard Version. The point seems to be that mankind had sunk to such a low level of carnal living that they were entirely given over to the flesh and there was no special point in God's Spirit any longer seeking to gain control of the inner spirit of sinful people who were entirely given over to the flesh: God's only recourse was to destroy the world by a cataclysmic judgment, the deluge.

Another activity of the Holy Spirit in the Old Testament is associated with the equipping of Bezalel for special service in connection with the construction of the tabernacle. Concerning him the LORD said to Moses: "I have filled him with the Spirit of God, with ability and intelligence, with knowledge and all craftsmanship, to devise artistic designs, to work in gold, silver, and bronze, in cutting stones for setting, and in carving wood, for work in every craft."[4]

1 Gen. 1:2.
2 Job 26:13.

3 Gen. 6:3.
4 Ex. 31:3-5.

259

The Lord also by His Spirit raised up deliverers for Israel in the days of the judges such as Gideon[5] and Jephthah[6] and Samson.[7] A number of passages in the Old Testament associate the gift of prophecy with the Holy Spirit.[8]

It is often stated by Christian teachers that prior to the day of Pentecost only a few outstanding leaders in Israel received the Holy Spirit. While it is true that special mention is made of the equipment for service of various leaders in Israel by Holy Spirit power,[9] yet the great leader Ezra in his notable prayer confessing the sin of Israel said to God: "Thou in thy great mercies didst not forsake them in the wilderness; the pillar of cloud which led them in the way did not depart from them by day, nor the pillar of fire by night which lighted for them the way by which they should go. Thou gavest thy good Spirit to instruct them, and didst not withhold thy manna from their mouth, and gavest them water for their thirst."[10]

The omnipresence of the Holy Spirit is beautifully expressed in Psalm 139:

> Whither shall I go from thy Spirit?
> Or whither shall I flee from thy presence?
> If I ascend to heaven, thou art there!
> If I make my bed in Sheol, thou art there!
> If I take the wings of the morning
>   and dwell in the uttermost parts of the sea,
> even there thy hand shall lead me,
>   and thy right hand shall hold me.
> If I say, "Let only darkness cover me,
>   and the light about me be night,"
> even the darkness is not dark to thee,
>   the night is bright as the day;
>   for darkness is as light with thee.[11]

The following Messianic prophecy was fulfilled in Jesus:

> There shall come forth a shoot from the stump of Jesse,
>   and a branch shall grow out of his roots.
> And the Spirit of the Lord shall rest upon him,
>   the spirit of wisdom and understanding,

---

5 Judg. 6:34.
6 Judg. 11:29.
7 Judg. 14:19; 15:14; etc.
8 Num. 11:29; I Sam. 10:6, 10.
9 E.g., David, I Sam. 16:13.
10 Neh. 9:19, 20.
11 Ps. 139:7-12.

the spirit of counsel and might,
the spirit of knowledge and the fear of the LORD.
And his delight shall be in the fear of the LORD.[12]

Also,

The Spirit of the Lord GOD is upon me,
because the LORD has anointed me
to bring good tidings to the afflicted;
he has sent me to bind up the brokenhearted,
to proclaim liberty to the captives,
and the opening of the prison to those who are bound;
to proclaim the year of the LORD's favor,
and the day of vengeance of our God;
to comfort all who mourn;
to grant to those who mourn in Zion—
to give them a garland instead of ashes,
the oil of gladness instead of mourning,
the mantle of praise instead of a faint spirit;
that they may be called oaks of righteousness,
the planting of the LORD, that he may be glorified.[13]

It must also be remembered that Christians today read the Old Testament, including its references to the Holy Spirit, with the full light of the New Testament revelation. It should not be supposed that the Old Testament saints were as conscious of the personality of the Holy Spirit as are Christian believers today. Were it not for the full revelation of God in the New Testament we would undoubtedly think that the Old Testament references to the Holy Spirit have no more significance than such expressions which God uses of Himself as, "my soul,"[14] meaning, "I myself." This is no denial of the fact that the Old Testament does definitely refer to the Holy Spirit; it is simply an acknowledgment that Christians are in a more favorable position to understand the Old Testament on this point, as on many others, than were the Israelites of old.

When we come to the New Testament we find the personality of the Holy Spirit clearly assumed; He is constantly spoken of as guiding,[15] speaking,[16] searching,[17] praying,[18] regenerating,[19] bearing witness to Christ,[20] teaching,[21] directing the church,[22] convicting of sin,[23] calling to office in the church,[24] bestowing various gifts for

12 Isa. 11:1-3.
13 Isa. 61:1-3.
14 Isa. 42:1.
15 John 16:13; Rom. 8:14.
16 Rev. 2:7.
17 I Cor. 2:10.
18 Rom. 8:26, 27.
19 John 3:5, 6; Titus 3:5.
20 John 15:26.
21 John 14:26.
22 Acts 13:2.
23 John 16:7-11.
24 Acts 20:28.

service,[25] and being grieved by sin.[26] These activities refer to what can be done only by a person.

Concerning the convicting power of the Holy Spirit, Jesus stated: "Nevertheless I tell you the truth: it is to your advantage that I go away, for if I do not go away, the Counselor will not come to you; but if I go, I will send him to you. And when he comes, he will convince the world of sin and of righteousness and of judgment: of sin, because they do not believe in me; of righteousness, because I go to the Father, and you will see me no more; of judgment, because the ruler of this world is judged."[27] And on the regenerating work of the Holy Spirit Jesus said: "Truly, truly, I say to you, unless one is born of water and the Spirit, he cannot enter the kingdom of God. . . . The wind blows where it wills, and you hear the sound of it, but you do not know whence it comes or whither it goes; so it is with every one who is born of the Spirit."[28] In this connection the Apostle Paul writes that God saved us, "not because of deeds done by us in righteousness, but in virtue of his own mercy, by the washing of regeneration and renewal in the Holy Spirit, which he poured out upon us richly through Jesus Christ our Savior."[29]

It is the Spirit of God who adds members to the church by convicting them of sin, by turning their hearts to accept and obey the Saviour, and who anoints each believer with a spiritual unction. "For just as the body is one and has many members, and all the members of the body, though many, are one body, so it is with Christ. For by one Spirit we were all baptized into one body—Jews or Greeks, slaves or free—and all were made to drink of one Spirit."[30] The New Testament knows nothing of converts to Christ receiving salvation and still standing in need of Holy Spirit baptism. Nowhere in the epistles does one read of Christians who are such without possessing the Holy Spirit. On the contrary, Paul says: "Any one who does not have the Spirit of Christ does not belong to him."[31]

The New Testament contains many references to the sanctifying work of the Holy Spirit. In his Letter to the Galatians Paul writes: "But I say, walk by the Spirit, and do not gratify the desires of the flesh. For the desires of the flesh are against the Spirit, and the desires of the Spirit are against the flesh; for these are opposed to each other, to prevent you from doing what you would. But if you are led by the Spirit you are not under the law. . . . But the

25 I Cor. 12:7-9.
26 Eph. 4:30.
27 John 16:7-11.
28 John 3:5-8.
29 Titus 3:5.
30 1 Cor. 12:12, 13.
31 Rom. 8:9.

fruit of the Spirit is love, joy, peace, patience, kindness, goodness, faithfulness, gentleness, self-control; against such there is no law. And those who belong to Christ Jesus have crucified the flesh with its passions and desires.

"If we live by the Spirit, let us also walk by the Spirit."[32]

Before His crucifixion Jesus promised the apostles: "These things I have spoken to you, while I am still with you. But the Counselor, the Holy Spirit, whom the Father will send in my name, he will teach you all things, and bring to your remembrance all that I have said to you."[33] And to the Christians at Corinth Paul wrote:

> What no eye has seen, nor ear heard,
> nor the heart of man conceived,
> what God has prepared for those who love him,

"God has revealed to us through the Spirit. For the Spirit searches everything, even the depths of God. . . . And we impart this in words not taught by human wisdom but taught by the Spirit, interpreting spiritual truths to those who possess the Spirit.

"The unspiritual man does not receive the gifts of the Spirit of God, for they are folly to him, and he is not able to understand them because they are spiritually discerned. The spiritual man judges all things, but is himself to be judged by no one. 'For who has known the mind of the Lord so as to instruct him?' But we have the mind of Christ."[34]

It was the confidence of the apostles that their readers as true Christians had all been anointed by the Spirit of God so that they were teachable and were actually taught of God themselves through the unction of the Holy Spirit which they had received. Paul writes: "But concerning love of the brethren you have no need to have any one write to you, for you yourselves have been taught by God to love one another. . . ."[35] And John states: "I write this to you about those who would deceive you; but the anointing which you received from him abides in you, and you have no need that any one should teach you; as his anointing teaches you about everything, and is true, and is no lie, just as it has taught you, abide in him."[36]

The New Testament regards every Christian as an object of the electing love and mercy of God, as having been anointed by the Holy Spirit, as enjoying His sanctifying and strengthening work, and as being guaranteed final and complete redemption by the present

32 Gal. 5:16-24.
33 John 14:25, 26.
34 I Cor. 2:9-16.

35 I Thess. 4:9.
36 I John 2:26, 27.

possession of the Holy Spirit. In other words, God puts His seal of ownership upon each one whom He calls into His kingdom by bestowing upon them the gift of the Holy Spirit.[37]

2. *THE UNIVERSALISM OF THE GOSPEL*

Theologians sometimes refer to the covenant of redemption, meaning the agreement between God and His eternal Son, that the latter would become incarnate in order to redeem the race. The plan of redemption is a divine arrangement, conceived "before the foundation of the world."[38]

The Covenant of Grace

The covenant of grace, on the other hand, is spoken of as being between God and mankind, meaning simply that God through all human history has accepted and saved those who put their faith in Him. The promise of the covenant of grace is sonship with God, together with all the blessings attending sonship.[39] The requirement is faith with its resultant obedience to God's Word. The condition of the covenant of grace is fundamentally the same in both Testaments, namely, the surrender of faith.[40] The covenant of grace had several preparatory stages, with Noah (its sign being the rainbow)[41]; with Abraham (its sign being circumcision)[42] with Isaac, and with Jacob.[43] The culmination of this covenant relationship with a national people came when the Old Covenant was made by God with Israel.[44] This Old Covenant was actually continuous with the Abrahamic covenant, according to Scripture.[45] The sign of the Old Covenant was the Jewish Sabbath.[46] This Old or "First" Covenant was ratified with blood.[47]

The New Covenant is with the "Israel of God,"[48] which is made up of believing Jews as heirs of Abraham, and of believing Gentiles who are now fellow heirs with the believing portion of Israel.[49] The fact that believing Gentiles should be fellow heirs with believing Israelites, the two groups comprising the church, is in the New Testament spoken of as a "mystery," that is, a truth which had not fully been made known by prophecy.[50] Paul does indicate, however, that there is justification in the Old Testament prophets for the reception

37 Rom. 8:23; II Cor. 1:22; 5:5; Eph. 1:14; 4:30.
38 I Pet. 1:20.
39 Jer. 31:31-34.
40 Rom. 4; Gal. 3:6-18.
41 Gen. 6:18; 9:9-17.
42 Gen. 12:2, 3; 15:18; 17:2, 9-14.
43 Ex. 3:6.
44 Ex. 24:7, 8.

45 Ex. 6:2-8; 19:3-6.
46 Ex. 31:12-17.
47 Ex. 24:8; Heb. 9:17-20.
48 Gal. 6:16.
49 Eph. 2:11—3:6.
50 Eph. 3:4.

of the Gentiles into the church.[51] The New Covenant was predicted in the Old Testament,[52] it was established by Christ,[53] it was continuous with the Old Covenant,[54] and it is eternal.[55]

Salvation for All

The Scriptures teach that Christ died for the world, "for all," and the Lord calls upon all men to accept the Gospel and be saved. According to the Word of God men are lost, not because of God, but because of their own choice of sin. It is true that there are a few statements in the Bible which if taken alone would seem to teach an election to damnation. For example, Acts 1 speaks of Judas turning aside or falling, "to go to his own place."[56] The meaning seems to be that Judas finally went to the place which was the predetermined end for anyone who puts sin first in his life, who chooses money, e.g., rather than the Lord. Similarly, the First Letter of Peter speaks of the wicked stumbling, "because they disobey the word, as they were destined to do."[57] Dr. Gerrit Verkuyl adds a note in his *Berkeley Version of the New Testament*: "Unbelievers will stumble; it is an eternal law."[58] In other words, a fall is predestined by God for everyone who rejects the Gospel of the Lord Jesus Christ.

Even in the Old Testament God declared: "Have I any pleasure in the death of the wicked, says the Lord God, and not rather that he should turn from his way and live?"[59] And again, "For I have no pleasure in the death of anyone, says the Lord God; so turn, and live."[60] Also, "Say to them, As I live, says the Lord God, I have no pleasure in the death of the wicked, but that the wicked turn from his way and live; turn back, turn back from your evil ways; for why will you die, O house of Israel?"[61] In the New Testament Paul states that God "desires all men to be saved and to come to the knowledge of the truth."[62] And Peter assures us that the Lord is forbearing toward men, "not wishing that any should perish, but that all should reach repentance."[63]

In line with the desire of God to see all men saved we find Jesus preaching: "The time is fulfilled, and the kingdom of God is at hand; repent, and believe in the gospel."[64] The promise of salvation is that "whoever drinks of the water that I shall give him will never

51 Rom. 15:9-12.
52 Jer. 31:31.
53 Heb. 8:6-13; 10:14-23; 12:24; I John 2:27.
54 Luke 1:72, 73; Acts 3:25; Rom. 9:4; 15:8-12; 16:25, 26; Gal. 3:6, 7, 14, 17, 27-29; 4:28; Eph. 2:12—3:11.
55 Heb. 13:20.
56 Acts 1:25.
57 I Pet. 2:8.
58 P. 596.
59 Ezek. 18:23.
60 Ezek. 18:32.
61 Ezek. 33:11.
62 I Tim. 2:4.
63 II Pet. 3:9.
64 Mark 1:15.

thirst; the water that I shall give him will become in him a spring of water welling up to eternal life."[65] To the Athenians Paul declared: "The times of ignorance God overlooked, but now he commands all men everywhere to repent, because he has fixed a day on which he will judge the world in righteousness by a man whom he has appointed, and of this he has given assurance to all men by raising him from the dead."[66] The invitation of the Saviour is: "Come to me, all who labor and are heavy-laden, and I will give you rest. Take my yoke upon you, and learn from me; for I am gentle and lowly in heart, and you will find rest for your souls. For my yoke is easy, and my burden is light."[67] According to the New Testament Christians are "ambassadors for Christ, God making his appeal through us. We beseech you on behalf of Christ, be reconciled to God."[68] One of the last messages of God's Word is: "The Spirit and the Bride say, 'Come.' And let him who hears say, 'Come.' And let him who is thirsty come, let him who desires take the water of life without price."[69]

One of the finest expositions of the universal love of God is found in the Fourth Gospel: "For God so loved the world that he gave his only Son, that whoever believes in him should not perish but have eternal life. For God sent the Son into the world, not to condemn the world, but that the world might be saved through him. He who believes in him is not condemned; he who does not believe is condemned already, because he has not believed in the name of the only Son of God."[70] "Truly, truly, I say to you, he who hears my word and believes him who sent me, has eternal life; he does not come into judgment, but has passed from death to life."[71]

3. ELECTION

The New Testament makes many references to the fact that Christians are elect or chosen, having been predestinated or fore-ordained to eternal life by a sovereign and loving God. In His final discourses to the apostles Jesus said: "If you were of the world, the world would love its own; but because you are not of the world, but I chose you out of the world, therefore the world hates you."[72] And the Apostle Paul exclaims: "Blessed be the God and Father of our Lord Jesus Christ, who has blessed us in Christ with every spiritual blessing in the heavenly places, even as he *chose* us in him before the foundation of the world, that we should be holy and blameless

---

65 John 4:14.
66 Acts 17:30, 31.
67 Matt. 11:28-30.

68 II Cor. 5:20.
69 Rev. 22:17.
70 John 3:16-18.

71 John 5:24.
72 John 15:19.

before him. He destined us in love to be his sons through Jesus Christ, according to the purpose of his will, to the praise of his glorious grace which he freely bestowed on us in the Beloved."[73]

From the Greek verb, to choose, is derived the adjective, chosen or elect. In His prophetic discourse on the Mount of Olives, Jesus spoke of the coming destruction of Jerusalem saying: "And if those days had not been shortened, no human being would be saved; but for the sake of the elect those days will be shortened. Then if any one says to you, 'Lo, here is the Christ!' or 'There he is!' do not believe it. For false Christs and false prophets will arise and show great signs and wonders, so as to lead astray, if possible, even the elect."[74] And in connection with His own return Jesus said: "And they will see the Son of man coming on the clouds of heaven with power and great glory; and he will send out his angels with a loud trumpet call, and they will gather his elect from the four winds, from one end of heaven to the other."[75] In teaching persistence in prayer Jesus declared: "And will not God vindicate his *elect,* who cry to him day and night?"[76]

The Apostle Paul frequently spoke of Christians as the elect: "Who shall bring any charge against God's elect? It is God who justifies."[77] "Put on then, as God's chosen ones, holy and beloved, compassion, kindness, lowliness, meekness, and patience."[78] Paul spoke of his own commission as an apostle of Christ, "to further the faith of God's elect and their knowledge of the truth."[79] And Peter described his readers as "chosen and destined by God the Father and sanctified by the Spirit for obedience to Jesus Christ and for sprinkling with his blood."[80]

In his First Letter to the Thessalonians Paul wrote these encouraging words: "For we know, brethren beloved by God, that he has *chosen* you; for our gospel came to you not only in word, but also in power and in the Holy Spirit and with full conviction."[81] Peter employs the same term for election when he writes: "Therefore, brethren, be the more zealous to confirm your call and *election,* for if you do this you will never fall; so there will be richly provided for you an entrance into the eternal kingdom of our Lord and Savior Jesus Christ."[82] Peter also employs a Greek word which might be translated, co-elect: "She who is at Babylon, who is likewise chosen, sends you greetings."[83]

73 Eph. 1:3-6.
74 Matt. 24:22-24.
75 Matt. 24:30, 31.
76 Luke 18:7.

77 Rom. 8:33.
78 Col. 3:12.
79 Titus 1:1.
80 I Pet. 1:1.

81 I Thess. 1:4.
82 II Pet. 1:10, 11.
83 I Pet. 5:13.

Paul uses still another Greek word meaning, to choose, when he writes in his Second Letter to the Thessalonians: "God *chose* you from the beginning to be saved, through sanctification by the Spirit and belief in the truth. To this he called you through our gospel, so that you may obtain the glory of our Lord Jesus Christ."[84]

The only time Paul arranged the steps of salvation into a series is in Romans 8: "We know that in everything God works for good with those who love him, who are called according to his purpose. For those whom he foreknew he also predestined to be conformed to the image of his Son, in order that he might be the firstborn among many brethren. And those whom he predestined he also called; and those whom he called he also justified; and those whom he justified he also glorified."[85] Paul employs the same term, to predestine, in his Letter to the Ephesians: "He destined us in love to be his sons through Jesus Christ."[86] Also, "We who first hoped in Christ have been *destined* and appointed to live for the praise of his glory."[87]

Perhaps the most striking example of Biblical election or predestination is found in the Book of Acts in connection with Paul's preaching of the Gospel at Antioch of Pisidia: "And when the Gentiles heard this, they were glad and glorified the word of God: and as many as were ordained to eternal life believed."[88] The term here translated "ordained" is elsewhere translated appointed,[89] set,[90] determined,[91] and addicted.[92] It is the same Greek word which is used in Romans 13 where Paul states that the governing authorities have been instituted by God. There seems to be nothing wrong with the translation of the Greek in Acts 13:48, the passage before us.

When one examines the general teaching of the New Testament one finds that the salvation of the righteous is regularly ascribed to the electing love and mercy and grace of God. "We love, because he first loved us."[93] The doctrine of election therefore becomes a means of ascribing to God the glory for the salvation of each Christian in that the believer's choice of Christ is grounded eternally in the love and goodness of God. The Bible is also entirely clear that if men are lost they alone are responsible. Acts 13:48 no more denies the fact that the Gentile converts accepted the Lord Jesus Christ as their Saviour, than does Acts 13:46 deny the universal love of God when the apostle described those who rejected the Gospel as "thrusting it from them and judging themselves unworthy of eternal

84 II Thess. 2:13, 14.
85 Rom. 8:28-30.
86 Eph. 1:5.
87 Eph. 1:12.
88 Acts 13:48.

89 Matt. 28:16; Acts 22:10; 28:23.
90 Luke 7:8.
91 Acts 15:2.
92 I Cor. 16:5.
93 I John 4:19.

life." In other words, if men are saved it is because God has loved them and bestowed on them the desire and the ability to respond to the offer of salvation. But if men are lost, it is because they reject Christ as their Saviour, choosing rather to live in sin. Divine grace is represented in the New Testament as being resistible. Felix was genuinely alarmed when Paul argued about justice and self-control and future judgment, but he did not accept the Lord Jesus.[94] Indeed, Luke's Gospel indicates that the Pharisees and lawyers frustrated God's purpose to save them by refusing baptism.[95]

When a sinner hears the Gospel and is convicted of sin by the Holy Spirit, there ensues in his bosom a more or less severe struggle as he attempts to decide for or against Jesus Christ. If he rejects, he is ever conscious thereafter that it was his decision, and his alone. But if he accepts, as he grows more mature in the Christian life and in his understanding of Christian doctrine, there will come to him a growing awareness that the decision which he made to accept Christ, although genuinely his, was ultimately due to the electing love and mercy of God. Mature Christians have a sense of God having chosen them as His own.[96]

Yet it must also be admitted that God has blessed some races and certain individuals with greater Gospel privileges than others. This is undoubtedly the point which Luke had in mind in describing the activities of Paul in Acts 16. The Holy Spirit blocked the way of the apostle by refusing to allow him to speak the word in Asia. "And when they had come opposite Mysia, they attempted to go into Bithynia, but the Spirit of Jesus did not allow them; so, passing by Mysia, they went down to Troas."[97] God was leading the apostle to the place of His own choosing, namely, Macedonia, where "the Lord opened [Lydia's] heart to give heed to what was said by Paul."[98]

It is also evident that in the New Testament the sovereignty of God is taught without apology. Before Jacob and Esau were born it had been determined by God to give the nation of Israel a higher place in His economy of history than the nation of Edom. It should be observed, of course, that Paul is speaking of the sovereignty of God in history, and the subject relates to the families of Jacob and

---

94 Acts 24:25.
95 Luke 7:30.
96 Cf. "Choose," in Alan Richardson, *A Theological Word Book of the Bible* (New York: Macmillan, 1951), pp. 43, 44.
97 Acts 16:7, 8.
98 Acts 16:14.

Esau and not merely to the individuals. It should also be noted that Romans 9 is not speaking of the eternal salvation of Jacob and Esau but of the greater prominence of Israel. Paul does not say: "The elder will be saved, while the younger will be damned"; he says: "The elder will serve the younger."[99] "Loving" and "hating" are used by Paul in their Oriental sense of giving primary versus secondary place. Compare, for example, the teaching of the Bible that one must "hate" the immediate members of his family if he wishes to be a disciple of Christ: the obvious meaning is, of course, that one dare not love brothers or sisters more than Christ.[1] The only way to interpret Romans 9 in harmony with the rest of Scripture is to regard the "vessels of wrath" as those who cling to sin and reject the Gospel, while the "vessels of mercy" are those whom God has loved from all eternity because in His foreknowledge He sees them as being in the Beloved, as being true believers on the Lord Jesus Christ.

It would appear that the Biblical doctrines of personal responsibility and human freedom, as well as the doctrines of sovereign grace and divine election, stand in a somewhat paradoxical relation to each other. Nevertheless, in order to present the nature of God fairly to the race, it is necessary to emphasize the centrality of the love of God in the same way as does the New Testament, to place the responsibility for the rejection of Christ squarely on the shoulders of those who refuse to yield to the Saviour, and to attribute the surrender of faith on the part of believers to the electing love and mercy of a gracious God.

4. *DIVINE CALLING*

The writers of the New Testament, especially Paul, frequently speak of the effectual call of God whereby a sinner is induced to accept the salvation which is offered in the Gospel of Christ. Usually the call is referred to God Himself, rather than to Christ or to the Holy Spirit. Sometimes the call is the external offer of salvation, and sometimes it is the inner call to the heart. Jesus Himself referred to the fact that "many are called, but few are chosen [elect]."[2] Our Lord evidently meant that the external call of the Gospel goes out to large numbers of people, but comparatively few show themselves believers, "elect," by turning to Christ in repentance and faith.

The Apostle Paul speaks of God extending His call to those whom He has predestined to salvation.[3] Paul also instructed each

---

99 Rom. 9:12.
1 Luke 14:26; cf. Matt. 10:37.

2 Matt. 22:14.
3 Rom. 8:30.

reader at Corinth to "lead the life which the Lord has assigned to him, and in which God has called him,"[4] whether married to an unbeliever, whether circumcised or uncircumcised, whether a slave or free. "Every one should remain in the state in which he was called."[5] Paul described the Christians at Corinth as being called by God "into the fellowship of his Son, Jesus Christ our Lord."[6] The Christians of Galatia were "deserting him who called [them] in the grace of Christ and turning to a different gospel."[7] Paul wrote to the Christians of Ephesus: "I therefore . . . beg you to lead a life worthy of the calling to which you have been called, with all lowliness and meekness, with patience, forbearing one another in love, eager to maintain the unity of the Spirit in the bond of peace."[8] In expressing the wish that God might sanctify the Christians of Thessalonica the apostle adds: "He who calls you is faithful, and he will do it."[9] And Paul told Timothy: "Take hold of the eternal life to which you were called when you made the good confession in the presence of many witnesses."[10]

The Letter to the Hebrews also refers to the divine calling of Christians,[11] as does Peter in both his letters.[12]

The Christian has been saved by God "and called . . . with a holy calling."[13] Christians as a class are spoken of as "the called."[14]

On at least one occasion the New Testament uses a compound verb to express the divine summons to enter the kingdom of Christ: "For the promise is to you and to your children and to all that are far off, every one whom the Lord our God calls to him."[15]

It is evident that the Biblical teaching on the effectual call of God to enter the body of Christ, His spiritual kingdom, is part and parcel of the total emphasis of the New Testament that salvation from beginning to end is the glorious work of God. This was well expressed by the Apostle Paul when he wrote:

And you he made alive, when you were dead through the trespasses and sins in which you once walked, following the course of this world, following the prince of the power of the air, the spirit that is now at work in the sons of disobedience. Among these we all once lived in the passions of our flesh, following the desires of body and mind, and so we were by nature children of wrath, like the rest of mankind. But God, who is rich in mercy, out of the great love with which he loved us, even when we were dead through our trespasses, made us alive together with Christ

4 I Cor. 7:17.
5 I Cor. 7:20.
6 I Cor. 1:9.
7 Gal. 1:6.
8 Eph. 4:1.
9 I Thess. 5:24.

10 I Tim. 6:12.
11 Heb. 9:15.
12 I Pet. 1:15; 2:9; 3:9; II Pet. 1:3.
13 II Tim. 1:9.
14 Rom. 8:28 (Greek).
15 Acts 2:39.

(by grace you have been saved), and raised us up with him, and made us sit with him in the heavenly places in Christ Jesus, that in the coming ages he might show the immeasurable riches of his grace in kindness toward us in Christ Jesus. For by grace you have been saved through faith; and this is not your own doing, it is the gift of God—not because of works, lest any man should boast. For we are his workmanship, created in Christ Jesus for good works, which God prepared beforehand, that we should walk in them.[16]

If human ingenuity and persuasiveness are not sufficient to summon a sinner out of his life of sin and to bring him to repentance and faith, it is evident that Christians should rely wholly upon God, beseeching Him in prayer in behalf of those who are yet "dead in trespasses and sins."[17] Only God can open the heart so that the sinner gives heed to the things which are spoken by the Lord's ambassadors.[18] The Christian worker is therefore absolutely dependent upon the blessing of the Lord in every evangelistic effort which he makes. It is God who must call sinners to repentance and faith.

On the other hand, one should not think of the election and calling of God as entitling the Christian to carelessness or indifference. One senses a warning on this point in the writings of Peter when he says: "Therefore, brethren, be the more zealous to confirm your call and election, for if you do this you will never fall; so there will be richly provided for you an entrance into the eternal kingdom of our Lord and Savior Jesus Christ."[19]

5. CHRISTIAN CONVERSION

By conversion is meant the response of a sinner under the conviction of the Holy Spirit, in which the sinner repents, renouncing his sin, and exercises faith in Christ as Saviour and Lord.

Repentance has at least three aspects: intellectual, emotional, and volitional. The intellectual aspect of repentance is a recognition of one's sinfulness and helplessness, a personal knowledge of sin. Paul's Letter to the Romans states that "through the law comes knowledge of sin."[20] Paul's own experience illustrates this truth. Paul stated that he would not have known sin had it not been for the law, because he would not have known what evil desires were had it not been that the law kept saying,[21] "You shall not have evil desire."[22] Many people have little or no conviction of sin until they see themselves in the mirror of God's holy law, whereupon they

16 Eph. 2:1-10.
17 Eph. 2:1.
18 Acts 16:14.

19 II Pet. 1:10, 11.
20 Rom. 3:20.

21 Force of Greek tense.
22 Rom. 7:7.

become stricken in conscience and exercised about their need of salvation. At this point, of course, the individual must have a knowledge of the Gospel of Christ if he is truly to be converted.

The emotional aspect of repentance consists of a godly sorrow for sin. To a repentant church Paul wrote: "As it is, I rejoice, not because you were grieved, but because you were grieved into repenting; for you felt a godly grief, so that you suffered no loss through us. For godly grief produces a repentance that leads to salvation and brings no regret, but worldly grief produces death."[23] Human nature is so constituted that men shrink from any contact with the supernatural. Were it not for the emotional aspect of repentance, no human being would accept Christ: he would rather flee from Him.

The final climax of conversion consists in the volitional element, the change of purpose, the inward turning from sin to Christ. The godly sorrow must lead to such spiritual nausea as shall compel the individual to desperately seek Christ and His salvation. The sorrow for sin is not in itself repentance, but it leads to repentance, which is the final turning to Christ in faith. Acts 2 contains a good example of Gospel conversion:

Now when they heard this they were cut to the heart, and said to Peter and the rest of the apostles, "Brethren, what shall we do?" And Peter said to them, "Repent, and be baptized every one of you in the name of Jesus Christ for the forgiveness of your sins; and you shall receive the gift of the Holy Spirit. . . ." And he testified with many other words and exhorted them, saying, "Save yourselves from this crooked generation." So those who received his word were baptized, and there were added that day about three thousand souls. And they devoted themselves to the apostles' teaching and fellowship, to the breaking of bread and the prayers.[24]

Here one observes the following steps in conversion: (1) the preaching of the Word of God; (2) Holy Spirit conviction and contrition; (3) repentance and faith; (4) Christian baptism; (5) Christian discipleship and fellowship.

What is the meaning of Christian faith? Faith is undoubtedly one of the least understood terms today. Faith is not an attitude of blind optimism while taking foolish chances; it is not a particular mood or feeling; nor is it an attitude of trying to do good and then hoping for the best on the judgment day. Faith is not to be contrasted with a reasonable ground of assurance. The elements of faith are probably four.

23 II Cor. 7:9, 10.   24 Acts 2:37-42.

1. Christian faith involves an attitude of confident trust in God and His Word. An excellent illustration of genuine faith is that of Abraham, the father of the faithful. God Almighty had promised Abraham that he would have a large family through Isaac. Before Isaac was ever married God tested the faith of Abraham by asking him to sacrifice his son. Abraham was convinced of the absolute faithfulness of God so that he expected the LORD to resurrect Isaac from the dead following his sacrifice. To the servants Abraham said, when they reached the foot of Moriah: "Stay here with the ass; I and the lad will go yonder and worship, and [we will] come again to you."[25] The Letter to the Hebrews comments thus: "By faith Abraham, when he was tested, offered up Isaac, and he who had received the promises was ready to offer up his only son, of whom it was said, 'Through Isaac shall your descendants be named.' He considered that God was able to raise men even from the dead; hence, figuratively speaking, he did receive him back."[26] The same letter speaks of the immutable purpose of God to save His people, confirmed by a divine oath, so that "we who have fled for refuge might have strong encouragement to seize the hope set before us. We have this as a sure and steadfast anchor of the soul, a hope that enters into the inner shrine behind the curtain, where Jesus has gone as a forerunner on our behalf, having become a high priest for ever after the order of Melchizedek."[27]

2. Christian faith includes also a continuing self-surrender to God. Again referring to Abraham, one observes that it would not have been sufficient for Abraham to have given himself to God initially in repentance and faith; it was also necessary for him to maintain his filial relationship to the LORD by remaining constantly surrendered to the divine will. The Letter of James comments: "Do you want to be shown, you foolish fellow, that faith apart from works is barren? Was not Abraham our father justified by works, when he offered his son Isaac upon the altar? You see that faith was active along with his works, and faith was completed by works, and the scripture was fulfilled which says, 'Abraham believed God, and it was reckoned to him as righteousness'; and he was called the friend of God."[28] It is not sufficient to have been gloriously saved at the time of one's conversion; it is also necessary to maintain a life of holiness and obedience. This is an aspect of saving faith.

3. Christian faith also involves a longing to please God. If one has been truly converted he will desire above all else to do the

25 Gen. 22:5.
26 Heb. 11:17-19.
27 Heb. 6:18-20.
28 Jas. 2:20-23.

things, and to be the person, which God desires. The testimony of the Apostle Paul was: "I always take pains to have a clear conscience toward God and toward men."[29] Unless this attitude is present, one cannot be certain that the individual is a person of true Christian faith. Paul constantly called himself a bond servant of Jesus Christ, undoubtedly meaning that he had no will of his own, that he belonged, body, soul, and spirit, to the Lord Jesus Christ, desiring only to do His blessed will.

4. Christian faith ventures obedience, ignoring consequences, desiring only to step forward at the command of Christ. In other words, he who has Christian faith does not live on the basis of prudence; he does not reckon with selfish outcomes. He serves God out of sheer love for Him, asking only for grace to perform whatever God asks. This is the emphasis of the excellent little tract of the Anabaptists, "Two Kinds of Obedience."[30]

It is important to recognize that while Christians are saved by the exercise of their faith, by putting their trust in God through the Lord Jesus Christ, they are not saved by the quality of their faith, by the perfection of their life, nor by the degree of perfection in which they resemble the Lord Jesus Christ in character. Salvation is not a matter which is achieved by merit; it is the gift of God. This gift is bestowed upon every honest soul who turns to Jesus Christ sincerely.

Christian faith is therefore never introspective. It is not in order for the child of God to anxiously inspect the quality of his faith, wondering whether it is sufficiently strong to save him. Saving faith does not have its eye on itself, but on its object, that is, God. The promise of eternal life is not given to those of exceptionally confident trust, but to everyone who believes on the Saviour and yields to Him sincerely. The Israelites who were "under the blood" were just as secure whether they were a bit anxious when the angel of death visited Egypt, or whether they were singing glorious songs of deliverance. So it is with the child of God: everyone who belongs to Jesus Christ will be saved, whether weak or strong.

In the case of children reared in Christian homes, brought up in the nurture of the Lord, conversion is usually not the strongly marked emotional crisis which it is in the case of hardened sinners or of former heathen. Many New Testament passages which describe in vigorous terms the profound conversion experiences of wicked

---

29 Acts 24:16.
30 Harry Emerson Fosdick, *Great Voices of the Reformation* (New York: Random House, 1952), pp. 296-99.

sinners refer to heathen and not to the children of Christians. All true converts, however, do experience repentance and faith.

The Scriptures do not assign any age as the normal one in which to accept Christ. Intelligent Christian parents and leaders therefore do not attempt to precipitate conversion before the child has reached a sufficient degree of maturity, intellectual, moral, and spiritual. Only the Holy Spirit is able to know when the proper time has arrived in the life of the individual to turn to Jesus. It would appear that frequently the Holy Spirit does begin His gracious work of repentance in the life of the adolescent about the time he enters puberty. Prior to the arrival of the age of accountability every child is safe in Christ, for Jesus died to redeem the entire race. One concludes from reading Romans 5 that so far as the curse had gone through the sin of Adam, so far does the atonement of Jesus Christ extend. All children prior to the age of accountability are therefore saved. They are saved without baptism, church membership, or any human activity whatever. It is cruel and unchristian to attempt to precipitate a conversion experience in those who are not sufficiently mature to experience conversion. Furthermore, it is actually impossible to bring an individual to Christ when the Holy Spirit is not working in his heart. To attempt to do so is either to bring the individual to despair, or to induce him to unite with the church without a real experience of conversion.

Inasmuch as young children are safe under the blood of Christ they should be taught from their earliest years that God loves them, that He hears their prayers, that He is able to assist them to be good, and that He forgives their sins. In other words, even prior to reaching the age of personal accountability, and experiencing genuine conversion, the child who is receiving a Christian nurture experiences on his child-level the love and goodness and forgiveness of God.[31] Later, when the spiritual awakening of the soul occurs, there will be an altogether new and profoundly deeper consciousness of sin, coupled with the awareness that God is now asking for the heart of the newly awakened youth, and asking for a public profession of faith in Jesus Christ. This is no longer the experience of a child, but of an individual who is personally accountable to God.

Genuine conversion results in a willingness to confess sin. All sin is, of course, to be confessed to God. The Apostle John writes: "If we say we have fellowship with him while we walk in darkness, we lie and do not live according to the truth; but if we walk in the

31 On this point I am indebted to my colleague, Dr. Paul Mininger, Professor of Practical Theology in the Goshen College Biblical Seminary.

light, as he is in the light, we have fellowship with one another, and the blood of Jesus his Son cleanses us from all sin. If we say we have no sin, we deceive ourselves, and the truth is not in us. If we confess our sins, he is faithful and just, and will forgive our sins and cleanse us from all unrighteousness."[32] To humbly confess one's shortcomings to a fellow believer is also a wholesome experience, and one which greatly relieves the conscience when peace cannot be secured otherwise. This truth is also recognized in the New Testament: "Therefore confess your sins to one another, and pray for one another, that you may be healed."[33] This might be called fraternal confession; it is not a matter of confessing to a priest. Where an individual has committed flagrant transgressions so as to publicly disgrace the name of the church, it is evident that he owes the brotherhood an apology. Not all sin, however, is to be confessed publicly. To desire to do so is often a reflection of wrong indoctrination, and sometimes is a manifestation of a sinful exhibitionism. Menno Simons was very clear on this matter. He wrote:

However should it ever happen that any one should sin against God in private, from which may His power preserve us all, and should the spirit of grace, which works repentance, again operate upon his heart and cause genuine repentance, of this we have not to judge; for it is a matter between him and God. For it is evident that we do not seek our righteousness and salvation, the remission of our sins, satisfaction, reconciliation and eternal life in or through excommunication, but alone in the righteousness, intercession, merits, death, and blood of Christ. There are but two objects and ends why the ban is commanded in the Scriptures, which can have no reference to such an one. Because in the first place his sins are private; hence no offense can follow. And secondly, because he is in deep contrition and is penitent in life. Therefore he has no need then of being brought to repentance. Nor are we anywhere commanded of Christ to put him to open shame before the church.[34]

In a letter of 1555 Menno attempted to correct the erroneous views of excommunication of the brethren of Franeker in Friesland:

I also understand that these same brethren are of the opinion that if some brother should secretly have transgressed in something or other, and in sorrow of heart should complain to one of his brethren that he had thus sinned against God, that then this same brother should tell it unto the church; and if he should fail to do so, that he then should be punished with the transgressor. This opinion is not only absurd but it sounds in my ears as a terrible one. For it is clearly against all Scriptures and love. Matt. 18; Jas. 5:19, 20.

---

32 I John 1:6-9.   33 Jas. 5:16.   34 *Complete Works*, I, p. 254.

Excommunication was, in one respect, instituted for the purpose of repentance. Now, if repentance is shown, namely, the contrite, sorrowing heart, how can excommunication, then, be pronounced against such? O my brethren, do not put this doctrine in force, for it will lead to sin and not to reformation.[35]

If we were thus to deal with poor, repenting sinners, whose transgressions were done in secret, how many would we keep from repentance, through shame. God forbid that I should ever agree with or act upon such doctrine! Lastly, I understand, they hold that if any one in his weakness, transgresses, and openly acknowledges his transgression, that they should consider him then as a worldling.

This again is an absurd doctrine; for if the transgression was done through weakness, then let us not be arrogant and too hard on the poor soul lest we commit a worse fault.

Not the weak but the corrupt members are cut off lest they corrupt the others. . . . I desire that excommunication be practiced in a sincere, paternal spirit, in faithful love according to the doctrine of Christ and His apostles. . . .

Follow this my brotherly admonition in this respect which has been acted upon for twenty-one years. I could give you no other and better advice.[36]

6. *THE NEW BIRTH*

The new birth or regeneration is the gracious act of God in which He implants spiritual life in the Christian convert and makes his governing disposition holy. This experience is referred to in the Scripture in many ways. It is called a new birth,[37] the circumcision of the heart,[38] the putting on of the new man,[39] the enlightenment of the eyes of the heart,[40] being washed,[41] receiving the washing of regeneration,[42] the illumination of the heart,[43] becoming a new creation,[44] having the heart sprinkled,[45] being risen with Christ,[46] etc. Regeneration was made necessary by the fall of original man into sin and the consequent depravity which has corrupted human nature since the Fall. While it is true that the Fall did not add any new organic desires to human nature, it did make men selfish and carnal. That is, because of depravity people are inclined to give undue place to the body and its desires, seeking to fulfill the cravings of flesh in ways that are contrary both to the will of God and to the promotion of personal happiness and peace. The body itself is neither sinful nor moral, but is used by the inner self either

---

35 *Ibid.*, I, p. 283.
36 *Ibid.*, I, pp. 283, 284.
37 John 3:3.
38 Rom. 2:29.

39 Eph. 4:24; Col. 3:10.
40 Eph. I:18.
41 I Cor. 6:11.
42 Titus 3:5.

43 II Cor. 4:6.
44 II Cor. 5:17; Gal. 6:15.
45 Heb. 10:22.
46 Rom. 6:4; Col. 2:12; 3:1.

for righteous or evil purposes. It is, therefore, the "heart" or true self which stands in need of spiritual regeneration.

The story is told of a slave owner who became converted. Someone asked one of his servants what had happened to his master. The servant replied: "Upon my word, I do not know! He's got the same skin, but there's a new man inside." The regenerated person has a new awareness of his own need of divine grace, he is now filled with love for God, he now has Christian love for his fellow believers on Christ, he now lives for the glory of God rather than for selfish pleasures and for self-interest, he is now united with Christ in a union of love, devotion, and obedience; in short, he is God's new creation.

In his booklet *The New Birth*, Menno Simons wrote:

That regeneration of which we write, of which comes the penitent, pious life having the promise, comes alone from the Word of the Lord if it be rightly taught and rightly understood and received in the heart by faith through the Holy Ghost. The first birth of man is out of the first, earthly Adam and therefore its nature is earthly and Adamic, that is, carnal-minded, unbelieving, disobedient and blind in divine things, deaf and foolish, whose end if not renewed by the Word will be damnation and eternal death. Would you therefore have your inbred, evil nature reformed and be free from eternal death and damnation so that you may obtain with all true Christians what is promised them, you must be born again. For the regenerated are in grace, and have the promise, as you have heard. They therefore lead a penitent and new life, for they are renewed in Christ and have received a new heart and spirit. Before, they were earthly, carnally minded, but now heavenly, spiritually; before, unrighteous, now righteous; before, evil, now good. And live no longer after the old, depraved nature of the first, earthly Adam, but after the new sincere nature of the new and heavenly Adam, Christ Jesus. . . . Their poor weak life they renew daily, more and more, and that after the image of Him who created them; their minds are after the mind of Christ, they gladly walk as He walked; crucify and mortify their flesh with its evil lusts; bury their sin with baptism in the Lord's death, and rise with Him to a new life; circumcise their hearts with the Word of the Lord, and are baptized with the Holy Ghost in the spotless, holy body of Christ, as obedient members and fellow-heirs of His church, according to the true ordinance and Word of the Lord. They put on Christ and manifest His Spirit, nature and power in all their fruits; fear God with all the heart, and seek in all their thoughts, words and works, nothing but the praise of God and the salvation of their beloved brethren. They know not hatred and vengeance, for they love those who hate them; do good to those who despitefully use them, and pray for those who persecute them; hate and resist avarice, pride, unchastity, pomp, drunkenness, fornication, adultery, hatred, envy, backbiting, lying, defrauding, quarreling, blood-shedding and idolatry, all impure, carnal works, and forsake the world with all its lusts; meditate upon the law of the Lord by day and by night; rejoice at the good, and are grieved at the evil; evil they do not repay with evil, but with good; they seek not self, nor their own good, but what is good for their neighbors, both as to body and soul; feed the hungry and give drink to the thirsty; entertain the needy, release prisoners, visit the sick, comfort the faint-hearted, admonish the erring, and are ready after their Master's example, to give their lives for their brethren. Again, their thoughts are pure and chaste, their words are true and seasoned with salt; with them *yea* is *yea*, and *nay* is *nay*, and their works are done in the fear of the Lord; their hearts are heavenly and new; their minds, peaceful and joyful; they seek righteousness with all their powers. In short, they are so assured in their faith through the Spirit and Word of God, that they will gallantly overcome, by virtue of their faith, all blood-thirsty, cruel tyrants, with all their tortures, punishment, exiling, plunder, stocks, stakes, executioners, tormentors and counsel; and out of a pure zeal, with an innocent, pure, simple *yea* and *nay* are willing to die. The glory of Christ, the sweetness of the Word, and the salvation of souls are dearer to them than anything under heaven.

Behold, worthy reader, all those who are born of God with Christ, who thus conform their weak life to the gospel, are thus converted, and follow the example of Christ, hear and believe His holy Word, follow His commands which He in plain words commanded us in the Holy Scriptures, form the holy Christian church which has the promise; the true children of God, brothers and sisters of Christ; for they are born with Him of one Father, and of the new Eve, the pure, chaste bride. They are flesh of Christ's flesh, and bone of His bone, the spiritual house of Israel, the spiritual city, Jerusalem, temple and Mount Zion, the spiritual ark of the Lord, in which are hidden the true bread of heaven, Christ Jesus and His blessed Word, the green, blossoming rod of faith, and the spiritual tables of stone, with the commands of the Lord written thereon; they are the spiritual seed of Abraham, children of the promise, confederates of the covenant of God, and partakers of the heavenly blessings.

These regenerated have a spiritual king over them who rules them by the unbroken scepter of His mouth, namely, with His Holy Spirit and Word, He clothes them with the garment of righteousness, of pure white silk; He refreshes them with the living water of His Holy Spirit, and feeds them with the bread of life. His name is Christ Jesus. They are the children of peace, who have beaten their swords into plow-shares, and their spears into pruning hooks, and know of no war; and give to Caesar the things that are Caesar's, and to God the things that are God's. Isa. 2:4; Matt. 22:21. Their sword is the sword of the Spirit, which they hold in a good conscience through the Holy Ghost. Their marriage is that of one man and one woman, according to the ordinance of God. Their kingdom is the kingdom of grace, here in hope, and after this in eternal life. Eph. 6:17; Matt. 19:5; 25:1.

Their citizenship is in heaven; and they use the creatures below, such as eating, drinking, clothing and dwelling with thanksgiving, and that to the necessary wants of their own lives, and to the free service of their neighbor, according to the Word of the Lord. Isa. 58:7. Their doctrine is the unadulterated Word of God, testified through Moses and the prophets, through Christ and the apostles, upon which they build their faith, and save their souls; and every thing that is contrary thereto, they consider accursed. They use and administer their baptism on the confession of their faith, according to the command of the Lord, and the doctrines and usages of the apostles. Mark 16:16.

The Lord's Supper they celebrate in remembrance of the favors and death of their Lord, and in reminding one another of true and brotherly love.

The ban [excommunication] extends to all the proud scorners, great and small, rich and poor, without any respect to person, who heard and obeyed the Word for a season, but have fallen off again, and in the house of the Lord, teach or live offensively, till they again sincerely repent.

They sigh and lament daily over their poor, displeasing, evil flesh, over the manifold errors and faults of their weak lives. They war inwardly and outwardly without ceasing. They seek and call the Most High; fight and struggle against the devil, world and flesh during their lives, press on towards the prize of the high calling that they may obtain it. And they prove by their actions that they believe the Word of the Lord; that they know and have Christ in power; that they are born of God and have Him as their Father.

Behold, worthy reader, as I said before, so I say again. These are the Christians who have the promise, and are assured by the Spirit of God, to whom are given and bestowed Christ Jesus, with all His merits, righteousness, intercessions, Word, cross, suffering, flesh, blood, death, resurrection, kingdom, and all His possessions, and this all without merit; given out of pure grace from God.[47]

In his booklet, *Christian Baptism,* Menno writes:

[Converts] therefore receive the holy baptism as a token of obedience which proceeds from faith, as proof, before God and His church that they firmly believe in the remission of their sins through Christ Jesus, as it was preached and taught them from the Word of God; therefore they receive remission of their sins in baptism, as the lovely promise of grace proclaims and represents; the same as the literal Israelites received remission of their sins by their offerings. For in case that we only sought outward baptism and trusted in the literal practice, and would yet continue in our old, corrupted walk, then indeed all would be in vain, the same as it was in such case, a vain offering amongst the ungodly and carnal Israelites. . . .

47 *Complete Works,* I. pp. 169-71.

Secondly, we are not cleansed in baptism of our inherited sinful nature which is in our flesh, so that it is entirely destroyed in us, for it remains with us after baptism; but since the merciful Father from whom are all good and perfect gifts has graciously given us the most holy faith, so we manifest in the baptism we receive, that we desire to die unto the inherent, sinful nature, and destroy it, so that it will not any longer be master of our mortal bodies. Rom. 6:12. . . .[48]

* * *

My worthy kind brethren, because the holy Christian baptism is a washing of regeneration, according to the doctrine of Paul, therefore none can be washed therewith, to the pleasure and will of God, but those alone who are regenerated through the Word of God; for we are not regenerated because of baptism, as may be perceived in the infants who have been baptized; but we are baptized because we are regenerated by faith in God's Word, as regeneration is not the result of baptism, but baptism the result of regeneration. . . .

Do you think, most beloved, that the new birth consists in nothing but in that which the miserable world hitherto has thought that it consists in, namely, baptism? Or in the expression, I baptize thee in the name of the Father, and of the Son, and of the Holy Ghost? No, worthy brother, no. The new birth consists, verily, not in water nor in words; but it is the heavenly, living and quickening power of God in our hearts, which comes from God, and which by the preaching of the divine Word, if we accept it by faith, quickens, renews, pierces and converts our hearts, so that we are changed and converted from unbelief unto faith, from unrighteousness into righteousness, from evil into good, from carnality into spirituality, from the earthly into the heavenly, from the wicked nature of Adam into the good nature of Jesus Christ; and of such Paul spoke in the alleged Scripture (Titus 3:5).[49]

But the little children, and particularly those of Christian seed, have a peculiar promise which was given them of God without any ceremony, but out of pure grace, through Christ Jesus our Lord who says, "Suffer little children, and forbid them not, to come unto me; for of such is the kingdom of heaven." Matt. 19:14; Mark 10:14; Luke 18:16. This promise makes glad and assures all the chosen saints of God, in regard to their children or infants; being assured that the true Word of our beloved Lord Jesus Christ can never fail. . . . Yea, by this same promise they are assured that their beloved children, so long as they are not of understanding years, are clean, holy, saved and pleasing unto God, be they alive or dead. Therefore they give thanks to the eternal Father through Jesus Christ our Lord for His inexpressibly great love to their children, and train them in the love of God and in wisdom, by correcting, chastising, teaching and admonishing them, and by walking before them with an unblameable life until they may hear the Word of God, believe it and

---

48 *Ibid.*, II, p. 201.   49 *Ibid.*, II, p. 215.

obey it in their works. Then is the time, of whatever age they may be, that they should receive the Christian baptism which Christ Jesus has commanded in obedience to His Word. . . .

Beloved brethren, if it should be said that we thus rob the children of the promise and of the grace of God, you will observe that they contradict us out of hatred and envy, and do not tell the truth. Say, who has the strongest ground and hope of the salvation of their children? Is it he who places his hopes upon an outward sign? Or is it he who bases his hopes upon the promise of grace, given and promised of Christ Jesus?[50]

In commenting on I Peter 3:21 Menno writes:

Here Peter teaches us how the inward baptism saves us by which the inner man is washed, and not the outer baptism by which the flesh is washed; for only this inward baptism . . . is of value in the sight of God, while outward baptism follows only as an evidence of obedience which is of faith; for could outward baptism save without the inner washing, the whole Scriptures which speak of the new man, would be spoken to no purpose. The kingdom of heaven would be bound to elementary water; the blood of Christ would be shed in vain, and no one that is baptized could be lost. No, no! Outward baptism avails nothing so long as we are not inwardly renewed, regenerated, and baptized of God with the heavenly fire and the Holy Ghost. But when we receive this baptism from above we will be constrained through the Spirit and Word of God, by a good conscience, which we thereby obtain, to believe sincerely in the merits of the death of the Lord, and in the power and benefits of His resurrection; and henceforth because we are inwardly cleansed by faith and the spiritual strength which we have received, we submissively covenant with the Lord, through the outward sign of baptism which is enjoined on all the believers in Christ, even as the Lord has covenanted with us in His grace through His Word that we will no longer live according to the evil, unclean lusts of the flesh but walk according to the witness of a good conscience before Him. . . .

The seal in our consciences is the Holy Ghost, but baptism is a sign of obedience commanded of Christ, by which we testify when we receive it that we believe the Word of the Lord, that we are sorry for and repent of our former life and conduct, that we desire to rise with Christ unto a new life, and that we believe in the forgiveness of sin through Jesus Christ. Not, my beloved, that we believe in the remission of sins through baptism; by no means; because by baptism we cannot obtain faith and repentance, neither do we receive the forgiveness of sins, nor peace, nor liberty of conscience, but we testify thereby that we have repented, received pardon and faith in Christ.[51]

After giving a number of Biblical passages assuring Christians of the gift of eternal life, Menno writes:

50 *Ibid.*, II, p. 226.　　　　51 *Ibid.*, I, p. 28.

All who believe this are those of whom the Scriptures say, "To them gave he power to become the sons of God, even to them that believe on his name, which were born, not of blood, nor of the will of the flesh, nor of the will of man, but of God." John 1:12, 13. These are they who are justified by faith, and have peace with God through our Lord Jesus Christ, by whom also we have access by faith into this grace wherein we stand, and rejoice in hope of the glory of God. . . . There is none that of himself can rejoice in or boast of this faith; it is the gift of God.[52] Eph. 2:8. All who receive faith from God, receive a tree full of all manner of good and delicious fruit; happy are they who receive this gift of God, for it is more precious than gold, silver or precious stones; it is incomparable, he that obtains it obtains Christ Jesus, forgiveness of sins, a new mind and eternal life. . . . Behold, such a faith, I say, is the gift of God. Eph. 2:8.[53]

7. JUSTIFICATION

By justification is meant the gracious act of God by which He declares every believer on Christ to have a perfect standing before Himself, the righteous judge. It is God's act of fully accepting a converted believer. The Greek word, to *justify,* is on the same stem as the adjective, *righteous,* or just and as the noun, *righteousness.* The term "forgiveness" refers to what might be called the negative aspect of acceptance with God, namely, the cancellation of guilt for one's sins. The term "justification," however, refers to the positive act of *declaring* the sinner *righteous* before God.

The Scriptures teach clearly that justification is a free gift bestowed by God on every one who puts his faith in Jesus Christ. The Fourth Gospel reports: "For God so loved the world that he gave his only Son, that whoever believes in him should not perish but have eternal life. For God sent the Son into the world, not to condemn the world, but that the world might be saved through him."[54] Again, "Truly, truly, I say to you, he who hears my word and believes him who sent me, has eternal life; he does not come into judgment, but has passed from death to life."[55] When the Jews came to Jesus asking what good works they needed to do in order to be "doing the work of God," Jesus replied: "This is the work of God, that you believe in him whom he has sent."[56]

One of the major purposes of the Letter to the Romans was to define the nature of salvation and to state how this gift is to be received by faith. The theme of the Letter to the Romans is that the gospel "is the power of God for salvation to every one who has faith . . . . For in it the righteousness of God is revealed through

52 Cf. *Ibid.,* I, p. 199.   54 John 3:16, 17.   56 John 6:28, 29.
53 *Ibid.,* I. p. 21.   55 John 5:24.

faith for faith; as it is written, 'He who through faith is righteous shall live.' "[57] After showing the futility of attempting to receive eternal life on the basis of character or merit because of depravity and moral inability Paul continues: "But now the righteousness of God has been manifested apart from law . . . , the righteousness of God through faith in Jesus Christ for all who believe. For there is no distinction; since all have sinned and fall short of the glory of God, they are justified by his grace as a gift, through the redemption which is in Christ Jesus, whom God put forward as an expiation by his blood, to be received by faith. . . . It was to prove at the present time that he himself is righteous and that he justifies him who has faith in Jesus."[58]

"For we hold that a man is justified by faith apart from works of law. . . . God will justify the circumcised on the ground of their faith and the uncircumcised because of their faith."[59]

"Therefore, since we are justified by faith, we have peace with God through our Lord Jesus Christ. Through him we have obtained access to this grace in which we stand."[60]

"For the wages of sin is death, but the free gift of God is eternal life in Christ Jesus our Lord."[61]

"There is therefore now no condemnation for those who are in Christ Jesus."[62]

"What then shall we say to this? If God is for us, who is against us? He who did not spare his own Son but gave him up for us all, will he not also give us all things with him? Who shall bring any charge against God's elect? It is God who justifies; who is to condemn? Is it Christ Jesus, who died, yes, who was raised from the dead, who is at the right hand of God, who indeed intercedes for us?"[63]

In describing the rejection of Christ by the Jews Paul writes: "For, being ignorant of the righteousness that comes from God, and seeking to establish their own, they did not submit to God's righteousness."[64] In his Letter to the Galatians Paul writes: "A man is not justified by works of the law but through faith in Jesus Christ, even we have believed in Christ Jesus, in order to be justified by faith in Christ, and not by works of the law, because by works of the law shall no one be justified."[65]

"Now it is evident that no man is justified before God by the law; for 'he who through faith is righteous shall live.' "[66]

57 Rom. 1:16, 17.
58 Rom. 3:21-26.
59 Rom. 3:28-30.
60 Rom. 5:1, 2.
61 Rom. 6:23.
62 Rom. 8:1.
63 Rom. 8:31-34.
64 Rom. 10:3.
65 Gal. 2:16.
66 Gal. 3:11.

"For by grace you have been saved through faith, and this is not your own doing, it is the gift of God—not because of works, lest any man should boast."[67]

Paul states in his Letter to the Philippians: "Indeed I count everything as loss because of the surpassing worth of knowing Christ Jesus my Lord. For his sake I have suffered the loss of all things, and count them as refuse, in order that I may gain Christ and be found in him, not having a righteousness of my own, based on law, but that which is through faith in Christ, the righteousness from God that depends on faith; that I may know him and the power of his resurrection, and may share his sufferings, becoming like him in his death, that if possible I may attain the resurrection from the dead."[68]

While the term *sanctification* refers to the holiness which God effects in the life of His saints, and although the term *justify* in itself refers to a reckoning as righteous rather than to a making righteous, yet these two aspects of salvation can be separated only in discussion and never in experience. In other words, the true convert to Jesus Christ who is justified by faith is also being transformed by the Spirit of God into a saint.[69] This fact has sometimes been lost sight of, with the unfortunate result that many teachers represent the possibility of being completely justified in God's sight without any spiritual transformation and without the obedience of faith. This the leading reformers did not teach. John Calvin, for example, wrote: "I confess that we are destitute of this incomparable blessing, till Christ becomes ours. I attribute, therefore, the highest importance to the connection between the head and members; to the inhabitation of Christ in our hearts; in a word, to the mystical union by which we enjoy Him, so that being made ours, He makes us partakers of the blessings with which He is furnished. We do not, then, contemplate Him at a distance out of ourselves, that His righteousness may be imputed to us; but because we have put Him on, and are ingrafted into His body, and because He has deigned to unite us to Himself, therefore we glory in a participation of His righteousness."[70] And Luther writes: "Christ is God's grace, mercy, wisdom, strength, comfort, and blessedness. I say not as some, *causaliter;* that is, that He gives righteousness, and remains without. For in that case righteousness is dead, nay, it is never given. Christ is there *Himself,* like the light and heat of the fire, which are not where the

---

67 Eph. 2:8, 9.
68 Phil. 3:8-11.
69 II Cor. 3:18.
70 *Institutes* (Allen translation), III, xi, 10 (Westminster Press, 1935, Vol. I, p. 660).

sun and the fire are not."[71] Justification, therefore, includes the glorious truths of our forgiveness in Christ, of the imputation of His righteousness to us, of our divine adoption, and of our being heirs of eternal life.

It is sometimes objected that the teaching of the doctrine of full justification on the basis of grace will lead to carelessness of life—a charge with which the apostle himself was familiar.[72] Nothing could be farther from the truth. The quality of obedience which springs from a union with Christ and a love for God, and which is constantly nourished by an awareness of the glorious grace of Christ, is infinitely more pure in quality and more earnest in devotion than is any type of obedience which is rendered on the basis of law or of a seeking for merit. Furthermore, the doctrine of free grace, the reception of salvation as a gift of grace, and the believer's perfect standing in Christ through grace: these great truths are held by evangelical Christians not for any personal satisfaction or philosophical purposes but out of sheer loyalty to the great emphases of the Scriptures.

Menno Simons writes:

They lead a pious, unblameable life before all men; suffer themselves to be baptized according to the commandment of the Lord, as proof that they bury their sins in the death of Christ, and are prepared to walk with Him in newness of life; they break the bread of peace with their beloved brethren as proof and testimony that they are one in Christ and His holy church and that they have, or know no other means of grace and remission of their sins, neither in heaven nor in earth, than the innocent flesh and blood of our Lord Jesus Christ alone, which He once, by His eternal Spirit in obedience to the Father, sacrificed and shed upon the cross for us poor sinners; they walk in all love and mercy, and serve their neighbors. In short, they suit themselves in their weakness to all words, commandments, ordinances, spirit, rule, example and measure of Christ, as the Scripture teaches; for they are in Christ and Christ is in them; and therefore they live no longer in the old life of sin after the first Adam (weakness excepted), but in the new life of righteousness which comes by faith, after the second and heavenly Adam, Christ. . . .

Think not, beloved reader, that we boast of being perfect and without sins, not at all. I for myself confess that often my prayer is mixed with sin and my righteousness with unrighteousness; for by the grace of God I feel, by the unction which is in me, when I compare my weak nature to

---

71 *Werke,* Erlangen Ausgabe, 37, p. 441. Cited in Marvin R. Vincent, *A . . . Commentary on . . . Philippians . . .* (New York: Scribner's, 1897), p. 127. Read the excursus, "Paul's Conception of Righteousness by Faith," pp. 123-28.

72 Rom. 3:8; 6:1.

Christ and His commandments, what kind of a flesh I inherited from Adam. Yea, if God should judge us according to our worthiness, righteousness, works and merits, and not according to His great goodness and mercy, then I confess with holy David that no man could stand before His judgment. Ps. 143:2; 130:3. Therefore it should be far from us that we should console ourselves with anything but the grace of God through Christ Jesus; for it is He alone and none other, who has perfectly fulfilled the righteousness required by God. We are also aware by the grace of God that all saints from the beginning have lamented the corruption of their flesh, as may be seen by the writings of Moses, David, Job, Isaiah, Paul, James, and John.

But for Christ's sake we are in grace; for His sake we are heard; and for His sake our failings and transgressions, which are committed involuntarily, are remitted. For it is He who stands between His Father and His imperfect children, with His perfect righteousness, and with His innocent blood and death; and intercedes for all those who believe on Him and who strive by faith in the divine Word to turn from evil, follow that which is good and who sincerely desire, with Paul, that they attain the perfection which is in Christ. Phil. 3:12.

Mark, beloved reader, that we do not believe nor teach that we are to be saved by our merits and works, as the envious accuse us of without truth; but that we are to be saved solely by grace, through Christ Jesus.[73]

In a private letter to a Christian woman who had a troubled conscience Menno wrote:

I understand that your conscience is troubled because you have not and do not now walk in such perfection as the Scriptures direct us; on which account I write the following to my faithful sister as a fraternal consolation from the true word and eternal truth of the Lord: The Scripture, says Paul, hath concluded all under sin. There is no man on earth, says Solomon, who does righteously and sinneth not. Eccl. 7. At another place, "A just man falls seven times, and riseth up again." Prov. 24:16. Moses says, "The Lord, the Lord God, merciful and gracious, longsuffering, and abundant in goodness and truth; keeping mercy for thousands, forgiving iniquity and transgression and sin, and that will by no means clear the guilty." Ex. 34:6, 7. . . .

As it is plain from all these Scriptures we must all acknowledge ourselves to be sinners, as we also are in fact; and as no one has perfectly fulfilled the righteousness required of God but Christ Jesus alone; therefore none can approach God, obtain grace and be saved except by the perfect righteousness, reconciliation and advocacy of Jesus Christ; however godly, righteous, holy and unblameable he is. We must all acknowledge, whosoever we are, that we are sinners in thoughts, words and works. Yea, if we had not before us the righteous Christ Jesus, no prophet nor apostle

73 *Complete Works*, II, p. 262, 263.

could be saved. Therefore be of good cheer and be consoled in the Lord. You can expect no greater righteousness in yourself than all the chosen of God had in them from the beginning. In and by yourself you are a poor sinner; and by the eternal righteousness, banished, accursed and adjudged to eternal death; but in and through Christ you are justified and pleasing unto God, and accepted of Him in eternal grace as a daughter and child. In this all saints have consoled themselves, trusted in Christ, esteemed their own righteousness as unclean, weak and imperfect, with contrite hearts approach the throne of grace, in the name of Christ, and with firm faith pray the Father: O, Father, forgive us our trespasses as we forgive those that trespass against us. Matt. 6; Luke 11....

I herewith pray you, and desire that you will wholly commend all your doings outward and inward unto Christ Jesus and His merits; believing and confessing that His precious blood alone is your cleansing; His righteousness your piety; His death your life; and His resurrection your justification; for He is the forgiveness of all your sin; His bloody wounds are your reconciliation; and His invincible strength the staff and consolation of your weakness, as we have in former days according to our small gift often shown you from the Scriptures. Yea, most beloved child and sister, so long as you find and feel such a spirit in yourself which is desirous of following that which is good, and abhorring that which is evil, notwithstanding the remnant of sin is not entirely dead in you, as also all the saints complained of from the beginning, so long you may rest assured that you are a child of God and that you will inherit the kingdom of grace in eternal joy with all the saints. . . .

I commend you, most beloved child and sister, to the faithful, merciful and gracious God, in Christ Jesus, now and forever. Let Him do with you and with all of us according to His blessed will. . . . Separation must once come. In the city of God, in the new Jerusalem, there we will wait on each other before the throne of God and of the Lamb; there sing hallelujah! and praise His name in perfect joy. Your husband and children I commend to Him who has given them to you, and He will do with them justly. The saving power of the most holy blood of Christ be with my most beloved child and sister, now and forever, Amen.[74]

Dirck Philips (c. 1504-68) also wrote:

It must therefore be recognized that every Christian has sin, and must confess himself a sinner, that he may humble himself under the mighty hand of God and pray the Lord for His mercy. Thus the Scripture remains true and unbroken which puts all men under condemnation and reproves them as sinners; but sin is not imputed to Christians, but has been forgiven them through the innocent death of Jesus Christ and is covered with His everlasting love, by which He offered Himself up for us for an everlasting atonement for our sins, taking upon Himself our

---

74 *Ibid.*, II, pp. 401, 402.

burden, and paying our debt with His bitter suffering, and making us a free gift of all that He has, so that He is one with us and we with Him, whereby we are made acceptable unto God, yea, accounted as saints of God.[75]

A Dutch Mennonite named Valerius, schoolmaster, who was martyred in 1568, wrote a book entitled, *The Proof of Faith,* in which is found the following:

If then we are to be saved through God's mercy, we must repent, must be obedient children of God, born again of Him, and must follow Christ in the regeneration and the footsteps of faith, through the narrow way unto eternal life; nor are we then saved through the merit of good works, but by the grace which came through Christ. Eph. 2:5. For though we lived holy, blameless, and perfect in all righteousness (as the Scriptures require), and suffered for the truth a death more bitter than that of Christ, which with us men is impossible, yet we could not be saved through our own good works, but only by God's mercy, and the grace of our Lord Jesus Christ, who alone has wrought out our salvation. And if we sought or placed our salvation in our good works or our sufferings, we should commit idolatry. . . . But now our salvation depends only on the mercy of God, and not on our running and following after. Rom. 9:16.[76]

8. *SANCTIFICATION*

Christian theologians use the word "sanctification" in two senses: first, of the initial setting apart by God of the believer as His exclusive possession: and second, that growth in holiness which extends from the conversion of the Christian to his death. Both the initial setting apart as God's and the progressive conformity of character to Jesus Christ, effected by the Holy Spirit in co-operation with the believer, are indiscriminately referred to as sanctification. The Bible seems to make little if any distinction between these two aspects of the experience.

It should also be noted that the Greek adjective *hagios* is translated *holy,* but when it is used as a substantive it is rendered, saint. A saint is therefore simply a holy person, one who belongs to God through faith in Jesus Christ. The Greek New Testament contains three nouns for holiness which are on this same stem.[77] The English words "holy," "saint," and "sanctification" refer to Greek words which are either identical or on the same stem. Sanctification is both the work of God and that of man; it is God's work in the sense that

75 *Op. cit.,* p. 282.
76 *Martyrs' Mirror,* p. 730.

77 1) I Cor. 1:30; Rom. 6:19, 22;
   2) II Cor. 1:12; Heb. 12:10;
   3) I Thess. 3:13; II Cor. 7:1.

it is He who sets us apart as His own; it is man's work in that the Christian believer co-operates with the Holy Spirit by yielding to Him in the ever progressively greater victory over sin which the growing child of God experiences. Paul speaks of sanctification as God's work when he writes to the Christians in Thessalonica: "May the God of peace himself sanctify you wholly; and may your spirit and soul and body be kept sound and blameless at the coming of our Lord Jesus Christ. He who calls you is faithful, and he will do it."[78] At the same time Paul recognized the obligation and the part which the Christian plays in the living of a holy life: "What shall we say then? Are we to continue in sin that grace may abound? By no means! How can we who died to sin still live in it? . . . So you also must consider yourselves dead to sin and alive to God in Christ Jesus."[79]

"Let not sin therefore reign in your mortal bodies, to make you obey their passions. Do not yield your members to sin as instruments of wickedness, but yield yourselves to God as men who have been brought from death to life, and your members to God as instruments of righteousness. For sin will have no dominion over you, since you are not under law but under grace."[80]

And to the Christians at Colossae, Paul wrote: "If then you have been raised with Christ, seek the things that are above, where Christ is, seated at the right hand of God. Set your minds on things that are above, not on things that are on earth. For you have died, and your life is hid with Christ in God. . . ."[81]

"Put to death therefore what is earthly in you: immorality, impurity, passion, evil desire, and covetousness, which is idolatry. On account of these the wrath of God is coming. In these you once walked, when you lived in them. But now put them all away: anger, wrath, malice, slander, and foul talk from your mouth. Do not lie to one another, seeing that you have put off the old nature with its practices and have put on the new nature, which is being renewed in knowledge after the image of its creator. . . ."[82]

"Put on then, as God's chosen ones, holy and beloved, compassion, kindness, lowliness, meekness, and patience, forbearing one another and, if one has a complaint against another, forgiving each other; as the Lord has forgiven you, so you also must forgive. And above all these put on love, which binds everything together in perfect harmony. And let the peace of Christ rule in your hearts, to which indeed you were called in the one body. . . . And whatever you do,

78 I Thess. 5:23, 24.   80 Rom. 6:12-14.   82 Col. 3:5-10.
79 Rom. 6:1-11.   81 Col. 3:1-3.

in word or deed, do everything in the name of the Lord Jesus, giving thanks to God the Father through him."[83]

It is thus evident that according to the New Testament sanctification involves a mortification of the old nature, and a reckoning of the sinful impulses as dead; it also involves a putting on of the new man in Christ and a cultivation of those attributes which resemble the Lord Jesus. There are a number of verses which, if taken alone, would give the impression that sanctification is perfect and complete in this life. After giving a list of gross sins which exclude people from the kingdom of God Paul adds: "And such were some of you. But you were washed, you were sanctified, you were justified in the name of the Lord Jesus Christ and in the Spirit of our God."[84] Paul also testified that "the law of the Spirit of life in Christ Jesus has set me free from the law of sin and death. For God has done what the law, weakened by the flesh, could not do: sending his own Son in the likeness of sinful flesh and for sin, he condemned sin in the flesh, in order that the just requirement of the law might be fulfilled in us, who walk not according to the flesh but according to the Spirit."[85] More specifically there are three verses in The First Letter of John which appear to teach perfectionism: (1) "No one who abides in him sins; no one who sins has either seen him or known him."[86] (2) "No one born of God commits sin; for God's nature abides in him, and he cannot sin because he is born of God."[87] (3) "We know that any one born of God does not sin, but He who was born of God keeps him, and the evil one does not touch him."[88]

Charles B. Williams[89] paraphrases these verses thus: (1) "No one who continues to live in union with Him practices sin." (2) "No one who is born of God makes a practice of sinning, because the God-given life-principle continues to live in him and so he cannot practice sinning, because he is born of God." (3) "We know that no one who is born of God makes a practice of sinning, but the Son who was born of God continues to keep him, and the evil one cannot touch him." The Greek, apart from any paraphrase, could be translated thus: (1) "Every one abiding in him is not sinning; every one sinning has not seen him neither known him." (2) "Every one who has been begotten of God is not doing sin, because his seed

83 Col. 3:12-17.
84 I Cor. 6:11.
85 Rom. 8:2-4.
86 I John 3:6.
87 I John 3:9.
88 I John 5:18.
89 In his excellent work, *The New Testament, A Translation in the Language of the People* (Chicago: Moody Press, 1949), pp. 532, 533, 536.

abides in him; and not is he able to be sinning, because it is from God that he has been begotten." (3) "We know that every one who has been begotten of God is not sinning, but he who was born of God keeps him, and the evil one does not touch him." The phrase, to sin, in verse nine should really be translated, "to be sinning," because this is the force of the Greek present infinitive here employed.

Whatever the particular explanations of these three verses may be it is obvious that this same Letter of John specifically denies perfectionism. For example, John wrote: "If we say we have no sin, we deceive ourselves, and the truth is not in us. If we confess our sins, he is faithful and just, and will forgive our sins and cleanse us from all unrighteousness."[90] Furthermore, there are a variety of statements in the New Testament from Jesus, from Paul, and from James, which specifically indicate the paradox that although Christians receive a divine nature in regeneration, together with supernatural grace to become victorious over temptation, nevertheless sanctification is ever imperfect in this life. Our Lord, for example, taught us to pray:

> And forgive us our debts,
> As we also have forgiven our debtors;
> And lead us not into temptation,
> But deliver us from the evil one [Greek].[91]

The Apostle Paul confessed: "For I know that nothing good dwells within me, that is, in my flesh."[92] Paul also stated that "we ourselves who have the first fruits of the Spirit, groan inwardly as we wait for adoption as sons, the redemption of our bodies."[93] And to the Christians of Galatia Paul wrote: "But I say, walk by the Spirit, and do not gratify the desires of the flesh. For the desires of the flesh are against the Spirit, and the desires of the Spirit are against the flesh; for these are opposed to each other, to prevent you from doing what you would."[94] (The meaning of the last phrase seems to be that should an individual become a bit careless and think to revert to carnal living, it is the faithful Holy Spirit who blocks the way against such an abandonment to sin. Yet at the same time, when a Christian seeks to push self and sin totally out of the picture and to act only from a pure love for God, he experiences some degree of frustration from his "flesh," so that there is thus more or less of a

90 I John 1:8, 9.
91 Matt. 6:11-13.
92 Rom. 7:18.
93 Rom. 8:23.
94 Gal. 5:16, 17.

struggle in the life of the child of God because of the fact of living "in the flesh.")[95]

James, our Lord's brother, states flatly: "For we all make many mistakes."[96] Also, "Confess your sins to one another, and pray for one another, that you may be healed."[97] If one is honest with the Word of God and with himself, and recognizes that God's holy law is absolute and not relative, and if he does not label sin by some other term, such as being human, every child of God must admit that he is not as perfect as Jesus Christ, that he continually stands in need of divine grace and forgiveness, and that he is saved only through the merits of Jesus Christ.

The attainment of a life of Christian victory over sin is achieved not merely by struggling with temptation, but rather by a height of spiritual devotion to Christ and His cause. In other words, if one wishes to live a more successful and radiant Christian life, one must cultivate the devotional life for faith to overcome temptation: reading God's Word, meditating on its message, waiting upon God in prayer, being obedient to all the light that one has, and seeking to witness in every way possible for Christ: only thus can the love of God drive sin from the human heart. Furthermore, in the New Testament victory does not refer to absolute perfection of life, but to perseverance in faith and loyal devotion to Christ and His cause.

Undoubtedly the most perfect description of Christian experience is that given by Paul in his Letter to the Philippians:

But whatever gain I had, I counted as loss for the sake of Christ. Indeed I count everything as loss because of the surpassing worth of knowing Christ Jesus my Lord. For his sake I have suffered the loss of all things, and count them as refuse, in order that I may gain Christ and be found in him, not having a righteousness of my own, based on law, but that which is through faith in Christ, the righteousness from God that depends on faith; that I may know him and the power of his resurrection, and may share his sufferings, becoming like him in his death, that if possible I may attain the resurrection from the dead.

Not that I have already obtained this or am already perfect; but I press on to make it my own, because Christ Jesus has made me his own. Brethren, I do not consider that I have made it my own; but one thing I do, forgetting what lies behind and straining forward to what lies ahead, I press on toward the goal for the prize of the upward call of God in Christ Jesus. Let those of us who are mature be thus minded; and if in anything you are otherwise minded, God will reveal that also to you. Only let us hold true to what we have attained.[98]

---

95 Cf. Ernest De Witt Burton, *Galatians* (I.C.C., New York: Scribner's, 1928), p. 302.
96 Jas. 3:2.　　　　97 Jas. 5:16.　　　　98 Phil. 3:7-16.

After quoting John 3:16-18, Menno Simons wrote:

> If you sincerely believe these words of Christ with the whole heart, that the almighty, eternal Father so loved you and the whole human family, that He sent His incomprehensible, almighty, eternal Word, wisdom, truth and Son, by whom He created the heavens, earth, the sea and the fulness thereof, and His eternal glory into this vale of misery; that He let Him become a poor, grieved, miserable man; that He let Him, for the sake of all our sins, suffer hunger and thirst; permitted Him to be slandered, apprehended, crowned with thorns, scourged, crucified and killed; then it cannot fail that your old carnal mind must become a regenerated, spiritual mind; your thoughts must become chaste and pure; your words must become discreet and well seasoned and your whole life pious and unblameable. . . .

> He sanctifies his body and heart as a habitation and temple of Christ and the Holy Ghost; hates all that is against God and His Word; honors, praises and thanks God with a sincere heart; and there is nothing to deter him, neither judgment, wrath, hell, devil, sin nor eternal death. For he knows that Christ is his Intercessor, Mediator and Propitiator. He acknowledges with holy Paul, that "there is, therefore, now no condemnation to them which are in Christ Jesus, who walk not after the flesh, but after the Spirit." Rom. 8:1. . . .

> Happy he who has such a faith and will salutarily retain it to the end. I repeat it, prove yourselves, whether you are in the faith; in Christ or out of Christ; penitent or impenitent. For in the mirror presented, you may view the whole face of your conscience and life, if you but believe that the Word of the Lord is true and right. Here notice how the true, Christian faith, is the only living fountain, whence flows, not only the penitent, new life, but also obedience to the evangelical ceremonies, such as baptism and the Lord's Supper will have to come and follow, not as those compelled through the law, for the rod of the oppressor is broken, but voluntarily, through the free will and submissive spirit of love, which is of a Christian nature, and is ready to all good works and obedience of the holy, divine Word.

> For all the truly regenerated and spiritual conform in all things to the word and ordinances of the Lord; not because they think to merit the propitiation of their sins and eternal life; by no means; in this matter they depend upon nothing except the true promise of the merciful Father, graciously given to all believers, through the blood and merits of Christ, which blood is, and ever will be the only eternal medium of our reconciliation, and not works, baptism or Lord's supper, as said above.

> For if our reconciliation depended upon works and ceremonies, then it would not be grace, and the merits and fruits of the blood of Christ would be void. O no! It is grace, and will be grace to all eternity; all that the merciful Father is doing or has done for us grievous sinners, through His beloved Son and Holy Spirit, is grace. Hence it is that they hear the

voice of the Lord, believe His Word, and therefore they should willingly observe and perform (although in weakness), the representation of both signs, under water, and bread and wine, set forth in obedience. For a truly believing Christian is thus minded, that he will not do otherwise than that which the Word of the Lord enjoins and teaches; for he knows that all presumption and disobedience, are like sins of witchcraft, and the end thereof is death.[99]

In another context Menno wrote:

Say, beloved brother, who can fully comprehend this grace, or relate these benefits? Again, formerly, we all strayed as lost sheep, which have no shepherd; we walked according to the lusts of our evil flesh, even as they all do, who know not the way of the Father; we were unbelievers in divine things, blind and without understanding, full of bruises and putre-fying sores from the sole of the foot to the crown of the head, and by nature, children of wrath like others. But blessed be the Lord, now we are washed, now we are sanctified, now we are justified in the name of our Lord Jesus Christ, through the Spirit of our God. I Cor. 6:11; in short, we are converted to the true Shepherd and preserver of our souls, Jesus Christ, who pastures us in the rich pastures of His truth, feeds us with the bread of His Word, sustains us with the tree of life, and refreshes us with the water of His Spirit. Who can comprehend and relate this grace?[1]

In discussing the four kinds of sin, Menno treats the short-comings of the saints thus:

The third kind are human frailties, errors and stumblings which are yet daily found among the saints and regenerated; such as untem-pered thoughts, careless words and rashness in our actions. These al-though they spring from those sins mentioned, as the sins of the unbe-lieving and impenitent, are yet not of the same kind; and have this differ-ence: the unbelieving which are yet unchanged in their first birth, com-mit sin unrestrainedly and fearlessly. . . .

But those who are born from above are fearful of all sin; they know by the law that all which is contrary to the first, righteousness, is sin, be it inwardly or outwardly, important or trifling; and therefore they daily fight, in spirit and faith with their weak flesh; sigh and lament about their errors, which they, with Paul, sincerely abhor. For they know them to be contrary to the first righteousness and God's law, and are therefore sins; they daily approach the throne of grace, with contrite hearts, and pray: Holy Father, forgive us our trespasses as we forgive those that trespass against us. And thus they are not rejected by the Lord on account of such transgressions which are not committed wilfully and intentionally, but contrary to their will, out of mere thoughtlessness and frailty. . . . For

99 *Complete Works*, I, pp. 157, 158.   1 *Ibid.*, I, p. 107.

they are under grace, and not under law, as Paul says. The seed of God, faith in Christ Jesus, the birth which is of God, and the unction of the Holy Spirit abide in them. They exercise themselves continually in warring against their flesh; die unto their lusts; watch and pray incessantly and although they are such poor weak children, they rejoice in the sure trust of the merits of Christ, and praise the Father for His grace. Heb. 4; Matt. 6; Luke 12; Rom. 6; I John 3; 5; Job 7; Eph. 6; II Tim. 2; Gal. 5; II Cor. 6; I Peter 5.[2]

9. *UNION WITH CHRIST*

Those who are not Christians frequently think of Christianity as being a set of rules for life or a particular philosophy of religion or a set of ritualistic forms. The most distinctive thing in Christianity, however, is not its philosophical theism, nor its lofty system of ethics, nor the few ceremonies of the Christian Church: that which is most distinctive in Christianity is salvation through union with the Lord Jesus Christ, the divine and eternal Son of God who became incarnate and by His redemptive death and glorious resurrection reconciled mankind unto God. The concept of Christian believers being *in Christ,* or being united with Him, runs through the New Testament like a golden chain.

The writings of John contain many illustrations of the intimate union between the Christian believer and his Lord. In the high priestly prayer of Jesus in John 17 He prayed that His disciples "may be one even as we are one, I in them and thou in me, that they may become perfectly one, so that the world may know that thou hast sent me and hast loved them even as thou hast loved me."[3] In His great sermon on the Bread of Life Jesus said: "He who eats my flesh and drinks my blood has eternal life, and I will raise him up at the last day. For my flesh is food indeed, and my blood is drink indeed. He who eats my flesh and drinks my blood abides in me, and I in him. As the living Father sent me, and I live because of the Father, so he who eats me will live because of me."[4]

In His beautiful discourse on the Vine and the Branches Jesus said: "Every branch of mine that bears no fruit, he takes away, and every branch that does bear fruit he prunes it, that it may bear more fruit. You are already made clean by the word which I have spoken to you. Abide in me, and I in you. As the branch cannot bear fruit by itself, unless it abides in the vine, neither can you, unless you abide in me. I am the vine, you are the branches. He who abides in me, and I in him, he it is that bears much fruit, for apart from me

2 *Ibid.,* II, p. 313. 3 John 17:22, 23. 4 John 6:54-57.

you can do nothing. If a man does not abide in me, he is cast forth as a branch and withers; and the branches are gathered, thrown into the fire and burned. If you abide in me, and my words abide in you, ask whatever you will, and it shall be done for you. By this my Father is glorified, that you bear much fruit, and so prove to be my disciples. As the Father has loved me, so have I loved you; abide in my love. If you keep my commandments, you will abide in my love, just as I have kept my Father's commandments and abide in his love."[5] Many years later the Apostle John wrote: "Let what you heard from the beginning abide in you. If what you heard from the beginning abides in you, then you will abide in the Son and in the Father. And this is what he has promised us, eternal life."[6]

The Apostle Paul spoke much of the union of the believer with Christ:[7] "Do you not know that all of us who have been baptized into Christ Jesus were baptized into his death? . . ."[8]

"For if we have been united with him in a death like his, we shall certainly be united with him in a resurrection like his. We know that our old self was crucified with him so that the sinful body might be destroyed [rendered powerless], and we might no longer be enslaved to sin. . . . But if we have died with Christ, we believe that we shall also live with him."[9] In another Letter Paul wrote as follows concerning the sin offering which Jesus made on Golgotha: "For our sake he made him to be sin who knew no sin, so that in him we might become the righteousness of God."[10] Paul indicated that he put no confidence in anything other than his union in Christ: "For his sake I have suffered the loss of all things, and count them as refuse, in order that I may gain Christ and be found in him, not having a righteousness of my own, based on law, but that which is through faith in Christ, the righteousness from God that depends on faith; that I may know him and the power of his resurrection, and may share his sufferings, becoming like him in his death, that if possible I may attain the resurrection from the dead."[11]

In other words, the sphere of the Christian is "in Christ." Christians are "sanctified in Christ Jesus."[12] Paul therefore found it appropriate to begin his Letter to the Ephesians: "To the saints who are also faithful in Christ Jesus."[13] And he addresses the Philippians thus: "To all the saints in Christ Jesus who are at Philippi."[14] In

---

5 John 15:2-10.
6 I John 2:24, 25.
7 Marvin R. Vincent, op. cit., p. 4, reports that "in Christ Jesus" occurs 48 times in Paul, "in Christ" 34 times, and "in the Lord" 50 times.

8 Rom. 6:3.
9 Rom. 6:5-8.

10 II Cor. 5:21.
11 Phil. 3:8-11.

12 I Cor. 1:2.
13 Eph. 1:1.
14 Phil. 1:1.

his Letter to the Colossians Paul writes: "To the saints and faithful brethren in Christ at Colossae."[15]

Perhaps the most beautiful testimony of the New Testament on the centrality of Christ in the life of the believer is that of Paul in his Letter to the Philippians: "For I know that through your prayers and the help of the Spirit of Jesus Christ this will turn out for my deliverance, as it is my eager expectation and hope that I shall not be at all ashamed, but that with full courage now as always Christ will be honored in my body, whether by life or by death. For to me to live is Christ, and to die is gain. . . . My desire is to depart and be with Christ, for that is far better."[16] The Christian life and faith involve a present union and fellowship with the Lord, a joy which will become even more intense in the glorious world of the future. The glorification of Jesus Christ by the Holy Spirit was promised by the Saviour before His passion: "When the Spirit of truth comes, he will guide you into all the truth; for he will not speak on his own authority, but whatever he hears he will speak, and he will declare to you the things that are to come. He will glorify me, for he will take what is mine and declare it to you. All that the Father has is mine; therefore I said that he will take what is mine and declare it to you."[17]

Union with Christ does not blur the integrity and distinction between the personality of Christ and that of the believer. Christ remains the Lord of glory, while the believer continues as a creature on earth. Union with Christ does not involve irresponsibility on the part of the Christian for holiness or for one's decisions. Christ remains Christ and the Christian remains Christ's disciple. Union with Christ is rather the attachment of faith. Becoming a believer is turning to the Lord. A large number of people at Antioch, upon hearing preaching about the Lord Jesus Christ, "turned to the Lord."[18] Having faith in Christ is one of the conditions for divine indwelling: "Whoever confesses that Jesus is the Son of God, God abides in him, and he in God."[19] Union with Christ also involves the devotion of love, for John also states: "God is love, and he who abides in love abides in God, and God abides in him."[20] Concerning Jesus Christ Peter writes: "Without having seen him you love him; though you do not now see him you believe in him and rejoice with unutterable and exalted joy."[21] Paul's prayer for the Christians of Ephesus was "that Christ may dwell in your hearts through faith;

---

15 Col. 1:2.
16 Phil. 1:19-23.
17 John 16:13-15.

18 Acts 11:21.
19 I John 4:15.

20 I John 4:16.
21 I Pet. 1:8.

that you, being rooted and grounded in love, may have power to comprehend with all the saints what is the breadth and length and height and depth, and to know the love of Christ which surpasses knowledge, that you may be filled with all the fullness of God."[22] Union with Christ is therefore the devotion of love.

To be united with Christ is not only to exercise faith in Him, and to love Him: it also involves an identity of will and intention, the rendering to Him of full obedience. "By this we may be sure that we are in him: he who says he abides in him ought to walk in the same way in which he walked."[23] John also wrote: "And this is his commandment, that we should believe in the name of his Son Jesus Christ and love one another, just as he has commanded us. All who keep his commandments abide in him, and he in them."[24] To be in Christ is therefore to be His disciple, His bond servant, completely united with Him in will and purpose: "If you keep my commandments, you will abide in my love, just as I have kept my Father's commandments and abide in his love."[25]

There is also a fourth aspect to union with Christ: the experience of the re-enactment of His passion, of His death and resurrection. Just as Christ died physically and rose again, so in our baptism we Christians died to sin and rose again to newness of life. "Do you not know that all of us who have been baptized into Christ Jesus were baptized into his death? We were buried therefore with him by baptism into death, so that as Christ was raised from the dead by the glory of the Father, we too might walk in newness of life.

"For if we have been united with him in a death like his, we shall certainly be united with him in a resurrection like his. We know that our old self was crucified with him so that the sinful body might be destroyed, and we might no longer be enslaved to sin."[26] This concept of the individual Christian being so vitally united with his Lord as to relive his life, even in suffering, was so vivid with the Apostle Paul that he thought of his sufferings as being in a sense an extension of the passion of Christ: "Now I rejoice in my sufferings for your sake, and in my flesh I complete what is lacking in Christ's afflictions for the sake of his body, that is, the church."[27] Union with Christ therefore involves such a love for the body of Christ that one comes to have the same self-sacrificing love which Jesus had when He went to the cross for the salvation of His church.

22 Eph. 3:17-19.
23 I John 2:5, 6.
24 I John 3:23, 24.
25 John 15:10.
26 Rom. 6:3-6.
27 Col. 1:24.

Union with Christ is many times spoken of by believers as being something mystical, as if Christians were in Christ in some sort of vague atmosphere, like a bird flies in the air or a fish swims in the sea. It is much more Biblical to think of union with Christ in terms of faith, love, obedience, and the suffering which results from following God's will in bringing men into a state of reconciliation with Him. The indwelling of Christ in the believer, and the believer's being in Christ, are aspects of the same basic reality. Union with Christ is not a matter of an occasional emotion, nor is it limited to exceptional saints who have had experiences of ecstasy with the Lord; it is rather the relationship of every Christian to his Lord and Saviour. This relationship is not dependent upon feeling or emotion, not even upon the awareness of that relation on the part of the believer: union with Christ is a blessed truth about the relationship of every one who has turned to Christ in repentance and faith. Jesus receives every such convert, becomes his Lord and Saviour, dwells in him, and grafts the believer into Himself. "He who believes in the Son has eternal life."[28] "For just as the body is one and has many members, and all the members of the body, though many, are one body, so it is with Christ. For by one Spirit we were all baptized into one body . . . and all were made to drink of one Spirit."[29] "For in Christ Jesus you are all sons of God, through faith. For as many of you as were baptized into Christ have put on Christ."[30] "He who has the Son has life."[31]

Menno Simons described God's chosen ones as "the church of Christ, His saints and beloved, who washed their clothes in the blood of the lamb, who are born of God, influenced by the Spirit of Christ; who are in Christ and He in them, who hear and believe His Word, who follow Him in their weakness, in His commandments, walk in His footsteps with all patience and humility, hate the evil, and love the good, earnestly desiring to apprehend Christ as they are apprehended of Him, for all who are in Christ are new creatures, flesh of His flesh, bone of His bone, and members of His body."[32]

10. ASSURANCE AND CONFIDENCE

It is perfectly evident from a reading of the New Testament that the apostles of Christ possessed the happy assurance that they were the children of God and that He who began a good work in them would also enable them to persevere to a happy end in Christ.

28 John 3:36.
29 I Cor. 12:12, 13.
30 Gal. 3:26, 27.

31 I John 5:12.
32 *Complete Works*, I, pp. 161, 162.

This type of assurance is possible only for those who understand the plan of salvation: that it is God who moves the sinner to repent, that it is God who bestows upon those who accept Jesus the gift of eternal life, that converts enjoy the forgiveness of their sins not through any merit of their own but alone through the redemptive death of Jesus, and that God is able to keep, and intends to keep, every one of His children. It should be noted that Christian assurance is not built upon a particular type of conversion; nowhere in Scripture is salvation made to depend upon any particular experience in connection with conversion, such as weeping, seeing a vision, or participating in an ecstasy. Christian assurance is also not based upon feeling. Certainly good health, physical, mental, and spiritual, tends to promote an attitude of optimism and euphoria, but the assurance of salvation is not dependent upon "feeling good." Least of all is salvation dependent upon any sort of merit; the notion that any human being can approach God through personal merit is absolutely unscriptural and untrue. The only way any believer throughout history has been able to stand before God is through the perfect righteousness of the Lord Jesus Christ. There is a certain sense in which evangelical theologians even speak of Christ "keeping the law for us."[33]

The causes of doubt are undoubtedly numerous. In some cases doubt is occasioned by ill health, especially that due to nervous and emotional difficulties. Doubt may also be occasioned by what could be called emotional trauma; that is, one calamity after another befalls a given individual in quick succession so that the person feels forsaken and crushed. At that point doubt is apt to come as to whether God loves the individual, or even as to whether there is a God who would permit such experiences to happen. Doubt is also commonly associated with the emotional instability of adolescence, particularly being a part of an intellectual awakening that frequently takes place in the latter teens or early twenties. Unfortunately human beings are also so constituted as to be capable of escape mechanisms; that is, when one has good reasons for dreading to face a certain situation or truth, the mind tends to subconsciously persuade one that the situation must be avoided through sickness, or that the truth can be escaped by the very "fact" that it is not the truth but falsehood! Consequently if one is living in sin one is inclined to rationalize that after all no one has ever seen God and it is altogether probable that He does not exist! This fact of escape

33 Menno Simons, *Complete Works,* I, pp. 44, 113, 154.

mechanisms must be cautiously kept in the background in any attempt to help an individual who is plagued with doubts, for there are many other reasons for doubting besides this moral occasion.

As a matter of fact when an individual is worried and distressed by his doubts it is sure evidence that he really is a believer, otherwise he would have no particular concern about his intellectual problems. Doubt is therefore a disguised form of faith, or faith manifesting itself in the life of one who is emotionally insecure or troubled.

Christian Assurance

What then are the factors which make possible Christian assurance? These factors are two: the Spirit and the Word. Ordinarily the Holy Spirit uses the Word of God to bring assurance to the Christian believer. The serenity of faith on the part of the Christian varies from person to person, depending undoubtedly in part on such factors as physical health, devotion to the means of grace, maturity of life and experience, and perhaps also temperament. In other words, the cure for doubt is not simple; each case must be treated as to its individual nature. Least of all dare one assert that doubt is necessarily an evidence of sin; on the contrary it is frequently found on the part of those who most earnestly desire to live a winsome Christian life.

Basically the only approach to the believer who lacks Christian assurance is to take the Scriptures and point out the clarity and simplicity of the promises of God to bestow salvation as a free gift on everyone who puts his trust in Jesus Christ. Statements to this effect run throughout the New Testament. Matthew quotes Jesus as saying: "Come to me, all who labor and are heavy-laden, and I will give you rest. Take my yoke upon you, and learn from me; for I am gentle and lowly in heart, and you will find rest for your souls. For my yoke is easy, and my burden is light."[34] Mark quotes Jesus thus: "Therefore I tell you, whatever you ask in prayer, believe that you receive it, and you will. And whenever you stand praying, forgive, if you have anything against any one; so that your Father also who is in heaven may forgive you your trespasses."[35] Luke quotes Jesus as stating that the very purpose of His incarnation was redemptive: "For the Son of man came to seek and to save the lost."[36] And John quotes the Saviour as saying: "Truly, truly, I say to you, he who hears my word and believes him who sent me, has eternal life;

---

34 Matt. 11:28-30; cf. John R. Mumaw, *Assurance of Salvation* (Scottdale, Pa.: Herald Press, 1950).
35 Mark 11:24-26.   36 Luke 19:10.

he does not come into judgment, but has passed from death to life."[37] When the Philippian jailer cried out to Paul and Silas: "Men, what must I do to be saved?"[38] the apostolic reply was: "Believe in the Lord Jesus, and you will be saved, you and your household."[39] The promise of the Apostle Paul in his Letter to the Romans is: "If you confess with your lips that Jesus is Lord and believe in your heart that God raised him from the dead, you will be saved. For man believes with his heart and so is justified, and he confesses with his lips and so is saved. The scripture says, 'No one who believes in him will be put to shame.' . . . For, 'every one who calls upon the name of the Lord will be saved.' "[40] And one must not forget the promise of the Saviour: "And him who comes to me I will not cast out."[41]

It should be noted again that salvation is not promised on the basis of any particular type of conversion, it does not rest upon feeling, and it is not achieved by merit: salvation is God's free gift promised unconditionally to everyone who accepts Christ as Saviour and Lord. It is the function of the Holy Spirit to take the precious promises of God's Word and enable the Christian believer to rest upon them. He who is troubled by doubts will therefore need to pray that God's Spirit might enable him to simply lay hold by faith on the promises of God, being willing to walk by faith and not by sight, renouncing feeling as the touchstone of his salvation, and seeking to live close to the Lord: for where worldliness and spiritual coldness enter a life, Christian assurance departs. The old Gospel song is theologically sound:

> Trust and obey, for there's no other way
> To be happy in Jesus, but to trust and obey.[42]

Even better is the doctrinal teaching of the poem of Edward Mote (1797—1874), "The Solid Rock," 1834:

> My hope is built on nothing less than Jesus' blood and right-
> eousness;
> I dare not trust the sweetest frame, but wholly lean on Jesus'
> name.

> When darkness seems to veil His face, I rest on His unchanging
> grace;

37 John 5:24.
38 Acts 16:30.
39 Acts 16:31.
40 Rom. 10:9-13.
41 John 6:37.
42 *Church and Sunday School Hymnal* (Scottdale, Pa.: Mennonite Publishing House, 1902; *Supplement,* 1911, No. 454).

In ev'ry high and stormy gale, my anchor holds within the
vail.

His oath, His covenant, and blood, support me in the whelming
flood;
When all around my soul gives way, He then is all my hope
and stay.

When He shall come with trumpet sound, O, may I then in
Him be found;
Clad in His righteousness alone, faultless to stand before the
throne.

On Christ, the solid Rock, I stand;
All other ground is sinking sand.[43]

As Christians become more mature, and in so far as they seek to
follow Jesus in every area of their lives, there gradually grows upon
them the quiet and happy assurance that they have been truly called
by God into His kingdom, and they learn to rely in simple faith
upon the blessed promises of His Word.

God's Keeping Power and Intention

Even to many sincere Christians, however, there come occasional periods of anxiety when fear is felt as to their ability to persevere in faith and holiness. This is where such believers need to be
taught the New Testament truth of divine preservation. Divine
preservation refers to the gracious operation of the Holy Spirit in
the believer which, if not persistently resisted, brings him unto a
happy end in Christ. This assurance that the God who has begun
the process of salvation in the child of God, will also continue the
same until death, is recognized throughout the New Testament.
Paul, for example, writes thus in the Letter to the Romans:

What then shall we say to this? If God is for us, who is against us?
He who did not spare his own Son but gave him up for us all, will he not
also give us all things with him? Who shall bring any charge against
God's elect? It is God who justifies; who is to condemn? Is it Christ Jesus,
who died, yes, who was raised from the dead, who is at the right hand of
God, who indeed intercedes for us? Who shall separate us from the love
of Christ? Shall tribulation, or distress, or persecution, or famine, or
nakedness, or peril, or sword? . . .
No, in all these things we are more than conquerors through him
who loved us. For I am sure that neither death, nor life, nor angels, nor

43 *Ibid.*, No. 458.

principalities, nor things present, nor things to come, nor powers, nor height, nor depth, nor anything else in all creation, will be able to separate us from the love of God in Christ Jesus our Lord.[44]

The Corinthian church manifested what is perhaps the lowest state of spirituality in any church in the New Testament. And yet Paul wrote in his First Letter to the Corinthians that God "will sustain you to the end, guiltless in the day of our Lord Jesus Christ. God is faithful, by whom you were called into the fellowship of his Son, Jesus Christ our Lord."[45] Similarly in his Letter to the Philippians the apostle wrote: "And I am sure that he who began a good work in you will bring it to completion at the day of Jesus Christ."[46] And in reference to the spiritual dangers which the Thessalonian Christians faced Paul wrote by way of assurance: "But the Lord is faithful; he will strengthen you and guard you from evil."[47] After referring to his own sufferings for Christ's sake Paul added: "But I am not ashamed, for I know whom I have believed and I am sure that he is able to guard until that Day what has been entrusted to me."[48] Again, "The Lord will rescue me from every evil and save me for his heavenly kingdom. To him be the glory for ever and ever. Amen."[49] The Apostle Peter speaks of the great mercy of God as having been manifested in the regeneration of his Christian readers, and of their inheritance which is being reserved in heaven "for you, who by God's power are guarded through faith for a salvation ready to be revealed in the last time."[50]

It is perfectly evident from dozens of statements in the New Testament that it is the will of God to keep Christians from apostasy, and that He is able to do so. Jesus Himself said: "My sheep hear my voice, and I know them, and they follow me; and I give them eternal life, and they shall never perish, and no one shall snatch them out of my hand. My Father, who has given them to me, is greater than all, and no one is able to snatch them out of the Father's hand."[51] In other words, God has saved us, He is able to keep us, and He intends to do so. God promises eternal security to those who are in Christ.

The Bible does not teach security in sin, however. In the strongest possible terms the Scriptures warn against not only the possibility but even the danger of apostasy. This is not because of a lack of ability on the part of God, nor a lack of faithfulness on His

44 Rom. 8:31-39.
45 I Cor. 1:8, 9.
46 Phil. 1:6; cf. 1:10.
47 II Thess. 3:3.
48 II Tim. 1:12.
49 II Tim. 4:18.
50 I Pet. 1:5.
51 John 10:27-29.

part to His promises. The possibility of apostasy arises from the fact that Christians are still in the flesh, still in need of the grace of God, and continually undergoing temptation and trial. The security of the child of God is in Christ and not in sin. The New Testament therefore warns against falling away. Jesus Himself said, in reference to the seed sown on rocky ground: "This is he who hears the word and immediately receives it with joy; yet he has no root in himself, but endures for a while, and when tribulation or persecution arises on account of the word, immediately he falls away. As for what was sown among thorns, this is he who hears the word, but the cares of the world and the delight in riches choke the word, and it proves unfruitful."[52] Paul wrote to the Christians of Colossae that God had now reconciled them "in order to present you holy and blameless and irreproachable before him," but then Paul adds by way of a warning, "provided that you continue in the faith, stable and steadfast, not shifting from the hope of the gospel which you heard."[53] Similarly, the Letter to the Hebrews warns: "Therefore we must pay the closer attention to what we have heard, lest we drift away from it."[54] And again, "Take care, brethren, lest there be in any of you an evil, unbelieving heart, leading you to fall away from the living God. But exhort one another every day, as long as it is called 'today,' that none of you may be hardened by the deceitfulness of sin. For we share in Christ, if only we hold our first confidence firm to the end."[55]

Perhaps the most startling warning in the New Testament against apostasy is found in Peter's Second Letter, where he speaks of a person being overcome and enslaved to sin: "For if, after they have escaped the defilements of the world through the knowledge of our Lord and Savior Jesus Christ, they are again entangled in them and overpowered, the last state has become worse for them than the first. For it would have been better for them never to have known the way of righteousness than after knowing it to turn back from the holy commandment delivered to them."[56] Peter then uses two illustrations of regeneration and sanctification: a dog who has been delivered from his sickness, and a sow who has been washed clean of the mire. Every honest exegete must admit that the illustrations are warnings about what can happen to the Christian who has been spiritually delivered from his sin and cleansed of his guilt.

James in his practical Letter speaks also of a Christian wandering from the truth.[57] And Jesus Himself spoke of the trying days that

---

52 Matt. 13:20-22.
53 Col. 1:22, 23.
54 Heb. 2:1.
55 Heb. 3:12-14.
56 II Pet. 2:20, 21.
57 Jas. 5:19.

were to come: "And because wickedness is multiplied, most men's love will grow cold. But he who endures to the end will be saved."[58] He also gave the following warning: "If a man does not abide in me, he is cast forth as a branch and withers; and the branches are gathered, thrown into the fire and burned."[59]

It is only fair to ask the question whether these warnings are merely theoretical, or whether individual Christians ever do actually lose out. On this point Paul says: "By rejecting conscience, certain persons have made shipwreck of their faith, among them Hymenaeus and Alexander, whom I have delivered to Satan that they may learn not to blaspheme."[60] In the same Letter Paul reports: "Now the Spirit expressly says that in later times some will depart from the faith by giving heed to deceitful spirits and doctrines of demons . . . ."[61] And in his Second Letter to Timothy, Paul writes about the godless chatter of the wicked, "and their talk will eat its way like gangrene. Among them are Hymenaeus and Philetus, who have swerved from the truth by holding that the resurrection is past already. They are upsetting the faith of some. But God's firm foundation stands, bearing this seal: 'The Lord knows those who are his,' and, 'Let every one who names the name of the Lord depart from iniquity.' "[62] When Paul wrote his Letter to the Colossians he was able to say: "Luke the beloved physician and Demas greet you,"[63] but when he wrote his Second Letter to Timothy he regretfully reported, "Demas, in love with this present world, has deserted me . . . ."[64] Judas himself is an example of a man whom Christ wished to transform into a mighty apostle but who allowed his love of money to transform him into a traitor, even "a devil."[65] Judas stooped so low in his thievery that he "used to take what was put" into the treasury of Christ and the apostles.[66] Instead of allowing Christ to make of him a powerful witness to His resurrection, Judas clung to his weakness, allowed it to overcome him, and finally "fell away" from his apostleship.[67]

Those who teach a doctrine of unconditional eternal security sometimes object to the possibility of apostasy by holding that a regenerated person would never *wish* to return to a life of sin and

58 Matt. 24:12, 13.
59 John 15:6.
60 I Tim. 1:19, 20.
61 I Tim. 4:1.
62 II Tim. 2:17-19.
63 Col. 4:14.
64 II Tim. 4:10.
65 John 6:70.
66 John 12:6.
67 Acts 1:25, ASV. The Greek implies a turning aside; here, an abandonment of one's trust (Thayer, p. 478).

to become an apostate. This fact is of course altogether true. The answer to the objection lies in the fact that believers can grow cold little by little, and ultimately find themselves with but little desire to return to Christ in penitence and renewed obedience. The steps in apostasy undoubtedly are somewhat as follows: first of all, the individual becomes too busy or unconcerned to maintain a faithful devotional life of Bible meditation and prayer. This results in a certain state of lukewarmness in which it becomes easy to harbor, if only briefly, a sinful desire or attitude. This attitude may be one of envy, pride, hatred, sensuality, or avarice. The unsanctified state of attempting to cling to a "minor sin" for a time in turn promotes the very neglect of Bible reading and prayer which brought about the state of lukewarmness to begin with. As the individual becomes more and more cold spiritually his zeal for the Lord's cause slackens. After a time overt acts of sin begin to occur in his life. These falls into sin are accompanied by a decreasing concern about sin and its guilt. There comes also a determination, and this is something new, to continue enjoying sin for the time being; the first intention was merely to indulge briefly. There is less and less interest in returning to a holy Christian life as time goes on and the apostasy becomes more severe. All this takes place in spite of fierce inner struggles of conscience, repeated chastisements of God, and generally the warnings of other Christians.

We are again reminded of Jeremy Taylor's (1613-67) description of the downward progress of the apostate: "First it startles him, then it becomes pleasing, then delightful, then frequent, then habitual, then confirmed; then the man is impenitent, then obstinate, then resolved never to repent, then damned."[68]

11. *A SUCCESSFUL CHRISTIAN LIFE*

As was noted above it is the desire of God to see every one of His children live a happy and successful Christian life, and He stands ready with His omnipotent resources to make this a reality. In His Word God has by the inspiration of the Holy Spirit indicated the basic steps one needs to take in order to be the kind of Christian, happy and victorious, which it is His will for His children to be. What are the "rules"?

1. First of all if one is to live a good life of Christian discipleship there must be from the beginning an open confession of Jesus Christ as Lord and Saviour. There have been those who thought that they

68 Strong, *Systematic Theology*, p. 651.

could be "secret believers," but this is one of the most awkward and impossible situations that any Christian can place himself into. This was the difficulty of Peter when he sought to deny his spiritual identity, a foolish step which led him into the awful sin of actually denying his Lord.[69] Even non-Christians respect a sincere and open confession of Jesus Christ.

2. If one's Christian life is to be robust and strong there must be no dallying with any known sin. The Bible represents that sin is an awful reality, a real danger for the child of God as long as he is in the flesh, and that it must be shunned. This ability to say a firm no to sin in all its forms comes only through such means of grace as prayer.

3. He who lives a happy and joyous Christian life is the believer who takes time to fellowship with God in prayer. Christian prayer is more than asking God for things; it is a fellowship between the saint and his God, a tarrying before Him in fellowship and thanksgiving and adoration even much more than in petition. The prayer life is a good barometer as to the vitality of an individual's Christianity.

4. He who wants to live a successful Christian life and become an effective worker for Christ must study his Bible, reading it meditatively, memorizing its choice passages, and seek to grasp its total message and its fundamental emphases. The outstanding Christian leaders in the history of the church have been men who took much time to read God's Word. It is said that Luther spent four hours a day in Bible reading, meditation, and prayer.

5. The church today needs many members who are not merely content to accept salvation as a ticket to heaven; it needs intelligent Christians, men and women who know what Christian theism is and what it involves, what its adversaries are in our time, and how to overcome them with the truth of God's Word. Just as the Christian apologists of the second century overcame their pagan enemies, so the church of today in the power of the Holy Spirit must also overcome the anti-Christian philosophies and theologies of this era.[70]

6. In order to become strong in faith and effective in service every true Christian needs to attend the public worship services of the church faithfully and purposefully. Church membership is no child's play; it calls for regular attendance, and the making of one's

---

69 Mark 14:66-72.
70 Cf. the books of Christian apologists such as Edward John Carnell, O. Hallesby, Carl F. H. Henry, C. S. Lewis, J. Gresham Machen, Bernard Ramm, and Wilbur M. Smith; also the symposium, *Modern Science and the Christian Faith* (Wheaton, Ill.: Van Kampen Press, 1948).

contribution to the life of the local congregation. Christians cannot afford to "shop around" from one assembly to the other; they need to anchor their membership in a local fellowship of believers and make their contribution there.

7. The child of God will seek to witness for Christ as God gives him opportunity and grace. As was noted above, salvation is not merely a private ticket to heaven; much more, it is a divine license to serve as a witness for Christ and His resurrection, spreading His Gospel, and inviting men to accept that Gospel and thereby become reconciled to God. Every Christian is an ambassador for Christ.

8. If one is to be a good disciple of Jesus Christ he must by the grace of God keep humble. He must flee from pride and conceit; at any cost he must avoid the "condemnation of the devil."[71] While it is true that this is perhaps the besetting temptation of the young believer, it is one against which every Christian must remain alert all his days.

9. Every disciple of Jesus Christ will want to exert his influence for righteousness and justice wherever he can do so as a Christian. While it is true that his major responsibility is to give a witness for the Gospel of Christ, it does not follow that his only calling is religious in the narrow sense. Rather the Christian will seek in his community to do what he can, without violating the Christian ethic, to bring about a more righteous and just social order.

10. The Bible teaches the principle of stewardship; consequently every Christian will wish to give systematically, sacrificially, and proportionately of his income for the extension of the kingdom of Christ. One cannot formulate a simple rule of the thumb such as the giving of ten per cent. The Christian should practice graduated giving: the higher one's income, the higher the proportion of that income that should be given to the cause of Christ. If even half the members of the Christian Church would but tithe, however, the number of foreign missionaries would undoubtedly be increased three or four fold.

11. The successful and victorious Christian is the one who chooses spiritual companions for his most intimate friends. He who selects as his companions those who are least spiritual is thereby indicating that for which he lives. The end of such choices is to become even more lukewarm or cold in the Christian life.

12. The Christian who is seeking to be like Jesus, and as much separated from the contemporary sinful world as Christ would be

71 I Tim. 3:6.

if He were living on earth now, will avoid all amusements and forms of recreation which spoil his taste for God's Word and prayer, or which would weaken his Christian witness and testimony. In the culture in which many of us live there are many spiritual Christians who feel that they can give their best witness by avoiding the dance, the theater, public bathing resorts, playing cards, and the use of alcohol and tobacco. The true child of God does not seek to indulge in as many "little sins" as possible; he seeks rather to follow Christ as closely as possible. This involves a wholesome respect for the general Christian conscience.

13. Every child of God must learn to bear the cross of Christ patiently, with quiet endurance. It was not only necessary for Jesus to go to the cross and there to die for the sins of the world; every believer follows his Lord in that he must be willing to bear whatever it costs to live a faithful Christian life.[72] Needless to say the cross of the believer is not redemptive; in that respect it differs from the cross of Christ.

14. The faithful disciple of Christ must learn to cultivate an attitude of implicit trust in God for forgiveness, for daily guidance, and for sustaining grace. It is not appropriate for the child of God to worry and to have anxiety as to the future. The resources of God will be adequate for whatever trials He allows to come into the life of His child.

15. The true Christian will seek to realize the fruit of the Spirit in his life. This means concretely that he will so surrender himself to Christ and so desire to be transformed into His image that the following attributes will become evident in his personality: "love, joy, peace, patience, kindness, goodness, faithfulness, gentleness, self-control."[73] In other words, the successful Christian is a growing Christian, one who is being progressively transformed into the image of Christ.

16. The successful Christian bears in mind that God is the real Author of his Christian life. He learns by bitter experience that the moment he begins to rely upon himself and his own ability to live the Christian life, he fails.

17. The victorious disciple of Christ also craves an awareness of the presence of God; he wants to be assured that he is continually in the will of God and that the blessing of God is resting upon him. This calls for a life of faithful discipleship, being careful about the

---

72 See Dietrich Bonhoeffer, *The Cost of Discipleship* (New York: Macmillan, 1949).

73 Gal. 5:22, 23.

so-called "little things" which many professing believers disregard entirely.

18. "Believe your beliefs and doubt your doubts." This is a recognition that most Christians at some time or other, usually many times, are troubled with doubt. The same God who delivers from sin is also able to bring one through these distressing moments in which one has to walk completely by faith, while being painfully aware that any feeling of the nearness of Christ is for the time being lacking.

The following two points of this discussion are generally neglected by the bulk of Christendom throughout the history of the church; consequently they deserve careful examination.

19. He who is seeking to be a faithful disciple of the Lord Jesus Christ can follow only the law of absolute love. This involves the rejection of force of every kind, even the resistance of evil men. Jesus Himself said:

You have heard that it was said, "An eye for an eye and a tooth for a tooth." But I say to you, Do not resist one who is evil. But if any one strikes you on the right cheek, turn to him the other also; and if any one would sue you and take your coat, let him have your cloak as well; and if any one forces you to go one mile, go with him two miles. Give to him who begs from you, and do not refuse him who would borrow from you.

You have heard that it was said, "You shall love your neighbor and hate your enemy." But I say to you, Love your enemies and pray for those who persecute you, so that you may be sons of your Father who is in heaven; for he makes his sun rise on the evil and on the good, and sends rain on the just and on the unjust. For if you love those who love you, what reward have you? Do not even the tax collectors do the same? And if you salute only your brethren, what more are you doing than others? Do not even the Gentiles do the same? You, therefore, must be perfect [in love], as your heavenly Father is perfect.[74]

A similar passage is found in Luke's Gospel.[75]

When Jesus was on trial before Pilate He stated: "My kingship is not of this world; if my kingship were of this world, my servants would fight, that I might not be handed over to the Jews; but my kingship is not from the world."

The Apostle Paul gave the following instruction to the Christians at Rome:

Bless those who persecute you; bless and do not curse them. Rejoice with those who rejoice, weep with those who weep. Live in harmony with one another; do not be haughty, but associate with the lowly; never

74 Matt. 5:38-48.   75 Luke 6:27-36.

be conceited. Repay no one evil for evil, but take thought for what is noble in the sight of all. If possible, so far as it depends upon you, live peaceably with all. Beloved, never avenge yourselves, but leave it to the wrath of God; for it is written, "Vengeance is mine, I will repay, says the Lord." No, "if your enemy is hungry, feed him; if he is thirsty, give him drink; for by so doing you will heap burning coals upon his head." Do not be overcome by evil, but overcome evil with good.[76]

In his Second Letter to the Corinthians Paul wrote: "For though we live in the world we are not carrying on a worldly war, for the weapons of our warfare are not worldly but have divine power to destroy strongholds. We destroy arguments and every proud obstacle to the knowledge of God, and take every thought captive to obey Christ . . . ."[77] And in another Letter Paul writes: "See that none of you repays evil for evil, but always seek to do good to one another and to all."[78] Similarly Paul told Timothy: "And the Lord's servant must not be quarrelsome but kindly to every one . . . ."[79]

The Apostle Peter gave the following instruction on the spirit which should characterize Christians: "Finally, all of you, have unity of spirit, sympathy, love of the brethren, a tender heart, and a humble mind. Do not return evil for evil or reviling for reviling; but on the contrary bless, for to this you have been called, that you may obtain a blessing."[80] Peter upheld the example of Jesus for his readers to follow, an example of patient suffering: "For to this you have been called, because Christ also suffered for you, leaving you an example, that you should follow in his steps. He committed no sin; no guile was found on his lips. When he was reviled, he did not revile in return; when he suffered, he did not threaten; but he trusted to him who judges justly."[81]

Historical research has demonstrated that in the first few centuries of the Christian era the members of the Christian Church generally understood these verses to involve the abandonment of force and violence, including military service.[82] This position has been held in recent centuries by three main Christian bodies: the Mennonites, the Church of the Brethren, and Society of Friends. Individual believers in nonresistance are today members of various other Christian groups, however. For example, one of the finest expositions of the doctrine of Biblical nonresistance has been re-

---

76 Rom. 12:14-21.
77 II Cor. 10:3-5.
78 I Thess. 5:15.
79 II Tim. 2:24.
80 I Pet. 3:8, 9.
81 I Pet. 2:21-23.
82 Cf. C. John Cadoux, *The Early Christian Attitude to War* (London: Allen & Unwin, 1940).

cently written by a Baptist Professor of the Philosophy of Religion.[83] The interested reader may also consult items three and four of the appendix of this book. Suffice it to say at this point that the absolutist holds that he cannot deal with anyone on any other basis than that of love; he therefore finds himself unable to go to the battlefield and deliberately seek to kill either Christians or non-Christians; much less is he able to rain death and destruction upon the noncombatant populations of cities during air raids. It is not that the Biblical nonresistant is unwilling to die for the sake of his loved ones; it is killing that he objects to, feeling that his calling is to follow the Prince of Peace at all times, to suffer wrong rather than to do wrong, and to commit himself and his loved ones into the providential care of an Almighty God rather than to resort to sub-Christian behavior to attempt to defend them.

The present writer is profoundly grateful to God for having been born and nurtured in a Christian home where Christian love and nonresistance were believed and taught. When his father was but a youth of fifteen he wrote:

> Though honors and glories never should cease,
> Be they ever so mighty, there's nothing like peace.
> Through battles and victories some honors are won:
> Be mine an honor of peace, or none.

20. The other distinctive point of ethics in the Anabaptist-Mennonite tradition relates to what is commonly called nonconformity to the world or separation from the world. The present writer confesses that he is a convinced Mennonite, holding that all through its history much of Christendom has too largely accommodated its life and ethic to the sub-Biblical standards of the contemporary world. A careful reading of the New Testament would indicate that the Christian must be different from the non-Christian in his speech, in recreation, in his attitude toward culture, in the care and treatment of his body, in the matter of proper adornment, in courtship and marriage, in the attitude toward wealth and possessions, in the exercise of one's duties to the state, and in a radical maintenance of belief in the sacred. There is a tremendous pressure in contemporary society toward a violent secularism which reduces Christianity down to a harmless cultivation of the fine arts for one hour each week. Inasmuch as the writer has attempted to write a monograph on the subject of nonconformity to the world,[84] he will not pursue the subject further here.

83 Culbert G. Rutenber, *The Dagger and the Cross* (New York: Fellowship Publications, 1950).
84 *Separated unto God* (Scottdale, Pa.: Mennonite Publishing House, 1952).

12. *THE CHRISTIAN IN SOCIETY*

It is the teaching of God's Word that the Lord wishes all men to come to a knowledge of the truth, to accept Christ as Saviour and Lord, to enter His church, and to build His kingdom on earth. The will of God for society is therefore its conversion, its turning to God, its obedience to His holy law. God wishes all men to be saved and to live by love, love for God and love for fellow man.

As a matter of fact, however, large numbers of people refuse to accept Jesus Christ, they will not enter the church, and they refuse to take God into account in the ordering of their lives. The result of this disobedience to the divine will is that mankind is divided into two realms: the kingdom of God and of Christ, constituted of those who have been baptized by the Holy Spirit into the body of Christ, His church[85]; and the kingdom of the world and of Satan, composed of all those who reject Christ and His salvation, and who decide to live in sin. What is the relation of these two kingdoms?

First of all, there is apt to be more or less antagonism and tension on the part of those who do not know Christ in their relation with Christians. Sometimes this amounts to actual persecution. Being a Christian always involves a certain reproach in the eyes of the "world." During part of church history the church has been sufficiently strong to influence society to adopt many of the principles of God's Word as its laws and standards. This has tended to reduce the tension between Christians and non-Christians. Unfortunately the church has sometimes linked hands with the state in an attempt to maintain purity of doctrine by force. To those who believe in the separation of church and state, this was a grievous error. It was the system which operated the Inquisition, and made possible the persecution of religious dissenters of all kinds. Thank God, the days of religious persecution, in which church and state co-operate in the enforcement of the Christian ethic and in the maintenance of orthodoxy, are for at least a part of the world gone.

What is the obligation of the Christian in a society made up partly of believers and partly of non-Christians? In a spiritual sense each Christian is by God called out of the world and into the church. God Himself "has delivered us from the dominion of darkness and transferred us to the kingdom of his beloved Son."[86] The Christian's first relationship to the world is therefore one of deliverance. Paul states that Jesus our Lord "gave himself for our sins to deliver us

---

85 See the excellent study by Geerhardus Vos, *The Teaching of Jesus Concerning the Kingdom of God and the Church* (New York: American Tract Society, 1903).
86 Col. 1:13.

from the present evil world, according to the will of our God and Father."[87] But this separation from the world is spiritual and not physical.

The Christian does not withdraw from society and live on a pillar or on an island, physical or cultural. It is the responsibility of the Christian to enter actively into the life of his community, maintaining a vital touch with his friends and neighbors, seeking to make effective a Christian witness at all times. Frankly, the Christian is interested in evangelizing his unchurched friends. It is his desire to win the confidence and trust of those who are not yet in Christ, to present to them the glorious Gospel of salvation through the Lord Jesus Christ, and to help them to make the good choice, the acceptance of Christ. It was none other than Jesus who commissioned His disciples as they would go over[88] the face of the earth to make disciples of all the nations and to baptize them in the name of the holy Trinity. Unfortunately the church has tended in every era of its existence to allow its members to sink too largely to the level of contemporary society, to become engrossed in the activities of acquiring economic security, etc., and to forget the basic commission of their Lord. But God never intended that His children should become indistinguishable from those who are not in His kingdom. God desires His sons and daughters to shine as lights in the world, illuminating the divine will for society, and exhibiting before men those attributes and relationships which it is God's will for all of society to possess and to maintain. In a corporate sense Christians therefore are set as a city upon a hill; they are commissioned and empowered by God to manifest what life can be like when men live by love rather than selfishness.

Individual Christians are also responsible to serve as healing agents in a society which is sick with selfishness and sin, living too largely for the pleasures of the senses, being too much engaged in activities associated with the acquisition of wealth, and giving no thought at all to love for God and one's neighbor. The individual Christian is therefore a sort of spiritual antibiotic, combating by a wholesome example and by the influence of his life and lips the selfishness and the greed of a wicked race. This means that the individual Christian has the same commission as the church. First of all he is seeking to carry out the Great Commission in his life. In the sight of God every Christian is responsible to do what he can by prayer, holiness of life, personal witnessing, giving to the support of

87 Gal. 1:4.
88 Matt. 28:19 (cf. Greek).

the work of the church, etc., in order that the kingdom of Christ may grow and spread throughout the earth. Perhaps this is as far as the responsibility of the church as an organization goes.

It is the general conviction of large numbers of Christian leaders that the individual Christian has a somewhat wider function than does the church. For example, the individual Christian is also concerned to provide for his family in an economic way, which is not the primary responsibility of the church as such. The individual Christian is also concerned to do all that love would suggest for the uplift of society, and for the alleviation of the ills of the race. This means that individual Christians can work for the elimination of the evils of poverty, such as slums; it means that individual Christians can seek to clean out of their communities the evils of strong drink, its manufacture and sale; it means that Christians may individually labor for the establishment and improvement of good schools in their communities; it may even lead to a concerted witness against the printing and distribution of impure literature; in other words, in every way that does not itself involve a stooping to a sub-Christian ethic. The individual Christian does not go through life with an attitude of social irresponsibility. It is rather his desire to do everything he can to improve the opportunity of children and young people to receive a good education, to live in communities where there is opportunity to earn a livelihood, to be able to establish homes and rear children without the degrading influence of pulp magazines being sold in half the stores of the community, etc.

The above does not mean that Christians abandon their central responsibility, the Great Commission, in order to devote themselves to secondary issues. In fact, it is undoubtedly true that the most effective way to deal with these secondary issues is by a vigorous promotion of personal and group witnessing, of actual evangelism. This means that all Christians, whether ordained as ministers or not, will be active in the establishment and support of mission outposts, of Sunday schools and summer Bible schools in unchurched communities, in helping to transform local congregations into vital units for the evangelization of their communities, etc. If this central responsibility is being faithfully attended to, then it would seem to follow that individual Christians can serve on school boards, can help to build community hospitals, can enter generally into the life of their communities, *in so far as the activities involved in community service do not call for the violation of any Christian principle.* God wants His children to be spiritual pilgrims in this world, that is, they are not to enter into the sins of the world and not abandon themselves to the standards and ideals of a non-Christian society. But it is surely not the will of God, and not the following of Christian love, to abandon the life and welfare of one's community in the name of separation from the world. God wants His children to be good "neighbors" in the best and most meaningful sense.

13. *RELATION TO GOVERNMENT*

Simply because of the general teaching of the Bible on the sovereignty of God it would be natural for Christians to believe that God exercises some control over the nations of the earth. According to the explicit teaching of the Scriptures this is the case. For example, when Daniel addressed King Nebuchadnezzar he said: "You, O king, the king of kings, to whom the God of heaven has given the kingdom, the power, and the might, and the glory, and into whose hand he has given, wherever they dwell, the sons of men, the beasts of the field, and the birds of the air, making you rule over them all . . . ."[89] And the prophet Jeremiah quotes the Word of the Lord thus: "It is I who by my great power and my outstretched arm have made the earth, with the men and animals that are on the earth, and I give it to whomever it seems right to me."[90] And even more specifically Daniel teaches the complete sovereignty of God in reference to the governments of this earth thus: "The Most High rules the kingdom of men, and gives it to whom he will, and sets over it the lowliest of men."[91] Wicked King Nebuchadnezzar was to lose his reason for a number of years, "till you know that the Most High rules the kingdom of men, and gives it to whom he will."[92] Nebuchadnezzar's own testimony became: "At the end of the days I, Nebuchadnezzar, lifted my eyes to heaven, and my reason returned to me, and I blessed the Most High, and praised and honored him who lives for ever;

> for his dominion is an everlasting dominion,
> and his kingdom endures from generation to generation;
> all the inhabitants of the earth are accounted as nothing;
> and he does according to his will in the host of heaven
> and among the inhabitants of the earth;
> and none can stay his hand
> or say to him, 'What doest thou?' "[93]

This teaching is repeated in the strongest possible way by the Apostle Paul in his Letter to the Romans: "Let every person be sub-

89 Dan. 2:37, 38.
90 Jer. 27:5.
91 Dan. 4:17.

92 Dan. 4:25; cf. 4:32.
93 Dan. 4:34, 35.

ject to the governing authorities. For there is no authority except from God, and those that exist have been instituted by God."[94]

The question naturally arises, In what sense are the governments of this earth ordained of God? Certainly not in the sense that only good men get into office. And certainly not in the sense that God approves how some rulers get into places of responsibility. Furthermore the expression, "minister of God,"[95] which Paul applies to the officials of government, cannot mean *per se*, saved men: otherwise there would be two plans of salvation, one being through faith in Christ, the other being through serving in government—and this is absurd. Furthermore, the expression, "minister of God," does not in itself constitute divine approval for Christians serving in every office of government; this expression designates no more than the fact that the officials of government are carrying out a work which God desires to be done. Thus the Assyrians of old were God's rod to punish Israel,[96] not in the sense that what they did was right, but in the sense that it was God's will for Israel to be punished. The Assyrians were not consciously doing the will of God, and what they did was not done for the purpose of pleasing God, and yet God in His sovereignty used wicked men and their wicked deeds to fulfill the good function of punishing His people for their sins. Thus it is with certain functions of government. Those who carry out these law-enforcement tasks are not necessarily children of God, often they do not do it for the glory of God, and they are sometimes not even professing believers. But they are "ministers of God" in the sense that God desires society to be characterized by law and order, not by violence and disorder. The further question as to whether regenerated Christians shall enter into every area of government, including that of law enforcement, cannot be settled by an appeal to the fact that governments are divinely ordained and that law-enforcement officers are "ministers of God."

It is therefore entirely clear from Scripture that God provides rulers for the various nations of the earth; evidently His sovereignty in this matter sometimes places into governmental office relatively good rulers who will constitute a blessing to their people, and sometimes God allows wicked men to rule over a nation to punish that nation for its secularism and its sin. (This is no denial of the fact that sin often brings its own punishment; concretely, that a wicked nation will create and tolerate such conditions as will permit the election of wicked men or the assumption of power by them. This

---

94 Rom. 13:1.   95 Rom. 13:6; cf. 13:4 (2x).   96 Isa. 10:5.

also is a part of the righteous moral government of this world by God. The sovereignty of God is never a denial of secondary causes, but frequently operates through them.)

It has been suggested that God has ordained government in a somewhat similar way to His ordination of marriage; that is, God created man with such a nature as would lead him to seek a companion and to establish a home; and human nature is also so constituted by God that men desire to live in a society of law and order, rather than as unmanaged "herds" of savages. The urge therefore for an orderly society, where people have an optimum amount of freedom, is a divinely given motivation. God wants men to dwell together as brothers, with freedom to marry and rear children, freedom to worship, and freedom to live in peace and security. In order to conquer sin and to enable men to live in holiness and peace, God gave His only Son to die on the cross. Few indeed are the people who have enough knowledge of history to realize the tremendous moral uplift which Christianity has brought to the world.

What then are the particular duties of the Christian to government? For one thing, the New Testament specifies plainly that Christians are to pay all taxes: "For the same reason you also pay taxes, for the authorities are ministers of God, attending to this very thing. Pay all of them their dues, taxes to whom taxes are due, revenue to whom revenue is due, respect to whom respect is due, honor to whom honor is due."[97] The present writer therefore cannot agree with those pacifists who reportedly refuse to pay that portion of their Federal Income Tax which they regard as being the percentage of the national budget which is being used for war or military purposes. Paul wrote the above words during the reign of Nero! It is therefore the responsibility of the Christian to pay all taxes, regardless of whether the government is being carried on in a way that is acceptable to the Christian in every respect or not.

A second obligation of the Christian to the government is mentioned by Paul in his First Letter to Timothy: "First of all, then, I urge that supplications, prayers, intercessions, and thanksgivings be made for all men, for kings and all who are in high positions, that we may lead a quiet and peaceable life, godly and respectful in every way. This is good, and it is acceptable in the sight of God our Savior, who desires all men to be saved and to come to the knowledge of the truth."[98] This is incidentally a point on which many Christians fall short; they fail to uphold in daily prayer before God those

97 Rom. 13:6, 7.   98 I Tim. 2:1, 2.

who are bearing an awful responsibility for the welfare of their subjects, and the determination of policies which shall lead either to calamity or blessing.

The third obligation of the Christian to his government is that of obedience, a point which has already been referred to. The apostle writes: "Let every person be subject to the governing authorities. . . . Therefore he who resists the authorities resists what God has appointed, and those who resist will incur judgment. . . . Therefore one must be subject, not only to avoid God's wrath but also for the sake of conscience."[99] Christians therefore are law-abiding citizens, seeking to render conscientious obedience to the laws of their respective countries, even when they personally might not be in sympathy with some of the laws. The only exception to this rule is that Christians are obligated to follow the higher law of God at any point where a national law actually conflicts with God's standards: a case in point being the attempt of the Jewish Sanhedrin to prohibit the preaching of the Gospel by the apostles of Christ. "So they called them and charged them not to speak or teach at all in the name of Jesus. But Peter and John answered them, 'Whether it is right in the sight of God to listen to you rather than to God, you must judge; for we cannot but speak of what we have seen and heard.' "[1] The apostles proceeded therefore to go out and evangelize widely in Jerusalem, the doing of which led to their rearrest: "And when they had brought them, they set them before the council. And the high priest questioned them, saying, 'We strictly charged you not to teach in this name, yet here you have filled Jerusalem with your teaching and you intend to bring this man's blood upon us.' But Peter and the apostles answered, 'We must obey God rather than men.' "[2]

The fourth obligation of the Christian to his government is the rendering of honor and respect. The Apostle Paul therefore wrote concerning the governing authorities: "Pay all of them their dues, taxes to whom taxes are due, revenue to whom revenue is due, respect to whom respect is due, honor to whom honor is due."[3] And Peter writes: "Honor all men. Love the brotherhood. Fear God. Honor the emperor."[4]

It should be observed that there is a marked contrast as between the church and the state. The state is made up of all people, good and bad, saints and sinners, the church and those who are still in the world. The state is entered by the natural birth, while one enters the church by the new birth, regeneration. The function of the state includes the maintenance of law and order, while the function of the church is to win souls for Christ and to nurture them in the Christian brotherhood. The state controls people by law, while the church uses only the Word of God. The state necessarily employs the sanction of force, using fines, prison, and even death, while the church can do no more than excommunicate the disobedient and the impenitent. The state has as its head a mere man or group of men, while the head of the church is the Lord Jesus Christ. The state will come to an end at the return of Christ, while the church will at that point enter into the life of glory and be with the Lord God forever. In view of these differences it is obvious that there are certain functions associated with the government which the Christian who accepts the doctrine of Biblical nonresistance cannot engage in. The position assumed in this book is that of the Swiss Brethren whose Schleitheim Confession of Faith, 1527, states:

The sword is ordained of God outside the perfection of Christ. It punishes and puts to death the wicked, and guards and protects the good. In the Law the sword was ordained for the punishment of the wicked and for their death, and the same [sword] is [now] ordained to be used by the worldly magistrates.

In the perfection of Christ, however, only the ban [excommunication] is used for a warning and for the excommunication of the one who has sinned, without putting the flesh to death—simply the warning and the command to sin no more.

Now it will be asked by many who do not recognize [this as] the will of Christ for us, whether a Christian may or should employ the sword against the wicked for the defense and protection of the good or for the sake of love. Our reply is unanimously as follows: Christ commands and teaches us to learn of Him, for He is meek and lowly in heart and so shall we find rest to our souls. Also Christ says to the heathenish woman who was taken in adultery, not that one should stone her according to the law of his father (and yet He says, as the Father has commanded me, thus I do), but in mercy and forgiveness and warning to sin no more. Such [an attitude] we also ought to take completely according to the rule of the ban.

Secondly, it will be asked concerning the sword, whether a Christian shall pass sentence in worldly disputes and strife such as unbelievers have with one another. This is our united answer. Christ did not wish to decide or pass judgment between brother and brother in the case of the inheritance but refused to do so. Therefore we should do likewise.

Thirdly, it will be asked concerning the sword, shall one be a magistrate if one should be chosen as such? The answer is as follows: they wished to make Christ king, but He fled and did not view it as the arrangement of His Father. Thus shall we do as He did, and follow Him, and so shall we not walk in darkness. For He Himself says, he who wishes to come after me, let him deny himself and take up his cross and follow me. Also He Himself forbids the [employment of] the force of the sword saying, The worldly princes lord it over them, etc., but not so shall it be with you. Further, Paul says, whom God did foreknow He also did predestinate to be conformed to the image of His Son, etc. Also Christ says, Christ has suffered (not ruled) and left us an example that ye should follow His steps.

Finally, it will be observed that it is not appropriate for a Christian to serve as a magistrate because of these points: the government magistracy is according to the flesh, but the Christians' is according to the Spirit; their houses and dwelling remain in this world, but the Christians' are in heaven; their citizenship is in this world, but the Christians' citizenship is in heaven; the weapons of their conflict and war are carnal and against the flesh only, but the Christians' weapons are spiritual, against the fortification of the devil. The worldlings are armed with steel and iron, but the Christians are armed with the armor of God, with truth, righteousness, peace, faith, salvation, and the Word of God. In brief, as is the mind of Christ toward us, so shall the mind of the members of the body of Christ be through Him in all things, that there may be no schism in the body through which it would be destroyed. For every kingdom divided against itself will be destroyed. Now since Christ is as it is written of Him, His members must also be the same, that His body may remain complete and united to its own advancement and upbuilding.[5]

It is perhaps in order to inquire whether there is no difference between serving as a policeman, a member of the constabulary, and serving as a soldier. In the opinion of the present writer there is some difference, but both the constabulary and the military fulfill purposes and employ methods which stand in contrast with the instructions of the New Testament for the Christian. Note the following comparisons and contrasts: the Christian has as his function the making of disciples to Jesus Christ; the constabulary has as its function the enforcement of law and order; the military serves a relatively wicked nation which is at war. The Christian depends on the power of the Holy Spirit in the performance of his work; the constabulary employs the threat of force and coercion; while the military aims to take life and destroy property and security. The Christian is according to the New Testament to be a suffering witness, even a martyr if need be; the constabulary must defend itself from

5 Cited in full in J. C. Wenger, *The Doctrines of the Mennonites* (Scottdale, Pa.: Mennonite Publishing House, 1952), pp. 74, 75.

criminals by the use of arms, even taking life if necessary; while in the waging of war the military employs violence against entire populations, both combatant and noncombatant. The Christian serves Christ and His church; the constabulary serves national or local government; while in the military men are *conscripted to kill.* The Christian offers salvation freely to all men; the constabulary seeks to compel men to live in obedience to law; while the military aims to break the enemy nation to the point of surrender. Although there is therefore a rather sharp contrast between the constabulary and the military, yet both necessarily employ force, including the possible taking of life, functions which make it impossible for the nonresistant Christian to serve either as a policeman or a soldier.

For a further review of the implications of the doctrine of nonresistance the interested reader is referred to the writings of such scholars as Culbert G. Rutenber, John Horsch, Edward Yoder, Melvin Gingerich, and especially Guy Franklin Hershberger and John H. Yoder.[6]

6 Their books are available from Mennonite Publishing House, Scottdale, Pa.

PART V

GOD AS ALL IN ALL

V. GOD AS ALL IN ALL

1. *THE HEREAFTER*

Throughout the Bible there is recognition that man dwells on this earth for a comparatively brief span, after which he enters into the eternal order. This truth is taught both in the Old Testament and in the New, although much more clearly and with greater fullness in the New Testament. A good sample of the Old Testament point of view is that of Ecclesiastes 12, where the following beautiful description of old age and death is given:

Remember also your Creator in the days of your youth, before the evil days come, and the years draw nigh, when you will say, "I have no pleasure in them"; before the sun and the light, and the moon, and the stars are darkened and the clouds return after the rain; in the day when the keepers of the house tremble, and the strong men are bent, and the grinders cease because they are few, and those that look through the windows are dimmed, and the doors on the street are shut; when the sound of the grinding is low, and one rises up at the voice of a bird, and all the daughters of song are brought low; they are afraid also of what is high, and terrors are in the way; the almond tree blossoms, the grasshopper drags itself along and desire fails; because man goes to his eternal home, and the mourners go about the streets; before the silver cord is snapped, or the golden bowl is broken, or the pitcher is broken at the fountain, or the wheel broken at the cistern, and the dust returns to the earth as it was, and the spirit returns to God who gave it. . . .

The end of the matter; all has been heard. Fear God, and keep his commandments; for this is the whole duty of man. For God will bring every deed into judgment, with every secret thing, whether good or evil.[1]

The above description agrees entirely with the succinct statement of the Letter to the Hebrews: "It is appointed for men to die once, and after that comes judgment."[2]

In the experience of death the individual lays aside the flesh, while the real self enters into the life of the hereafter. This life in

1 Eccl. 12:1-9, 13, 14.   2 Heb. 9:27.

the hereafter is one of conscious bliss or conscious suffering as the discussion below will indicate. Death also marks the end of probation, there being no more opportunity in the hereafter to repent and believe. The Scriptures therefore uniformly urge proper faith and life here and now in order to be prepared for the judgment which is to come. At the judgment seat of Christ everyone will receive his just retribution or reward according to the deeds done in the body. "For we must all appear before the judgment seat of Christ, so that each one may receive good or evil, according to what he has done in the body."[3]

Old Testament Teaching

According to the Old Testament, when a man dies his spirit goes to *Sheol*, the abode of the dead. An examination of the use of the word "Sheol" in the Old Testament reveals that it is not always employed in the same sense. Sometimes it refers indifferently to the abode of all the dead, being used both of the good and the wicked, and sometimes it is applied in a special way to the state of the wicked dead. The former usage is found in the Book of Genesis. Jacob, for example, stated when his sons and daughters rose up to comfort him: "No, I shall go down to Sheol to my son, mourning."[4] Jacob also forbade Reuben to take Benjamin into Egypt, saying: "My son shall not go down with you, for his brother is dead, and he only is left. If harm should befall him on the journey that you are to make, you would bring down my gray hairs with sorrow to Sheol."[5] Similarly, the Messianic prophecy of Psalm 16:10 indicates that the Christ should not remain in Sheol.

On the other hand, many Scriptures in the Old Testament speak of Sheol as the end of a life of sin. The Proverbs, for example, frequently speak of harlots as leading men to Sheol:

Her feet go down to death;
    her steps follow the path to Sheol.[6]

Her house is the way to Sheol,
    going down to the chambers of death.[7]
The Psalmist David announced:
    The wicked shall depart to Sheol,
        all the nations that forget God.[8]

3 II Cor. 5:10.
4 Gen. 37:35.
5 Gen. 42:38.

6 Prov. 5:5.
7 Prov. 7:27.
8 Ps. 9:17.

The Old Testament also employs words for grave,[9] sepulcher,[10] and pit,[11] as well as a more obscure term[12] which is used only once.

The Old Testament uses five or six different Hebrew words which may be translated heaven.[13] The Hebrew words for heaven sometimes refer to the sky, sometimes to the starry universe, and sometimes to the abode of God. It is this last usage which particularly interests us at this point. One of the best illustrations of this last usage is found in the prayer of Solomon at the dedication of the temple. "When thy people Israel are defeated before the enemy because they have sinned against thee, if they turn again to thee, and acknowledge thy name, and pray and make supplication to thee in this house; then hear thou in heaven, and forgive the sin of thy people Israel . . . ."[14]

The basic teaching of the Old Testament on the hereafter does not depend upon the word *Sheol* nor upon any of the Hebrew words for grave, death, pit, or heaven; it depends rather on comforting statements such as the following:

> Thou dost show me the path of life;
> in thy presence there is fullness of joy,
> in thy right hand are pleasures for evermore.[15]

Even more impressive is the testimony of David:
> As for me, I shall behold thy face in righteousness;
> when I awake, I shall be satisfied with beholding thy form.[16]

And the Psalmist Asaph writes:

> Thou dost guide me with thy counsel,
> and afterward thou wilt receive me to glory.
> Whom have I in heaven but thee?
> And there is nothing upon earth that I desire besides thee.[17]

And Job sings concerning the hereafter:

> There the wicked cease from troubling,
> and there the weary are at rest.[18]

---

9 Gen. 35:20.
10 Gen. 23:4.
11 Isa. 51:14.
12 Job 30:24.
13 (1) Heavens, sky, starry sky, *heaven*, Gen. 1:1; Ps. 19:1; (2) *Heaven*, starry sky, sky, Ezra 5:11; Jer. 10:11; (3) Clouds?, Ps. 36:5; (4) Plain, desert, sky?, Ps. 68:4; (5) Sky, whirlwind?, wheel, Ps. 77:18; (6) Clouds?, Isa. 5:30.

14 I Kings 8:33, 34.
15 Ps. 16:11.
16 Ps. 17:15.

17 Ps. 73:24, 25.
18 Job 3:17.

One of the most striking examples of the belief in life in the hereafter is found in the account of David's behavior when one of his sons died:

And the LORD struck the child that Uriah's wife bore to David, and it became sick. David therefore besought God for the child; and David fasted, and went in and lay all night upon the ground. And the elders of his house stood beside him, to raise him from the ground; but he would not, nor did he eat food with them. On the seventh day the child died. And the servants of David feared to tell him that the child was dead; for they said, "Behold, while the child was yet alive, we spoke to him, and he did not listen to us; how then can we say to him the child is dead? He may do himself some harm." But when David saw that his servants were whispering together, David perceived that the child was dead; and David said to his servants, "Is the child dead?" They said, "He is dead." Then David arose from the earth, and washed, and anointed himself, and changed his clothes; and he went into the house of the LORD, and worshiped; he then went to his own house; and when he asked, they set food before him, and he ate. Then his servants said to him, "What is this thing that you have done? You fasted and wept for the child while it was alive; but when the child died, you arose and ate food." He said, "While the child was still alive, I fasted and wept; for I said, 'Who knows whether the LORD will be gracious to me, that the child may live?' But now he is dead; why should I fast? Can I bring him back again? I shall go to him, but he will not return to me."[19]

New Testament Teaching

The New Testament equivalent in Greek of the Sheol of the Hebrew Old Testament is *Hades,* which is also the usual translation of Sheol in the Septuagint. Sometimes Hades in the New Testament is the translation of a Sheol quotation from the Old Testament, for example, in the Messianic prophecy concerning the resurrection of Jesus[20]; sometimes it refers to the underworld, but usually with a rather strong flavor of the place of the wicked dead. Capernaum, for example, is to be brought down to Hades[21]; and the "gates" of Hades (that is, the schemings made at its gates) will not prevail against the church.[22] Furthermore, when the rich man died in his sin he opened his eyes in Hades, being in torment.[23] The Book of Revelation makes frequent mention of "Death and Hades."[24]

In the New Testament the place of eternal punishment is generally designated by the Greek word *Gehenna.* Unfortunately the Hades and Gehenna passages are not distinguishable in the King

19 II Sam. 12:15-23.   21 Matt. 11:23.   23 Luke 16:23.
20 Acts 2:27, 31; Ps. 16:10.   22 Matt. 16:18.   24 Rev. 1:18; 6:8; 20:13, 14.

James Version. Jesus warned that anyone calling a person a fool would be liable to the Gehenna of fire,[25] and He also stated that it was better to practice severe self-discipline now than to have the whole body "thrown into Gehenna."[26] A wicked person is designated as a child of Gehenna,[27] and Jesus warned the wicked Pharisees of the damnation of Gehenna.[28]

There is a third word in the New Testament which is translated hell, namely, *Tartarus*: Peter speaks in his Second Letter of the angels who sinned and were by God cast "into Tartarus" and committed to "pits of nether gloom to be kept until the judgment."[29]

Jesus also spoke several times of unquenchable fire,[30] and the Book of Revelation mentions the lake of fire.[31] Jesus expressly stated that the lost will go away into "eternal punishment, but the righteous into eternal life."[32]

The usual term for the eternal home of the saints in the New Testament is simply *heaven,* but Paul also speaks of a third heaven and uses it as equivalent to Paradise. In a rather obscure passage in which he apparently refers to himself Paul says: "I know a man in Christ who fourteen years ago was caught up to the third heaven . . . . And I know that this man was caught up into Paradise . . . and he heard things that cannot be told, which man may not utter."[33]

Concerning the eternal home of the saints in heaven Jesus remarked that the reward of the saints there is great.[34] God is there.[35] The angels of God are in heaven.[36] The treasures of the saints are there.[37] Christ is in heaven.[38] The hope of the saints is in heaven.[39] The inheritance of Christians is in heaven.[40]

We therefore conclude the following about the hereafter: at death the inner self, the real person, enters into conscious bliss with Christ, vastly superior to this life (II Corinthians 5:8; Philippians 1:23; Luke 23:43; II Corinthians 5:1), or into conscious suffering (Luke 16:22, 23), awaiting the final resurrection at Christ's coming on the Last Day. John 5:28, 29; 6:39, 40, 44, 54; 11:24; I Thessalonians 4:13—5:4. This "interval" which the New Testament seems to presuppose between the death of the body and the resurrection at the second coming of Jesus is commonly spoken of by theologians as the "Intermediate State," although it must be admitted that the

25 Matt. 5:22.
26 Matt. 10:28; 18:9; Mark 9:43.
27 Matt. 23:15.
28 Matt. 23:33.
29 II Pet. 2:4.
30 Mark 9:43, 44, 45, 46, 48.
31 Rev. 19:20; 20:10, 14, 15.
32 Matt. 25:46.

33 II Cor. 12:2-4; cf. Luke 23:43; Rev. 2:7.
34 Matt. 5:12; Luke 6:23.
35 Matt. 5:48; 6:9, 10.
36 Matt. 22:30; Mark 12:25.
37 Matt. 6:20; Mark 10:21; Luke 18:22.
38 Eph. 6:9; Col. 4:1; Heb. 9:24.
39 Col. 1:5.
40 I Pet. 1:4.

Bible does not seem to treat the problem of the relationship of time to eternity in any complete manner.

By way of summary we may say that the eternal states are heaven and hell: heaven being a place and state of bliss with God, with Christ, with the holy angels, and with all the believers of human history. Matthew 8:11; 13:43; 25:10; John 14:1, 2; I Peter 1:4; Revelation 7:15; 19:9; 21:3, 4, 23; 22:3-5. Furthermore, heaven will undoubtedly involve joyful service, not static inactivity.[41] The other eternal destiny is hell, according to the Scriptures a place of torment, of banishment from God and the society of heaven, where the wrath of God, remorse of conscience, and anguish and misery will be endured forever. Matthew 13:41, 42; 18:9; 22:12, 13; 24:50, 51; 25:30, 46; Revelation 20:14, 15.

It is sometimes objected that it is unthinkable that a God of love should consign sinners to a place of torment forever and ever, where there is no longer any opportunity to repent, and where the punishment is obviously not redemptive. It should be observed that the doctrine of eternal punishment is not arrived at through philosophy, or through a vindictive spirit on the part of theologians. This doctrine is taught simply because it is the clear representation of the New Testament. Man is made with "a never-dying soul to save" and God has made that salvation possible through the giving of His only Son on Calvary. Life on this earth is a probation for eternity. It is obvious that the righteous must be severed from the wicked, else heaven would not be a place of bliss. Furthermore heaven would actually be at least as great a punishment for an unregenerated man as would hell; in his wickedness of character the presence of a holy God and His glorified saints would be agony. The awful issues of heaven and hell ought therefore be powerful factors to move unsaved people to accept Christ and His free salvation. They should also, as Paul remarks, move Christians to be active ambassadors, entreating sinners to accept Christ and "be reconciled to God."[42]

2. THE RETURN OF JESUS

Every attempt to write a theology of God's Word must be made humbly, for one is dealing with the very "oracles of God,"[43] and the responsibility of attempting to present the truth of God so as to honestly represent Him before men is formidable indeed. In no area of Christian truth is the propriety of humility greater than in eschatology. This means that there is no place for sharp judgments

41 Rev. 7:15; cf. 22:3.   42 II Cor. 5:20; cf. 5:11.   43 Rom. 3:2.

on fellow Christians with whom one may differ as to the exact order of events for the return of Jesus.

In the judgment of many sound students of the Bible, prophecy does not constitute pre-written history. Take the Old Testament prophecies of the Messiah, for example. One can learn a few details about the earthly life of Jesus, and somewhat more about His spiritual ministry, from the Old Testament prophets, but it would simply have been impossible to write the life of Christ on the basis of Old Testament prophecy before the incarnation and passion of our Lord. After He had lived on earth it became possible to write the story of Jesus with a richness and completeness that would have been utterly impossible before His incarnation. So it is with prophecy now. Only when Jesus has come again will the complete account of events associated with His coming be possible. Furthermore, it should be perfectly obvious that every generation throughout the Christian era should not expect the fulfillment of every prophecy in the contemporary world.

Eschatology is one area of Christian truth where there is not perfect agreement among all professing Christians, not even among those who otherwise rather closely resemble one another theologically. These differences relate mostly to the view that is taken of Revelation 20, but are not exclusively related to the doctrine of a millennium.

The Signs of His Coming

The Scriptures give a number of signs of the return of Jesus.

1. One of these is the world-wide proclamation of the Gospel. Matthew 24:14; Mark 13:10. "And this gospel of the kingdom will be preached throughout the whole world, as a testimony to all nations; and then the end will come."

2. Another sign of the return of Jesus will be the fact that many Gentiles will have come into the church. Matthew 8:11; Luke 2:32; Acts 15:14; Romans 9:24-26; 11:25; 15:8-12; Ephesians 2:11-20. Paul states "A hardening has come upon part of Israel, until the full number of the Gentiles come in."

3. The Scriptures also indicate that before Jesus returns many Israelites will also turn to Christ in faith. Romans 11:14, 15, 25-32; II Corinthians 3:14-16. Again Paul states: "And so all Israel will be saved; as it is written,

'The Deliverer will come from Zion,
he will banish ungodliness from Jacob';

'and this will be my covenant with them
when I take away their sins.'

As regards the gospel they are enemies of God, for your sake; but as regards election they are beloved for the sake of their forefathers. For the gifts and the call of God are irrevocable."[44] Paul also remarks concerning the ultimate acceptance of the Gospel by the Jews, in contrast with their present rejection of the Gospel: "For if their rejection means the reconciliation of the world, what will their acceptance mean but life from the dead?"[45]

It should be observed that this discussion relates to the spiritual conversion of Israel, and it is not an attempt to answer the question as to the political restoration of Israel. Some theologians regard certain passages as suggesting that such a political restoration may be a part of the ultimate mercy of God to be shown to the Jews. Matthew 19:28; Luke 22:29, 30; 21:24; Acts 1:6. Other Bible students feel that Israel will never be restored by God as a political entity. Matthew 8:11, 12; 21:28-46; 22:4-9; Luke 13:6-9; I Thessalonians 2:14-16.

4. A fourth sign of the return of Christ will be apostasy and tribulation. Matthew 24:9-12; Mark 13:9-13; Luke 21:22-24; II Thessalonians 2:3, 4; I Timothy 4:1-3; II Timothy 3:1-5.

5. The Scriptures also seem to indicate that shortly before the return of Christ an antichrist, "the man of sin," will appear. II Thessalonians 2:1-12; I John 2:18, 21, 22; 4:3; II John 7; Revelation 13. It cannot be stated with dogmatism whether the antichrist is an institution, a series of institutions, or a particular individual, although many theologians today believe that it will be some one particular person.

6. A sixth and final sign of the return of Jesus will be the series of things described in the Olivet Discourse of our Lord which is recorded in Matthew 24, Mark 13, and Luke 21. These signs and wonders include such evils as war, famine, and earthquakes; false prophets and heresies; and "astronomical disturbances," though in what sense is not entirely clear. A study of the Old Testament would suggest the possibility that the astronomical signs might refer to what we today would call "world-shaking" events.[46]

The Nature of His Coming

A careful study of the passages of the New Testament that refer to the return of Jesus indicates that it will be personal and visible

44 Rom. 11:26-29.   45 Rom. 11:15.
46 Cf. God's wrath with the nations, esp. Edom, Isa. 34:4; and with Egypt, Ezek. 32:7, 8.

(Matthew 24:44; 26:64; Mark 13:26; Luke 21:27; Acts 1:11; 3:20, 21; I Corinthians 15:23; Philippians 3:20; Colossians 3:4; I Thessalonians 2:19; 3:13; 4:13—5:4; II Timothy 4:8; Titus 2:13; Hebrews 9:28; Revelation 1:7), sudden and unannounced (Matthew 24:27-44; 25:1-13; Mark 13:32-37; I Thessalonians 5:2, 3; Revelation 3:3; 16:15), and glorious and triumphant (Matthew 24:30; I Thessalonians 4:16; II Thessalonians 1:7-10). Perhaps one single passage on the return of Jesus will suffice to indicate its nature:

But we would not have you ignorant, brethren, concerning those who are asleep, that you may not grieve as others do who have no hope. For since we believe that Jesus died and rose again, even so, through Jesus, God will bring with him those who have fallen asleep. For this we declare to you by the word of the Lord, that we who are alive, who are left until the coming of the Lord, shall not precede those who have fallen asleep. For the Lord himself will descend from heaven with a cry of command, with the archangel's call, and with the sound of the trumpet of God. And the dead in Christ will rise first; then we who are alive, who are left, shall be caught up together with them in the clouds to meet the Lord in the air; and so we shall always be with the Lord. Therefore comfort one another with these words.

But as to the times and the seasons, brethren, you have no need to have anything written to you. For you yourselves know well that the day of the Lord will come like a thief in the night. When people say, "There is peace and security," then sudden destruction will come upon them as travail comes upon a woman with child, and there will be no escape. But you are not in darkness, brethren, for that day to surprise you like a thief.[47]

The Purposes of His Coming

According to the New Testament the purposes of the return of Christ are threefold: (1) to raise the dead (John 5:28, 29; 6:39, 40, 44. 54; 11:24; Acts 24:15; I Corinthians 15:23; I Thessalonians 4:15-17); (2) to hold judgment (Matthew 13:30, 40-43, 49; 25:31-46; John 12:48; Acts 24:25; Romans 2:5-16; I Thessalonians 4:14-5:4; II Thessalonians 1:7-10; II Peter 3:3-13). This judgment will involve the full and final salvation of the saints (Luke 21:25-28; Romans 8:23; Ephesians 1:13, 14; 4:30; Philippians 3:20, 21; I Peter 1:3-5), also the punishment and damnation of the wicked (Matthew 13:37-43; 25:31-46; II Thessalonians 1:7-10; Romans 2:5-16). (3) The third purpose of the return of Jesus is to restore the creation to its original purity and harmony (Matthew 19:28; Acts 3:21; Romans 8:21; Hebrews 1:10-12; 12:26-28; II Peter 3:13; Revelation 21:1).

47 I Thess. 4:13-5:4.

The Scriptures show that because of the fall of man a curse was put on the ground. Paul states that not only the Christian, but the whole creation, groans and travails together in pain until now; furthermore "the creation itself will be set free from its bondage to decay and obtain the glorious liberty of the children of God."[48]

Undoubtedly the main emphases of the New Testament as to the purposes of Christ's return are the resurrection of the dead and the judgment of all men. Let us look at each of these briefly.

The great chapter on the resurrection from the dead is I Corinthians 15:

Now if Christ is preached as raised from the dead, how can some of you say that there is no resurrection of the dead? But if there is no resurrection of the dead, then Christ has not been raised . . . .

But in fact Christ has been raised from the dead, the first fruits of those who have fallen asleep. For as by a man came death, by a man has come also the resurrection of the dead. For as in Adam all die, so also in Christ shall all be made alive. But each in his own order: Christ the first fruits, then at his coming those who belong to Christ. Then comes the end, when he delivers the kingdom to God the Father after destroying every rule and every authority and power. For he must reign until he has put all his enemies under his feet. The last enemy to be destroyed is death. "For God has put all things in subjection under his feet." But when it says, "All things are put in subjection under him," it is plain that he is excepted who put all things under him. When all things are subjected to him, then the Son himself will also be subjected to him who put all things under him, that God may be everything to every one. . . .

But some one will ask, "How are the dead raised? With what kind of body do they come?" You foolish man! What you sow does not come to life unless it dies. And what you sow is not the body which is to be, but a bare kernel, perhaps of wheat or of some other grain. But God gives it a body as he has chosen, and to each kind of seed its own body. For not all flesh is alike, but there is one kind for men, another for animals, another for birds, and another for fish. There are celestial bodies and there are terrestrial bodies; but the glory of the celestial is one, and the glory of the terrestrial is another. There is one glory of the sun, and another glory of the moon, and another glory of the stars; for star differs from star in glory.

So is it with the resurrection of the dead. What is sown is perishable, what is raised is imperishable. It is sown in dishonor, it is raised in glory. It is sown in weakness, it is raised in power. It is sown a physical body, it is raised a spiritual body. If there is a physical body, there is also a spiritual body. Thus it is written, "The first man Adam became a living being"; the last Adam became a life-giving spirit. But it is not the spirit-

48 Rom. 8:21, 22.

ual which is first but the physical, and then the spiritual. The first man was from the earth, a man of dust; the second man is from heaven. As was the man of dust, so are those who are of the dust; and as is the man of heaven, so are those who are of heaven. Just as we have borne the image of the man of dust, we shall also bear the image of the man of heaven. I tell you this, brethren: flesh and blood cannot inherit the kingdom of God, nor does the perishable inherit the imperishable.

Lo! I tell you a mystery. We shall not all sleep, but we shall all be changed, in a moment, in the twinkling of an eye, at the last trumpet. For the trumpet will sound, and the dead will be raised imperishable, and we shall be changed. For this perishable nature must put on the imperishable, and this mortal nature must put on immortality. When the perishable puts on the imperishable, and the mortal puts on immortality, then shall come to pass the saying that is written:

> "Death is swallowed up in victory."
> "O death, where is thy victory?
> O death, where is thy sting?"[49]

Perhaps the fullest description of the judgment, and the one employing the most literal language is that found in Romans 2:

Do you suppose, O man, that when you judge those who do such things and yet do them yourself, you will escape the judgment of God? Or do you presume upon the riches of his kindness and forbearance and patience? Do you not know that God's kindness is meant to lead you to repentance? But by your hard and impenitent heart you are storing up wrath for yourself on the day of wrath when God's righteous judgment will be revealed. For he will render to every man according to his works: to those who by patience in well-doing seek for glory and honor and immortality, he will give eternal life; but for those who are factious and do not obey the truth, but obey wickedness, there will be wrath and fury. There will be tribulation and distress for every human being who does evil, the Jew first and also the Greek, but glory and honor and peace for every one who does good, the Jew first and also the Greek. For God shows no partiality.

All who have sinned without the law will also perish without the law, and all who have sinned under the law will be judged by the law. For it is not the hearers of the law who are righteous before God, but the doers of the law who will be justified. When Gentiles who have not the law do by nature what the law requires, they are a law to themselves, even though they do not have the law. They show that what the law requires is written on their hearts, while their conscience also bears witness and their conflicting thoughts accuse or perhaps excuse them on that day when, according to my gospel, God judges the secrets of men by Christ Jesus.[50]

49 I Cor. 15:12, 13, 20-29, 35-55.　　50 Rom. 2:3-16.

The Revelation contains the following description of the final judgment:

Then I saw a great white throne and him who sat upon it; from his presence earth and sky fled away, and no place was found for them. And I saw the dead, great and small, standing before the throne, and books were opened. Also another book was opened, which is the book of life. And the dead were judged by what was written in the books, by what they had done. And the sea gave up the dead in it, Death and Hades gave up the dead in them, and all were judged by what they had done. Then Death and Hades were thrown into the lake of fire. This is the second death, the lake of fire; and if any one's name was not found written in the book of life, he was thrown into the lake of fire.[51]

Paul also says earnestly: "Why do you pass judgment on your brother? Or you, why do you despise your brother? For we shall all stand before the judgment seat of God; for it is written,

'As I live, says the Lord, every knee shall bow to me,
    and every tongue shall give praise to God.'

So each of us shall give account of himself to God."[52]

Major References to the Return of Jesus

All evangelical theologians agree that Christ will come again visibly and in person to take His bride, the church, unto Himself; that Jesus will also raise up the wicked dead and serve as their judge. The major point of disagreement centers in whether or not there will be an earthly reign of Jesus for a thousand years with Christ's throne being located in Jerusalem. Before taking up the three main schools of thought on this "millennial reign" it would seem desirable to review the main eschatological passages of the New Testament in order to allow the reader to judge for himself what the teaching of the Scriptures is on the return of Christ, the resurrection of the dead, and the final judgment.

The Gospels

The following statements from the lips of Jesus are arranged in the chronological order in which they are placed by Professor A. T. Robertson in his *Harmony of the Gospels for Students of the Life of Christ*.[53] In a general way parallel passages will be ignored in this study.

51 Rev. 20:11-15.
52 Rom. 14:10-12.
53 Pub. by Harper & Brothers, New York and London, 1912. An excellent work.

The very first statement in the Gospels comes from the lips of John the Baptist and concerns the judgment which Jesus will hold when He returns: "His winnowing fork is in his hand, to clear his threshing floor, and to gather the wheat into his granary, but the chaff he will burn with unquenchable fire."[54]

The first statement which Jesus made on eschatology has to do with the resurrection: "For as the Father has life in himself, so he has granted the Son also to have life in himself, and has given him authority to execute judgment, because he is the Son of man. Do not marvel at this; for the hour is coming when all who are in the tombs will hear his voice and come forth, those who have done good, to the resurrection of life, and those who have done evil, to the resurrection of judgment."[55]

At the end of the Sermon on the Mount Jesus said: "Not every one who says to me, 'Lord, Lord,' shall enter the kingdom of heaven, but he who does the will of my Father who is in heaven. On that day many will say to me, 'Lord, Lord, did we not prophesy in your name, and cast out demons in your name, and do many mighty works in your name?' And then will I declare to them, 'I never knew you; depart from me, you evildoers.' "[56]

Matthew also records the following: "Then he began to upbraid the cities where most of his mighty works had been done, because they did not repent. 'Woe to you, Chorazin! woe to you, Bethsaida! . . . But I tell you, it shall be more tolerable on the day of judgment for Tyre and Sidon than for you. And you, Capernaum, will you be exalted to heaven? You shall be brought down to Hades. For if the mighty works done in you had been done in Sodom, it would have remained until this day. But I tell you that it shall be more tolerable on the day of judgment for the land of Sodom than for you.' "[57]

Concerning the matter of speech Jesus said: "I tell you, on the day of judgment men will render account for every careless word they utter; for by your words you will be justified, and by your words you will be condemned."[58]

In rebuking the unbelieving scribes and Pharisees Jesus declared: "The men of Nineveh will arise at the judgment with this generation and condemn it; for they repented at the preaching of Jonah, and behold, something greater than Jonah is here. The queen of the South will arise at the judgment with this generation and condemn it; for she came from the ends of the earth to hear the

54 Luke 3:17 (p. 18, Robertson's *Harmony*).   57 Matt. 11:20-24 (p. 59).
55 John 5:26-29 (p. 43).   58 Matt. 12:36, 37 (p. 62).
56 Matt. 7:21, 22 (p. 54).

wisdom of Solomon, and behold, something greater than Solomon is here."[59]

Matthew 13 contains considerable teaching in the form of parables, one of the most significant being the parable of the tares or weeds. Jesus Himself gave the following interpretation: "He who sows the good seed is the Son of man; the field is the world, and the good seed means the sons of the kingdom; the weeds are the sons of the evil one, and the enemy who sowed them is the devil; the harvest is the close of the age, and the reapers are angels. Just as the weeds are gathered and burned with fire, so will it be at the close of the age. The Son of man will send his angels, and they will gather out of his kingdom all causes of sin and all evildoers, and throw them into the furnace of fire; there men will weep and gnash their teeth. Then the righteous will shine like the sun in the kingdom of their Father. He who has ears, let him hear."[60]

In interpreting a similar parable Jesus said: "So it will be at the close of the age. The angels will come out and separate the evil from the righteous, and throw them into the furnace of fire; there men will weep and gnash their teeth."[61]

When Jesus sent out His twelve disciples on a preaching mission He stated: "And if any one will not receive you or listen to your words, shake off the dust from your feet as you leave that house or town. Truly, I say to you, it shall be more tolerable on the day of judgment for the land of Sodom and Gomorrah than for that town."[62]

In His great sermon on "The Bread of Life," Jesus stated "All that the Father gives me will come to me; and him who comes to me I will not cast out. . . . And this is the will of him who sent me, that I should lose nothing of all that he has given me, but raise it up at the last day. For this is the will of my Father, that every one who sees the Son and believes in him should have eternal life; and I will raise him up at the last day. . . . No one can come to me unless the Father who sent me draws him; and I will raise him up at the last day. . . . He who eats my flesh and drinks my blood has eternal life, and I will raise him up at the last day."[63]

In connection with making the point of what a tremendous loss it is to lose one's soul Jesus said: "For the Son of man is to come with his angels in the glory of his Father, and then he will repay every man for what he has done."[64] Mark states this truth as follows: "For whoever is ashamed of me and of my words in this adulterous

59 Matt. 12:41, 42 (p. 63).
60 Matt. 13:37-43 (p. 69).
61 Matt. 13:49, 50 (p. 70).

62 Matt. 10:14, 15 (p. 80).
63 John 6:37-40, 44, 54 (pp. 91, 92).
64 Matt. 16:27 (pp. 101, 102).)

and sinful generation, of him will the Son of man also be ashamed, when he comes in the glory of his Father with the holy angels."[65]

When Jesus sent out His seventy disciples to preach the Gospel He said: "But whenever you enter a town and they do not receive you, go into its streets and say, 'Even the dust of your town that clings to our feet, we wipe off against you; nevertheless know this, that the kingdom of God has come near.' I tell you, it shall be more tolerable on that day for Sodom than for that town."[66]

On another occasion Jesus declared: "The queen of the South will arise at the judgment with the men of this generation and condemn them; for she came from the ends of the earth to hear the wisdom of Solomon, and behold, something greater than Solomon is here. The men of Nineveh will arise at the judgment with this generation and condemn it; for they repented at the preaching of Jonah, and behold, something greater than Jonah is here."[67]

To His believing disciples our Lord gave the following instructions: "Let your loins be girded and your lamps burning, and be like men who are waiting for their master to come home from the marriage feast, so that they may open to him at once when he comes and knocks. Blessed are those servants whom the master finds awake when he comes; truly, I say to you, he will gird himself and have them sit at table, and he will come and serve them. If he comes in the second watch, or in the third, and finds them so, blessed are those servants! But know this, that if the householder had known at what hour the thief was coming, he would have been awake and would not have left his house to be broken into. You also must be ready; for the Son of man is coming at an hour you do not expect."[68]

Luke reports that when Jesus was on His way to Jerusalem, teaching in various towns and villages, someone asked Jesus, "Lord, will those who are saved be few?" Jesus replied: "Strive to enter by the narrow door; for many, I tell you, will seek to enter and will not be able. When once the householder has risen up and shut the door, you will begin to stand outside and to knock at the door, saying, 'Lord, open to us.' He will answer you, 'I do not know where you come from.' Then you will begin to say, "We ate and drank in your presence, and you taught in our streets.' But he will say, 'I tell you, I do not know where you come from; depart from me, all you workers of iniquity!' There you will weep and gnash your teeth, when you see Abraham and Isaac and Jacob and all the prophets in the kingdom of God and you yourselves thrust out. And men will come

65 Mark 8:38 (pp. 101, 102).   67 Luke 11:31, 32 (p. 124).
66 Luke 10:10-12 (p. 121); cf. 10:14.   68 Luke 12:35-40 (p. 127).

from east and west, and from north and south, and sit at table in the kingdom of God. And behold, some are last who will be first, and some are first who will be last."[69]

When Lazarus died Martha said to Jesus: " 'Lord, if you had been here, my brother would not have died. And even now I know that whatever you ask from God, God will give you.' Jesus said to her, 'Your brother will rise again.' Martha said to him, 'I know that he will rise again in the resurrection at the last day.' Jesus said to her, 'I am the resurrection and the life; he who believes in me, though he die, yet shall he live, and whoever lives and believes in me shall never die.' "[70]

In speaking of the divine rescue of the righteous and the judgment and destruction of the wicked at His return, Jesus said: "The days are coming when you will desire to see one of the days of the Son of man, and you will not see it. And they will say to you, 'Lo, there!' or 'Lo, here!' Do not go, do not follow them. For as the lightning flashes and lights up the sky from one side to the other, so will the Son of man be in his day. But first he must suffer many things and be rejected by this generation. As it was in the days of Noah, so will it be in the days of the Son of man. They ate, they drank, they married, they were given in marriage, until the day when Noah entered the ark, and the flood came and destroyed them all. Likewise as it was in the days of Lot—they ate, they drank, they bought, they sold, they planted, they built, but on the day when Lot went out from Sodom fire and brimstone rained from heaven and destroyed them all—so will it be on the day when the Son of man is revealed. On that day, let him who is on the housetop, with his goods in the house, not come down to take them away; and likewise let him who is in the field not turn back. Remember Lot's wife. Whoever seeks to gain his life will lose it, but whoever loses his life will preserve it. I tell you, in that night there will be two men in one bed; one will be taken and the other left. There will be two women grinding together; one will be taken and the other left." And they said to Him, "Where, Lord?" He said to them, "Where the body is, there the eagles will be gathered together."[71]

On another occasion Peter asked Jesus what the reward of the apostles would be for having left everything in order to follow Him. Jesus replied: "Truly, I say to you, in the new world ['the regeneration'] when the Son of man shall sit on his glorious throne, you who have followed me will also sit on twelve thrones, judging the twelve

---

69 Luke 13:23-30 (pp. 131, 132).
70 John 11:21-26 (p. 138).

71 Luke 17:22-37 (p. 140).

tribes of Israel. And every one who has left houses or brothers or sisters or father or mother or children or lands, for my name's sake, will receive a hundredfold, and inherit eternal life. But many that are first will be last, and the last first."[72]

Before giving the parable of the pounds, the Scripture says that Jesus "proceeded to tell a parable, because he was near to Jerusalem, and because they supposed that the kingdom of God was to appear immediately,"[73] the parable being the fact that the servant who received five pounds was faithful as was the one who received two; but he who received one was inactive and unfaithful. Jesus concluded the parable by saying: "I tell you, that to every one who has will more be given; but from him who has not, even what he has will be taken away. But as for these enemies of mine, who did not want me to reign over them, bring them here and slay them before me."[74]

On another occasion Jesus declared: "If any one hears my sayings and does not keep them, I do not judge him; for I did not come to judge the world but to save the world. He who rejects me and does not receive my sayings has a judge; the word that I have spoken will be his judge on the last day. For I have not spoken on my own authority . . . ."[75]

In answer to the silly story of the Sadducees who ridiculed the idea of the resurrection of the dead, Jesus replied: "The sons of this age marry and are given in marriage; but those who are accounted worthy to attain to that age and to the resurrection from the dead neither marry nor are given in marriage, for they cannot die any more, because they are equal to angels and are sons of God, being sons of the resurrection. But that the dead are raised, even Moses showed, in the passage about the bush, where he calls the Lord the God of Abraham and the God of Isaac and the God of Jacob. Now he is not God of the dead, but of the living; for all live to him."[76]

In His stern denunciation of the hypocritical scribes and Pharisees Jesus declared: "You serpents, you brood of vipers, how are you to escape being sentenced to hell?"[77]

In His great Olivet Discourse on the destruction of Jerusalem and His return at the end of the world, Jesus gave the following teachings:

And many false prophets will arise and lead many astray. And because wickedness is multiplied, most men's love will grow cold. But he who endures to the end will be saved. And this gospel of the kingdom

72 Matt. 19:28-30 (pp. 145, 146).
73 Luke 19:11 (p. 150).
74 Luke 19:26, 27 (p. 151).

75 John 12:47-49 (p. 158).
76 Luke 20:34-38 (pp. 166, 167).
77 Matt. 23:33 (p. 171).

will be preached throughout the whole world, as a testimony to all nations; and then the end will come. . . .

For as the lightning comes from the east and shines as far as the west, so will be the coming of the Son of man. Wherever the body is, there the eagles will be gathered together.

Immediately after the tribulation of those days the sun will be darkened, and the moon will not give its light, and the stars will fall from heaven, and the powers of the heavens will be shaken; then will appear the sign of the Son of man in heaven, and then all the tribes of the earth will mourn, and they will see the Son of man coming on the clouds of heaven with power and great glory; and he will send out his angels with a loud trumpet call, and they will gather his elect from the four winds, from one end of heaven to the other. . . .

But of that day and hour no one knows, not even the angels of heaven, nor the Son, but the Father only. As were the days of Noah, so will be the coming of the Son of man. . . . Watch therefore, for you do not know on what day your Lord is coming. But know this, that if the householder had known in what part of the night the thief was coming, he would have watched and would not have let his house be broken into. Therefore you also must be ready; for the Son of man is coming at an hour you do not expect.

Who then is the faithful and wise servant, whom his master has set over his household, to give them their food at the proper time? Blessed is that servant whom his master when he comes will find so doing. Truly, I say to you, he will set him over all his possessions. But if that wicked servant says to himself, "My master is delayed," and begins to beat his fellow servants, and eats and drinks with the drunken, the master of that servant will come on a day when he does not expect him and at an hour he does not know, and will punish him, and put him with the hypocrites; there men will weep and gnash their teeth.[78]

Undoubtedly all of Matthew 25 should be quoted in any study of the eschatological teaching of Christ. However, only the first and last sections of the chapter will be given here:

Then the kingdom of heaven shall be compared to ten maidens who took their lamps and went to meet the bridegroom. Five of them were foolish, and five were wise. For when the foolish took their lamps, they took no oil with them; but the wise took flasks of oil with their lamps. As the bridegroom was delayed, they all slumbered and slept. But at midnight there was a cry, "Behold, the bridegroom! Come out to meet him." Then all those maidens rose and trimmed their lamps. And the foolish said to the wise, "Give us some of your oil, for our lamps are going out." But the wise replied, "Perhaps there will not be enough for us and for you; go rather to the dealers and buy for yourselves." And while

78 Matt. 24:11-14, 27-31, 36, 37, 42-51 (pp. 176-84).

they went to buy, the bridegroom came, and those who were ready went in with him to the marriage feast; and the door was shut. Afterward the other maidens came also, saying, "Lord, lord, open to us." But he replied, "Truly, I say to you, I do not know you." Watch therefore, for you know neither the day nor the hour.[79]

When the Son of man comes in his glory, and all the angels with him, then he will sit on his glorious throne. Before him will be gathered all the nations, and he will separate them one from another as a shepherd separates the sheep from the goats, and he will place the sheep at his right hand, but the goats at the left. Then the King will say to those at his right hand, "Come, O blessed of my Father, inherit the kingdom prepared for you from the foundation of the world; for I was hungry and you gave me food, I was thirsty and you gave me drink, I was a stranger and you welcomed me, I was naked and you clothed me, I was sick and you visited me, I was in prison and you came to me." . . . Then he will say to those at his left hand, "Depart from me, you cursed, into the eternal fire prepared for the devil and his angels . . . ." And they will go away into eternal punishment, but the righteous into eternal life.[80]

At the Last Supper Jesus told the apostles: "You are those who have continued with me in my trials; as my Father appointed a kingdom for me, so do I appoint for you that you may eat and drink at my table in my kingdom, and sit on thrones judging the twelve tribes of Israel."[81]

When Jesus instituted His Supper He said: "For as often as you eat this bread and drink the cup, you proclaim the Lord's death until he comes."[82]

Before going to the Garden of Gethsemane Jesus said: "Let not your hearts be troubled; believe in God, believe also in me. In my Father's house are many rooms; if it were not so, would I have told you that I go to prepare a place for you? And when I go and prepare a place for you, I will come again and will take you to myself, that where I am you may be also."[83]

When Caiaphas who was presiding over the Sanhedrin asked Jesus whether He was the Christ, the Son of God, Jesus answered that He was, "But I tell you, hereafter you will see the Son of man seated at the right hand of Power, and coming on the clouds of heaven,"[84] an obvious allusion to Psalm 110:1 and Daniel 7:13.

Finally, just before the ascension, Jesus told His disciples: "All authority in heaven and on earth has been given to me. Go therefore and make disciples of all nations, baptizing them in the name

---

79 Matt. 25:1-13 (p. 184).
80 Matt. 25:31-46 (pp. 185, 186).
81 Luke 22:28, 29 (p. 190).

82 I Cor. 11:26 (p. 196).
83 John 14:1-3 (p. 197).
84 Matt. 26:64 (p. 211).

of the Father and of the Son and of the Holy Spirit, teaching them to observe all that I have commanded you; and lo, I am with you always, to the close of the age."[85]

The Acts

Following the ascension of our Lord two angels told the apostles: "Men of Galilee, why do you stand looking into heaven? This Jesus, who was taken up from you into heaven, will come in the same way as you saw him go into heaven."[86]

In one of his powerful evangelistic appeals to the Jews Peter said: "Repent therefore, and turn again, that your sins may be blotted out, that times of refreshing may come from the presence of the Lord, and that he may send the Christ appointed for you, Jesus, whom heaven must receive until the time for establishing [the restoration of] all that God spoke by the mouth of his holy prophets from of old."[87]

To the house of Cornelius Peter reported the commission which Christ gave to the apostles: "And he commanded us to preach to the people, and to testify that he is the one ordained by God to be judge of the living and the dead."[88]

In his sermon on Mars' Hill Paul declared that God "commands all men every where to repent, because he has fixed a day on which he will judge the world in righteousness by a man whom he has appointed, and of this he has given assurance to all men by raising him from the dead."[89]

When Paul was giving his defense before Felix he declared: "But this I admit to you, that according to the way, which they call a sect, I worship the God of our fathers, believing everything laid down by the law or written in the prophets, having a hope in God which these themselves accept, that there will be a resurrection of both the just and the unjust."[90]

The Epistles

The Letter to the Romans gives the following description of "the day of wrath when God's righteous judgment will be revealed. For he will render to every man according to his works: to those who by patience in well-doing seek for glory and honor and immortality, he will give eternal life; but for those who are factious and do not obey the truth, but obey wickedness, there will be wrath and fury. There will be tribulation and distress for every human being who

85 Matt. 28:18-20 (p. 250).   87 Acts 3:19-21.   89 Acts 17:31.
86 Acts 1:11 (p. 251).   88 Acts 10:42.   90 Acts 24:14, 15.

does evil . . . , but glory and honor and peace for every one who does good . . . . For God shows no partiality." God will judge "the secrets of men by Christ Jesus."[91]

As he looked forward to the return of Jesus and the restoration of the creation to its pristine beauty Paul wrote: "I consider that the sufferings of this present time are not worth comparing with the glory that is to be revealed to us. For the creation waits with eager longing for the revealing of the sons of God; for the creation was subjected to futility, not of its own will but by the will of him who subjected it in hope; because the creation itself will be set free from its bondage to decay and obtain the glorious liberty of the children of God. We know that the whole creation has been groaning in travail together until now; and not only the creation, but we ourselves, who have the first fruits of the Spirit, groan inwardly as we wait for adoption as sons, the redemption of our bodies."[92]

Paul also makes the following appeal to the Christians at Rome: "Why do you pass judgment on your brother? Or you, why do you despise your brother? For we shall all stand before the judgment seat of God; for it is written,

'As I live, says the Lord, every knee shall bow to me,
and every tongue shall give praise to God.'

So each of us shall give account of himself to God."[93]

In his First Letter to the Corinthians Paul speaks of the spiritual sufficiency which the Christians at Corinth have in Jesus, "So that you are not lacking in any spiritual gift, as you wait for the revealing of our Lord Jesus Christ; who will sustain you to the end, guiltless in the day of our Lord Jesus Christ."[94]

In speaking of the contribution which each believer makes to the Lord's temple Paul declared: "Each man's work will become manifest; for the Day will disclose it, because it will be revealed with fire, and the fire will test what sort of work each one has done."[95]

Paul also writes to the Corinthians in a vein similar to Romans 14: "Therefore do not pronounce judgment before the time, before the Lord comes, who will bring to light the things now hidden in darkness and will disclose the purposes of the heart. Then every man will receive his commendation from God."[96]

Concerning the open sinner in the church at Corinth Paul instructed the church, "To deliver this man to Satan for the destruction

91 Rom. 2:5-16. 93 Rom. 14:10-12. 95 I Cor. 3:13.
92 Rom. 8:18-23. 94 I Cor. 1:7, 8. 96 I Cor. 4:5.

of the flesh, that his spirit may be saved in the day of the Lord Jesus."[97]

On the subject of the resurrection from the dead Paul wrote:

But in fact Christ has been raised from the dead, the first fruits of those who have fallen asleep. For as by a man came death, by a man has come also the resurrection of the dead. For as in Adam all die, so also in Christ shall all be made alive. But each in his own order: Christ the first fruits, then at his coming those who belong to Christ. Then comes the end, when he delivers the kingdom to God the Father after destroying every rule and every authority and power. For he must reign until he has put all his enemies under his feet. The last enemy to be destroyed is death. . . . When all things are subjected to him, then the Son himself will also be subjected to him who put all things under him, that God may be everything to every one.[98]

Lo! I tell you a mystery. We shall not all sleep, but we shall all be changed, in a moment, in the twinkling of an eye, at the last trumpet. For the trumpet will sound, and the dead will be raised imperishable, and we shall be changed. For this perishable nature must put on the imperishable, and this mortal nature must put on immortality. When the perishable puts on the imperishable, and the mortal puts on immortality, then shall come to pass the saying that is written:

"Death is swallowed up in victory."
"O death, where is thy victory?
O death, where is thy sting?"[99]

In the Second Letter to the Corinthians Paul wrote: "For we write no other things unto you, than what you read or even acknowledge, and I hope you will acknowledge unto the end: as also you did acknowledge us in part, that we are your glorying even as you also are ours, in the day of our Lord Jesus Christ."[1]

In the same Letter Paul spoke of his confidence in the resurrection thus: "Knowing that he who raised the Lord Jesus will raise us also with Jesus and bring us with you into his presence."[2] And after speaking of the glorified body which each Christian shall receive Paul adds: "So we are always of good courage; we know that while we are at home in the body we are away from the Lord, for we walk by faith, not by sight. We are of good courage, and we would rather be away from the body and at home with the Lord. So whether we are at home or away, we make it our aim to please him. For we must all appear before the judgment seat of Christ, so that each one may receive good or evil, according to what he has done in the body."[3]

97 I Cor. 5:5.
98 I Cor. 15:20-28.
99 I Cor. 15:51-55.

1 II Cor. 1:13, 14 (adapted from ASV).
2 II Cor. 4:14.
3 II Cor. 5:6-10.

In the Letter to the Ephesians Paul makes the following appeal: "And do not grieve the Holy Spirit of God, in whom you were sealed for the day of redemption." [4]

In his Letter to the Philippians Paul expressed the firm confidence, "That he who began a good work in you will bring it to completion at the day of Jesus Christ. . . . And it is my prayer that your love may abound more and more, with knowledge and all discernment, so that you may approve what is excellent, and may be pure and blameless for the day of Christ."[5] And in the same Letter Paul wrote: "But our commonwealth is in heaven, and from it we await a Saviour, the Lord Jesus Christ, who will change our lowly body to be like his glorious body, by the power which enables him even to subject all things to himself."[6]

To the Christians at Colossae Paul wrote the happy assurance: "When Christ who is our life appears, then you also will appear with him in glory."[7]

Paul describes the Christians at Thessalonica as having turned to God from idols, "to serve a living and true God, and to wait for his Son from heaven, whom he raised from the dead, Jesus who delivers us from the wrath to come."[8] A little later in the same Letter Paul exclaims: "For what is our hope or joy or crown of glorying before our Lord Jesus at his coming? Is it not you? For you are our glory and joy."[9] The prayer of Paul for his readers was that God "may establish your hearts unblameable in holiness before our God and Father, at the coming of our Lord Jesus with all his saints."[10] Paul's First Letter to the Thessalonians also contains his longest discourse on the return of Christ:

But we would not have you ignorant, brethren, concerning those who are asleep, that you may not grieve as others do who have no hope. For since we believe that Jesus died and rose again, even so, through Jesus, God will bring with him those who have fallen asleep. For this we declare to you by the word of the Lord, that we who are alive, who are left until the coming of the Lord, shall not precede those who have fallen asleep. For the Lord himself will descend from heaven with a cry of command, with the archangel's call, and with the sound of the trumpet of God. And the dead in Christ will rise first; then we who are alive, who are left, shall be caught up together with them in the clouds to meet the Lord in the air; and so we shall always be with the Lord. Therefore comfort one another with these words.

4 Eph. 4:30.
5 Phil. 1:6, 9, 10.
6 Phil. 3:20, 21.
7 Col. 3:4.

8 I Thess. 1:9, 10.
9 I Thess. 2:19.
10 I Thess. 3:13.

But as to the times and the seasons, brethren, you have no need to have anything written to you. For you yourselves know well that the day of the Lord will come like a thief in the night. When people say, "There is peace and security," then sudden destruction will come upon them as travail comes upon a woman with child, and there will be no escape. But you are not in darkness, brethren, for that day to surprise you like a thief.[11]

Near the close of the Letter Paul writes: "May the God of peace himself sanctify you wholly; and may your spirit and soul and body be kept sound and blameless at the coming of our Lord Jesus Christ. He who calls you is faithful, and he will do it."[12]

In his Second Letter to the Thessalonians Paul writes concerning the time "when the Lord Jesus is revealed from heaven with his mighty angels in flaming fire, inflicting vengeance upon those who do not know God and upon those who do not obey the gospel of our Lord Jesus. They shall suffer the punishment of eternal destruction and exclusion from the presence of the Lord and from the glory of his might, when he comes on that day to be glorified in his saints, and to be marveled at in all who have believed, because our testimony to you was believed."[13]

The Second Letter to the Thessalonians also contains the longest section in the epistles on the antichrist:

Now concerning the coming of our Lord Jesus Christ and our assembling to meet him, we beg you, brethren, not to be quickly shaken in mind or excited, either by spirit or by word, or by letter purporting to be from us, to the effect that the day of the Lord has come. Let no one deceive you in any way; for that day will not come, unless the rebellion comes first, and the man of lawlessness is revealed, the son of perdition, who opposes and exalts himself against every so-called god or object of worship, so that he takes his seat in the temple of God, proclaiming himself to be God. Do you not remember that when I was still with you I told you this? And you know what is restraining him now so that he may be revealed in his time. For the mystery of lawlessness is already at work; only he who now restrains it will do so until he is out of the way. And then the lawless one will be revealed, and the Lord Jesus will slay him with the breath of his mouth and destroy him by his appearing and his coming. The coming of the lawless one by the activity of Satan will be with all power and with pretended signs and wonders, and with all wicked deception for those who are to perish, because they refused to love the truth and so be saved.[14]

In his First Letter to Timothy Paul gave Timothy the following

---

11 I Thess. 4:13—5:5.
12 I Thess. 5:23.

13 II Thess. 1:7-10.
14 II Thess. 2:1-10.

charge: "To keep the commandment unstained and free from reproach until the appearing of our Lord Jesus Christ; and this will be made manifest at the proper time by the blessed and only Sovereign, the King of kings and Lord of lords, who alone has immortality and dwells in unapproachable light. . . ."[15]

In his Second Letter to Timothy Paul makes mention of the courage and kindness of Onesiphorus, adding: "May the Lord grant him to find mercy from the Lord on that Day."[16] Paul also renewed his charge to Timothy: "I charge you in the presence of God and of Christ Jesus who is to judge the living and the dead, and by his appearing and his kingdom: preach the word, be urgent in season and out of season, convince, rebuke, and exhort, be unfailing in patience and in teaching. . . .

"For I am already on the point of being sacrificed; the time of my departure has come. I have fought the good fight, I have finished the race, I have kept the faith. Henceforth there is laid up for me the crown of righteousness, which the Lord, the righteous judge, will award to me on that Day, and not only to me but also to all who have loved his appearing."[17]

In his Letter to Titus Paul speaks of the grace of God teaching us "to renounce irreligion and worldly passions, and to live sober, upright, and godly lives in this world, awaiting our blessed hope, the appearing of the glory of our great God and Saviour Jesus Christ, who gave himself for us to redeem us from all iniquity and to purify for himself a people of his own who are zealous for good deeds."[18]

The Letter to the Hebrews states that Christ "has appeared once for all at the end of the age to put away sin by the sacrifice of himself. And just as it is appointed for men to die once, and after that comes judgment, so Christ, having been offered once to bear the sins of many, will appear a second time, not to deal with sin but to save those who are eagerly waiting for him."[19] He also wrote of "the Day drawing near."[20]

James exhorts his readers thus: "Be patient, therefore, brethren, until the coming of the Lord. Behold, the farmer waits for the precious fruit of the earth, being patient over it until it receives the early and the late rain. You also be patient. Establish your hearts, for the coming of the Lord is at hand. Do not grumble, brethren, against one another, that you may not be judged; behold, the Judge is standing at the doors."[21]

15 I Tim. 6:14-16.
16 II Tim. 1:18.
17 II Tim. 4:1, 2, 6-8.
18 Titus 2:12-14.

19 Heb. 9:26-28.
20 Heb. 10:25.
21 Jas. 5:7-9.

In his First Letter Peter describes Christians as being guarded by God's power "through faith for a salvation ready to be revealed in the last time. In this you rejoice, though now for a little while you may have to suffer various trials, so that the genuineness of your faith, more precious than gold which though perishable is tested by fire, may redound to praise and glory and honor at the revelation of Jesus Christ. . . . Therefore gird up your minds, be sober, set your hope fully upon the grace that is coming to you at the revelation of Jesus Christ."[22]

In reference to the wicked Peter states: "But they will give account to him who is ready to judge the living and the dead. . . .

"The end of all things is at hand; therefore keep sane and sober for your prayers."[23]

"Beloved, do not be surprised at the fiery ordeal which comes upon you to prove you, as though something strange were happening to you. But rejoice in so far as you share Christ's sufferings, that you may also rejoice and be glad when his glory is revealed."[24]

To the elders Peter wrote: "And when the chief Shepherd is manifested you will obtain the unfading crown of glory."[25]

The Second Letter of Peter states: "And we have the prophetic word made more sure. You will do well to pay attention to this as to a lamp shining in a dark place, until the day dawns and the morning star rises in your hearts,"[26] and by way of assuring his readers of God's keeping power: "For if God did not spare the angels when they sinned, but cast them into hell and committed them to pits of nether gloom to be kept until the judgment; if he did not spare the ancient world, but preserved Noah, a herald of righteousness, with seven other persons, when he brought a flood upon the world of the ungodly . . . then the Lord knows how to rescue the godly from trial, and to keep the unrighteous under punishment until the day of judgment."[27] Concerning the return of Christ Peter's Second Letter states:

First of all you must understand this, that scoffers will come in the last days with scoffing, following their own passions and saying, "Where is the promise of his coming? For ever since the fathers fell asleep, all things have continued as they were from the beginning of creation." They deliberately ignore this fact, that by the word of God heavens existed long ago, and an earth formed out of water and by means of water, through which the world that then existed was deluged with water and perished. But by the same word the heavens and earth that now

22 I Pet. 1:5-7, 13.   24 I Pet. 4:12, 13.   26 II Pet. 1:19.
23 I Pet. 4:5, 7.   25 I Pet. 5:4.   27 II Pet. 2:4, 5, 9.

exist have been stored up for fire, being kept until the day of judgment and destruction of ungodly men.

But do not ignore this one fact, beloved, that with the Lord one day is as a thousand years, and a thousand years as one day. The Lord is not slow about his promise as some count slowness, but is forbearing toward you, not wishing that any should perish, but that all should reach repentance. But the day of the Lord will come like a thief, and then the heavens will pass away with a loud noise, and the elements will be dissolved with fire, and the earth and the works that are upon it will be burned up.

Since all these things are thus to be dissolved, what sort of persons ought you to be in lives of holiness and godliness, waiting for and hastening the coming of the day of God, because of which the heavens will be kindled and dissolved, and the elements will melt with fire! But according to his promise we wait for new heavens and a new earth in which righteousness dwells.[28]

In his First Letter John writes: "And now, little children, abide in him, so that when he appears we may have confidence and not shrink from him in shame at his coming. . . . Beloved, we are God's children now; it does not yet appear what we shall be, but we know that when he appears we shall be like him, for we shall see him as he is. And every one who thus hopes in him purifies himself as he is pure."[29]

John also writes: "God is love, and he who abides in love abides in God, and God abides in him. In this is love perfected with us, that we may have confidence for the day of judgment, because as he is so are we in this world."[30]

Concerning the wicked Jude writes: "It was of these also that Enoch in the seventh generation from Adam prophesied, saying, 'Behold, the Lord came with his holy myriads, to execute judgment on all, and to convict all the ungodly of all their deeds of ungodliness which they have committed in such an ungodly way, and of all the harsh things which ungodly sinners have spoken against him.' "[31]

The Revelation

The Book of Revelation is devoted largely to events associated with the return of Christ; more particularly, to the intense struggle between the forces of God and those of Satan just prior to the end of the world. Revelation was evidently written to assure the church during persecution that God's cause will yet triumph on earth.

28 II Pet. 3:3-13.
29 I John 2:28; 3:2, 3.
30 I John 4:16, 17.
31 Jude 14, 15.

Certain references to the coming of Jesus in the Book of Revelation are somewhat obscure in that it is difficult to know whether the Lord means that He will visit judgment upon a given church, or whether the reference is to His personal second coming at the end of time. Examples of these references to a coming in judgment to a given church are Revelation 2:5, "Remember then from what you have fallen, repent and do the works you did at first. If not, I will come to you and remove your lampstand from its place, unless you repent"; and 2:16: "Repent then. If not, I will come to you soon and war against them with the sword of my mouth."

One of the most striking references to the coming of Jesus is this: "Behold, he is coming with the clouds, and every eye will see him, every one who pierced him; and all tribes of the earth will wail on account of him. Even so. Amen."[32]

To the church at Thyatira Jesus declared: "Only hold fast what you have, until I come."[33] And to the church at Philadelphia: "I am coming soon; hold fast what you have, so that no one may seize your crown."[34]

The following quotation, although not referring explicitly to the return of Christ, seems nevertheless to be a description of it:

Then I looked, and lo, a white cloud, and seated on the cloud one like a son of man, with a golden crown on his head, and a sharp sickle in his hand. And another angel came out of the temple, calling with a loud voice to him who sat upon the cloud, "Put in your sickle, and reap, for the hour to reap has come, for the harvest of the earth is fully ripe." So he who sat upon the cloud swung his sickle on the earth, and the earth was reaped.

And another angel came out of the temple in heaven, and he too had a sharp sickle. Then another angel came out from the altar, the angel who has power over fire, and he called with a loud voice to him who had the sharp sickle, "Put in your sickle, and gather the clusters of the vine of the earth, for its grapes are ripe." So the angel swung his sickle on the earth and gathered the vintage of the earth, and threw it into the great wine press of the wrath of God; and the wine press was trodden outside the city . . . .[35]

In the midst of an awful description of the gathering of the forces of evil at Armageddon,[36] Jesus suddenly interrupts to say: "Lo, I am coming like a thief: Blessed is he who is awake, keeping his garments . . . ."[37]

32 Rev. 1:7.
33 Rev. 2:25.
34 Rev. 3:11.
35 Rev. 14:14-20.
36 Armageddon is the Mt. Megiddo of the Old Testament.
37 Rev. 16:15.

In one of the many passages of Scripture that refer to the church as a bride, the Revelation looks forward to the victorious union of the bride of Christ with her Lord in heaven:

After this I heard what seemed to be the mighty voice of a great multitude in heaven, crying,
"Hallelujah! Salvation and glory and power belong to our God, for his judgments are true and just;
he has judged the great harlot who corrupted the earth with her fornication,
and he has avenged on her the blood of his servants."
Once more they cried,
"Hallelujah! The smoke from her goes up for ever and ever." And the twenty-four elders and the four living creatures fell down and worshiped God who is seated on the throne, saying, "Amen. Hallelujah!" And from the throne came a voice crying,
"Praise our God, all you his servants,
you who fear him, small and great."
Then I heard what seemed to be the voice of a great multitude, like the sound of many waters and like the sound of mighty thunderpeals, crying,
"Hallelujah! For the Lord our God the Almighty reigns.
Let us rejoice and exult and give him the glory,
for the marriage of the Lamb has come,
and his Bride has made herself ready;
it was granted her to be clothed with fine linen, bright and pure"—
for the fine linen is the righteous deeds of the saints.

And the angel said to me, "Write this: Blessed are those who are invited to the marriage supper of the Lamb." And he said to me, "These are true words of God."[38]

In Revelation 20, following the binding of Satan, the reign of the martyrs with Christ for a thousand years, and the final judgment of Satan, John presents the following vision of the judgment of men:

Then I saw a great white throne and him who sat upon it; from his presence earth and sky fled away, and no place was found for them. And I saw the dead, great and small, standing before the throne, and books were opened. Also another book was opened, which is the book of life. And the dead were judged by what was written in the books, by what they had done. And the sea gave up the dead in it, Death and Hades gave up the dead in them, and all were judged by what they had done. Then Death and Hades were thrown into the lake of fire. This

---

38 Rev. 19:1-9.

is the second death, the lake of fire; and if any one's name was not found written in the book of life, he was thrown into the lake of fire.[39]

One of the last things in the Revelation is the message of Christ: "And, behold, I am coming soon";[40] and again: "He who testifies to these things says, 'Surely I am coming soon.' "[41]

The response of John was: "Amen. Come, Lord Jesus!"[42]

Eschatological Terminology

Eight main expressions or groups of terms are used in the New Testament to refer to the return of Jesus.

1. The first of these relates to the term *day* which is used in a variety of combinations such as the following: the day of the Lord (I Thessalonians 5:2; II Peter 3:10; II Thessalonians 2:2); the day of our Lord Jesus Christ (I Corinthians 1:8); the day of the Lord Jesus (II Corinthians 1:14); the day of Jesus Christ (Philippians 1:6); the day of Christ (Philippians 1:10; 2:16); the day when the Son of man is revealed (Luke 17:30); the Son of man in His day (Luke 17:24); the day of God (II Peter 3:12); the day when God shall judge . . . by Jesus Christ (Romans 2:16; cf. Acts 17:31); the day of judgment (Matthew 10:15; 11:22, 24; 12:36, 41, 42; II Peter 2:9; 3:7; I John 4:17); the judgment of the great day (Jude 6); the great day of God the Almighty (Revelation 16:14); the day of wrath and revelation (Romans 2:5); the great day of their wrath (Revelation 6:17); the day of visitation (I Peter 2:12); the day of redemption (Ephesians 4:30); the last day (John 6:39, 40, 44, 54; 11:24; 12:48); that day (Matthew 7:22; 24:36; Mark 13:32; Luke 10:12; 17:31; 21:34; II Thessalonians 1:10; II Timothy 1:12, 18; 4:8); the day (Matthew 25:13; Romans 13:12; I Corinthians 3:13; I Thessalonians 5:4; Hebrews 10:25; II Peter 1:19).

The expression, *day of the Lord*, originated in the Old Testament. The emphasis implied in the term seems to be the fact that Christ is coming as judge and as Saviour of the church. The term "day" is used about fifty times in the New Testament to refer to the coming of Jesus.

2. The New Testament also speaks frequently of the return of Christ using the verb, *to come*, although the expression "second coming" is not found in the New Testament. The verb, to come, is used of the coming of Christ about three dozen times; the emphasis seems to lie on the personal character of His return. Some of the

39 Rev. 20:11-15.
40 Rev. 22:7.
41 Rev. 22:20.
42 Rev. 22:20.

references which refer to the fact that Christ will come are: Matthew 16:27, 28; 24:30, 42, 44; 25:31; 26:64; Mark 8:38; 13:26, 36; 14:62; Luke 9:26; 12:37, 40; 18:8; 21:27; John 14:3, 18; I Corinthians 11:26; II Thessalonians 1:10; Hebrews 10:37; Jude 14; Revelation 1:5; 3:11; 4:8; 16:15; 22:7, 12, 20.

3. The New Testament also employs a Greek word *Parousia,* which is translated *Coming.* This term seems to refer to the majesty in which Jesus shall return. It is used about seventeen times in the New Testament: Matthew 24:3, 27, 37, 39; I Corinthians 15:23; I Thessalonians 2:19; 3:13; 4:15; 5:23; II Thessalonians 2:1, 8; James 5:7, 8; II Peter 1:16; 3:4, 12; I John 2:28.

4. Nine times the New Testament uses a Greek word *Telos* which is translated *end.* The word itself seems to refer to a termination, to an end point. It is used of the return of Christ in Matthew 10:22; 24:6, 14; Mark 13:7, 13; Luke 21:9; I Corinthians 1:8; 15:24, and I Peter 4:7.

5. The New Testament also uses a Greek word *Sunteleia,* which is translated *end* but which really signifies a consummation, a drawing together, a final conclusion. It is used in the following six places of the return of Christ: Matthew 13:39, 40, 49; 24:3; 28:20, and Hebrews 9:26.

6. Five times the New Testament uses the Greek word *Apokalupsis* which is translated *revelation* or unveiling. The emphasis seems to lie on the majesty and glory in which Jesus shall come: I Corinthians 1:7; II Thessalonians 1:7; I Peter 1:7, 13; 4:13.

7. Five times also the New Testament uses the Greek word *Epiphaneia* which is translated *appearing.* The term seems to refer to the dignity and splendor in which Jesus shall come: II Thessalonians 2:8; I Timothy 6:14; II Timothy 4:1, 8; Titus 2:13.

8. The New Testament also employs the verb *Phaneroō,* which is translated *to be manifested.* The emphasis seems to be on the open display of Christ's glory at His return: Colossians 3:4; I Peter 5:4; I John 2:28; 3:2.

An examination of the references which employ these eight different terms referring to Christ's return will reveal the fact that they seem to be frequently used more or less interchangeably. In Matthew 24, for example, the apostles asked Jesus about His *Parousia* and the *Consummation* of the world; in verse six Jesus said that the end *(Telos)* is not yet; in verse 14 Jesus said, "Then comes the end" *(Telos),* in verse 27 Jesus again speaks of His *Parousia,* and in verse 30 He says they will see the Son of man *coming* on the clouds of heaven; in verse 36 Jesus speaks of *that day,* and in verse 44 He says:

"The Son of man is *coming* at an hour you do not expect." In other words, in this discourse one finds the terms *Parousia, Telos, Consummation,* and the verb, *to come,* used more or less interchangeably. Similarly, in I Corinthians 1:7, 8, the terms, *revelation* and end *(Telos),* are used interchangeably; in I Thessalonians 4:13—5:4 the terms *Parousia* and *Day of the Lord* are used interchangeably; in II Thessalonians Paul uses *revelation, Parousia, Day of the Lord,* etc. In II Peter 3 one also finds a variety of terms used interchangeably of the return of Christ.

3. *MILLENNIAL THEORIES*

Premillennialism

At various times in the history of the Christian Church, as early as the second century, and rather widespreadly in the nineteenth and twentieth centuries, the view has been held that prior to the final resurrection of the (wicked) dead Christ will reign on earth for a thousand years with His saints. The basis for this view is Revelation 20:1-10:

Then I saw an angel coming down from heaven, holding in his hand the key of the bottomless pit and a great chain. And he seized the dragon, that ancient serpent, who is the Devil and Satan, and bound him for a thousand years, and threw him into the pit, and shut it and sealed it over him, that he should deceive the nations no more, till the thousand years were ended. After that he must be loosed for a little while.

Then I saw thrones, and seated on them were those to whom judgment was committed. Also I saw the souls of those who had been beheaded for their testimony to Jesus and for the word of God, and who had not worshiped the beast or its image and had not received its mark on their foreheads or their hands. They came to life again, and reigned with Christ a thousand years. The rest of the dead did not come to life again until the thousand years were ended. This is the first resurrection. Blessed and holy is he who shares in the first resurrection! Over such the second death has no power, but they shall be priests of God and of Christ, and they shall reign with him a thousand years.

And when the thousand years are ended, Satan will be loosed from his prison and will come out to deceive the nations which are at the four corners of the earth, that is, Gog and Magog, to gather them for battle; their number is like the sand of the sea. And they marched up over the broad earth and surrounded the camp of the saints and the beloved city; but fire came down from heaven and consumed them, and the devil who had deceived them was thrown into the lake of fire and brimstone where the beast and the false prophet were, and they will be tormented day and night for ever and ever.

Those who hold to the premillennial interpretation of prophecy also regard many other passages in the Scriptures as referring to this "golden age" in the history of the church on earth. Among the statements of Jesus which are held to apply to this period are the following: "And the angel said to her, 'Do not be afraid, Mary, for you have found favor with God. And behold, you will conceive in your womb and bear a son, and you shall call his name Jesus.

> He will be great, and will be called the Son of the Most High; and the Lord God will give to him the throne of his father David, and he will reign over the house of Jacob for ever; and of his king-dom there will be no end.' "[43]

Furthermore Jesus Himself promised: "Truly, I say to you, in the new world, when the Son of man shall sit on his glorious throne, you who have followed me will also sit on twelve thrones, judging the twelve tribes of Israel."[44] Also, "You are those who have continued with me in my trials; as my Father appointed a kingdom for me, so do I appoint for you that you may eat and drink at my table in my kingdom, and sit on thrones judging the twelve tribes of Israel."[45] It is also pointed out that Jesus did not argue against the funda-mental assumption of the apostles when they asked Him: "Lord, will you at this time restore the kingdom to Israel?"[46] Finally, we have the promises of Jesus in the Revelation: "He who conquers and who keeps my works until the end, I will give him power over the nations, and he shall rule them with a rod of iron, as when earthen pots are broken in pieces, even as I myself have received power from my Father"[47]; also, "He who conquers, I will grant him to sit with me on my throne, as I myself conquered and sat down with my Fa-ther on his throne."[48] It should also be stated that many passages from the Old Testament are also fitted into the premillennial un-derstanding of prophecy.

Typical of the Chiliasm in the second century are the views of Irenaeus who became a bishop in Gaul in A.D. 177 and who evident-ly died around 200. Irenaeus believed that (1) the world would last six thousand years; he based this view on his understanding of Psalm 90:4; II Peter 3:8, and Hebrews 4:9. (2) Near the end of the present world the antichrist will appear. (3) Christ will appear in glory and triumph over His enemies. (4) Christ will then reign as

43 Luke 1:30-33.
44 Matt. 19:28.
45 Luke 22:28-30.
46 Acts 1:6.
47 Rev. 2:26, 27.
48 Rev. 3:21.

king on earth for one thousand years. (5) Jerusalem will be rebuilt and the earth will become very fruitful. (6) Peace and righteousness will prevail during the millennial reign of Christ. (7) Following the millennial kingdom of Christ the final judgment will be held and the new creation will follow. It is said that the Chiliasm of Irenaeus was not Jewish in character; that is, he had no emphasis on the Jews displacing the church as the people of God, nor on the observance of Jewish feasts, temple worship, observance of the Jewish holy year, etc.

In the ancient church the chief adherents of Chiliasm were Papias, who lived in the first half of the second century; Tertullian (c. 160-c. 230); Barnabas, who wrote somewhere between A.D. 70 and 150; Justin Martyr (c. 100-c. 165); Irenaeus (c. 130-c. 200); Hippolytus of the early third century; Montanus, who flourished the middle of the second century; Cyprian (martyred at Carthage in A.D. 258); Lactantius (c. 260-c. 325); Commodianus of the early fourth century; Victorinus, who was martyred in A.D. 304; Apollinaris (c. 310-c. 392); Cerinthus of the first century, and whose followers were called Cerinthians.[49]

In more modern times the chief adherents of Chiliasm, now commonly called premillennialism, have been the German Pietists, Philip Jacob Spener (1635-1705) and J. A. Bengel (1687-1752); Ann Lee (1736-84) and her English Shakers; Edward Irving (1792-1834) and his "Irvingite" followers; John Nelson Darby (1800-82) and his so-called Plymouth Brethren; William Miller (1782-1849), prominent leader of the Adventist bodies; Johann Heinrich Jung, commonly called Jung-Stilling (1740-1817), the German mystic; Karl A. Auberlen (1824-64), of Basel; August Hahn (1792-1863); Rudolf E. Stier (1800-62); Ludwig Ross (1806-59); Friedrich S. Oetinger (1702-82); Richard Rothe (1799-1867); Johann Peter Lange (1802-84), the Bible commentator; Johann C. K. von Hofmann (1810-77); the prominent commentators Franz Delitzsch (1813-90) and Heinrich A. W. Meyer (1800-73); Dean Henry Alford (1810-71); Robert Jamieson (1802-80), the commentator; Charles H. Spurgeon (1834-92), the English Baptist preacher; D. L. Moody (1837-99); and C. I. Scofield (1843-1921), author of the famous *Scofield Reference Bible*, 1909. The famous Prophetic Bible Conferences of the last seventy-five years have also promoted premillennialism, as well as the various Bible schools of North America, such as Moody Bible Institute and the Bible Institute of Los Angeles.

---

49 Note Menno Simons' sharp words about the Chiliasm of the Cerinthians, *Complete Works*, I, p. 82.

According to premillennialism the prophetic order of events will be as follows: (1) the resurrection of the saints at Christ's "Rapture" (I Thessalonians 4:14-18); (2) the return of the Jews to Palestine (Ezekiel 37:21-28); (3) the tribulation period under the antichrist (II Thessalonians 2:3; Revelation 7:14); (4) the "Revelation" of Christ and the judgment of the living nations (I Thessalonians 3:13; Matthew 25:31-46); (5) the resurrection of the tribulation saints (Revelation 6:11); (6) the millennial reign of Christ followed by the "little season" (Revelation 20:1-10); (7) the battle of Armageddon (Revelation 16:16; 20:7-10)[50]; (8) the resurrection of the wicked dead (Revelation 20:5); (9) the judgment of the great white throne (Revelation 20:11-15); and (10) the eternal states, heaven and hell (Matthew 25:46; Revelation 20:14, 15).

Those who do not accept the premillennial view charge the Chiliast with approaching the bulk of the New Testament eschatological sections and references with a system of interpretation based too largely on the visions of Daniel, the Book of Revelation, and other figurative passages. Those who are not premillennial hold that the Gospels and the Epistles consistently represent the hope, the reward, and the inheritance of the saints as being eternal in heaven, not in an earthly and temporal kingdom. They believe also that the Gospels and Epistles present the *Parousia* of Christ as ushering in the eternal state with a universal resurrection and judgment. Those who reject premillennialism believe that Chiliasm finds more support in the Jewish apocalypses than in the canonical Scriptures.[51] They believe further that the Book of Revelation is too figurative and symbolic to erect from it a system of interpretation which they think conflicts with the plain, didactic, and literal portions of the New Testament. Another factor which puzzles those who are not premillennial in their thinking is that the millennial reign of Christ is supposed to include glorified saints who have been in heaven during the seven-year tribulation period and who have again returned to a world of sin and death, as well as unconverted Jews, and Christians who will be offering animal sacrifices, keeping Jewish feasts and sabbaths, etc., as though Christianity had not displaced Judaism!

Inasmuch, however, as premillennialism has been held by such Christian leaders as Justin, Tertullian, and Irenaeus, as well as many

50 Often the battle of Armageddon is placed immediately after the "Revelation" of Christ which is to take place after the "tribulation period" (*Scofield Reference Bible*, pp. 1348, 1349).

51 Papias actually quoted the apocryphal book of Baruch (29:1-8) in support of his Chiliasm. Cf. Ira D. Landis, *The Faith of Our Fathers on Eschatology* (Lititz, Pa.: Published by the author, 1946), pp. 31, 32, 371, etc.; also D. H. Kromminga, *The Millennium in the Church* (Grand Rapids, Mich.: Eerdmans, 1945), pp. 54, 55; William H. Rutgers, *Premillennialism in America* (Goes, Holland: Oosterbaan & Le Cointre, n.d. but about 1930), pp. 56, 57.

nineteenth-century exegetes, even those who reject Chiliasm must respect their premillennial brethren, recognize them as sincere, and grant them the full right to believe and teach the prophetic Word as they understand it.

Dispensationalism

Dispensationalism arose in Ireland in 1825, but by 1832 the chief center of the movement had become Plymouth in England.[52] The "Brethren" who held to the philosophy of history known as Dispensationalism therefore came to be nicknamed "Plymouth Brethren." The chief founder of the movement seems to have been Edward Cronin, who was a minister in Dublin, Ireland, but the main promoter was John Nelson Darby (1800-82), who was active both in England and on the continent. According to dispensationalism redemptive history is divided into seven dispensations in each of which God deals with man on different terms, and each of which ends in human failure and divine judgment. These dispensations are carefully delineated in the *Scofield Reference Bible*.[53]

One of the distinctive positions of Dispensationalism is the postponement theory: the concept that Jesus first offered the kingdom to the Jews but when they rejected Him He postponed His Jewish kingdom until the millennial reign[54] and inserted in its place for the present the church, an institution which had not been foreseen by the Old Testament prophets.[55] Dispensationalism therefore holds that the church is not in Old Testament prophecy, is not obligated to keep "kingdom ethics,"[56] that the church age will end in failure and judgment just as all the other dispensations have[57]; and that the church will necessarily give way and be displaced by the Jewish kingdom after the "revelation" of Christ at the end of the tribulation period.

Dispensationalism teaches that the Jews will be converted *en masse* at the sight of Christ at His "revelation," apart from the work of the church and the Holy Spirit.[58] The Jewish kingdom of the millennium will be established by "power not persuasion."[59] During the millennium the Jews will lead the nations, the Gentiles will keep the Jewish feasts, Jewish sacrifices and temple worship will be

52 H. A. Ironside, *A Historical Sketch of the Brethren Movement* (Grand Rapids, Mich.: Zondervan Publishing House, 1942), *passim*.
53 See pp. 5, 10, 16, 20, 94, 1115, 1250.
54 *Scofield Reference Bible*, pp. 723, 998, etc.
55 *Ibid.*, pp. 982, 1015, 1252, etc.
56 *Ibid.*, pp. 990, 999, 1000, 1089, 1090.
57 *Ibid.*, pp. 115, 1276.
58 *Ibid.*, pp. 976-78; cf. 1205, 1337.
59 *Ibid.*, p. 977.

reconstituted, and the Jewish sabbath will once more be observed; in other words, the millennial reign is strongly Jewish in character, according to Dispensationalism.[60] Old Testament prophecies such as Isaiah 11 and 35 are regarded as descriptions of the glorious condition of nature during Christ's millennial reign with the Jews. Scofield holds that only in the writings of Paul can one find the "doctrine, position, walk, and destiny" of the church.[61]

Whatever else may be said about Dispensationalism, it is obviously not the teaching of the Bible itself, but a strange system of interpretation superimposed upon the Scriptures. Among the objections to Dispensationalism may be mentioned the following: (1) According to Scripture there is but one means of salvation all through history: personal faith in God. Romans 4 seems to teach this principle with great clarity, although the rest of the New Testament assumes the same position. (2) There are but two major covenants, the Old and the New, separated by the death of Jesus, although there were preparatory stages to the Old Covenant. According to Scofield, however, there are seven dispensations, seven judgments, eight covenants, four forms of the Gospel, etc., etc. (3) The ethics of the Bible are basically uniform, although more clearly and fully revealed in the New Testament than in the Old. New Testament writers base their teaching squarely on the Old Testament. It is not the case that God's standards and requirements vary from each age to the next, nor does the Scripture divide human history into seven "dispensations." (4) The cross of Jesus, far from being a calamity due merely to Jewish unbelief, was the pre-determined end of Jesus, prophesied in the Old Testament, taught consistently by Christ Himself; the divinely provided and eternal sacrifice for human sin. (5) The church is, according to the New Testament, the final goal of God's redemptive work in the world. It is no mere parenthesis between a supposed rejection of the kingdom offered by Jesus and a future Jewish kingdom. (As a matter of fact, the Gospels teach that it was Jesus who rejected the intention of the Jews to make Him an earthly king.)[62] (6) There is no salvation apart from the word of the cross as proclaimed by the church before the second coming of Christ. Now is the day of salvation. The return of Jesus will close the offer of salvation through the Gospel. (7) Judaism as a religious system was merely preparatory in character and will never displace its fulfillment, Christianity. Anyone who has read the Letter to the Gala-

60 *Ibid.*, pp. 714, 725, 747, 890, 922, 956, 963, 1011, 1150, 1343, etc.
61 *Ibid.*, p. 1252.
62 John 6:15.

tians as well as the Hebrew Letter should fully understand this great truth. (8) The apostles, after Pentecost, betray no interest in a Jewish and earthly kingdom and in the fulfillment of so-called "unfulfilled prophecy," except the return of Jesus.

In the judgment of the present writer Dispensationalism is a serious departure from Biblical truth, an unsound system of interpretation, a depreciation of the church of Christ as an institution of God, a low view of the competence of the Old Testament prophets to predict the future through Holy Spirit inspiration, an undue emphasis on the primacy of the Jews in the program of God, a misunderstanding of the relationship of Judaism to Christianity, and a fanciful system of interpretation in general. It is probably only a matter of time until Christian theologians will have been able to overcome this fanciful and unscriptural system of interpretation.

Postmillennialism

The present discussion will ignore those liberal and unsound types of postmillennialism which do not acknowledge the truth of regeneration, its need and its reality, and which hold an unscriptural view of man's natural goodness, together with the possibility of creating millennial conditions on earth through education and culture. Many Christians do not seem to be aware, however, that originally postmillennialism, when it appeared in the seventeenth century in Lutheran and Reformed circles, was an evangelical movement. Evangelical postmillennialism rejected the concept of a visible reign of Christ on earth for a thousand years, but held that before the return of Jesus, and before the end of the world, there would be an era of great prosperity for the church (not for the Jews). It was held that peace and righteousness would prevail on earth through the spread of the church and the effective ministry of the Gospel and the blessed work of the Holy Spirit. The era of prosperity thus anticipated was held to be the fulfillment of the thousand-year reign of Revelation 20.

In the last seventy-five years the modern liberal brand of postmillennialism arose which held that through human effort a new social order, glorious in character, will be created. Therefore it is the task of the Christian Church to preach a "social gospel."[63]

Returning to the evangelical postmillennialists one may mention such scholars as the following: Daniel Whitby (1638-1726), an English divine; Campegius Vitringa (1659-1722), a Dutch theologian; George Stanley Faber (1773-1854), an Anglican theologian;

---

63 See W. Rauschenbusch, *A Theology for the Social Gospel* (New York: Macmillan, 1918).

Charles Hodge (1797-1878), the great theologian of Princeton Seminary; David Brown (1803-97), the Scotch professor and Bible commentator; Patrick Fairbairn (1805-74), the Scotch nonconformist; Benjamin B. Warfield (1851-1921), one of the outstanding theologians of the entire English-speaking world, who served long at Princeton Seminary; and Richard Watson (1781-1833), the Methodist theologian.

By way of critique of evangelical postmillennialism, one may say that the New Testament does not seem to anticipate any such golden age as the above evangelical writers looked for. On the contrary, the New Testament represents the church as a body of pilgrims, apparently always more or less a minority in the world; at least they dwell in the midst of a more or less hostile world. It is true that the New Testament does promise great growth for the kingdom of Christ; on the other hand, it also anticipates that evil men will "wax worse and worse."[64] In the judgment of the present writer the postmillennial viewpoint cannot be harmonized with divine revelation. Nevertheless, it would not seem to be just to accuse such outstanding evangelical scholars as Charles Hodge and B. B. Warfield with being "unsound." The evangelical postmillennial view should be rejected as not in harmony with the New Testament, but in no sense should it be considered a heresy.

Amillennialism

Amillennialism, as it is now called, is the view which has been held by many leaders in the Christian Church from the second century until the present. It is a rejection of both premillennialism and postmillennialism, denying that there will be any golden age for the church prior to the return of Jesus, and rejecting also the view that Christ will reign on earth as a political king for one thousand years after His return. This was the view of Gaius or Caius of the early third century, of Origen (c. 185-c. 254), of Jerome (c. 340-420), of Clement of Alexandria (c. 150-c. 220), and of the great Augustine (354-430).

What is now called amillennialism is also the view of the historic creeds of the Christian Church. The so-called Apostles' Creed says that Jesus "ascended into heaven, and sitteth at the right hand of the Father; from thence He shall come to judge the quick and the dead."[65] The Nicaeno-Constantinopolitan Creed of A.D. 381 says

---

64 II Tim. 3:13.

65 Philip Schaff, *The Creeds of Christendom* (New York: Harper & Brothers, 1877, 1919), II, p. 48.

that Jesus "ascended into heaven, and sitteth on the right hand of the Father; and He shall come again, with glory, to judge both the quick and the dead; whose kingdom shall have no end."[66] The so-called Athanasian Creed states that Jesus "ascended into heaven, He sitteth on the right hand of the Father God almighty. From whence He shall come to judge the quick and the dead. At whose coming all men shall rise again with their bodies; and shall give account for their own works. And they that have done good shall go into life everlasting: and they that have done evil, into everlasting fire."[67]

All the major leaders of the Swiss Brethren, the Hutterian Brethren, and the Dutch Mennonites were amillennial in faith.[68] Menno Simons explicitly rejected Chiliasm.[69] All the Mennonite confessions of faith are amillennial: Schleitheim (1527), Twisck (1617), the Dutch Mennonite Deposition of 1626, the Olive Branch (1627), Jan Cents (1630), Dordrecht (1632), Ris (1766), etc.

Amillennialism was also the view of such recent leaders in the Mennonite Church as: John F. Funk (1835-1930), John S. Coffman (1848-99), Daniel Kauffman (1865-1944), John Horsch (1867-1941), Andrew S. Mack (1836-1917), Abner G. Yoder (1879-1942), and E. L. Frey (1856-1942). On the other hand, the following outstanding leaders in the Mennonite Church were premillennial: A. D. Wenger (1867-1935), Aaron Loucks (1864-1945), E. J. Berkey (1874-1954), S. F. Coffman (1872-1954), A. I. Yoder (1866-1932), J. B. Smith (1870-1951), J. A. Ressler (1867-1936), John Thut (1879-1950), George R. Brunk (1871-1938), and J. D. Charles (1878-1923).

As to the views of the amillennialists, it may be said simply that they believe in only one coming of Christ, one glorious return at the end of the world, at which time they believe that Christ will close the door of grace, that He will raise all the dead, that He will judge all men, that He will create "new heavens and a new earth," and that He will usher in the two eternal states, heaven and hell. Amillennialists do not expect world evangelization ever to create a golden age of any sort on earth. They hold that the only glory that Christians have is that of membership in Christ's church here and now, together with the bliss of heaven for all eternity.

The amillennial view has been held by most systematic theologians in recent centuries of the church, and it is the official posi-

---

66 *Ibid.*, II, p. 59.
67 *Ibid.*, II, p. 69.
68 See the article, "Chiliasm," in the four-volume *Mennonite Encyclopedia*, Harold S. Bender and C. Henry Smith. Editors (Scottdale, Pa.; Mennonite Publishing House, 1955-59). c. 1954).
69 Relevant citations in Landis, *op. cit.*, pp. 14-20. Note especially Menno's *Complete Works*, I, pp. 82, 95, 170, 171, etc.

tion of most of the older Protestant denominations. The Lutheran Augsburg Confession of 1530 says that "in the consummation of the world [at the last day], Christ shall appear to judge, and shall raise up all the dead, and shall give unto the godly and elect eternal life and everlasting joy; but ungodly men and the devils shall He condemn unto endless torments."[70]

The Heidelberg Catechism of 1563, a Reformed document, asks as Question 52: "What comfort is it to thee that Christ shall come again to judge the quick and the dead?" *Answer*: "That in all my sorrows and persecutions with uplifted head, I look for the self-same One who has before offered Himself for me to the judgment of God, and removed from me all curse, to come again as Judge from heaven; who shall cast all His and my enemies into everlasting condemnation, but shall take me, with all His chosen ones, to Himself, into heavenly joy and glory."[71]

The Belgic Confession of 1561 states: "Finally, we believe, according to the Word of God, when the time appointed by the Lord (which is unknown to all creatures) is come, and the number of the elect complete, that our Lord Jesus Christ will come from heaven, corporally and visibly, as He ascended with great glory and majesty, to declare Himself Judge of the quick and the dead, burning this old world with fire and flame to cleanse it. And then all men will personally appear before this great Judge, both men and women and children, that have been from the beginning of the world to the end thereof, being summoned by the voice of the archangel, and by the sound of the trumpet of God. For all the dead shall be raised out of the earth, and their souls joined and united with their proper bodies in which they formerly lived. As for those who shall then be living, they shall not die as the others, but be changed in the twinkling of an eye, and from corruptible become incorruptible.

"Then the books (that is to say, the consciences) shall be opened, and the dead judged according to what they shall have done in this world, whether it be good or evil. Nay, all men shall give an account of every idle word they have spoken, which the world only counts amusement and jest; and then the secrets and hypocrisy of men shall be disclosed and laid open before all.

"And, therefore, the consideration of this judgment is justly terrible and dreadful to the wicked and ungodly, but most desirable and comfortable to the righteous and the elect; because then their full deliverance shall be perfected, and there they shall receive the

---

70 Schaff. *op. cit.*, III, pp. 17, 18.
71 *Ibid.*, III, p. 324.

fruits of their labor and trouble which they have borne. Their innocence shall be known to all, and they shall see the terrible vengeance which God shall execute on the wicked, who most cruelly persecuted, oppressed, and tormented them in this world; and who shall be convicted by the testimony of their own consciences, and, being immortal, shall be tormented in that everlasting fire which is prepared for the devil and his angels.

"But on the contrary, the faithful and elect shall be crowned with glory and honor; and the Son of God will confess their names before His Father, and His elect angels; all tears shall be wiped from their eyes; and their cause, which is now condemned by many judges and magistrates as heretical and impious, will then be known to be the cause of the Son of God. And, for a gracious reward, the Lord will cause them to possess such a glory as never entered into the heart of man to conceive.

"Therefore we expect that great day with a most ardent desire, to the end that we may fully enjoy the promises of God in Christ Jesus our Lord. Amen.

"Even so, come Lord Jesus. Revelation xxii. 20."[72]

Other historic creeds such as the Scotch,[73] Westminster,[74] Irish,[75] Moravian,[76] Methodist,[77] etc., teach the same amillennial faith.

In spite of a rather weighty support for the amillennial position in the ancient church, as well as in the standard Protestant denominations, it must be confessed that amillennialism manifests some uncertainty regarding the meaning of certain passages in the Gospels, such as those which refer to the promise of Christ that the apostles would sit on twelve thrones, judging the twelve tribes of Israel,[78] as well as an apparent neglect of much Old Testament prophecy. Perhaps the greatest difficulty faced by amillennialism is its lack of an adequate interpretation of Revelation 20. It is sometimes also pointed out that amillennialism manifests at least a partial inability to provide a philosophy of history which fully vindicates the sovereignty of God on earth.

In spite of these difficulties which the amillennialist must humbly acknowledge, it is held by amillennialists that they accept what they feel are the basic presuppositions of New Testament writers as to prophecy and the church:

1. The New Covenant was intended by God to include Israelites. Acts 2:39; 3:25; Luke 19:9.

72 *Ibid.*, III, pp. 433-36.
73 *Ibid.*, III, pp. 477, 478.
74 *Ibid.*, III, pp. 671-73.
75 *Ibid.*, III, p. 544.
76 *Ibid.*, III, p. 801.
77 *Ibid.*, III, p. 807.
78 Matt. 19:28.

2. It was only the believing remnant of Israel, however, which was to enter the New Covenant through faith in Christ. Isaiah 53:1; 10:21; Romans 2:28, 29; 9:27; 11:5, 15, 17-20; 15:8.

3. Believing Gentiles also were to enter the New Covenant by God's intention. Acts 15:16-18; Romans 15:8-12; Galatians 3:5-8.

4. The New Covenant is in some sense continuous with the Old. Luke 1:72; Romans 9:8; Galatians 3:6, 7, 29; 4:7; 6:16; Hebrews 12:22.

5. In Christ national and racial distinctions are obliterated, and all those rejecting Him, whether Jew or Gentile, are lost. Matthew 3:7-10; 8:11, 12; John 8:39; Romans 10:11-13; I Corinthians 12:12, 13; Galatians 3:28; Philippians 3:2, 3.

6. That believing Gentiles should be fellow heirs with believing Israel in the New Covenant was not fully revealed in the Old Testament but is a New Testament "mystery." Ephesians 3:1-10.

7. Christ's headship of the church is in the New Testament spoken of as a reign, and His saints constitute a kingdom in fulfillment of Old Testament Messianic prophecy. Matthew 3:2; 4:17; Romans 14:17; 15:12; Matthew 28:18; Ephesians 1:20-23; Psalm 110:1; Colossians 1:13, 18; I Peter 2:9, 10.

8. In some respects the reign of Christ over the church will terminate at His return. I Corinthians 15:20-28.

9. The return of Christ will usher in an eternal reign. Luke 19:11-27; Matthew 19:28-30; Acts 1:6, 7; Revelation 19:6; 5:11-13; 4:2, 3, 11; 21:3-5.

10. In a spiritual sense the New Testament calls the church of Christ "Zion" and "Jerusalem." Galatians 4:26; Hebrews 12:22. Christians whether Jew or Gentile are the "Israel of God," continuous with Israel of old in God's covenant of grace. That is, the spiritual blessings promised to Israel are fulfilled in God's present "Israel," the church. Romans 9—11; Galatians 3:29; 4:26; 6:16; Ephesians 1:9; Philippians 3:3, etc., etc.

11. The New Testament apostles after the Day of Pentecost indicate no interest whatever in a *political* restoration of Israel; they are concerned rather to lead the Jews to saving faith in the Lord Jesus, to a *spiritual* restoration to God's heavenly "Jerusalem," the spiritual "Zion," not the Palestinian city.

12. In spite of the general outline of events to come, particularly those associated with the return of Jesus, the New Testament indicates that God has not seen fit to reveal fully what the future will bring. "Beloved, we are God's children now; it does not yet appear

what we shall be, but we know that when he appears we shall be like him, for we shall see him as he is."[79]

This last point being true, it behooves Christians not to waste time arguing at length about details associated with the coming of Jesus, but to engage themselves in the evangelization of the lost and in the Christian nurture of the saints. Least of all will there be a disposition on the part of humble children of God to pass sharp judgments on those whose understanding of the prophecies of Scripture may differ from their own.

The present writer feels that the tone of Article XVIII of the Dordrecht Confession of Faith of the Mennonite Church is truly Christian:

> Finally, concerning the resurrection of the dead, we confess with the mouth, and believe with the heart, according to Scripture, that in the last day all men who shall have died, and fallen asleep, shall be awaked and quickened, and shall rise again, through the incomprehensible power of God; and that they, together with those who will still be alive, and who shall be changed in the twinkling of an eye, at the sound of the last trump, shall be placed before the judgment seat of Christ, and the good be separated from the wicked; that then everyone shall receive in his own body according to that he hath done, whether it be good or evil; and that the good or pious, as the blessed, shall be taken up with Christ, and shall enter into life eternal, and obtain that joy, which eye hath not seen, nor ear heard, neither hath entered into the heart of man, to reign and triumph with Christ forever and ever. Matthew 22:30, 31; Daniel 12:12; Job 19:26, 27; Matthew 25:31; John 5:28; II Corinthians 5:10; I Corinthians 15; Revelation 20:12; I Thessalonians 4:15; I Corinthians 2:9.
>
> And that, on the other hand, the wicked or impious, as accursed, shall be cast into outer darkness, yea, into the everlasting pains of hell, where their worm shall not die, nor their fire be quenched, and where they, according to holy Scripture, can nevermore expect any hope, comfort, or redemption. Mark 9:44; Revelation 14:11.
>
> May the Lord, through His grace, make us all worthy and meet, that this may befall none of us; but that we may thus take heed unto ourselves, and use all diligence, that on that day we may be found before Him unspotted and blameless in peace. Amen.[80]

> *And when all things shall be subdued unto*
> *him, then shall the Son also himself be subject*
> *unto him that put all things under him, that*
> *God may be all in all.—I Corinthians 15:28.*[81]

79 I John 3:2.
80 *Martyrs' Mirror,* pp. 43, 44.   81 A.V.

Appendixes

APPENDIXES

1. THE DORDRECHT CONFESSION OF FAITH, 1632

Adopted April 21, 1632, by a Dutch Mennonite Conference held at Dordrecht, Holland. Translated from the Dutch by Joseph F Sohm, 1855-1902.

I. Of God and the Creation of All Things

Since we find it testified that without faith it is impossible to please God, and that he that would come to God must believe that there is a God, and that He is a rewarder of them that seek Him; therefore, we confess with the mouth, and believe with the heart, with all the pious, according to the holy Scriptures, in one eternal, almighty, and incomprehensible God, the Father, Son, and Holy Ghost, and in none more, nor in any other; before whom no God was made or existed, nor shall there be any after Him: for of Him, and through Him, and in Him, are all things; to Him be praise and honor forever and ever, Amen. Heb. 11:6; Deut. 6:4; Gen. 17:1; Isa. 46:8; I John 5:7; Rom. 11:36.

Of this same one God, who worketh all in all, we believe and confess that He is the Creator of all things visible and invisible; that He, in six days, created, made, and prepared, heaven and earth, and the sea, and all that in them is; and that He still governs and upholds the same and all His works through His wisdom, might, and the word of His power. I Cor. 12:6; Gen. 1; Acts 14:15.

And when He had finished His works, and had ordained and prepared them, each in its nature and properties, good and upright, according to His pleasure, He created the first man, the father of us all, Adam; whom He formed of the dust of the ground, and breathed into his nostrils the breath of life, so that he became a living soul, created by God in His own image and likeness, in righteousness and holiness, unto eternal life. He regarded him above all other creatures, endowed him with many high and glorious gifts, placed him in the pleasure garden or Paradise, and gave him a command and prohibition; afterwards He took a rib from Adam, made a woman therefrom, and brought her to him, joining and giving her to him for a helpmate, companion, and wife; and in consequence of this He also caused, that from this one man Adam, all men that dwell upon the whole earth have descended. Gen. 1:27; 2:7, 17, 18, 22.

II. Of the Fall of Man

We believe and confess, according to the holy Scriptures, that these our first parents, Adam and Eve, did not continue long in this glorious state in which they were created, but that they, seduced by the subtlety and deceit of the serpent, and the envy of the devil, transgressed the high commandment of God and became disobedient to their Creator; through which disobedience sin has come into the world, and death by

375

sin, which has thus passed upon all men, for that all have sinned, and, hence, brought upon themselves the wrath of God, and condemnation; for which reason they were of God driven out of Paradise, or the pleasure garden, to till the earth, in sorrow to eat of it, and to eat their bread in the sweat of their face, till they should return to the earth, from which they were taken; and that they, therefore, through this one sin, became so ruined, separated, and estranged from God, that they, neither through themselves, nor through any of their descendants, nor through angels, nor men, nor any other creature in heaven or on earth, could be raised up, redeemed, or reconciled to God, but would have had to be eternally lost, had not God, in compassion for His creatures, made provision for it, and interposed with His love and mercy. Gen. 3:6; IV Esd. 3:7; Rom. 5:12, 18; Gen. 3:23; Ps. 49:8; Rev. 5:9; John 3:16.

III. Of the Restoration of Man Through the Promise of the Coming Christ

Concerning the restoration of the first man and his posterity we confess and believe, that God, notwithstanding their fall, transgression, and sin, and their utter inability, was nevertheless not willing to cast them off entirely, or to let them be forever lost; but that He called them again to Him, comforted them, and showed them that with Him there was yet a means for their reconciliation, namely, the immaculate Lamb, the Son of God, who had been foreordained thereto before the foundation of the world, and was promised them while they were yet in Paradise, for consolation, redemption, and salvation, for themselves as well as for their posterity; yea, who through faith, had, from that time on, been given them as their own; for whom all the pious patriarchs, unto whom this promise was frequently renewed, longed and inquired, and to whom, through faith, they looked forward from afar, waiting for the fulfillment, that He by His coming, would redeem, liberate, and raise the fallen race of man from their sin, guilt, and unrighteousness. John 1:29; I Pet. 1:19; Gen. 3:15; I John 3:8; 2:1; Heb. 11:13, 39; Gal. 4:4.

IV. Of the Coming of Christ into This World, and the Purpose for Which He Came

We believe and confess further, that when the time of the promise, for which all the pious forefathers had so much longed and waited, had come and was fulfilled, this previously promised Messiah, Redeemer, and Saviour, proceeded from God, was sent, and, according to the prediction of the prophets, and the testimony of the evangelists, came into the world, yea, into the flesh, was made manifest, and the Word, Himself became flesh and man; that He was conceived in the virgin Mary, who was espoused to a man named Joseph, of the house of David; and that she brought Him forth as her first-born son, at Bethlehem, wrapped Him in swaddling clothes, and laid Him in a manger. John 4:25; 16:28; I Tim. 3:16; John 1:14; Matt. 1:23; Luke 2:7.

We confess and believe also, that this is the same whose goings forth have been from of old, from everlasting, without beginning of days, or end of life; of whom it is testified that He Himself is the Alpha and Omega, the beginning and the ending, the first and the last; that He is the same, and no other, who was foreordained, promised, sent, and came into the world; who is God's only, first and own Son; who was before John the Baptist, before Abraham, before the world; yea, who was David's Lord, and the God of the whole world, the first-born of every creature; who was brought into the world, and for whom a body was prepared, which He yielded up as a sacrifice and offering, for a sweet savor unto God, yea, for the consolation, redemption, and salvation of all mankind. John 3:16; Heb. 1:6; Rom. 8:32; John 1:30; Matt. 22:43; Col. 1:15; Heb. 10:5.

But as to how and in what manner this precious body was prepared, and how the Word became flesh, and He Himself man, in regard to this we content ourselves with the statement pertaining to this matter which the worthy evangelists have left us in their accounts, according to which we confess with all the saints, that He is the Son of the living God, in whom alone consist all our hope, consolation, redemption, and salvation, which we neither may nor must seek in any other. Luke 1:31, 32; John 20:31; Matt. 16:16.

We furthermore believe and confess with the Scriptures, that, when He had finished His course, and accomplished the work for which He was sent and came into the world, He was, according to the providence of God, delivered into the hands of the unrighteous; suffered under the judge, Pontius Pilate; was crucified, dead, was buried, and on the third day, rose from the dead, and ascended to heaven; and that He sits on the right hand of God the Majesty on high, whence He will come again to judge the quick and the dead. Luke 22:53; 23:1; 24:6, 7, 51.

And that thus the Son of God died, and tasted death and shed His precious blood for all men; and that He thereby bruised the serpent's head, destroyed the works of the devil, annulled the handwriting and obtained forgiveness of sins for all mankind; thus becoming the cause of eternal salvation for all those who, from Adam unto the end of the world, each in his time, believe in, and obey Him. Gen. 3:15; I John 3:8; Col. 2:14; Rom. 5:18.

V. Of the Law of Christ, i.e., the Holy Gospel or the New Testament

We also believe and confess that before His ascension He instituted His New Testament, and, since it was to be and remain an eternal Testament, that He confirmed and sealed the same with His precious blood, and gave and left it to His disciples, yea, charged them so highly with it, that neither angel nor man may alter it, nor add to it nor take away from it; and that He caused the same, as containing the whole counsel and will of His heavenly Father, as far as is necessary for salvation to be proclaimed in His name by His beloved apostles, messengers, and ministers—whom He called, chose, and sent into all the world for that purpose—among all peoples, nations, and tongues; and repentance and remission of sins to be preached and testified of; and that He accordingly has therein declared all men without distinction, who through faith, as obedient children, heed, follow, and practice what the same contains, to be His children and lawful heirs; thus excluding no one from the precious inheritance of eternal salvation, except the unbelieving and disobedient, the stiff-necked and obdurate, who despise it, and incur this through their own sins, thus making themselves unworthy of eternal life. Jer. 31:31; Heb. 9:15-17; Matt. 26:28; Gal. 1:8; I Tim. 6:3; John 15:15; Matt. 28:19; Mark 16:15; Luke 24:47; Rom. 8:17; Acts 13:46.

VI. Of Repentance and Reformation of Life

We believe and confess, that, since the imagination of man's heart is evil from his youth, and, therefore, prone to all unrighteousness, sin, and wickedness, the first lesson of the precious New Testament of the Son of God is repentance and reformation of life, and that, therefore, those who have ears to hear, and hearts to understand, must bring forth genuine fruits of repentance, reform their lives, believe the Gospel, eschew evil and do good, desist from unrighteousness, forsake sin, put off the old man with his deeds, and put on the new man, which after God is created in righteousness and true holiness: for, neither baptism, supper, church [membership], nor any other outward ceremony, can without faith, regeneration, change or renewing of life, avail anything to please God or to obtain of Him any consolation or promise of salvation; but we must go to God with an upright heart, and in perfect faith, and believe in Jesus Christ, as the Scripture says, and testifies of Him; through which faith we obtain forgiveness of sins, are sanctified, justified, and made children of God, yea, partake of His mind, nature, and image, as being born again of God from above, through incorruptible seed. Gen. 8:21; Mark 1:15; Ezek. 12:2; Col. 3:9, 10; Eph. 4:22, 24; Heb. 10:22, 23; John 7:38.

VII. Of Holy Baptism

Concerning baptism we confess that all penitent believers, who, through faith, regeneration, and the renewing of the Holy Ghost, are made one with God, and are written in heaven, must, upon such Scriptural confession of faith, and renewing of life, be baptized with water, in the most worthy name of the Father, and of the Son, and of the Holy Ghost, according to the command of Christ, and the teaching, example, and practice of the apostles, to the burying of their sins, and thus be incorporated into the communion of the saints; henceforth to learn to observe all things which the Son of God has taught, left, and commanded His disciples. Acts 2:38; Matt. 28:19, 20; Rom. 6:4; Mark 16:16; Matt. 3:15; Acts 8:16; 9:18; 10:47; 16:33; Col. 2:11, 12.

VIII. *Of the Church of Christ*

We believe in, and confess a visible church of God, namely, those who, as has been said before, truly repent and believe, and are rightly baptized; who are one with God in heaven, and rightly incorporated into the communion of the saints here on earth. These we confess to be the chosen generation, the royal priesthood, the holy nation, who are declared to be the bride and wife of Christ, yea, children and heirs of everlasting life, a tent, tabernacle, and habitation of God in the Spirit, built upon the foundation of the apostles and prophets, of which Jesus Christ Himself is declared to be the cornerstone (upon which His church is built). This church of the living God, which He has acquired, purchased, and redeemed with His own precious blood; with which, according to His promise, He will be and remain always, even unto the end of the world, for consolation and protection, yea, will dwell and walk among them, and preserve them, so that no floods or tempests, nay, not even the gates of hell, shall move or prevail against them—this church, we say, may be known by their Scriptural faith, doctrine, love, and godly conversation, as, also, by the fruitful observance, practice, and maintenance of the true ordinances of Christ, which He so highly enjoined upon His disciples. I Cor. 12; I Pet. 2:9; John 3:29; Rev. 19:7; Titus 3:6, 7; Eph. 2:19-21; Matt. 16:18; I Pet. 1:18, 19; Matt. 28:20; II Cor. 6:16; Matt. 7:25.

IX. *Of the Election, and Offices of Teachers, Deacons, and Deaconesses, in the Church*

Concerning the offices and elections in the church, we believe and confess, that, since without offices and ordinances the church cannot subsist in her growth, nor continue in building, therefore the Lord Jesus Christ Himself, as a husbandman in His house, has instituted, ordained, enjoined, and commanded His offices and ordinances, how everyone is to walk therein, and give heed to and perform His work and calling, as is meet, even as He Himself, as the faithful, great, chief Shepherd and Bishop of our souls, was sent, and came into the world, not to bruise, break, or destroy the souls of men, but to heal and restore them, to seek the lost, to break down the middle wall of partition, to make of twain one, and thus to gather of Jews, Gentiles, and all nations, one flock, for a church in His name, for which—that no one should err or be lost— He Himself laid down His life, thus ministering to their salvation, and liberating and redeeming them, (mark) wherein no one else could help or assist them. Eph. 4:10-12; I Pet. 2:25; Matt. 12:19; 18:11; Eph. 2:14; Gal. 3:28; John 10:9, 11, 15; Ps. 49:8.

And that He, moreover, before His departure, left His church supplied with faithful ministers, apostles, evangelists, pastors, and teachers, whom He before, through the Holy Ghost, had chosen with prayer and supplication; that they might govern the church, feed His flock, and watch over, protect, and provide for it, yea, do in all things, as He had done before them, had taught, by example shown, and charged them, to teach to observe all things whatsoever He had commanded them. Luke 10:1; 6:12, 13; John 2:15.

That the apostles, likewise, as faithful followers of Christ, and leaders of the church, were diligent in this respect, with prayer and supplication to God, through the election of brethren, to provide every city, place, or church, with bishops, pastors, and leaders, and to ordain such persons thereto, who would take heed unto themselves, and unto the doctrine and flock, who were sound in faith, pious in life and conversation, and of good report without as well as in the church; that they might be an example, light, and pattern in all godliness and good works, worthily administering the Lord's ordinances—baptism and supper—and that they might everywhere (where such could be found) appoint faithful men who would be able to teach others also, as elders, ordaining them by the laying on of hands in the name of the Lord, and provide for all the wants of the church according to their ability; so that, as faithful servants, they might husband well their Lord's talent, get gain with it, and, consequently, save themselves and those who hear them. I Tim. 3:1; Acts 23:24; Titus 1:5; I Tim. 4:16; Titus 2:1, 2; I Tim. 3:7; II Tim. 2:2; I Tim. 4:14; 5:2; Luke 19:13.

That they should also see diligently to it, particularly each among his own over whom he has the oversight, that all places be well provided with deacons (to look after and care for the poor), who may receive the contributions and alms, in order to dispense them faithfully and with all propriety to the poor and needy saints. Acts 6:3-6.

And that also honorable aged widows should be chosen and ordained deaconesses, that they with the deacons may visit, comfort, and care for, the poor, feeble, sick, sorrowing and needy, as also the widows and orphans, and assist in attending to other wants and necessities of the church to the best of their ability. I Tim. 5:9; Rom. 16:1; Jas. 1:27.

Furthermore, concerning deacons, that they, especially when they are fit, and chosen and ordained thereto by the church, for the assistance and relief of the elders, may exhort the church (since they, as has been said, are chosen thereto), and labor also in the Word and in teaching; that each may minister unto the other with the gift he has received of the Lord, so that through mutual service and the assistance of every member, each in his measure, the body of Christ may be improved, and the vine and church of the Lord continue to grow, increase, and be built up, according as it is proper.

X. Of the Holy Supper

We also confess and observe the breaking of bread, or Supper, as the Lord Christ Jesus before His suffering instituted it with bread and wine, and observed and ate with His apostles, commanding them to observe it in remembrance of Him; which they accordingly taught and practiced in the church, and commanded that it should be kept in remembrance of the suffering and death of the Lord; and that His precious body was broken, and His blood shed, for us and all mankind, as also the fruits hereof, namely, redemption and eternal salvation, which He purchased thereby, showing such great love toward us sinful men; whereby we are admonished to the utmost, to love and forgive one another and our neighbor, as He has done unto us, and to be mindful to maintain and live up to the unity and fellowship which we have with God and one another, which is signified to us by this breaking of bread. Matt. 26:26; Mark 14:22; Acts 2:42; I Cor. 10:16; 11:23.

XI. Of the Washing of the Saints' Feet

We also confess a washing of the saints' feet, as the Lord Christ not only instituted, enjoined and commanded it, but Himself, although He was their Lord and Master, washed His apostles' feet, thereby giving an example that they should likewise wash one another's feet, and do as He had done unto them; which they accordingly, from this time on, taught believers to observe, as a sign of true humility, and, especially, to remember by this feet washing, the true washing, whereby we are washed through His precious blood, and made pure after the soul. John 13:4-17; I Tim. 5:10.

XII. Of the State of Matrimony

We confess that there is in the church of God an honorable state of matrimony, of two free, believing persons, in accordance with the manner after which God originally ordained the same in Paradise, and instituted it Himself with Adam and Eve, and that the Lord Christ did away and set aside all the abuses of marriage which had meanwhile crept in, and referred all to the original order, and thus left it. Gen. 1:27; Mark 10:4.

In this manner the Apostle Paul also taught and permitted matrimony in the church, and left it free for every one to be married, according to the original order, in the Lord, to whomsoever one may get to consent. By these words, *in the Lord*, there is to be understood, we think, that even as the patriarchs had to marry among their kindred or generation, so the believers of the New Testament have likewise no other liberty than to marry among the chosen generation and spiritual kindred of Christ, namely, such, and no others, who have previously become united with the church as one heart and soul, have received one baptism, and stand in one communion, faith, doctrine and practice, before they may unite with one another by marriage. Such are then joined by God in His church according to the original order; and this is called, marrying in the Lord. II Cor. 7:2; I Cor. 9:5; Gen. 24:4; 28:2; I Cor. 7:39.

XIII. Of the Office of the Secular Authority

We believe and confess that God has ordained power and authority, and set them to punish the evil, and protect the good, to govern the world, and maintain countries and cities, with their subjects, in good order and regulation; and that we, therefore, may not despise, revile, or resist the same, but must acknowledge and honor them as the ministers of God, and be subject and obedient unto them, yea, ready for all good works, especially in that which is not contrary to the law, will, and commandment of God; also faithfully pay custom, tribute, and taxes, and to render unto them their dues, even also as the Son of God taught and practiced, and commanded His disciples to do; that we, moreover, must constantly and earnestly pray to the Lord for them and their welfare, and for the prosperity of the country, that we may dwell under its protection, earn our livelihood, and lead a quiet, peaceable life, with all godliness and honesty; and, furthermore, that the Lord would recompense unto them, here, and afterwards in eternity, all benefits, liberty, and favor which we enjoy here under their praiseworthy administration. Rom. 13:1-7; Titus 3:1; I Pet. 2:17; Matt. 22:21; 17:27; I Tim. 2:1.

XIV. Of Revenge

As regards revenge, that is, to oppose an enemy with the sword, we believe and confess that the Lord Christ has forbidden and set aside to His disciples and followers all revenge and retaliation, and commanded them to render to no one evil for evil, or cursing for cursing, but to put the sword into the sheath, or, as the prophets have predicted, to beat the swords into ploughshares. Matt. 5:39, 44; Rom. 12:14; I Pet. 3:9; Isa. 2:4; Micah 4:3; Zech. 9:8, 9.

From this we understand that therefore, and according to His example, we must not inflict pain, harm, or sorrow upon any one, but seek the highest welfare and salvation of all men, and even, if necessity require it, flee for the Lord's sake from one city or country into another, and suffer the spoiling of our goods; that we must not harm any one, and, when we are smitten, rather turn the other cheek also, than take revenge or retaliate. Matt. 5:39.

And, moreover, that we must pray for our enemies, feed and refresh them whenever they are hungry or thirsty, and thus convince them by well-doing, and overcome all ignorance. Rom. 12:19, 20.

Finally, that we must do good and commend ourselves to every man's conscience; and, according to the law of Christ, do unto no one that which we would not have done to us. II Cor. 4:2; Matt. 7:12.

XV. Of the Swearing of Oaths

Concerning the swearing of oaths we believe and confess that the Lord Christ has set aside and forbidden the same to His disciples, that they should not swear at all, but that yea should be yea, and nay, nay;

from which we understand that all oaths, high and low, are forbidden, and that instead of them we are to confirm all our promises and obligations, yea, all our declarations and testimonies of any matter, only with our word yea, in that which is yea, and with nay, in that which is nay; yet, that we must always, in all matters, and with everyone, adhere to, keep, follow, and fulfill the same, as though we had confirmed it with a solemn oath. And if we do this, we trust that no one, not even the Magistracy itself, will have just reason to lay a greater burden on our mind and conscience. Matt. 5:34, 35; Jas. 5:12; II Cor. 1:17.

XVI. Of the Ecclesiastical Ban, or Separation from the Church

We also believe in, and confess, a ban, separation, and Christian correction in the church, for amendment, and not for destruction, in order to distinguish that which is pure from the impure: namely, when any one, after he is enlightened, has accepted the knowledge of the truth, and been incorporated into the communion of the saints, sins again unto death, either through willfulness, or through presumption against God, or through some other cause, and falls into the unfruitful works of darkness, thereby becoming separated from God, and forfeiting the kingdom of God, that such a one, after the deed is manifest and sufficiently known to the church, may not remain in the congregation of the righteous, but, as an offensive member and open sinner, shall and must be separated, put away, reproved before all, and purged out as leaven; and this for his amendment, as an example, that others may fear, and to keep the church pure, by cleansing her from such spots, lest, in default of this, the name of the Lord be blasphemed, the church dishonored, and offense given to them that are without; and finally, that the sinner may not be condemned with the world, but become convinced in his mind, and be moved to sorrow, repentance, and reformation. Jer. 59:2; I Cor. 5:5, 13; I Tim. 5:20; I Cor. 5:6; II Cor. 10:8; 13:10.

Further, concerning brotherly reproof or admonition, as also the instruction of the erring it is necessary to exercise all diligence and care, to watch over them and to admonish them with all meekness, that they may be bettered, and to reprove, according as is proper, the stubborn who remain obdurate; in short, the church must put away from her the wicked (either in doctrine or life), and no other. Jas. 5:19; Titus 3:10; I Cor. 5:13.

XVII. Of Shunning the Separated

Concerning the withdrawing from, or shunning the separated, we believe and confess, that if any one, either through his wicked life or perverted doctrine, has so far fallen that he is separated from God, and, consequently, also separated and punished by the church, the same must, according to the doctrine of Christ and His apostles, be shunned, without distinction, by all the fellow members of the church, especially those to whom it is known, in eating, drinking, and other similar intercourse, and no company be had with him that they may not become contaminated by intercourse with him, nor made partakers of his sins; but that the sinner may be made ashamed, pricked in his heart, and convicted in his conscience, unto his reformation. I Cor. 5:9-11; II Thess. 3:14.

Yet, in shunning as well as in reproving, such moderation and Christian discretion must be used, that it may conduce, not to the destruction, but to the reformation of the sinner. For, if he is needy, hungry, thirsty, naked, sick, or in any other distress, we are in duty bound, necessity requiring it, according to love and the doctrine of Christ and His apostles, to render him aid and assistance; otherwise, shunning would in this case tend more to destruction than to reformation.

Therefore, we must not count them as enemies, but admonish them as brethren, that thereby they may be brought to a knowledge of and to repentance and sorrow for their sins, so that they may become reconciled to God, and consequently be received again into the church, and that love may continue with them, according as is proper. II Thess. 3:15.

XVIII. Of the Resurrection of the Dead, and the Last Judgment

Finally, concerning the resurrection of the dead, we confess with the mouth, and believe with the heart, according to Scripture, that in the last day all men who shall have died, and fallen asleep, shall be awaked and quickened, and shall rise again, through the incomprehensible power of God; and that they, together with those who then will still be alive, and who shall be changed in the twinkling of an eye, at the sound of the last trump, shall be placed before the judgment seat of Christ, and the good be separated from the wicked; that then everyone shall receive in his own body according to that he hath done, whether it be good or evil; and that the good or pious, as the blessed, shall be taken up with Christ, and shall enter into life eternal, and obtain that joy, which eye hath not seen, nor ear heard, neither hath entered into the heart of man, to reign and triumph with Christ forever and ever. Matt. 22:30, 31; Dan. 12:12; Job 19:26, 27; Matt. 25:31; John 5:28; II Cor. 5:10; I Cor. 15; Rev. 20:12; I Thess. 4:15; I Cor. 2:9.

And that, on the other hand, the wicked or impious, as accursed, shall be cast into outer darkness, yea, into the everlasting pains of hell, where their worm shall not die, nor their fire be quenched, and where they, according to holy Scripture, can nevermore expect any hope, comfort, or redemption. Mark 9:44; Rev. 14:11.

May the Lord, through His grace, make us all worthy and meet, that this may befall none of us; but that we may thus take heed unto ourselves, and use all diligence, that on that day we may be found before Him unspotted and blameless in peace. Amen.

These, then, as has been briefly stated before, are the principal articles of our general Christian faith, as we teach and practice the same throughout in our churches and among our people; which, in our judgment, is the only true Christian faith, which the apostles in their time believed and taught, yea, testified with their life, confirmed with their death, and, some of them, also sealed with their blood; wherein we in our weakness with them and all the pious, would fain abide, live, and die, that we may afterwards obtain salvation with them through the grace of the Lord.

Thus done and finished in our united churches, in the city of Dordrecht, the 21st of April, 1632, new style.

[Signers given in Van Braght: *Martyrs' Mirror*, page 44.]

ADOPTION BY THE ALSATIAN MENNONITES, 1660

We, the undersigned, ministers of the word of God, and elders of the church in Alsace, hereby declare and make known, that being assembled this 4th of February in the year of our Lord 1660, at Ohnenheim in the principality of Rappoltstein, on account of the Confession of Faith, which was adopted at the Peace Convention of the *Tauffs-gesinnten* which are called the Flemish, in the city of Dort, on the 21st day of April in the year 1632, and which was printed at Rotterdam by Franciscus von Hochstraten, Anno 1658; and having examined the same, and found it in agreement with our judgment, we have entirely adopted it as our own.

[Signers given in Wenger: *Glimpses of Mennonite History and Doctrine* (Scottdale, Pa.: Mennonite Publishing House, 1949), page 227.]

ADOPTION BY THE MENNONITES OF AMERICA, 1725

We the hereunder written Servants of the Word of God, and Elders in the Congregation of the People called, *Mennonists,* in the Province of *Pennsylvania,* do acknowledge, and herewith make known, That we do own the afore-going *Confession, Appendix,* and *Menno's* Excusation, to be according to our Opinion: and also have took the same to be wholly ours.

[Signers given in Wenger: *History of the Mennonites of the Franconia Conference* (Telford, Pa.: Franconia Mennonite Historical Society, 1937), page 318.]

Note: See also the *Mennonite Confession of Faith* adopted by Mennonite General Conference, 1963, and published as a pamphlet by Herald Press, Scottdale, Pennsylvania.

2. THE SHORTER CATECHISM, c. 1690

Question 1. [The following is asked the person desiring to unite with the church:] *What has induced you to desire to unite with the communion of believers and be baptized?**

Answer. I am impelled by faith, to separate myself from the world and its sinful lusts, and to submit in obedience to my Lord, Redeemer, and Saviour, for the salvation of my soul. Heb. 5:9.

2. What has induced you to do this?

The will and good pleasure of God, which were proclaimed and demonstrated to me through the preaching of the holy Gospel; in which were also revealed unto me the laws and commandments of Christ, which I am bound to receive and observe in true faith. Matt. 7:21; 19:17.

3. Do you then expect to be justified and saved through your good works and the keeping of the commandments of Christ?

No. For through our good works alone we cannot merit heaven, for salvation is the unmerited grace of God purchased for us by Jesus Christ. Eph. 2:8.

4. For what purpose then are good works, or the keeping of the commandments of Christ necessary?

They are evidence of true faith in Jesus Christ; for obedience out of love to God, is the light and life of faith without which "faith is dead." Jas. 2:20.

5. Through what is man justified before God?

Through the Lord Jesus Christ alone, of whose righteousness we must become partakers through "faith which worketh by love." Gal. 5:6.

6. What is true faith?

It is a certain knowledge, whereby we hold everything as true that is revealed to us in Holy Scripture, and whereby we cherish a full confidence that the pardon of our sins, righteousness, and eternal life are granted unto us by God through our Lord Jesus Christ. Eph. 2:5.

7. What do you believe?

I believe in God the Father, Son, and Holy Ghost.

8. How do you believe in God the Father?

I believe with the heart, and confess with the mouth, that He is one, eternal, almighty, and just God the Creator and Preserver of heaven and earth, together with all things visible and invisible. Gen. 14:17.

9. How do you believe in the Son?

I believe that He is Jesus Christ, the Son of the living God, our Saviour and Redeemer; who has been with the Father from eternity, and who, at "the fullness of time," was sent into the world; that He was conceived by the Holy Ghost, born of the blessed Virgin Mary; suffered for us under Pontius Pilate; was crucified, dead and buried, rose again from the dead on the third day, ascended into heaven, and sits at the

---

* In the original this question is asked in the third person rather than the second.

right hand of God, the almighty Father, whence He will again come to judge the living and the dead. Matt. 25:31; John 17:5; Gal. 4:4.

10. How do you believe in the Holy Ghost?

I believe and confess that the Holy Ghost proceedeth from the Father and the Son, and is of a divine nature; therefore I also believe in God, Father, Son, and Holy Ghost, as being one true God. Besides I also confess a general, holy Christian church, the communion of saints, the remission of sins, the resurrection of the flesh, and thereafter eternal life. I John 5:20; John 5:29.

11. What do you confess of the Christian church, or the congregation of the Lord?

I confess by my faith that there is a Church of God, which the Lord Jesus purchased with His own blood, and which He sanctified and cleansed with the washing of water by the Word, that He might present it to Himself a glorious church. Eph. 5:26, 27.

12. In what does the Church of God consist?

In a number of persons, who, through faith in Jesus Christ, have withdrawn from a sinful world and submitted in obedience to the Gospel, not to live any more to themselves, but to Christ, in true humility; who also give diligence to exercise Christian virtues, by observing God's holy ordinances. Such are members of the body of Christ, and heirs of eternal life. II Pet. 1:11.

13. How, and through what, is the Church of God upheld?

Through the preaching of the holy Gospel and the instruction of the Holy Ghost, for the purpose of carrying on and maintaining which, teachers and ministers are elected by the church. Eph. 4:11.

14. Who has given power to the church to choose teachers?

I confess that, as the apostles were accustomed to do, so has God also given power to His church to do, namely, to elect teachers and ministers, that the body of Christ may be edified and preserved. Wherefore the election of such teachers and ministers also takes place according to the example which the apostles were accustomed to observe in such matters. Eph. 4:12; Acts 1:15-26.

15. Whence comes the ordinance of the service to the poor?

Of this service we have an example in the Acts of the Apostles, where the apostles, when the "number of the disciples was multiplied," called together the multitude and caused to be "appointed from among them, seven men," who took charge of the necessary "business," which example is still observed; so that that which is contributed by Christian hearts is properly applied to the relief of the necessities of the poor members of the church. Acts 6:1; Eph. 4:28.

16. How, and through what means, are the members of the body of Christ incorporated into the church?

Through the ordinance of Christian baptism, on confession of their faith and repentance of their past sins, whereupon they are baptized in the name of the Father, the Son, and the Holy Ghost. Matt. 28:19.

17. What is baptism properly?

I confess that it is an external ordinance of Christ, a sign of a spiritual birth from God, a "putting on of Christ," and an incorporation into His church, an evidence that we have established a covenant with Christ. Rom. 6:4; Gal. 3:27; I Pet. 3:21.

18. Of what use is baptism?

It represents to true believers the washing away of the impurity of their souls through the blood of Christ, namely, the pardon of their sins, whereupon they console themselves with the hope of eternal salvation through Jesus Christ, whom they have "put on" in baptism. Gal. 3:27.

19. To what are the members of the church of Christ bound by baptism?

To the act of suffering their past sins to be buried into Christ's death by baptism, and of binding themselves to Christ in a new life and conversation—a life of obedience—in order that they may follow His will and do what He has commanded them to do. Matt. 28:20.

20. What is the Lord's Supper?

I confess that it is an external ceremony and institution of Christ, administered to believers in the form of bread and wine; in the partaking of which the death and sufferings of Christ are to be declared and observed to His memory. I Cor. 11:26.

21. What purpose does the observance of this ordinance subserve?

It is thereby represented to us how Christ's holy body was sacrificed on the cross, and His precious blood shed for us for the pardon of our sins. I John 1:7.

22. What is the use of the observance of the Lord's Supper?

We thereby bear witness to our simple obedience to Christ, our Saviour and Redeemer; which has the promise of eternal salvation. Further, it secures unto us, through faith, the communion of the body and blood of Christ, and comforts us with the benefit of His death; that is, the assurance of the pardon of our sins. I Cor. 10:16; Heb. 5:9.

23. Is marriage also an institution of God?

Yes. For it is instituted by God Himself, and confirmed in the case of Adam and Eve in the Garden of Eden. Gen. 1:27, 28.

24. For what purpose is marriage instituted?

For the purpose of increasing the human race, so that the earth may thereby be peopled with inhabitants; also that fornication may be avoided. Therefore "every man" is to "have his own wife," and "every woman her own husband" (I Cor. 7:2).

25. How must such marriage be begun so that it does not clash with the institution?

Persons who are not too nearly related by consanguinity, may, after diligent prayer to God, enter into this state, and endeavor to live therein, in a Christian manner, to the end of their days; provided that they, as members of the Christian Church, enter into marriage only with members of the church. Lev. 18:6-17; I Cor. 7:39; 9:5.

26. Is a member of the church not at all allowed to enter into matrimony with a person who is not agreed with him in faith and doctrine?

No. For this is contrary to the marriage institution; and he who thus enters into matrimony, acts contrary to the law of God, and the doctrine of the apostles. Deut. 7:3, 4; Judg. 3:6, 7; I Cor. 1:10; 7:39; Phil. 2:1, 2.

27. Can also a lawful marriage, for any cause, be divorced?

No. For the persons united by such marriage are so closely bound to each other that they can in no wise separate, except in case of fornication. Matt. 19:9.

28. What do you confess in regard to the power of civil government?

I confess, from the testimony of Holy Scripture, that kings and governments are instituted by God for the welfare and common interest of the countries over which they rule; and that he who resists such authorities, "resists the ordinance of God." Rom. 13:1. Wherefore we are under obligation to fear and honor government, and obey the same in all things that do not militate against the Word of God. So we are also commanded to pray for the same. I Tim. 1:2.

29. Is it allowed to swear an oath?

No. For although this was allowed to the fathers of the Old Testament, yet has our Lord and institutor of the New Testament, Christ Jesus, expressly forbidden it, Matt. 5:33-37, which is confirmed by the Apostle James, when he says: "Above all things, my brethren, swear not . . . but let your yea be yea; and your nay, nay; lest ye fall into condemnation" (Jas. 5:12).

30. Is it allowed to take revenge?

No; although there was liberty to do so under the Old Testament dispensation. But now that it is totally forbidden by Christ and His apostles, we must not lust after it, but in meekness do good unto our neighbor; yea also to our enemies. Matt. 5:38, 39; Rom. 12:19-21.

31. If a member of the church fall into some sin or misdeed, what is to be done in such case?

I confess by virtue of the doctrine of Christ and His apostles that reproof and discipline must be fostered and maintained among believers, so that the headstrong, as well as such as have committed gross sins and works of the flesh, whereby they have separated themselves from God, may not be suffered in the communion of believers; but may, for their own amendment, be rebuked before all, "that others also may fear." Matt. 18:15-18; Isa. 59:2; I Tim. 5:20.

32. How must we demean ourselves toward such as are thus separated from the church?

According to the doctrine of the apostles, the true members of the church of Christ are to withdraw from such reproved and impenitent offenders, and have no spiritual communion with them, except by chance or occasion, when they may be exhorted in love, compassion, and Christian discretion again to rise from their fallen state, and return to the church. Rom. 16:17; Titus 3:10.

33. How long is the avoiding of such offenders to be observed?

Until they return again, give evidence of repentance—sorrow for their sins—and earnestly desire again to be admitted into the communion of the church. In such case they are, after solemn prayer to God, again to be received and admitted. II Cor. 2:6, 7.

34. What do you believe concerning the second coming of Christ, and the resurrection of the dead?

I believe that Christ, our Head, Lord and Saviour, will just as He visibly ascended to heaven, again appear from thence in great power and glory, "with a shout . . . and with the trump of God" (I Thess. 4:16). "For the hour is coming, in the which all that are in the graves shall hear his voice, and shall come forth; they that have done good, unto the resurrection of life; and they that have done evil, unto the resurrection of damnation" (John 5:28, 29). "For we must all appear before the judgment seat of Christ; that every one may receive the things done in his body, according to that he hath done, whether it be good or bad" (II Cor. 5:10).

35. [Now as this confession agrees with the doctrine of Christ and His apostles, the question is finally put to the disciple:] Are you inclined with your whole heart, to submit yourself to the will of your Redeemer and Saviour, Jesus Christ, to deny yourself together with all sinful lusts, and to strive by the grace of God, in true faith and heartfelt humility, to lead a pious and godly life and holy behavior, according to the commandments of God, as long as you shall live?*

Yes. [To which are heartily wished God's grace and rich blessings, through the power of the Holy Spirit, to salvation, to whom be honor and praise for ever and ever. Amen.]

---

* In the original this question is written in the third person rather than the second.

3. PEACE, WAR, AND MILITARY SERVICE, 1937

A STATEMENT OF THE POSITION OF THE MENNONITE CHURCH

Resolutions adopted by the Mennonite General Conference at Turner, Oregon, August, 1937

Introduction

In view of the present troubled state of world affairs, with wars and rumors of wars threatening the peace of the world, we, the representatives of the Mennonite Church, assembled in General Conference near Turner, Oregon, on August 25 and 26, 1937, and representing sixteen conferences in the United States and Canada, one in India and one in Argentina, S.A., do desire to set forth in the following statement our faith and convictions in the matter of peace and nonresistance as opposed to participation in war and military service, earnestly admonishing our membership to order their lives as becometh Christians in accord with these principles.

In doing so we do not establish a new doctrine among us, but rather give fresh expression to the age-old faith of the church which has been held precious by our forefathers from the time that the church was founded in Reformation times in Switzerland (1525) and in Holland (1533), at times even at the cost of despoiling of goods and exile from native land, and in some cases torture and death. On a number of former occasions since our settlement in America we have set forth our nonresistant, peaceful faith in memorials to officers of state, such as the petition of 1775 to the colonial assembly of Pennsylvania, and in addresses to the President of the United States and to the Governor-General of Canada during and after the World War in 1915, 1917, and 1919, and at other times, thus testifying to our rulers and to our fellow citizens of our convictions. Since our position has been fully and authoritatively expressed in our confession of faith, known as "The Eighteen Articles," adopted in Dortrecht, Holland, in 1632 and confirmed at the first Mennonite Conference held in America in Germantown in 1725, reaffirmed in the declaration of the 1917 General Conference at Goshen, Indiana, and in the statement of faith adopted by the General Conference at Garden City, Missouri, in 1921, we do not consider it necessary at this time to set forth our position in detail, but rather merely to affirm in clear and unmistakable terms the main tenets of our peaceful and nonresistant faith as they apply to present conditions.

Our Position on Peace and War

1. Our peace principles are rooted in Christ and His Word, and in His strength alone do we hope to live a life of peace and love toward all men.

2. As followers of Christ the Prince of Peace, we believe His Gospel to be a Gospel of Peace, requiring us as His disciples to be at peace with all men, to live a life of love and good will, even toward our enemies, and to renounce the use of force and violence in all forms as contrary to the spirit of our Master. These principles we derive from such Scripture teachings as: "Love your enemies"; "Do good to them that hate you"; "Resist not evil"; "My kingdom is not of this world: if my kingdom were of this world, then would my servants fight"; "Put up thy sword into its place; for all they that take the sword shall perish with the sword"; "Dearly beloved, avenge not yourselves"; "If thine enemy hunger, feed him; if he thirst, give him drink: for in so doing thou shalt heap coals of fire on his head"; "Be not overcome of evil, but overcome evil with good"; "The servant of the Lord must not strive; but be gentle to all men"; "The weapons of our warfare are not carnal"; "Christ also suffered for us, leaving us an example, that ye should follow his steps, who did no sin, neither was guile found in his mouth; who . . . when he was reviled, reviled not again; when he suffered, he threatened not"; "Not rendering evil for evil, or railing for railing: but contrariwise blessing"; "If a man say I love God and hateth his brother, he is a liar . . . and this commandment have we from him, that he who loveth God love his brother also"; and other similar passages, as well as from the whole tenor of the Gospel.

3. Peace within the heart as well as toward others is a fruit of the Gospel. Therefore he who professes peace must at all times and in all relations with his fellow men live a life that is in harmony with the Gospel.

4. We believe that war is altogether contrary to the teaching and spirit of Christ and the Gospel, that therefore war is sin, as is all manner of carnal strife, that it is wrong in spirit and method as well as in purpose, and destructive in its results. Therefore, if we profess the principles of peace and nevertheless engage in warfare and strife we as Christians become guilty of sin and fall under the condemnation of Christ, the righteous Judge.

Our Position on Military Service

In the light of the above principles of Scripture we are constrained as followers of Christ to abstain from all forms of military service and all means of support of war, and must consider members who violate these principles as transgressors and out of fellowship with the church. Specifically our position entails the following commitments:

1. We can have no part in carnal warfare or conflict between nations, nor in strife between classes, groups, or individuals. We believe that this means that we cannot bear arms personally nor aid in any way those who do so, and that as a consequence we cannot accept service under the military arm of the government, whether direct or indirect, combatant or noncombatant, which ultimately involves participation in any operation

aiding or abetting war and thus causes us to be responsible for the destruction of the life, health, and property of our fellow men.

2. On the same grounds consistency requires that we do not serve during wartime under civil organizations temporarily allied with the military in the prosecution of the war, such as the YMCA, the Red Cross, and similar organizations which, under military orders, become a part of the war system in effect, if not in method and spirit, however beneficial their peacetime activities may be.

3. We can have no part in the financing of war operations through the purchase of war bonds in any form or through voluntary contributions to any of the organizations or activities falling under the category described immediately above, unless such contributions are used for civilian relief or similar purposes.

4. We cannot knowingly participate in the manufacture of munitions and weapons of war either in peacetime or in wartime.

5. We can have no part in military training in schools and colleges, or in any other form of peacetime preparation for service as part of the war system.

6. We ought carefully to abstain from any agitation, propaganda, or activity that tends to promote ill will or hatred among nations which leads to war, but rather endeavor to foster good will and respect for all nations, peoples, and races, being careful to observe a spirit of sincere neutrality when cases of war and conflict arise.

7. We ought not to seek to make a profit out of war and wartime inflation, which would mean profiting from the shedding of the blood of our fellow men. If, however, during wartime, excess profits do come into our hands, such profits should be conscientiously devoted to charitable purposes, such as the bringing of relief to the needy, or the spreading of the Gospel of peace and love, and should not be applied to our own material benefit.

Our Willingness to Relieve Distress

According to the teaching and spirit of Christ and the Gospel we are to do good to all men. Hence we are willing at all times to aid in the relief of those who are in need, distress, or suffering, regardless of the danger in which we may be placed in bringing such relief, or of the cost which may be involved in the same. We are ready to render such service in time of war as well as in time of peace.

Our Attitude During Wartime

If our country becomes involved in war, we shall endeavor to continue to live a quiet and peaceable life in all godliness and honesty; avoid joining in the wartime hysteria of hatred, revenge, and retaliation; manifest a meek and submissive spirit, being obedient unto the laws and regulations of the government in all things, except in such cases where obedience to the government would cause us to violate the teachings of the

Scriptures so that we could not maintain a clear conscience before God. Acts 5:29. We confess that our supreme allegiance is to God, and that we cannot violate this allegiance by any lesser loyalty, but rather must follow Christ in all things, no matter what it cost. We love and honor our country and desire to work constructively for its highest welfare as loyal and obedient citizens; at the same time we are constrained by the love of Christ to love the people of all lands and races and to do them good as opportunity affords rather than evil, and we believe that this duty is not abrogated by war. We realize that to take this position may mean misunderstanding and even contempt from our fellow men, as well as possible suffering, but we hope by the grace of God that we may be able to assume, as our forefathers did, the sacrifices and suffering which may attend the sincere practice of this way of life, without malice or ill will toward those who may differ with us.

If once again conscription should be established, we venture to express the hope that if service be required of us it may not be under the military arm of the government, and may be such that we can perform it without violating our conscience, and that we may thus be permitted to continue to enjoy that full liberty of religious faith and conscience which has been our privilege hitherto.

Resolution of Appreciation

We desire to express our appreciation for the endeavors of our governments, both in the United States and Canada, to promote peace and good will among nations, and to keep from war. In particular, do we desire to endorse the policy of neutrality and nonparticipation in disputes between other nations. We invoke the blessings of God upon the President of the United States and the Prime Minister of Canada as well as upon the heads of state in the various lands in which our missionaries are serving, in their difficult and arduous duties as chief executives, and pray that their endeavors toward peace may be crowned with success.

We cherish our native lands, the United States of America, and the Dominion of Canada, as homelands to which our forefathers fled for refuge in times of persecution in Europe, and we are deeply grateful for the full freedom of conscience and liberty of worship which has been our happy privilege ever since the days of William Penn and which is vouchsafed to us as well as to all our fellow citizens by the national constitutions and the constitutions of the several states and provinces. We pray that the blessings and guidance of a beneficent God may continue to rest upon our nations, their institutions and their peoples.

Adopting Resolution

We hereby adopt the above statement as representing our position on peace, war, and military service, and we instruct the Peace Problems Committee to bring this statement to the attention of the proper governmental authorities of the United States and Canada and other lands in which our missionaries are laboring. We would likewise suggest to each of our district conferences that they endorse this statement of position and bring it to the attention of every congregation and of all the members individually, in order that our people may be fully informed of our position and may be strengthened in conviction, that we may all continue in the simple, peaceful, nonresistant faith of the Scripture as handed down to us by our forefathers of former times.

As a matter of practical application, we request our Peace Problems Committee, as representing the church in these problems, to carefully and prayerfully consider the problems which may arise in case our members become involved in conscription, giving particular attention to the proposed legislation on this matter which is now before congress or its committees.

4. A DECLARATION OF CHRISTIAN FAITH AND COMMITMENT

WITH RESPECT TO PEACE, WAR, AND NONRESISTANCE, 1951

The Position of the Mennonite Church
as adopted by the Mennonite General Conference
at Goshen, Indiana, August 23, 1951

Introduction

In August, 1937, the Mennonite Church through its General Conference assembled at Turner, Oregon, in the face of approaching war, adopted *A Statement of Position—Peace, War, and Military Service,* in which it set forth its faith and committed itself clearly on the issues of the time. Since then we have passed through a grievous world conflict, and after a few years of uneasy peace find ourselves again in a limited war and in dread of a third world war, with constantly growing world armaments and tensions. The United States government has repeatedly extended the military service law of 1940 and now plans to establish a permanent military training system. Other nations are committed to enlarged military programs. In the face of these conditions, a renewed statement of position is desirable, setting forth more completely the full meaning of our nonresistant faith, both for the strengthening of the faith and life of our membership and for a more adequate testimony to others. Therefore, we, the representatives of the Mennonite Church, assembled in General Conference at Goshen, Indiana, August 21-24, 1951, do adopt the following *Declaration of Christian Faith and Commitment with Respect to Peace, War, and Nonresistance.*

Basic Central Truths

The peace principles of the Mennonite Church, including its historic four-century-old witness against all war, are an integral part of the Gospel of Jesus Christ and of the discipleship which we believe the lordship of Christ requires of all of His followers. They derive directly from a Christian faith which holds as central truths:

(1) That one is our Master, even Christ, who is our only Saviour and Lord, and to whom alone supreme loyalty and obedience is due. He is the basis for our faith and commitment to the nonresistant way of life, and in His strength alone do we hope to live in peace and love toward all men. "For other foundation can no man lay than that is laid, which is Jesus Christ."

(2) That by the atoning and renewing grace of God which makes us new creatures in Christ, and through the power of the indwelling Spirit, we *can* live the life of holy obedience and discipleship to which all the children of God are called.

(3) That redeeming love is at the heart of the Gospel, and that the life of love and peace is God's plan for the individual and the race.

(4) That Christ has established in the church, which is His body, a universal community and brotherhood of the redeemed, within which the fullness of His lordship must be practiced and from which must go out into all human society the saving and healing ministry of the Gospel.

(5) That war is altogether contrary to the teaching and spirit of Christ and the Gospel, and to God's will as revealed in His Word; that therefore war is sin, as is all manner of carnal strife; that it is wrong in spirit and method as well as in purpose, and destructive in its results; and that if we profess the principles of peace and nevertheless engage in warfare and strife we become guilty of sin and fall under the just condemnation of God.

Scriptural Basis: The Old Testament

While we believe that the Old Testament Scriptures are divine in origin and authoritative in character, we nevertheless hold that these Scriptures are but a part of the progressive revelation of the nature and will of God leading to the full and final revelation found in the New Testament under the new covenant. Therefore Old Testament Scriptures which are sometimes cited in support of Christian participation in war may not be used to contradict clear New Testament teaching, but must be interpreted in the light of the teaching of Christ and the apostles, for in Christ we find the norm for the whole of Scripture. The national history of Israel as recorded in the Old Testament cannot be an example for us, for under the new covenant the people of God, the church, are of every nation, and are separate from the world and its institutions; church and state are separate. But even in the Old Testament it is clear that it was God's original will that there should be no killing and warfare; and that man, made in God's image, should be governed by love.

Scriptural Basis: The New Testament

Among the many New Testament passages which clearly show the sinfulness of all war and strife, and the requirement of creative Christian love, we point to the following: "Blessed are the peacemakers"; "Love your enemies . . . do good to them that hate you . . . that ye may be the children of your Father which is in heaven"; "Resist not him that is evil"; "Whatsoever ye would that men should do to you, do ye even so to them"; "If any man will come after me, let him deny himself, and take up his cross daily, and follow me"; "My kingdom is not of this world: if my kingdom were of this world, then would my servants fight"; "Put up thy sword into its place; for all they that take the sword shall perish with the sword"; "Dearly beloved, avenge not yourselves"; "If thine enemy hunger, feed him; if he thirst, give him drink; for in so doing thou shalt heap coals of fire on his head"; "Be not overcome of evil, but overcome evil with good"; "The servant of the Lord must not strive; but be gentle to all men"; "The weapons of our warfare are not carnal"; "Christ also suffered for us, leaving us an example, that ye should follow his steps, who did no sin, neither was guile found in his mouth; who, when he was reviled, reviled not again; when he suffered, he threatened not"; "Not rendering evil for evil, or railing for railing: but contrariwise blessing"; "From whence come wars and fightings among you, come they not hence even of your lusts"; "Hereby perceive we the love of God because he laid down his life for us: and we ought to lay down our lives for the brethren"; "If a man say, I love God, and hateth his brother, he is a liar. . . . And this commandment have we from him, That he who loveth God love his brother also"; "But the greatest of these is love" (Matt. 5:9; Matt. 5:44, 45; Matt. 5:39; Matt. 7:12; Luke 9:23; John 18:36; Matt. 26:52; Rom. 12:20, 21; II Tim. 2:24; II Cor. 10:4; I Pet. 2:21-23; I Pet. 3:9; Jas. 4:1; I John 3:16; I John 4:20, 21; I Cor. 13:13).

Christ, the Example of Suffering Love

All these words Christ brought to living expression in Himself. In the life and work of Him, who in His incarnation became one with man, is given the full revelation of God's will, reaching its supreme meaning at Calvary. Integral to this divine-human life of our Lord was His innocent and nonresistant endurance of the evil inflicted upon Him, His identification of Himself in His suffering with all sinners, thus bearing man's sin in His own body on the cross, and His triumphant victory over sin by the very means of His death. What He taught in the Sermon on the Mount He fulfilled in His life and practice, including the cross. As those who believe in this Christ are united with Him in death and resurrection experience, they also will become identified with Him in His way of nonresistant suffering and triumphant overcoming. In this "way" of Christ, war and its related evils can have no place.

The Way of the Cross

But beyond the specific New Testament words and even the example of Christ, we hold that the whole tenor of the Gospel, being redemptive, forbids the destructiveness of war and calls for love. The very cross of Christ itself, the means by which God's love operates redemptively in a world of sinful men, speaks against war; for it stands for the acceptance of unlimited suffering, the utter denial of self, and the complete dedication of life to the ministry of redemption for others. This way of self-sacrifice is the cross which Christ lays upon us when He calls us to take up our cross daily and follow Him in the discipleship of self-denial, nonresistance, and suffering love.

The Way of Discipleship

We believe further that the Christian, having been laid hold of by God through Christ, must follow his Lord in all things regardless of consequences. He must pay the price of complete discipleship, for to him the commands of Christ and the principles of the Gospel are not mere counsels to be accepted or rejected as may seem good at the moment, but rather imperatives which must be followed to the end. Once the premise is accepted that Christ speaks with authority from heaven, only one thing remains, that is to obey His command. And this the new man in Christ will desire from his heart to do.

But this way of discipleship is not only a command to be obeyed; it is the way of victory and peace for the individual and society, to be practiced in the here and now and not to be postponed to some future kingdom. With a joyful belief in the reality of God's reign, we therefore forthrightly establish our lives on the power of Christ. We are convinced that the teachings of Jesus and the power of the Gospel are the solution to the problems of sin in man and society; and that the reason society is still in its broken state is either because men reject Christ and His Gospel or because those who have taken the name of Christ will not live that Gospel and take up the cross of utter discipleship laid upon them by their Lord. The true Christian must move out into the world of sin and need and there apply the Gospel to its fullest extent, uncompromisingly, and in and through his own life. This calls for an action program requiring the full unfolding of divine grace and power through man, but it is the only hope of the world.

The Problem of the Use of Force in an Evil World

We recognize that in a world where the evil and the good exist side by side, there is a necessary place, authorized by God Himself, for the use of force by the state in the restraint of evil and the protection of the good, though always under restrictions deriving from the higher laws of God. But we hold that the Christian cannot be the executor of this force, his call being to operate on the basis of love. If he abandons this way, he effectually destroys the only hope for the world, since force can never create righteousness or a Christian society; it can at best only restrain the evil in varying degrees.

Our Commitment to Total Discipleship

These declarations of faith and conviction give no blueprint for permanent peace nor do they assume that human endeavor alone can bring about a warless and sinless world within history, for only when men come under the lordship of Christ can they make peace and fulfill the prayer of our Lord, "Thy kingdom come, thy will be done in earth as it is in heaven." They do, however, require certain positive attitudes, duties, and ministries by Christian disciples toward all men which have far larger scope than only a testimony against war, and which call for consistent demonstration of sacrificial Christian love in all relationships. We believe, however, that the tremendous demands of this way of total love and total discipleship can by God's help be met, and we do here by God's grace declare our renewed acceptance of these demands and our determination to undertake their fulfillment in His name. Specifically, we understand this commitment to mean:

A. IN OUR OWN SPIRIT

(1) that we have peace with God.

(2) that the peace of God shall keep our hearts and minds through Christ Jesus.

(3) that the love of Christ shall reign in our natures and be the controlling motive in all our relations with our fellow men, in the family, in the church, in the community, in society, in all of our daily life.

B. IN OUR SERVICE AND WITNESS

(4) that we are bound in loving outreach to all to bear witness to Christ and to serve in His name, bringing the Gospel and all its benefits to everyone, and summoning men everywhere to the life of full discipleship and to the pursuit of peace and love without limit. For this ministry we mean to use every feasible way and facility: the spoken and written word; the demonstration of holiness and love in family, church, and community; relief work and Christian social service; and all other ways. In this service our youth can play a great part; they should give themselves to it in large numbers both in shorter or longer terms of special service, and in lifetime dedication.

(5) that we have the responsibility to bring to the total social order in which we live, and from which we receive so much, the utmost of which we are capable in Christian love and service. Seeking for all men first the kingdom of God and His righteousness, we should hold together in one united ministry the evangelism which brings men to Christ and the creative application of the Gospel to cultural, social, and material needs. This ministry will go to all alike regardless of race, class, or condition.

C. IN OUR SOCIAL, ECONOMIC, AND POLITICAL RELATIONS

(6) that we practice a sharper Christian control of our economic, social, and cultural practices, to make certain that love truly operates to work no ill to our neighbor, either short-range or long-range. Knowing how much the selfishness, pride, and greed of individuals, groups, and nations, which economic systems often encourage, help to cause carnal strife and warfare, we propose not to contribute thereto or to anything which destroys property or causes hurt or loss of human life.

(7) that Christian love must hold primacy in all our economic and labor relations, that we cannot participate in activities, organizations, investments, or systems which use the methods of force and violence, compromise Christian ethics, or do not permit the full exercise of Christian love and brotherhood, and that we seek in our own practices to work out this love and brotherhood in concrete applications.

(8) that though we recognize fully that God has set the state in its place of power and ministry, we cannot take part in those of its functions or respond to any of its demands which involve us in the use of force or

frustrate Christian love; but we acknowledge our obligation to witness to the powers-that-be of the righteousness which God requires of all men, even in government, and beyond this to continue in earnest intercession to God on their behalf.

(9) that while rejecting any social system or ideology which opposes the Gospel and would destroy the true Christian faith and way of life, we cannot take attitudes or commit acts contrary to Christian love against those who promote such views or practices, but must seek to overcome their evil and win them through the Gospel.

D. IN WAR AND MILITARY SERVICE

(10) that we can have no part in carnal warfare or conflict between nations, nor in strife between classes, groups, or individuals, and that we can therefore not accept military service, either combatant or noncombatant, or preparation or training therefor in any form.

(11) that we cannot apply our labor, money, business, factories, nor resources in any form to war or military ends, either in war finance or war industry, even under compulsion.

(12) that we cannot take part in scientific, educational, or cultural programs designed to contribute to war, nor in any propaganda or activity that tends to promote ill will or hatred among men or nations.

(13) that while we witness against conscription in any form and cannot lend ourselves to be a channel for its compulsions, we shall seek to find ways to serve in wartime as well as peacetime, through which the demands of the state may be both satisfied and transcended. We both expect and desire that this service be sacrificial on the part of our young men and that the church go with them all the way in their service and witness sharing in the sacrifice.

(14) that if war does come, with its possible serious devastation from bombings or other forms of destruction, such as atomic blasts, germ warfare, poison gas, etc., we will willingly render such civilian help as conscience permits, sacrificially and without thought of personal safety, so long as we thereby help to preserve and restore life and not to destroy it.

(15) that in wartime, as well as in peacetime, we shall endeavor to continue to live a quiet and peaceable life in all godliness and honesty; avoid joining in the wartime hysteria of hatred, revenge, and retaliation; and manifest a meek and submissive spirit, being obedient to the laws and regulations of the government in all things, including the usual taxes, except when obedience would cause us to violate the teachings of the Scripture and our conscience before God.

Conclusion

While we are deeply grateful to God for the precious heritage of faith, including the principle of love and nonresistance, which our Swiss, Dutch, and German Anabaptist-Mennonite forefathers purchased for us by their faith, obedience, and sacrifice, and which we believe is again expressed in the above declarations and commitments, we are convinced that this faith must be repossessed personally by each one out of his own reading and obeying of God's Word, and must ever be wrought out in practice anew. Hence we summon our brotherhood to a deeper mastery of the Scriptures as the infallible revelation of God's will for us, and to find afresh under Holy Spirit guidance its total message regarding Christ's way and its application in our present world.

We humbly confess our inadequacies and failures both in understanding and in following this way of love, peace, and nonresistance, knowing well that we have come short in demonstration and proclamation of Christian love. As we renew our commitment of discipleship and ambassadorship for Christ, we entreat God for the grace we so much need, and pledge each other our mutual help in learning and obedience.

We also appeal to all Christians to re-examine the full meaning of the Gospel of the cross and Christian discipleship, to proclaim this Gospel in its fullness for the saving of men and the healing of the nations, and to exercise the entire ministry of reconciliation of man to God and man to man which is entrusted to all the followers of Jesus Christ.

5. INDUSTRIAL RELATIONS, 1941

A STATEMENT OF THE POSITION OF THE
MENNONITE AND BRETHREN IN CHRIST CHURCHES

Introduction

A most significant development of the past seventy-five years has been the growing industrialization of America, the concentration of large populations in our cities, and the creation of great corporations, employing large masses of workingmen who, as individuals, are no longer in a position to bargain on a basis of equality with their employers. This condition has given rise first to trade unionism and then more recently to industrial organizations of a more comprehensive type as a means of restoring the balance of bargaining power. While these developments are understandable as an accompaniment of the economic growth of the nation, it is, nevertheless, our conviction that industrial organization in its present form involves a class struggle and conflict which is ultimately due to an absence of the Christian principle of love.

Our respective confessions of faith are a witness to the fact that from their earliest history the Mennonite and Brethren in Christ churches in their religious faith and practice have emphasized the principle of love and nonresistance which abjures the spirit of retaliation in all human relations, and which manifests a spirit of good will toward all men, including even their enemies, if there be such.

From time to time in recent years our conferences have reaffirmed this faith with special reference to its applications in the modern world. And believing sincerely that the coercive methods employed by industrial organizations are out of harmony with this faith which we profess we desire herewith to set forth a fresh statement of our faith and convictions in the matter of love and nonresistance as applied to industrial relations, earnestly admonishing our membership to order their lives as becometh Christians in accord with these principles.

Our Position on Industrial Relations

Our principles are based on the teachings of Christ who commands His disciples to live peaceably with all men. The Scripture specifically enjoins us to put away "all bitterness, and wrath, and anger, and clamour, and evil speaking" and says "be ye kind one to another." And again, "the servant of the Lord must not strive; but be gentle unto all men."

This way of peace which the Gospel enjoins is especially applicable to economic and industrial relations. Many Scriptures admonish Christians to brotherly love in business relations, particularly in the relations of employer and employee: "Whatsoever ye would that men should do to you, do ye even so to them"; "He that hath two coats, let him impart to him that hath none"; "Exact no more than that which is appointed you";

"Do violence to no man, neither accuse any falsely; and be content with your wages"; "Be kindly affectioned one to another with brotherly love; in honour preferring one another"; "Servants, be obedient to them that are your masters . . . not with eyeservice, as menpleasers; but as servants of Christ"; "Masters, give unto your servants that which is just and equal; knowing that ye also have a Master in heaven."

We believe that industrial strife, unfair and unjust practices by employers or employees, and every economic and social condition and practice which makes for suffering or ill will among men is altogether contrary to the teaching and spirit of Christ and the Gospel. Therefore if we profess the principle of Christian peace and nevertheless engage in industrial warfare and strife, we as Christians become guilty of sin and fall under the condemnation of Christ, the righteous Judge.

Our Position on Industrial Unionism

We believe the industrial conflict to be a struggle for power with which to achieve social justice, whereas Biblical nonresistance enjoins submission even to injustice rather than to engage in conflict. We find these two principles directly opposed to each other, mutually exclusive. We believe that the aim of coercive methods, both of labor and capital, is to compel the opposition to do one good. As Christians, however, we are commanded to love our opponent, not that he may do us good, but that we may do him good and so obey the will of God. The Christian's first task, as we understand it, is to obey the will of God, whether the immediate consequence is justice or injustice for himself. For these reasons our position involves the following specific commitments:

1. As employers we can have no part in manufacturers' or employers' associations in so far as they are organized for the purpose of fighting the labor movement, using such well-known methods as the lockout, the black list, detective agencies, espionage, strikebreakers, and munitions. Rather we consider ourselves under obligation to heed the Scriptural injunction, "Give unto your servants that which is just and equal." We regard ourselves duty-bound to exemplify the industrial way of life herein implied, through the payment of such wages, the maintenance of such working conditions, and the provision of such measures for the social and economic security of the workingman as shall remove every occasion for grievance, strife, or conflict. Furthermore we can have no part in any program designed to evade or oppose the government in matters of taxation, and the regulation of hours, wages, and working conditions.

2. As employees we can have no part in labor organizations in so far as their sanctions ultimately rest on force, making use of such well-known methods as the monopolistic closed shop, the boycott, the picket line, and the strike.

3. As agriculturalists we can have no part in farmers' organizations in so far as they are organized for monopolistic or coercive purposes, ultimately employing such methods as the boycott and the strike.

4. On the same ground, consistency with this position and with our convictions against the purposes and methods of these organizations requires that we have no part in financing them.

Our Attitude

We shall endeavor at all times to live the principles which we profess, to avoid involvement in any industrial relations which may compromise our faith, and to obey the letter and the spirit of the laws of the government for the regulation of taxes, hours and wages, and labor relations in general, unless there should be a case where such obedience would cause us to violate the teachings of the Scripture which commands us to obey God rather than men. We shall endeavor by official presentation of our position to industrial and labor organizations and to government officials to negotiate arrangements for such relationships as will not require us to violate our conscience, that we may thus be permitted to continue to enjoy that full liberty of religious faith and conscience which has been our condition hitherto. However, in cases where we find ourselves unable to negotiate such arrangements, making it necessary for us to suffer privation and loss for the sake of conscience, we hope by the grace of God that we may be able to assume, as our forefathers did, the sacrifices and suffering which may attend the sincere practice of this peaceful and nonresistant way of life, without malice or ill will toward those who differ with us.

Adopting Resolution

We hereby adopt the above statement as representing our position on industrial relations and we authorize the Committee on Industrial Relations to bring this statement to the attention of the proper officials and leaders in industry and labor in all areas where our people are in any way connected with industry or labor. We also request the committee, as representing the church in these matters, to consider carefully and prayerfully all problems of industrial relations which may arise from time to time. We would likewise suggest to each of our district conferences that they indorse this statement of position and bring it to the attention of every congregation and of all members individually, in order that our people may be fully informed of our position and may be strengthened in conviction, that we may continue in the simple, peaceful, nonresistant faith of the Scriptures.

Adopted June 6, 1941, by the General Conference of the Brethren in Christ Church and on August 26, 1941, by the General Conference of the Mennonite Church.

ADOPTED AT A STUDY CONFERENCE

ON CHRISTIAN COMMUNITY RELATIONS

AT

LAURELVILLE MENNONITE CAMP

July 24-27, 1951

Sponsored by the
Committee on Industrial Relations of the Mennonite Church
Goshen, Indiana

Doctrine and Practice

I. We recognize a tendency in current Christianity to make social betterment a chief concern, on the assumption that natural human goodness will assert itself if the machinery of environment is adjusted. We recognize also another tendency to emphasize exclusively the vertical relationship of man to God, on the assumption that if a man gets right with God his horizontal relationships with his fellows will automatically adjust themselves. We believe that the "social Gospel" is basically in error; but we also believe that the non-social Gospel is inadequate. We believe the statement of James that faith and works must go together. We therefore wish to express our deep concern that as a church we should not depart from the basic assumption that good social behavior must be secured as the outworking of a regenerated heart, that only the Spirit of God can produce the fruit of the Spirit. We would warn our people against any program of social or economic improvement which is divorced from the evangelizing purpose to bring men to Christ as both Saviour from sin and the Lord of their conduct.

We are further concerned that the church should acquire a better understanding of the principles of social justice contained in the Gospel of Christ, and urge our preachers and teachers to study and to set forth the social obligations expressed and implied in the teachings of the Old Testament prophets, of our Lord, and of all the apostles. We are deeply concerned that the social conscience of all our people may be aroused and sharpened, so that we may sense more and more the implications of Christian love and brotherhood in the complex details of modern life. We believe that our Christian testimony to the world about us can be effective only as we confess unsocial conduct to be sin and cleanse our lives of its defilement.

Nonresistance in Daily Life

II. In view of the fact that nonresistance is seen, not only in one's attitude toward war, but still more in the total spirit of the life in times of peace and war; and in view of the fact that the considerable failure of our members to take a consistent peace stand during the wars of the past decades argues a general failure in the more inclusive nonresistant life, this study conference expresses its concern:

1. That the principle of nonresistance become deeply imbedded in the thinking of our people as a result of regeneration and a continued program of teaching.

2. That our young men be encouraged and helped to such a daily behavior as will give them no embarrassment when they are asked in Form SSS-150 to describe actions and behavior which demonstrate their nonresistant conviction.

3. That our people carefully avoid every manifestation of covetousness, greed, and oppression; all willful neglect of duty by employer or employed; any relationship with agricultural, mercantile, industrial, or labor associations involving a compromise of principle; or any pressure methods designed at bettering themselves at the expense of others.

4. That we be more concerned about acting justly than about being treated justly, looking for every opportunity to witness for our Master as we overcome evil with good.

5. That we give a better demonstration of our unwillingness to profit through products of our labor or capital which contribute directly to military operations or to the destruction of property or life, or to participate in any program which tends to promote ill will or hatred among men or nations.

Christian Ethics in Business and Professions

III. In view of the extent to which the organization of modern life has been carried in the areas of business, industry, and the professions, and in view of the policies, methods, and procedures frequently used by these business and professional organizations, we are concerned with the necessity of examining with care, in the light of Christian ethics, the policies and methods of every such organization with which they have to do, to the end that all organization relationships be such as will not violate the Christian ethic. In this area we wish to state the following concerns in particular:

1. That a careful study be made of the various business, agricultural, and professional organizations affecting our brotherhood to the end that we be better informed as to their objectives, policies, and methods, enabling us to evaluate them in the light of our Christian ethic.

2. That business connections be avoided among us which would involve responsibility for unethical practices over which the individual has no control.

3. That great care be exercised in the investment of capital in large corporations and that this be done only when it is certain that business practices of the corporation, its policies with respect to competitors, and its labor policies are such as can be approved by the Christian conscience.

4. That our farmers and business and professional men exercise great care that no relations be maintained with agricultural, business, and professional organizations which will make them party to unchristian pressure tactics, unfair competition, unfair labor policies, or other unchristian methods and procedures.

5. That we seek to promote a diversification of small industries and businesses in our various communities to the end that as many as possible of our people engaged in business and industry may be so engaged in small community industries in preference to the large-scale corporations in our larger industrial centers.

6. That our brethren in the operation of their own business organizations seek to enlighten their consciences as to the best type of internal organization and administration for the maintenance of Christian labor relations, and that they continually seek to improve these relations.

7. That as a brotherhood we continually seek to discover ways and means of bringing the economic life of our brethren more completely into the way of Christian stewardship and Christian discipleship.

Organized Labor

IV. The rise of the labor movement, accompanied by an industrial trend among our own people, has created problems arising out of our relations with organized labor. While recognizing the benefits which the workers have realized from the efforts of the labor unions, we recognize also that some of the methods employed are not in harmony with Scriptural principles, and therefore cannot be endorsed, and should not be participated in, by the Christian.

In relation to the problem thus existing and in our effort to adjust ourselves to it, we feel that we should have a concern in the following areas:

1. That our present "Statement of Position on Industrial Relations" should be re-examined with a view to its improvement as a piece of literature which will serve our purposes well in our contacts with labor leaders or the general public.

2. That a study should be made as to indoctrination literature which is needed for the instruction and guidance of our people.

3. That consideration should also be given as to effective ways and means whereby a conscience and personal convictions on this question can be developed, which we recognize as being a basic requisite in the solution of the problem.

4. That further clarification should be made as to what kinds of working arrangements can be accepted without compromise of Scriptural principles.

5. Since the lack of uniformity in attitude and practice throughout the church presents an inconsistent testimony, and since the acceptance of unqualified union membership by members of the church may well have serious implications in weakening the position of the church on the entire

question of nonresistance and the recognition we seek to obtain for that position, we feel it should be our sincere concern that the position and practice of the church as a whole may become more fully unified in harmony with Scriptural principles which should guide our relations in this area.

Race and Minority Group Relations

V. In view of the clear Scriptural teachings that God is no respecter of persons, and that there is no Jew nor Greek but that all are one in Christ Jesus; in view of the widespread prevalence of race animosity in the world of today and especially in our own country; and in view of the impact which race animosities have produced in our own brotherhood, it is the concern of those here assembled:

1. That we study means of bringing the Gospel of Christ to racial and minority groups such as Negroes, Jews, and Japanese-Americans, and that the Gospel message be accompanied where necessary with service activities designed to raise their standard of living.

2. That we study means of better informing our brotherhood, (a) of the disabilities suffered by racial and minority groups, (b) of the lack of scientific basis for making differences between races, and (c) of the Scriptural teachings on race and minority group relationships.

3. That we witness against racial segregation or discrimination at every opportunity, and that we seek to abolish it wherever it may exist in our own brotherhood.

4. That we study means of providing opportunities for fellowship between Christians of different races and minority groups, to enable them to learn to know each other better as fellow saints.

Other Related Concerns

VI. In view of the striking increase in material prosperity in the United States and Canada and the enormous disparity in the standard of living between these areas and many other areas of the world which have urgent needs not only for the message of the Gospel of Jesus Christ but for material necessities requisite for the maintenance of life on a plane of health and decency, it is the concern of those here assembled:

1. That continued study of disparities in standards of living be made so that we may be aware of the true circumstances of other peoples.

2. That we teach without ceasing the true principles and practice of Christian stewardship of the possessions which have been entrusted to us.

3. That we recognize the great material prosperity of our countries to be the result primarily of the abundance of our natural resources provided by our benevolent heavenly Father rather than the accumulated work of our own minds or bodies or of our righteous living.

4. That we practice sharing our technical abilities and our accumulated possessions with those who are less fortunate in such a way as to enable them to exert their own efforts to raise their standards of living.

5. That we refrain from assenting to policies of selfish nationalism embodied in such devices as the protective tariff and other restrictions on the free flow of international trade, the imperialistic exploitation of colonial peoples, and the discriminatory restriction of immigration of peoples from underprivileged countries to our own.

VII. In view of the tendency of modern governments in the United States and Canada to assume an increasingly paternalistic attitude toward their subjects, especially as related to the care of dependent aged, children, widows, and to the provision of insurances against contingencies of storm, flood, unemployment, disease, and accidents, and in view of the resulting tendency among the masses of people and even among many members of our own communion to look to the government rather than to the church for help in time of need, it is the concern of those here assembled:

1. That a study be made of the extent to which members of our own brotherhood are availing themselves of the benefits of governmental assistance.

2. That we look with favor upon the present mutual assistance activities of our local congregations, our district conferences, and other church organizations; that we urge these groups and others to study ways and means of making their present work more effective and to extend their scope of activities to other needed areas.

3. That we seek to decrease rather than increase disparity of wealth in our brotherhood, recognizing the responsibility of each member for the welfare of the household of faith.

VIII. In view of the Scriptural Mennonite emphasis upon simplicity of life, it is the concern of those here assembled that Mennonite productive resources of land, labor, and capital be engaged in the production of those goods and services which contribute more directly to the promotion of the Gospel of Jesus Christ in the world and to the supplying of the necessities for sustaining and enriching life rather than to the production of those things which weaken the mind or the body or which supply the trivial, superficial, or peripheral wants of man.

IX. In view of the rapidly changing standards of the world about us relative to rights, privileges, and obligations of women and children in the community and in the family and in view of the lofty standards of the Scriptures with respect to the status of all human personality regardless of age or sex, it is the concern of those here assembled:

1. That there be a continued study of ways of strengthening family relationships.

2. That we maintain a consistent witness to the world of the effectiveness of the power of devotion to the kingdom of God, of the power of love and respect among all the members of the family group in building homes which will endure and will show forth the regenerated life.

X. In view of the gross immorality manifest in our country through such sins as the liquor and narcotic traffic, gambling, and white slavery, and in view of dangers which these evils present to the welfare of our country, it is the concern of those here assembled:

1. That we maintain a continued strict and absolutist position against these evils as they appear in our brotherhood.

2. That we witness against these evils in the communities, states, and nations where we live.

INDEX

Index

415